o Contract

gation of chattel status lay in the con
riage. Signifying self ownership, voliti
among formally equal individuals, contract became the dominant
metaphor for social relations and the very symbol of freedom.

This book explores how a generation of American thinkers and
reformers – abolitionists, former slaves, feminists, labor advocates,
jurists, moralists, and social scientists – drew on contract to condemn
the evils of chattel slavery as well as to measure the virtues of free
society. Their arguments over the meaning of slavery and freedom
were grounded in changing circumstances of labor and home life
on both sides of the Mason–Dixon line. At the heart of these arguments lay the problem of defining which realms of self and social
existence could be rendered market commodities and which could
not. *From Bondage to Contract* reveals how the problem of distinguishing between what was saleable and what was not reflected the ideological and social changes wrought by the concurrence of abolition
in the South and burgeoning industrial capitalism in the North.

Amy Dru Stanley is an Associate Professor of History at the University of Chicago. She has received fellowships from the American
Council of Learned Societies, the Woodrow Wilson National Fellowship Foundation, the Smithsonian Institution, and the American Bar
Foundation.

From Bondage to Contract

*Wage Labor, Marriage, and the Market
in the Age of Slave Emancipation*

Amy Dru Stanley

CAMBRIDGE
UNIVERSITY PRESS

PUBLISHED BY THE PRESS SYNDICATE OF THE UNIVERSITY OF CAMBRIDGE
The Pitt Building, Trumpington Street, Cambridge CB2 1RP, United Kingdom

CAMBRIDGE UNIVERSITY PRESS
The Edinburgh Building, Cambridge CB2 2RU, UK   http://www.cup.cam.ac.uk
40 West 20th Street, New York, NY 10011-4211, USA   http://www.cup.org
10 Stamford Road, Oakleigh, Melbourne 3166, Australia

© Amy Dru Stanley 1998

First published 1998

Printed in the United States of America

Typeset in New Baskerville 10/12 pt, in DeskTopPro$_{/UX}$®

A catalog record for this book is available from the British Library

Library of Congress Cataloging in Publication Data

Stanley, Amy Dru.
From bondage to contract : wage labor, marriage, and the market in
the age of slave emancipation / Amy Dru Stanley.
p.   cm.
Includes bibliographical references and index.
ISBN 0 521 41470 9 (hb). – ISBN 0 521 63526 8 (pbk.)
1. Labor – United States – History.   2. Slavery – United States –
History.   3. Contract labor – United States – History.   4. Marriage –
United States – History.   5. Women – United States – Social
conditions.   I. Title.
HD8066.S68   1998
306.3'6'0973–dc21   98-39348
CIP

ISBN 0 521 41470 9 (hardback)
ISBN 0 521 63526 8 (paperback)

To Craig, Tom, and Isaac

Contents

Preface

Slave emancipation ended the contradictory coexistence of freedom and slavery in the American republic. But a central paradox of emancipation was nullifying the buying and selling of chattel slaves while consecrating the market as a model of social relations among free persons. For Americans who came of age in the postbellum era, the problem was distinguishing between what was saleable and what was not. That problem reflected the concurrence of abolition in the South and burgeoning industrial capitalism in the North, and was grounded in changing circumstances of wage labor and home life on both sides of the Mason–Dixon line. At stake were matters of property, political economy, law, and morals. This book studies how a generation who argued over the meaning of slavery and emancipation drew on contract to describe the changes in their world and to distinguish between the commodity relations of freedom and bondage.[1]

---

[1] On the momentous moral and cultural implications of the rise of free market relations, see J.G.A. Pocock, *Virtue, Commerce, and History* (New York, 1985), 103–23; Jean-Christophe Agnew, *Worlds Apart: The Market and the Theater in Anglo-American Thought, 1550–1750* (New York, 1986); C.B. Macpherson, *The Political Theory of Possessive Individualism: Hobbes to Locke* (Oxford, 1962); David Brion Davis, *The Problem of Slavery in the Age of Revolution, 1770–1832* (Ithaca, 1975); Karl Polanyi, *The Great Transformation: The Political and Economic Origins of Our Time* (Boston, 1944); Sean Wilentz, *Chants Democratic: New York City and the Rise of the American Working Class* (New York, 1984); David R. Roediger, *The Wages of Whiteness: Race and the Making of the American Working Class* (London, 1991); Nancy F. Cott, *The Bonds of Womanhood: "Woman's Sphere" in New England, 1780–1835* (New Haven, 1977); Mary P. Ryan, *Cradle of the Middle Class: The Family in Oneida County, New York, 1790–1865* (New York, 1981); Steven Hahn, *The Roots of Southern Populism: Yeoman Farmers and the Transformation of the Georgia Upcountry, 1850–1890* (New York, 1983); Christine Stansell, *City of Women: Sex and Class in New York, 1789–1860* (New York, 1986); Jeanne Boydston, *Home and Work: Housework, Wages, and the Ideology of Labor in the Early Republic* (New York, 1990); Steven Hahn and Jonathan Prude, eds., *The Countryside in the Age of Capitalist Transformation: Essays in the Social History of Rural America* (Chapel Hill, 1985); Karen Haltunnen, *Confidence Men and Painted Women: A Study of Middle-Class Culture in America, 1830–1870* (New Haven, 1982); Thomas Bender, ed., *The Antislavery Debate: Capitalism and Abolitionism as a Problem in Historical Interpretation* (Berkeley, 1992); Thomas L. Haskell and Richard F. Teichgraeber III, eds., *The Culture of the Market: Historical Essays* (New York, 1993); Melvyn Stokes and Stephen

This is a study, then, of contract as a worldview. That worldview idealized ownership of self and voluntary exchange between individuals who were formally equal and free. It had roots in ancient notions of covenant, but its modern origins lay in Enlightenment traditions of liberal thought. Through the lens of contract many Americans conceptualized the transition from slavery to freedom and pondered the ambiguities of a culture that deplored the traffic in slaves while pushing nearly all else to sale in the free market. Most interested in these issues were freed slaves and Yankee hirelings, statesmen and feminists, and all kinds of moral reformers and social scientific thinkers. Contract offered them less a common vantage point than common principles for expressing their differing visions of freedom and slavery. In the realm of law the nineteenth century has long been deemed the age of contract – with contract standing as the legal paradigm of classical liberalism. Yet the ideal of contract transcended the boundaries of law.[2] It represented the antithesis of the "traffic in bodies and souls of men and women" decried by slavery's critics, as well as the essence of free society celebrated by capitalism's exponents as "one vast hive of buyers and sellers."[3] In the age of slave emancipation contract became a dominant metaphor for social relations and the very symbol of freedom.

But contract was not only a worldview, entailing images, symbolism, and a descriptive vocabulary. For a contract is a palpable transaction, a social relation assumed in American culture to rest on principles of self ownership, consent, and exchange. And the antislavery claim of the nineteenth century was that abstract rights of freedom found concrete embodiment in the contracts of wage labor and mar-

Conway, eds., *The Market Revolution in America: Social, Political, and Religious Expressions, 1800–1880* (Charlottesville, 1996).

[2] J. Willard Hurst, *Law and the Conditions of Freedom in the Nineteenth Century United States* (Madison, 1956); Lawrence Friedman, *Contract Law in America: A Social and Economic Case Study* (Madison, 1965); Morton J. Horwitz, *The Transformation of American Law, 1780–1860* (Cambridge, Mass., 1977); Patrick Atiyah, *The Rise and Fall of Freedom of Contract* (Oxford, 1979); Anthony T. Kronman, "Paternalism and the Law of Contract," *Yale Law Journal*, 92 (1983), 763–98; Martha Minow, *Making All the Difference: Inclusion, Exclusion, and American Law* (Ithaca, 1990), 121–29, 146–56; Robert J. Steinfeld, *The Invention of Free Labor: The Employment Relation in English and American Law and Culture, 1350–1870* (Chapel Hill, 1991); Christopher Tomlins, *Law, Labor and Ideology in the Early American Republic* (New York, 1993). On the broader ideological significance of contract, see Christopher Hill, *Puritanism and Revolution: Studies in Interpretation of the English Revolution of the 17th Century* (New York, 1958), 278–83; Perry Miller, *Errand into the Wilderness* (Cambridge, 1956); Edmund Morgan, *Puritan Political Ideas 1558–1794* (Indianapolis, 1965); Gordon Wood, *The Creation of the American Republic 1776–1787* (New York, 1972); Macpherson, *Possessive Individualism*; Carole Pateman, *The Sexual Contract* (Cambridge, 1988).

[3] Sarah Parker Remond quoted in Dorothy Sterling, ed., *We Are Your Sisters: Black Women in the Nineteenth Century* (New York, 1984), 177; Arthur Latham Perry, *Elements of Political Economy* (New York, 1868), 78.

riage – that the negation of chattel status lay in owning oneself, in selling one's labor as a free market commodity, and in marrying and maintaining a home. This book is also about postbellum debates over emancipation evoked by the material circumstances and legal terms of wage labor and marriage in both the North and the South. Framing those debates was the antislavery assumption that contract freedom precluded the sale of human beings.

Thus both ideas and experience are central in this study, which reconsiders the meaning of freedom after slavery's downfall and elucidates past arguments over the moral boundaries of market relations by exploring the problem of contract.[4] The ideas in question revolved around autonomy and dependence, volition and coercion, equality and inequality, entitlement and dispossession, self proprietorship and alienation – dualisms at the heart of classical liberal theory. The account treats both plebeian and elite viewpoints, mainly analyzing the insights of people who were not philosophers but who meditated on philosophical themes while encountering conditions outside the world of ideas. In some instances they reflected upon their own lives. In others, their thoughts on contract freedom were occasioned by experiences such as touring the homes of ex-slaves, inspecting Yankee sweatshops, or confronting beggars and prostitutes who violated the rules of legitimate trade.

As these practical philosophers argued over the broad outcomes of emancipation they brought to light the ambiguities of wage labor and marriage in a society that counted itself free because it had replaced bondage with contract. Not all Americans wholly accepted the antislavery claim that abolition had ended the buying, selling, and owning of human chattel. Instead many critics of postbellum life used slavery as a metaphor to assail conditions in both the North and the South. A common endeavor of former slaves, northern labor

---

[4] On the meaning of freedom in the aftermath of slave emancipation, see Ira Berlin et al., eds., *Freedom: A Documentary History of Emancipation* (4 vols., Cambridge, 1982–   ); Barbara Jeanne Fields, *Slavery and Freedom on the Middle Ground: Maryland during the Nineteenth Century* (New Haven, 1985); Eric Foner, "The Meaning of Freedom in the Age of Emancipation," *Journal of American History*, 81 (September 1994), 435–60; Eric Foner, *Nothing But Freedom: Emancipation and Its Legacy* (Baton Rouge, 1983); Thomas C. Holt, *The Problem of Freedom: Race, Labor, and Politics in Jamaica and Britain, 1832–1938* (Baltimore, 1992); Julie Saville, *The Work of Reconstruction: From Slave to Wage Labor in South Carolina, 1860–1870* (New York, 1994); Ellen Carol DuBois, "Outgrowing the Compact of the Fathers: Equal Rights, Woman Suffrage, and the United States Constitution, 1820–1878," *Journal of American History*, 74 (December 1997), 836–62; Laura T. Edwards, *Gendered Strife and Confusion: The Political Culture of Reconstruction* (Urbana, 1997); Frank McGlynn and Seymour Drescher, eds., *The Meaning of Freedom: Economics, Politics, and Culture after Slavery* (Pittsburgh, 1992); Rebecca J. Scott et al., *The Abolition of Slavery and the Aftermath of Emancipation in Brazil* (Durham, 1988).

radicals, and feminist reformers was illuminating the unfreedoms of existing contracts. Testing antislavery ideals against conditions at work and at home, they pointed to enduring traffic in bodies and souls, dispossession of self, and relations of personal dominion and dependence. Hirelings entitled to possess their own persons spoke of themselves as slaves because their labor was for sale. Feminists spoke of wives as slaves because, by law, both their persons and labor belonged to their husbands. And these arguments joined in revealing the conflict between contract freedom and marriage bonds – in showing that husbands must lose their rights as masters when wives sold their labor as a market commodity.

This book has above all been shaped by historical studies of the simultaneous transformations – ideological and material – wrought by the ascendance of industrial capitalism and the abolition of slavery. Yet it differs from those studies in placing marriage and home life alongside labor as focal points of analysis.[5] It begins with the antislavery idea of contract as distinguishing between freedom and bondage; it ends with the efforts of postbellum Americans to draw boundaries between the sale of labor and the sale of sex in the free marketplace. It explores why the moral legitimacy of commodity relations in a society purged of chattel slavery rested on establishing such boundaries.

The chapters that follow study contract freedom as a problem distilled by a set of very particular debates over what contemporaries knew as the "social questions" of the day. The first chapter introduces the fundamental contract principles of self ownership, consent, and exchange and illuminates the equation of freedom with contract in postbellum thought. This chapter traces the development of modern contract doctrine from its origins in Puritan theology and Enlightenment political theory through its dissemination in arguments over slave emancipation. It reveals how market theories of contract displaced earlier notions of the social compact and Puritan covenant, and it argues that ideological conflict over chattel slavery

---

[5] See Davis, *Slavery in the Age of Revolution*; David Montgomery, *Beyond Equality: Labor and the Radical Republicans, 1862–1872* (New York, 1967); Eric Foner, *Reconstruction: America's Unfinished Revolution 1863–1877* (New York, 1988); Saville, *Work of Reconstruction*; Holt, *Problem of Freedom*. For scholarship on labor and households, see Stansell, *City of Women*; Boydston, *Home and Work*; Alice Kessler-Harris, *Out to Work: A History of Wage-Earning Women in the United States* (New York, 1982); Eugene D. Genovese, *Roll, Jordan, Roll: The World the Slaves Made* (New York, 1972); Elizabeth Fox-Genovese, *Within the Plantation Household: Black and White Women of the Old South* (Chapel Hill, 1988); Stephanie McCurry, *Masters of Small Worlds: Yeoman Households, Gender Relations and the Political Culture of the Antebellum South Carolina Low Country* (New York, 1995); Edwards, *Gendered Strife*; Eileen Boris, *Home to Work: Motherhood and the Politics of Industrial Homework in the United States* (New York, 1994); Joan Wallach Scott, *Gender and the Politics of History* (New York, 1988), 53–163.

made marriage and the property rights of free men in their wives as central as was labor to the understanding of contract freedom.

The second and third chapters concentrate on the wage contract and the contradictions of freedom and dependence. Chapter 2 examines public inquiry into the "labor question" of the postbellum era, focusing on doctrines of law and political economy that defined commerce in free labor as emancipation and the claims of hireling men that in selling their labor they were no more self-owning than slaves. Chapter 3 analyzes anxiety created by the figure of the beggar, who did not enter into the matrix of contract relations. It deals with laws enacted after abolition that imposed forcible labor as a punishment for dependence, exposing the links between the coercions of free contract in the North and the South.

The fourth and fifth chapters turn to the consequences of wage labor for home life. Both address the counterpoint between contract freedom and marriage bonds. Chapter 4 explores social investigations into hireling domesticity in light of the antislavery postulate that freedom made home life inviolable by the market. It concerns the predicaments of postbellum households in which nothing was exempt from sale – in which the circumstances of wage work denied husbands ownership of their wives' labor. Chapter 5 considers public debate over the marriage contract and the wife's emancipation. It illuminates the dilemmas posed by the wife's status as a hireling and the conflicting resolutions offered at law and by feminism.

The last chapter reveals why the prostitute came to embody all the ambiguities of contract freedom defined as the negation of the traffic in slaves. It analyzes postbellum concern with her presence in the streets, revealing how she stood as the beggar's legal counterpart, outside the world of legitimate contracts, but was also represented as equivalent to the hireling, wife, and slave. It dwells on conceptions of the prostitute as a figure of free society who was nonetheless bought, body and soul.

At the moment of emancipation former slaves rejoiced that they would no longer be auctioned:

> Tain't no mo' sellin' today,
> Tain't no mo' hirin' today,
> Tain't no pullin' off shirts today,
> It's stomp down freedom today.[6]

Understanding the fate of this antislavery vision in a culture that enshrined free market relations is the task of this study of contract in the age of emancipation.

---

[6] Quoted in Sterling, ed., *We Are Your Sisters*, 244.

Acknowledgments

For their insights, criticisms, and faith in this project over the years, I am grateful to my teachers at Yale University: David Brion Davis, Nancy Cott, and David Montgomery. As my dissertation advisor, David Brion Davis asked expansive questions and also knew when to leave me alone. For research assistance, I am grateful to librarians and archivists at the Boston Public Library, the Massachusetts Historical Society, the Massachusetts State Archives, the Houghton Library of Harvard University, the New York City Municipal Archives, the Wisconsin State Historical Society, the Regenstein Library of the University of Chicago, and especially the Library of Congress. For fellowship support, I am grateful to the Charlotte W. Newcombe Foundation, the National Museum of American History, the Golieb Program at New York University School of Law, the American Bar Foundation, the National Endowment for the Humanities in conjunction with the Institute for Legal History at the University of Wisconsin School of Law, the University of California at Irvine, the American Council of Learned Societies, and the Humanities Institute of the University of Chicago.

As this project took shape as a dissertation and then as a book, many people helped me in many ways. For offering ideas, phrases, queries, guidance on sources, or simply encouragement, I am grateful to Sam Becker, Iver Bernstein, George Chauncey, Judy Coffin, Kathleen Conzen, Lorraine Daston, Eric Foner, Lori Ginzberg, Lucy Gorham, Michael Johnson, Elaine Karp-Gelernter, Jerry Kleiner, Stephanie McCurry, Kathy Peiss, Daniel Rodgers, Lisa Ruddick, Leslie Rowland, Dorothy Ross, Julie Saville, Christine Stansell, and Nomi Stolzenberg. I have been most fortunate in having the research assistance of Matthew Lindsay, Kim Reilly, and Rebecca Roiphe. I am very grateful to Dirk Hartog, Willy Forbath, and Eileen Boris for their readings of the entire book manuscript.

I am at a loss to thank Kristin Warbasse, who has immeasurably sustained this project. Nor can I fully thank my parents, Sylvia Gelernter Stanley and Lewis Stanley, or my brothers, Glenn and Lee, who have shaped my intellectual and moral convictions for as long as I can remember.

And my sons, Tom and Isaac, how can I thank you? No words are equivalent to all I wish to express. As for Craig Becker, my thanks begin in ending this project, which has been both of ours.

1

Legends of Contract Freedom

"What do social classes owe to each other?" Two decades after the Emancipation Proclamation the sociologist William Graham Sumner, an influential, if somewhat eccentric, exponent of classical liberalism, undertook to answer what many saw as the central social question of the age. His answer sought to dispel "muddling and blundering" notions of paternalism, relics of the feudal past. "In our modern state," he argued, "and in the United States more than anywhere else, the social structure is based on contract."[1]

For Sumner the virtues of contract were nothing less than freedom. A disciple of Charles Darwin and Herbert Spencer, he recognized few absolutes other than the properties of the physical universe. Yet he placed contract at the center of his social cosmology, and he took it as an article of faith that the ascendance of contract would destroy bonds of personal dependence based on status, law, or custom. "A society based on contract," he wrote, "is a society of free and independent men." Sumner granted that the new order entailed losses, that there was "more poetry and romance" in "feudal ties." But unlike some of his antimodernist contemporaries, he was not drawn to medieval idylls. The "sentimental relations which once united baron and retainer, master and servant," were antithetical to a society founded on contract.[2]

Rather, the ideal of contract freedom was modeled on classical political economy's rules of market exchange. As opposed to enduring ties of dominion and dependence, contract expressed obligations arrived at through competitive bargaining between formally equal and autonomous individuals. Contracting parties were held together only by "impersonal force – supply and demand," wrote Sumner. The contract relation was "rationalistic . . . realistic, cold, and matter-of-fact." It was also transitory, lasting "only so long as the

---

[1] William Graham Sumner, *What Social Classes Owe to Each Other* (New York, 1972; orig. pub. 1883), 118, 24. Some of the themes of this chapter are addressed in Amy Dru Stanley, "Conjugal Bonds and Wage Labor: Rights of Contract in the Age of Emancipation," *Journal of American History*, 75 (September 1988), 471–500.

[2] Sumner, *Social Classes*, 24–26.

reason for it endures." Sentiment belonged strictly to "the sphere of private and personal relations." The image of the contracting subject was an "isolated man," implying that the sentimental realm, where contract did not prevail, was woman's sphere.[3]

Supposedly, the historical progress toward freedom culminated in the regime of contract. Sumner subscribed to the theory, epigrammatically stated by the English jurist Sir Henry Maine, that progressive societies moved "from Status to Contract." Just as John Locke had once viewed America as embodying the state of nature, Sumner now saw his own country as the most perfect existing specimen "of a society of free men united by contract."[4]

This worldview was by no means idiosyncratic. Sumner was hardly alone in using contract to decipher social relations and to symbolize individual rights. In the aftermath of slave emancipation ideas of freedom were disseminated through the language of contract. That language reflected traditions of common law, Anglo-American political economy and political theory, and Puritan theology. But it was the debate over slavery and emancipation – the endeavor of defining the rights contrary to bondage – that rooted contract principles in everyday thought and speech while at the same time exposing the ambiguities and contradictions of contract freedom.

In postbellum America contract was above all a metaphor of freedom. In principle, contract reconciled human autonomy and obligation, imposing social order through personal volition rather than external force. To contract was to incur a duty purely by choice and establish its terms without the constraints of status or legal prescription. As the liberal pundit E.L. Godkin set forth this principle in 1871: "A contract, both in law and in political economy, is an agreement entered into by two perfectly free agents, with full knowledge of its nature, and under no compulsion either to refuse it or accept it."[5] Contract marked the difference between freedom and coercion.

If contract epitomized freedom, it also entailed exchange. The mechanism of exchange established the symmetry of the relation, entailing a reciprocity of rights and duties while also testifying to the mutual consent of the contracting parties. In his 1878 book, *Political Science; or, The State Theoretically and Practically Considered,* the Yale University professor Theodore Dwight Woolsey defined the principle of exchange essential to free contract: "A contract is a transaction in

---

[3] Ibid., 39, 150, 64, 25, 66, and see 73.
[4] Sir Henry Maine, *Ancient Law: Its Connection with the Early History of Society and Its Relation to Modern Ideas* (London, 1930; orig. pub. 1861), 182; Sumner, *Social Classes,* 26.
[5] E.L. Godkin, "The Labor Crisis," *North American Review,* 105 (1867), 184.

which at least two persons . . . acting freely, give to one another rights and impose on one another obligations." Reciprocity mitigated contract obligations by making them mutual.[6]

As a relation of voluntary exchange, contract was premised on self ownership. In order to surrender rights and accept duties, parties to contracts had to be sovereigns of themselves, possessive individuals entitled to their own persons, labor, and faculties. It was an axiom of Enlightenment philosophy that contract derived from and governed individual will and that free will was intimately connected to rights of proprietorship. As Woolsey restated this principle: "I cannot make that the property of another *by contract* which is not *mine* already." And the property at stake constituted not simply tangible commodities but rights in the self:

a man is a source of power over himself; he transfers something to another on purpose, just as if he gave away a piece of property out and out. . . . [S]o he gives a right over himself to another.

It was also axiomatic that men were the propertied individuals who ordered free society by contract.[7]

Both contract treatises and less formal expositions of social theory represented contract as the pith of social existence. "All social life presumes it and rests upon it," wrote Theophilus Parsons in *The Law of Contracts*. "Almost the whole procedure of human life implies, or rather is, the continual fulfillment of contracts." Catechisms on freedom taught the same principle to former slaves after the Civil War: "You have all heard a great deal about contracts, have you not, since you have been free? . . . Contracts are very numerous; numerous as the leaves on the trees almost; and, in fact, the world could not get on at all without them." This principle also underlay visions of freedom that challenged inequalities of sex as well as of race. "There is neither right nor duty," proclaimed the feminist reformer Victoria Woodhull in 1871, "beyond the uniting – the contracting – individuals." Such aphorisms celebrated a cultural code that identified contract with personal freedom and social progress, that found a metaphor for human relations in market transactions.[8]

[6] Theodore Dwight Woolsey, *Political Science; or, The State Theoretically and Practically Considered* (2 vols., New York, 1878), 1: 72.

[7] Ibid., 1: 74–76. See also William Paley, *The Principles of Moral and Political Philosophy* (2 vols., Hartford, England, 1850), 1: 102. See T.M. Knox, trans., *Hegel's Philosophy of Right* (London, 1952), 58, 38; Sir Frederick Pollack, *Principles of Contract at Law and in Equity* (Cincinnati, 1885), ix; A.W.B. Simpson, *A History of the Common Law of Contract: The Rise of the Action of Assumpsit* (Oxford, 1975), 9–21.

[8] Theophilus Parsons, *The Law of Contracts* (3 vols., Boston, 1873), 1: 3; Clinton B. Fisk, *Plain Counsels for Freedmen: In Sixteen Brief Lectures* (Boston, 1866), 47; Victoria Woodhull, "The Principles of Social Freedom," reprinted in *Woodhull's & Claflin's Weekly*, August 16, 1873; and see Woolsey, *Political Science* 1: 75. On classical liberal

In the eyes of most Americans it was the abolition of slavery that assured the ascendance of contract. Emancipation apocalyptically achieved the transition from status to contract, appearing to destroy all traces of bondage in the republic by affording freed slaves the right to own themselves and enter into voluntary relations of exchange. Here was the epic downfall of ties of dominion and dependence. "Where are the slave auction-blocks . . . the slave-yokes and fetters. . . . They are all gone! From chattels to human beings. . . . Freedmen at work as independent laborers by voluntary contract!" declared the abolitionist leader William Lloyd Garrison. "Away, then, with all croaking, all dismal forebodings, all depressing prophecies!"[9]

To its witnesses, then, slave emancipation distilled the forward sweep of history, and contract the nature of freedom that was established by abolition. In an 1867 essay on labor Godkin expressed the faith of the era. He wrote that the triumph of contract over status had occurred in "the lifetime of the present generation" and that the tendency of modern times was to "submit our social relations more and more to the dominion of contract simply."[10] This faith assumed the inevitability of contract freedom. Yet, as with most faiths, there were agnostics and dissenters, as well as those who interpreted contract principles in heterodox ways.

The intellectual roots of contract freedom extended back to antebellum debates over slavery, twisting along the paths of the common law to the liberal political thought of the seventeenth century. Throughout, the principles of self ownership, consent, and exchange remained central to this body of doctrine. Yet the meaning of these principles altered as they were enlisted to validate changing institutions and relations. In modern thought contract first represented an account of the origins of the state and the Puritan church. By the late eighteenth century, it had become a paradigm of the free market economy.[11]

In Enlightenment thought contract explained the mysteries of political obligation and the logic of individual rights. As social contract theory was formulated by Thomas Hobbes and John Locke, a con-

---

thought, market relations, and contract, see Thomas Holt, *Problem of Freedom: Race, Labor, and Politics in Jamaica and Britain, 1832–1938* (Baltimore, 1992), 5; Charles Fried, *Contract as Promise* (Cambridge, 1981); Thomas Haskell, "Capitalism and the Origins of the Humanitarian Sensibility," 2 pts., *American Historical Review*, 90 (1985), pt. 2, 547, 551–56; John R. Commons, *Legal Foundations of Capitalism* (New York, 1924), 248–51.

[9] "Is the Cause Onward," *Independent,* January 14, 1869.

[10] E.L. Godkin, "The Labor Crisis," *North American Review,* 105 (July 1867), 181, 183.

[11] On the historical significance of contract as a theory of political obligation, see John Gough, *The Social Contract: A Critical Study of Its Development* (Oxford, 1936).

tract among the people gave contractual justification to the sovereignty of the state and the submission of citizens. Individuals left a state of nature and consented to government, giving up some of their liberties in return for protection. Yet notions of reciprocal obligation were of far older lineage, extending back to feudal compacts between lord and serf and to biblical covenants. What distinguished Enlightenment contract doctrine was the idea of personal volition, the idea that obligation was created by free will rather than arising from relations of authority and subjection. Legitimate political power arose from consent, and contract elucidated why citizens accepted the rule of law. In exchange for security of person and property, they pledged obedience to the authority of their own voluntary creation. As Hobbes wrote, the multitude joins in "a real unity . . . made by covenant of every man with every man."[12]

In this theory of political sovereignty, contract remained indispensable well after the founding of the state. Justice was held to entail the fulfillment of contract, which the state had power to enforce in order to "make good that propriety," as Hobbes explained, "which by mutual contract men acquire." By contract, Hobbes meant the free and mutual "transferring of right."[13] Not only was

[12] Thomas Hobbes, *Leviathan: Or the Matter, Forme and Power of a Commonwealth Ecclesiastical and Civil* (New York, 1962; orig. pub. 1651); John Locke, *Second Treatise of Government*, ed. C.B. Macpherson (Indianapolis, 1980; orig. pub. 1690), 66. See Mary Lyndon Shanley, "Marriage Contract and Social Contract in Seventeenth-Century English Political Thought," in *The Family in Political Thought*, ed. Jean B. Elshtain (Amherst, 1982), 80–95; Christopher Hill, "Covenant Theology and the Concept of 'A Public Person,' " in *The Collected Essays of Christopher Hill, Volume 3: People and Ideas in 17th Century England* (Brighton, England, 1986), 300–302; Perry Miller, *Errand into the Wilderness* (Cambridge, 1956), 48–98; Gough, *Social Contract*, 5, 39, 41–45, 86–89; Patrick Atiyah, *The Rise and Fall of Freedom of Contract* (Oxford, 1979), 40–41; Edmund Morgan, *Puritan Political Ideas 1558–1794* (Indianapolis, 1965), xxiv; Immanuel Wallerstein, *The Capitalist World-Economy: Essays by Immanuel Wallerstein* (London, 1979), 147; E.P. Thompson, "Patrician Society, Plebeian Culture," *Journal of Social History*, 7 (1974), 382, 383–87; Fernand Braudel, *The Wheels of Commerce: Civilization and Capitalism, 15th–18th Centuries* (New York, 1979), 2: 260, 464; Sir Fredrick Pollack and Fredrick Maitland, *The History of English Law Before the Time of Edward I* (2 vols., Cambridge, 1923; orig. pub. 1895), 2: 216–33; Maine, *Ancient Law*, 340–86; Simpson, *Common Law of Contract*, 199–466; Hill, "Covenant Theology," 301–3; Morgan, *Puritan Political Ideas*, xx; Kohachiro Takahashi, "A Contribution to the Discussion," in *The Transition from Feudalism to Capitalism*, ed. Rodney Hilton (London, 1976), 68, 81; David Brion Davis, *The Problem of Slavery in the Age of Revolution 1770–1823* (Ithaca, 1975), 263, 166–67; Martyn P. Thompson, "The History of Contract as a Motif in Political Thought," *American Historical Review*, 84 (1979), 919–44. On the significance of absolute rights of personal security and liberty and the right of private property, see William Blackstone, *Commentaries on the Laws of England* (4 vols., Chicago, 1979; orig. pub. 1765–69), 1: 120–35.

[13] Hobbes, *Leviathan*, 113, 114, 104–6, 129. See Christopher Hill, *Puritanism and Revolution: Studies in Interpretation of the English Revolution of the 17th Century* (New York, 1958), 278–83; C.B. Macpherson, *The Political Theory of Possessive Individualism: Hobbes to Locke* (New York, 1962), esp. pp. 96–98.

the state the creature of covenant, it also found its purpose in binding citizens to fulfill contracts governing rights and relations of
property.

Whether free persons could contract away all their rights and
thereby voluntarily become slaves was a point of theoretical dispute.
For Hobbes and the natural law theorist Samuel Pufendorf, slavery
was consistent with consent and could arise from a contract in
which one freely relinquished all one's liberty. But for Locke,
though the political contract represented submission to a sovereign,
the essence of contract was freedom. Locke maintained that consent – the ideal of voluntary subordination – rendered contract
wholly inconsistent with slavery, and he stressed the limits on subjugation and self alienation inhering in contract: "if once *compact*
enter . . . and make an agreement for a limited power on the one
side, and obedience on the other, *slavery* ceases, as long as the compact endures." Yet consent legitimated various degrees and forms
of obedience that fell short of enslavement. Transforming submission into freedom, contract precluded unlimited, predetermined,
and arbitrary power. "*The liberty of man,* in society," Locke wrote, "is
to be under no other legislative power, but that established, by consent." In other words, being free was being bound purely by a voluntary compact.[14]

The political theory of the Enlightenment gave secular formulation to the Puritan doctrine of covenant, a doctrine at the core of
dissenting Protestantism. Puritan ministers imagined the relation between God and humanity as a bargain and the complexity of salvation as a set of mutual obligations, a contract reconciling human
agency and divine supremacy. They designated covenant the foundation for both church and state, holding that each institution rested
on the agreement of its members to obey biblical injunctions and
the laws enacted by magistrates. Aboard the *Arbella* on the way to the
New World, John Winthrop sanctified the mission through contract
imagery: "Thus stands the cause betweene God and use, wee are
entered into Covenant with him for this worke. . . . [W]ee must be
knitt together in this worke as one man." Other dissenting clerics
used more profane images in explaining the sanctity of contract,

---

[14] Locke, *Second Treatise,* 17. On Hobbes's differing conception, see *Leviathan,* 132,
153–54; David Brion Davis, *The Problem of Slavery in Western Culture* (Ithaca, 1966),
116–20. Blackstone also saw contract as the obverse of slavery: see *Commentaries* 1:
411. On the difference between the views of Hobbes and Pufendorf on slavery and
reciprocal contract obligations, see Gough, *Social Contract,* 112–18. On the idea of
consent as the antithesis of slavery, see Davis, *Slavery in the Age of Revolution,* 266–67.
On the theoretical links among contract, slavery, and natural law doctrine, see
Robert Cover, *Justice Accused: Antislavery and the Judicial Process* (New Haven, 1975),
12–19.

teaching that God dealt with men "as we do by way of commerce one with another, propounding mercy by covenant."[15]

The fashioning of Puritan doctrines of contract and consensual government shaped the British conflict over absolute monarchy. A century later these doctrines provided a legacy for American revolutionaries who gave them a more radical meaning. By basing political obedience on a voluntary pact between rulers and ruled, covenant theory could serve either to justify or to restrict absolute sovereignty. But in the course of experimenting with self government and resisting British rule, American political thinkers rejected the idea of a political compact between rulers and ruled, and introduced instead the idea of a social contract. This theory retained the emphasis on consent and reciprocal obligation but replaced the concept of absolute governmental supremacy with that of popular sovereignty. In Revolutionary America the dominant conception of covenant no longer was a relation of submission and dominion premised on protection and obedience. Rather, it suggested a voluntary association created by citizens equal under the law, a compact guaranteeing inalienable individual rights as well as the private contract relations arising from those rights.[16]

These private contracts governed both property relations, founded on ownership and exchange of wealth, and domestic relations, rooted in marriage and the household. According to William Blackstone's *Commentaries on the Laws,* the most influential legal treatise in the Anglo-American world of the late eighteenth century,

[15] Preston quoted in Miller, *Errand,* 60; see also p. 39; Sibbes quoted in Hill, "Covenant Theology," 302; Winthrop quoted in Morgan, *Puritan Political Ideas,* 90–92. See also Gough, *Social Contract,* 82–92, 69; David Zaret, *The Heavenly Contract: Ideology and Organization in Pre-Revolutionary Puritanism* (Chicago, 1985); Hill, *Puritanism and Revolution,* 278; Edmund Morgan, *The Puritan Family: Religion and Domestic Relations in Seventeenth-Century New England* (New York, 1944), 17–28.

[16] On contract principles in the political thought of the English and American Revolutions, see Hill, *Puritanism and Revolution,* 278; and Hill, "Covenant Theology"; Gough, *Social Contract,* 137–53; Miller, *Errand,* 48–98, 141–52; Bernard Bailyn, *Ideological Origins of the American Revolution* (Cambridge, 1967), 32–33; Shanley, "Marriage Contract and Social Contract." On Winthrop's notion of voluntary submission, see Miller, *Errand,* 89–90, 161–62. It is beyond the scope of this chapter to deal with the many discussions of contract ideas by Enlightenment theorists and their adoption by thinkers in the United States (especially in the early years of constitution making). However, for discussions of the fundamental shift in contract political principles, from a contract of voluntary subordination to government to a contract in which the populace retains its sovereignty, see Gordon Wood, *The Creation of the American Republic 1776–1787* (New York, 1972), esp. pp. 268–73, 282–91, 540–43, 600–615; Morgan, *Puritan Political Ideas,* xxiv–xxv, xl–xlvii; Bailyn, *Ideological Origins,* esp. pp. 198–229; Miller, *Errand,* 97–98, 150–52; Gough, *Social Contract,* 119–52; Rhys Isaac, *The Transformation of Virginia 1740–1790* (Chapel Hill, 1982), 205, 244, 291–95, 309–11, 318–19; Macpherson, *Possessive Individualism;* Commons, *Legal Foundations,* esp. pp. 248–49.

these contract relations concerned the *"rights of things"* acquired over "external objects" and the *"rights of persons"* attached to the "persons of men." Hobbes had explained that all property transactions were "acts of contract" – "buying and selling; hiring, and letting to hire; lending and borrowing; exchanging, bartering." And the Puritans had rejected older Christian doctrines of marriage as a sacrament, reinterpreting the relation in light of covenant theology. Secular theorists adopted this model in defining the marriage contract as the foundation of property rights within the family. Yet both Puritanism and classical liberal theory recognized crucial distinctions between a contract of sale and a marriage contract – not least that commerce presumed a bargain between equals whereas marriage established the dominion of men and the dependence of other household members. The *"master of a family,"* as Locke wrote, was a man "with all these subordinate relations of *wife, children, servants* and *slaves"* gathered under his "domestic rule."[17]

Yet in contracts involving rights to both "things" and "persons" the principles of self ownership, consent, and exchange were preeminent. Ownership lay at the heart of all rights. What Blackstone called the "despotic dominion" over property derived from an even more basic proprietary right: entitlement to oneself and one's labor. In liberal theory the individual was quintessentially an owner; selfhood counted as entitlement. As Locke postulated, by being "master of himself," the *"proprietor of his own person, and the actions or labour of it,"* each individual had *"in himself the great foundation of property."* The labor theory of wealth rested on the premise that a man possessed *"property* in his own person," and therefore, by mixing his labor with nature, made the proceeds his property. A century later, in the course of expounding the new system of law in the American republic, the jurist Jesse Root affirmed the connection between self ownership, property, and contract: "we have a property in our persons, in our powers and faculties, and in the fruits and effects of our industry," a property that enabled the law to "construe contracts and agreements."[18]

---

[17] Blackstone, *Commentaries* 1: 118; Hobbes, *Leviathan*, 118, 152–55; Locke, *Second Treatise*, 46. See also Blackstone, *Commentaries*, 1: 410–33; Paley, *Principles* 1: 5, 11, 13, 15–16; Morgan, *Puritan Family*; Carole Pateman, *The Sexual Contract* (Stanford, 1988).

[18] Blackstone, *Commentaries* 2: 2; Locke, *Second Treatise*, 27, 19; Paley, *Principles* 1: 142; Jesse Roote, "The Origin of Government and Laws in Connecticut," in *The Legal Mind in America*, ed. Perry Miller (Ithaca, 1962), 31, 36. See also Macpherson, *Possessive Individualism*, 197–220. On links between the rise of the capitalist market economy and ideas of free contract and ownership of one's own labor, see C.B. Macpherson, "A Political Theory of Property," in *Democratic Theory: Essays in Retrieval* (Oxford, 1973), esp. pp. 127–31. See also William B. Scott, *The Pursuit of*

Because labor was imagined as property, it was imagined, too, as a commodity. Self proprietors were entitled to put their labor and its fruits up for sale. As with other commodities, one could contract to exchange labor for a wage. Under the common law a master acquired a property right in his servants' labor "by the contract of hiring, and purchased by giving them wages."[19] The contract transaction – the fact that servants consented to the sale and received something in exchange – legitimated the master's title to their time and industry. Striking a balance between property rights seemingly in conflict, contract adjusted self ownership with the master's right to the servant's labor, the part of self that the servant put on the market.

Such an adjustment, hinging on consent and exchange, was precisely what the slave relation purportedly lacked. The absence of contract marked the slave. In the famous formulation of the philosopher William Paley, which abolitionists later quoted widely, slavery constituted "an obligation to labour for the benefit of the master, without the contract or consent of the servant." Locke had reasoned similarly: "freemen" were bound merely by "what is contained in the *contract*." According to such arguments, which reflected and justified the rise of capitalist relations and an expanding market in free labor, the wage contract distinguished freedom from slavery.[20]

If the wage status represented slavery's opposite, it nonetheless appeared incompatible with the rights of citizenship in the eyes of most political thinkers in the seventeenth and eighteenth centuries. Although only free and self-owning persons could enter into wage contracts, as hirelings they forfeited not simply property in their own labor but also economic independence and thus the franchise. However voluntary the transaction, to work for wages was to be dependent, to lose the autonomy requisite to citizenship – the autonomy associated with title to property, including one's productive capacities. Carrying a social meaning beyond the mere exchange of property, the contract between master and servant created a relationship of authority and submission, a voluntary and limited form of self

Happiness: American Conceptions of Property from the Seventeenth to the Twentieth Century (Bloomington, 1977), 24–75.

[19] Blackstone, *Commentaries* 1: 416–17.

[20] Paley, *Principles* 1: 150, and see p. 114; Locke, *Second Treatise*, 45. See also Davis, *Slavery in the Age of Revolution*, esp. pp. 262–70, 381–82, 455–62, 489–501; David Brion Davis, "Reflections on Abolitionism and Ideological Hegemony," *American Historical Review*, 92 (October 1987), 797–812; Macpherson, *Democratic Theory*, 129; Macpherson, *Possessive Individualism*, 48–68, 194–231, 263–77. On the tension between individual property rights and a master's property in his servants and their proceeds, see Richard T. Ely, *Property and Contract in Their Relations to the Distribution of Wealth* (2 vols., New York, 1914), 2: 542.

alienation that combined freedom and dependency. By selling his labor, as Locke observed, the servant granted his master "a temporary power over him." The servant put himself "into the family of his master, and under the ordinary discipline thereof."[21]

What is striking about Locke's language is not only his blunt statement of the power exercised in the wage relation but also his depiction of that power as a form of family discipline. In the earliest formulations of liberalism the wage contract appeared as a hybrid: a composite of commercial and household conventions. It shared the characteristics of the marketplace; yet it also had much in common with marriage. For both the wage contract and the marriage contract vested paternal dominion in the master of the household; as Locke stated, the husband's authority mirrored that of "a *master* over his servant." The symmetry of the two contracts was codified in the common law, which classified the wage contract as a domestic relation – along with husband and wife and parent and child. In Blackstone's phrase, these were the three great "oeconomical relations" of "private life."[22]

In classical contract theory, then, the wife was the analog of the servant, and marriage was the analog of the wage relationship. Like the wage contract, the marriage contract was founded on consent and created a relation of authority and subordination premised on reciprocal exchange: the common law named the wife a dependent and bound her to serve and obey her husband in return for his protection. Like the servant, she owed her husband her labor and its proceeds, though in exchange not for wages but for subsistence. Even thinkers such as Locke, who argued that spouses should have the legal right to devise their own conjugal agreements and alter or dissolve them at will, affirmed the rule of female subordination. Authority had to lie somewhere, and though not absolute, wrote Locke,

---

[21] Locke, *Second Treatise*, 45. See Thomas Jefferson, *Notes on the State of Virginia*, ed. William Pedan (New York, 1954), 164–65; Christopher Hill, "Pottage for Freeborn Englishmen: Attitudes to Wage Labor in the Sixteenth and Seventeenth Centuries," in *Socialism, Capitalism and Economic Growth* (Cambridge, 1967), 338–50; Hill, "James Harrington and the People," in *Puritanism and Revolution*, 299–313; Macpherson, *Possessive Individualism*, 107–59; C.B. Macpherson, "Servants and Labourers in Seventeenth-Century England," in *Democratic Theory*, 207–23; Scott, *Pursuit of Happiness*, 24–30.

[22] Locke, *Second Treatise*, 7; Blackstone, *Commentaries* 1: 410. See Nancy Cott, "Divorce and the Changing Status of Women in Eighteenth-Century Massachusetts," in *The American Family in Social-Historical Perspective*, ed. Michael Gordon (New York, 1978), 115–39; Morgan, *Puritan Family*, esp. pp. 19–64, 109–32; George Stroud, *A Sketch of the Laws Relating to Slavery* (New York, 1968; orig. pub. 1856), 41; Davis, *Slavery in Western Culture*, 102–6, 252–54; Orlando Patterson, *Slavery and Social Death: A Comparative Study* (Cambridge, 1982), 188–90; Pateman, *Sexual Contract*; Christopher Tomlins, "Subordination, Authority, Law: Subjects in Labor History," *International Labor and Working-Class History*, 47 (Spring 1995), 56–90.

it was "the man's share, as the abler and the stronger." Just as in the bargains between ruler and ruled and between master and servant, the wife ostensibly accepted submission by freely entering the marriage contract.[23]

According to Blackstone's *Commentaries*, the law treated marriage like any other contract. But this was something of a misstatement, as Blackstone's own exposition of the marital rule of coverture disclosed. Under this rule the marriage contract incorporated the wife's person into that of her husband, making them one at law, suspending her legal existence: her "very being" was merged into his. No other contract contained a rule obliterating the identity and autonomy of one party to the contract. Coverture had no parallel in commercial contracts; and for all the symmetries between marriage and the wage contract, the legal disabilities of the wife were far more severe than those of the hireling. Unlike the waged servant, the wife was not only bound to serve and obey the master of the household, she was also obliged to yield all she owned – her person, her body, her "being." As the protagonist in Daniel Defoe's novel *Roxana* explained, "if I shou'd be a Wife, all I had then, was given up to the Husband, and I was thenceforth to be under his Authority, only." Like all other contracts, marriage hinged on the principles of mutual consent and exchange. But, unlike any other contract, the marriage contract ordained male proprietorship and absolute female dispossession, establishing self ownership as the fundamental right of men alone.[24]

That contract conferred an unequal sort of freedom based on sexual difference was a proposition assumed by Enlightenment thinkers. Though they thought of contract as a universal right, they understood marriage as the sovereignty of husbands over wives. Yet the difference between the sexes was not their central concern. Rather, the critical difference was between slavery and freedom, a distinction that overshadowed differences of sex and degrees of unfreedom and freedom. Stripped of all rights of property and volition, slaves had utterly no contractual capacity; by contrast, free persons of both sexes could marry and (if a woman chose not to marry) both could contract to sell their labor for wages. Enlightenment writers saw slavery as exceptional among relations of personal dependence, a view that led them to elide the differences between the status of the wife and that of the servant. In their eyes what made the depen-

---

[23] Locke, *Second Treatise*, 44. See also Blackstone, *Commentaries* 1: 421, 430; Paley, *Principles* 1: 197–98; Paley, *Principles* 1: 204.

[24] Blackstone, *Commentaries* 1: 430; Daniel Defoe, *Roxana* (New York, 1982; orig. pub. 1724), 183.

dencies of marriage and labor unlike slavery, and therefore essentially similar, was that slavery alone rested on coercion – "a principle independent of the contract."[25]

In his *Lectures on Jurisprudence* delivered in the 1760s Adam Smith, the father of classical political economy, discredited social contract theory as a myth. His mentor, David Hume, had raised both philosophical and historical objections to contract as the basis for political obligation, and Smith, along with his disciples in both England and America, followed Hume's teachings. Thus by the late eighteenth century the doctrine of a political contract no longer held sway among social theorists. Yet Smith had not rejected all versions of contractualism. His writings celebrate relations of voluntary exchange and rights of proprietorship. While dissociating contract from the problem of political sovereignty, Smith linked it to the creation of wealth, a displacement emblematic of changing intellectual currents at the end of the eighteenth century. As the theory of a social compact came to appear a political fiction, the ideal of contract was newly embodied in the marketplace. Freedom of contract formed the crux of classical economics.[26]

Arguably, the founding of the American republic presented a semblance of an original political compact, as even critics of such accounts allowed. Moreover, well into the nineteenth century American political thinkers continued to speak of the political contract as fact, particularly during constitutional crises provoked by slavery and sectional conflict. Nevertheless, by the end of the Civil War, leading publicists of contractualism had dismissed the social contract as a figment of philosophers' imagination, and instead hailed the ascendance of market conceptions of contract.[27]

---

[25] Paley, *Principles* 1: 150. In return for his wife's voluntary surrender of her person and labor, the husband was bound to protect her and provide her with necessaries. See Pollack and Maitland, *History of English Law* 1: 585. On the refusal of the political theorists of the American Revolution to destabilize the rules of coverture or reenvision the status of women, see Linda Kerber, "The Paradox of Women's Citizenship in the Early Republic: The Case of *Martin vs. Massachusetts, 1805*," *American Historical Review,* 97 (April 1992), 349–78.

[26] Adam Smith, *Lectures on Jurisprudence,* ed. R.L. Meek, D.D. Raphael, and P.G. Stein (Oxford, 1978), 316–18. See also Robert Heilbroner, *The Worldly Philosophers: The Lives, Times and Ideas of the Great Economic Thinkers* (New York, 1972), 49–51; Atiyah, *Freedom of Contract,* 294; Gough, *Social Contract,* 174–222; Ely, *Property and Contract,* 107; Commons, *Legal Foundations,* lol.

[27] See E.L. Godkin, "The Democratic View of Democracy," *North American Review,* 101 (1965), 103, 107; Paley, *Principles* 1: 71–73. Both antislavery and proslavery advocates employed contractual imagery and justifications. See, for example, *Proceedings of the Anti-Slavery Convention Assembled at Philadelphia, December 4, 5, and 6, 1833* (New York, 1833), 14–15; Wendell Phillips, *Review of Webster,* 9–13, Pamphlet Collection, Wisconsin State Historical Society, Madison, Wisc.; "Immoral Contracts Not Bind-

Classical political economy forged the connection between contract and market relations as industrial capitalism developed on both sides of the Atlantic. Contract ratified free commerce in land, labor, money, and commodities, emerging as the dominant model of economic exchange, supplanting the older cultural power of the gift. It gave legal form and protection to market exchange. "Every man . . . lives by exchanging, or becomes in some measure a merchant, and the society itself grows to be . . . a commercial society," wrote Adam Smith in *The Wealth of Nations*.[28] Thus a contract transaction – commercial exchange – marked the advent not of religious community or political society but rather of acquisitive culture.

The market concept of contract did not so much as hint at reciprocity among unequals as a justification for relations of authority and obedience, which had been a principal meaning of contractualism in Puritan and Enlightenment social thought. To the contrary, as formulated by Adam Smith and his followers, contract stood for sharp bargaining, liberty, and formal equality among individuals burdened only by the goods they had for sale and ruled only by the laws of supply and demand. This form of exchange, wrote Smith, necessarily had a "rough equality" assured by the bargaining of the market, the competitive ritual of offer and acceptance – "Give me that which I want, and you shall have this which you want." The division of labor guaranteed that each person needed what others sold; consequently, all came to the market on "equal terms," as Smith's American disciples affirmed. "The parties in contract . . . stand on a footing of equality." In his 1848 treatise, *The Principles of Political Economy*, John Stuart Mill was just as positive that contract implied not only "free consent" but also the exchange of "an equivalent" in return for the right to the fruits of another's labor.[29] Such an express emphasis on the rule of equality, or equivalence in exchange, had belonged neither to covenant theology nor to secular social contract doctrine. By the mid-nineteenth century, the orthodoxy of market economics had come to eclipse philosophical and even religious

ing," *Liberator*, December 23, 1842; *Congressional Globe*, 39th Cong., 1st sess., 1866, 36, pt. 1: 477. On the representation of the Civil War as a crisis of contract, see Perry Miller, *The Life of the Mind in America from the Revolution to the Civil War* (New York, 1965), esp. p. 116; Gough, *Social Contract*, 214–22.

[28] Adam Smith, *An Inquiry into the Nature and Causes of the Wealth of Nations*, ed. Edwin Cannan (New York, 1937; orig. pub. 1776), 22.

[29] Ibid., 31, 14; Francis Wayland, *The Elements of Political Economy* (Boston, 1852; orig. pub. 1837), 301; Calvin Colton, *The Junius Tracts*, no. 7, "Labor and Capital" (1844; reprint New York, 1974), 7, and see p. 9; John Stuart Mill, *The Principles of Political Economy with Some Applications to Social Philosophy*, ed. Sir W.J. Ashley (New York, 1965; orig. pub. 1848), 221, 220. A cardinal tenet of classical economy states that only items with exchange value create wealth. See Smith, *Wealth of Nations*, 314–15; Mill, *Political Economy*, 4–9.

truths about human nature and social exchange, and contract theory registered this intellectual transformation.

Some aspects of classical political economy's construction of contract, however, closely echoed earlier contract doctrine. Adam Smith defined the individual subject of contract transactions as a masculine proprietor, agreeing with Locke that the right to contract derived from self ownership and that the source of all property was the title "every man has in his own labour." Mill alone among the Manchester school recognized woman as a self-owning individual by ascribing the natural right of property to the right of each to "his (or her) own faculties" and to the "fruits of their own labour." Mill also directly engaged the apparent conflict between the labor theory of property and the wage contract, a problem addressed by earlier thinkers. Observing that wage earners created the "whole produce" by their labor but were entitled merely to "their stipulated hire," he explained that laborers transferred part of their product to employers by "voluntary contract." Not only did the contract principle of voluntary exchange justify property in the fruits of another's labor, ostensibly reconciling the competing claims of buyers and sellers of labor; it also authorized wages unequal to the value of that labor.[30]

Precisely because the market economy pivoted on highly contradictory principles – competition and reciprocity, advantage and equivalence, suspicion and faith – the coercive power of law was required to safeguard contracts. For when contracts became dead letters, trust was broken and commerce obstructed; the uncertainties of language, appearance, and identity characteristic of market culture grew still more intense. In a commercial society, "held together by . . . feelings arising out of pecuniary interests," wrote Mill, the purpose of government was "enforcing contracts." Whether or not contracting parties trusted each other, the law would protect their bargains. Contract rights were inextricable from contract law.[31]

[30] Smith, *Wealth of Nations*, 121–22, and see p. 66; Mill, *Political Economy*, 218, 219. Seen also Wayland, *Political Economy*, 114, 154. The concept of property in labor was Smith's justification for repudiating laws that regulated the labor market and the wage relation as an interference with the "liberty" of both laborers and employers. Quoted a century later in Justice Field's famous dissent in the *Slaughterhouse Cases*, it rapidly became a bedrock of American judicial rulings striking down labor regulations in the name of "liberty of contract" well into the twentieth century. See William Forbath, "The Ambiguities of Free Labor: Labor and Law in the Gilded Age," *Wisconsin Law Review*, no. 4 (1985), 767–817; Charles McCurdy, "The Roots of 'Liberty of Contract' Reconsidered: Major Premises in the Law of Employment, 1867–1937," *Supreme Court Historical Society Yearbook* (Washington, D.C., 1984), 20–33; Roscoe Pound, "Liberty of Contract," *Yale Law Journal*, 8 (1909), 454–87.

[31] Smith, *Lectures on Jurisprudence*, 86–87; Mill, *Political Economy*, 754, 798. On the profound cultural confusion – the ambiguity of social roles, relations, and identities – wrought by the predominance of the market economy, see Jean-Christophe Agnew,

By a strict legal definition, contract signified "an agreement, upon sufficient consideration, to do or not do a particular thing." Such was Blackstone's classic formulation, the key components of a legal contract being volition and exchange. Each contracting party had freely to give "consideration," the thing exchanged for a promise, or quid pro quo. In Blackstone's reading of the law, any degree of reciprocity, if reached by agreement and not unlawful, created a binding contract. Blackstone's treatment of the subject in his *Commentaries* was rather sketchy; it was left to later jurists to elaborate his outline into an intricate common law of contract responsive to a swiftly expanding market economy. The contract law that came to be identified with nineteenth-century jurisprudence valorized classical economic precepts and lent order and certainty to impersonal market transactions.[32]

Still, the legal essence of contract remained as Blackstone had defined it. The United States Supreme Court quoted his phrasing, and American law treatises reiterated that consent and reciprocity constituted a contract. Later commentators elaborated the precept that the equities of contract, like the market itself, were self-regulating: the courts could only prevent outright fraud, not judge if bargains were unfair. However much economic theorists might stress equivalence as an element of contract, the exchange of perfect equivalents was not a legal requirement of contract. Every contract originated from "the mutual agreement of the parties," explained American law writers of the early nineteenth century. There also had to be "something given in exchange," as Chancellor James Kent stated, "something that is mutual, or something which is the induce-

---

Worlds Apart: The Market and the Theater in Anglo-American Thought (New York, 1986). On the dissolution of all social relations into proprietary exchange relations, see Knox, trans., *Hegel's Philosophy of Right*, 57–64; Karl Polanyi, *The Great Transformation* (New York, 1944), 163; Karl Marx, *Capital*, trans. Ben Fowkes (3 vols., New York, 1977; orig. pub. 1867), 1: 178. On the significance of contract law to the development of the market economy – the crucial importance of certainty, predictability, and security of promises and contract obligations to capital accumulation, investment, and development, see Commons, *Legal Foundations*, 90–91, 125, 246–54, 302; Mill, *Political Economy*, 165–67; Macpherson, *Democratic Theory*, 242; Atiyah, *Freedom of Contract*, 102, 230–31, 398–417; Haskell, "Humanitarian Sensibility," pt. 2.

[32] Blackstone, *Commentaries* 2: 442–45. See Atiyah, *Freedom of Contract*, esp. pp. 85–89, 102–3, 146–77, 215–16, 230–31, 300–393; A.W.B. Simpson's introduction to Book 2 of Blackstone, *Commentaries* 2: iii, xiii-xiv, and also his *Common Law of Contract*; Pollack and Maitland, *History of English Law* 2: 184–233; Pollack, *Principles of Contract*. On the history of contract law in America, see J. Willard Hurst, *Law and the Conditions of Freedom in the Nineteenth Century United States* (Madison, 1956), esp. pp. 9–22, 75–77; Morton Horwitz, *The Transformation of American Law 1780–1860* (Cambridge, 1977), 160–210; Grant Gilmore, *The Death of Contract* (Columbus, 1974); Lawrence Friedman, *Contract Law in America: A Social and Economic Case Study* (Madison, 1965); Anthony T. Kronman, "Paternalism and the Law of Contracts," *Yale Law Journal*, 92 (April 1983), 763–98.

ment to the contract." But jurists did not specify the substance of mutuality. And presuming the autonomy and equality of contracting parties, the courts refused to command exact reciprocity as a condition of the contract. What mattered at law was that the contract involved consent and some kind of consideration.[33]

In political economy and law the equation of contract with commodity relations was paramount, but not absolute. Nor was every type of contract presumed to entail the equality of the contracting parties, despite the fact of reciprocity. Both classical economics and common law rules treated contract as the axis not simply of the marketplace but of marriage and the household. Yet the marriage contract, contrary to market exchanges, continued to be understood as a dependency relation, for political economy did not reformulate domestic doctrine. Affirming the husband's "great power" as master of the household, Adam Smith conceptualized marriage as a starkly unequal relationship, which, along with the rights of liberty and property, represented one of the fundamental "priviledges [*sic*] of free men."[34]

American authors of common law treatises in the nineteenth century also found contract tenets fully complementary with the subordination of wives and servants. Following Blackstone, they underscored the principles of consent and reciprocity that marriage and wage labor shared with other contracts. However, these writers sharply distinguished the wage contract and marriage contract from purely commercial transactions, defining both as *domestic relations* that presupposed not simply consent and exchange but unique rights of authority and obligations of obedience. Chancellor Kent wrote that the wife's duty to serve and obey was the "consideration" she owed in return for her husband's protection. Tapping Reeve wrote of the husband's property in the "person of his wife" and all she acquired by "labor, service or act," and of the wife's incapacity to own anything or to make contracts. The hireling's legal dependency was not held to be as complete and permanent as that of the wife. Yet the master's right to "command," as Kent declared, was

---

[33] William W. Story, *A Treatise on the Law of Contracts Not under Seal* (New York, 1972; orig. pub. 1844), 4; James S. Kent, *Commentaries on American Law* (4 vols., New York, 1832), 2: 463. See *Sturges v. Crowningshield*, 17 U.S. 122, 197 (1819); Parsons, *Contracts*, 458, 8, 447–52, 499. The language of the *Sturges* holding was widely restated; see, for example, Gulian C. Verplanck, *An Essay on the Doctrine of Contracts: Being an Inquiry on How Contracts Are Affected in Law and Morals by Concealment, Error, or Inadequate Price* (New York, 1972; orig. pub. 1825), 224; Parsons, *Contracts*, 6. On the dissolution of fixed notions of value and fairness in contract law, see Horwitz, *Transformation*, 160–210.

[34] Smith, *Lectures on Jurisprudence*, 176, 191, and see pp. 86, 141, 176–78.

fitting in a labor contract where "one is bound to render service, and the other to pay the stipulated consideration."[35]

Law writers in America adhered to contract as the basis for domestic authority, at a time when few thinkers still found it a convincing theory of political sovereignty. Simultaneously, however, they clung to the idea that contract represented the boundary between slavery and freedom. The obligations of only one "species of servants" – chattel slaves – was "not founded on compact," declared Tapping Reeve. Nor could the slave, being dispossessed of self, enter any binding contracts, even marriage, for the husband's rights and duties were "incompatible with a state of slavery."[36] Positive that contract signified freedom, legal thinkers found no need to justify the asymmetry between rules of voluntary exchange that assumed equality in the marketplace and that assured subordination in the household.

Nor had this contradiction posed a dilemma for Adam Smith. He contrasted free men to slaves, emphasizing that even lowly hirelings were entitled to the "benefit of marriage," an institution in which the wife toiled "under the husband as his servant" in exchange for the subsistence he provided. Thus Smith explained the material reasons for the wife's submission – the economic connection between the wage contract and the marriage contract. Unlike the female slave, whose master supplied her needs, the wife was instead bound to her husband as his dependent. In such market representations of contract freedom, women, as wives, were never fully free.[37]

With the rise of radical abolitionism in the 1830s issues of contract came to bear much of the weight of the protracted contest over chattel slavery. In turn, the conflict over slavery infused the principles of self ownership, consent, and exchange with new ideological urgency. As abolitionists asserted that the slave system was at war with funda-

---

[35] Kent, *Commentaries* 2: 76–77, 147; Tapping Reeve, *The Law of Baron and Femme, of Parent and Child, Guardian and Ward, Master and Servant and of the Powers of the Court of Chancery* (Albany, 1862), 220, 139, 182, and see p. 482; Kent, *Commentaries* 2: 76–77, 147, 258. See also Story, *Treatise on the Law of Contracts*, 43; John C. Hurd, *The Law of Freedom and Bondage in the United States* (2 vols., Boston, 1858), 1: 137; Maxwell Bloomfield, *American Lawyers in a Changing Society, 1776–1876* (Cambridge, 1976), 105–7; Linda K. Kerber, "A Constitutional Right to Be Treated Like American Ladies: Women and the Obligations of Citizenship," in *U.S. History as Women's History: New Feminist Essays*, ed., Linda K. Kerber, Alice Kessler-Harris, and Kathryn Kish Sklar (Chapel Hill, 1995), 17–35.

[36] Reeve, *Baron and Femme*, 482–83. See also Kent, *Commentaries* 2: 247–58; Story, *Treatise on Contracts*, 50; Stroud, *Laws Relating to Slavery*, 41. See Hurd, *Law of Freedom and Bondage*.

[37] Smith, *Lectures on Jurisprudence*, 191, 162.

mental contract rights, contract became the language of insurgent popular politics. But this was not antislavery's only influence on contract doctrine. Abolitionism also reshaped the meaning of contract freedom by dissociating wage labor from relations of personal dependency while at the same time placing the contract between husband and wife at the forefront of the debate over slavery and freedom.

According to the Declaration of Sentiments set forth by the American Antislavery Society in 1833, all the evils of slavery accrued from converting human beings into "marketable commodities." As objects owned and exchanged by masters, slaves had no right to their own bodies, their households were torn apart, and they were robbed of the fruits of their labor – this was "a daring infringement on the law of nature, a base overthrow of the very foundations of the social compact." By 1840 abolitionists had split into factions clashing over political goals and tactics; nonetheless, they still shared the view that slavery annihilated rights long associated with contract. The "infernal catalogue" drawn up by Frederick Douglass in 1849 listed the wrongs of bondage that he had escaped: "To buy and sell, to brand and scourge human beings . . . to rob them of all the just rewards of their labor . . . to blot out the institution of marriage." Speaking of the slave's misery, William Goodell simply asked, "Can a chattel make a contract?"[38]

The slave codes of the Old South articulated the dispossessions and disabilities of bondage. As a species of property, slaves had no legal control of their own persons and no proprietary rights or contractual capacities. "A slave is one who is in the power of a master to whom he belongs," the Louisiana Code declared. "All that a slave possesses belongs to his master; he possesses nothing of his own." Southern courts recognized no volition in slaves; the master's total dominion dictated the slave's "want of free consent," ruled the North Carolina high court. Without legal power to assert rights or incur duties, slaves could neither marry nor lay claim to wages. As a treatise on slave law explained the essence of bondage, "One general principle predominates in all the slave states, and that is, that a slave cannot make a contract."[39]

[38] *The Antislavery Argument,* ed. William H. Pease and Jane H. Pease (New York, 1965), 67, 68; Frederick Douglass, "The Address of Southern Delegates in Congress to Their Constituents; or, the Address of John C. Calhoun and Forty Other Thieves," *North Star,* February 9, 1849, in Philip S. Foner, *The Life and Writings of Frederick Douglass* (4 vols.; New York, 1950–1955), 1: 358; "Goodell's Anti-Slavery Lectures," reprinted in *Liberator,* April 5, 1839. See also Aileen Kraditor, *Means and Ends in American Abolitionism: Garrison and His Critics on Strategy and Tactics, 1834–1850* (New York, 1967); Ronald G. Walters, *The Antislavery Appeal: American Abolitionism after 1830* (Baltimore, 1976).
[39] Stroud, *Laws Relating to Slavery,* 10, 31; *State v. Samuel,* 2 Devereux and Battle's *Law Review,* cited in James Bradwell, *Validity of Slave Marriages* (Chicago, 1866), 15;

Even in justifying slavery, southerners agreed that contract marked the line between freedom and bondage. In an 1850 sermon on "The Rights and Duties of Masters" James Henley Thornwell, who was one of slavery's most formidable advocates, decried the abolitionist theory that the slaveowner held property in the slave's limbs, organs, and soul. Arguing from the standpoint of moral philosophy, he insisted that no human spirit, not even the slave's, could be owned by another or transformed into "an article of barter or exchange." Slavery, he maintained, consisted simply of the absence of contract. "What is it that makes a man a slave? We answer, the obligation to labour for another, determined by the Providence of God, independently of the provisions of a contract." His point was that, just as under the wage system, the slave master was entitled only to labor (however forcibly extracted), not to the slave's person, which was understood as distinct from labor.[40]

Such arguments cut to the heart of abolitionist faith. For Thornwell preached that the difference between labor systems expressed by contract did not bear upon issues of human agency, responsibility, or subjectivity. Whether laborers were slaves or hirelings, they were "equally moral, equally responsible, equally men. But they work upon different principles." Although slavery was opposed to contract, it did not divest slaves "of humanity," or degrade "them from the rank of responsible and voluntary agents to the condition of tools or brutes," or annul their "personal rights" and "moral obligation." Like the free laborer, the slave was self-owning – as Thornwell said, the slave's body was "not mine, but his." This creed deemed contract insignificant as a principle of moral and social order, challenging the idea that self entitlement and personal autonomy derived solely from contract.[41]

Where southern arguments converged with northern labor reform was in assailing the unfreedom of voluntary contract relations. Both slaveholders and Yankee hirelings sought to reveal the coercions and dependencies of wage labor while deploring free market relations that treated impersonal commodity exchange as a model

---

Jacob D. Wheeler, *A Practical Treatise on the Law of Slavery* (New York, 1837), cited in "Slavery as Created and Established by Law," *Emancipator*, September 19, 1839. See Hurd, *Law of Freedom and Bondage*, 42, 44; Mark Tushnet, *The American Law of Slavery, 1810–1860: Considerations of Humanity and Interest* (Princeton, 1981); Alan Watson, *Slave Law in the Americas* (Athens, Ga., 1989).

[40] James H. Thornwell, *The Rights and the Duties of Masters: A Sermon Preached at the Dedication of a Church, Erected in Charleson, S.C., for the Benefit and Instruction of the Coloured Population* (Charleston, 1850), 22, 24. See also Eugene D. Genovese, *The Slaveholders' Dilemma: Freedom and Progress in Southern Conservative Thought, 1820–1860* (Columbia, S.C., 1992).

[41] Thornwell, *Rights and Duties*, 24, 22, 24.

for contract rights and duties. The most famous southern indictment
was George Fitzhugh's *Cannibals All!*, a tract that contrasted slavery's
benevolent mutualism to the brutality of free labor.

Capital exercises a more perfect compulsion over free laborers than human
masters over slaves; for free laborers must at all times work or starve, and
slaves are supported whether they work or not. . . . Though each free laborer
has no particular master, his wants and other men's capital make him a slave
without a master.

For northern critics, the object was not to defend slavery with wage
labor as the foil; nor did they hold that slaves and hirelings were
equally self owning and capable of personal agency. But they did
argue that contract was a precarious basis for freedom. "There may
be those who believe that wages slaves work when and for whom they
please – make their own contracts," wrote the labor reformer William West during his famous controversy with the abolitionist leader
William Lloyd Garrison in 1847. "This apparent freedom of the
wage slaves is wholly fictitious," for the lash of "bitter necessity" fell
on them. The doctrine of labor spokesmen such as West was the
older republican one that defined ownership of productive property
as the foundation of individual independence – a doctrine that conflated slavery and freedom by calling into question wage labor's guarantee of contract rights.[42]

The response of most abolitionists was to utter even more categorical tributes to contract freedom. While not insensitive to the plight
of the laboring poor, they claimed that the wage–slavery argument
obscured the singular evils of chattel slavery and confused the true
meaning of freedom. As the former slave Ellen Craft avowed in 1852,
"I had much rather starve . . . a free woman, than be a slave." Most
abolitionists championed the commerce in free labor, extolling its
voluntary and equitable aspects.[43] Indeed, they argued that the wage
contract eradicated personal dominion and subordination – an idea

[42] George Fitzhugh, *Cannibals All! or, Slaves without Masters*, ed. C. Vann Woodward
(Cambridge, 1960; orig. pub. 1857), 32; William West, "Wages Slavery and Chattel
Slavery," *Liberator*, April 2, 1847. See also Eugene Genovese, *The World the Slaveholders Made: Two Essays in Interpretation* (New York, 1971), 118–244; Eric Foner, "Abolitionism and the Labor Movement in Ante-Bellum America," in *Politics and Ideology
in the Age of the Civil War* (New York, 1980), 57–76; David Roediger, *The Wages of
Whiteness: Race and the Making of the American Working Class* (London, 1991); Sean
Wilentz, *Chants Democratic: New York City and the Rise of the American Working Class,
1788–1858* (New York, 1984).
[43] "Letter from Ellen Craft," reprinted in *Pennsylvania Freeman*, December 23, 1852.
See Davis, *Slavery in the Age of Revolution*, 455–501; Davis, "Reflections"; Jonathan
A. Glickstein, *Concepts of Free Labor in Antebellum America* (New Haven, 1991); Foner,
"Abolitionism and the Labor Movement."

that defied Enlightenment political theory and common law precepts that did not recognize hirelings as fully autonomous.

By no means did abolitionists equate hirelings with wives or classify them as subordinate members of a master's household. Rather,
through their attack on slavery they transformed the cultural meaning of wage labor, dissociating it from domestic dependency – removing the free labor contract from the household's shadow. Garrison contrasted the condition of the wage laborer to that of a
"domestic animal," a metaphor that could have denoted either a
chattel slave or a wife. Was the hireling not a "free agent?" he asked.
"May he not contract for his wages? . . . Are his movements dependent on the will and pleasure of another? . . . Does he not own himself? Is he not 'lord of his presence,' at least, though he may be lord
'of no land beside'?" Instead of defining a condition of dependency
less profound than chattel slavery, the wage contract had become
the very token of freedom.[44]

Legitimating wage labor was a central part of the abolitionist project, but never its sum total. Other dimensions of the argument
against slavery were at least as culturally significant as the problem
posed by labor discipline. For most abolitionists, the autonomy expressed in wage labor was but an offshoot of the underlying right of
property in the self that constituted the taproot of contract freedom.
Despite proslavery rebuttals, they yoked self ownership solely to freedom and prized it as the most indispensable right.[45]

"SELF-RIGHT is the *foundation* right – *the post in the middle,* to
which all other rights are fastened," declared Theodore Weld in
1838. The same year the Second National Anti-Slavery Convention
of American Women declared that women had the authority to assert the core right of self ownership on the slave's behalf, to ask
whether a man's "bones and sinews shall be his own, or another's."
Black abolitionists, born both free and slave, also adopted the rhetoric of possessive individualism. Free blacks considered self entitlement an essential aspect of liberty, though recognizing that it hardly
toppled the barriers of racial prejudice or economic privilege. Nancy
Prince, a free black born in Massachusetts, wrote that freed slaves in
Jamaica were "determined to possess themselves, and to possess
property besides." Fugitive slaves advocated the right of self sover-

---

[44] "Chattel Slavery and Wages Slavery," *Liberator,* March 26, 1847, October 1, 1847.
[45] See Jonathan A. Glickstein, " 'Poverty Is Not Slavery': American Abolitionists and
the Competitive Labor Market," in *Anti-Slavery Reconsidered: New Perspectives on the
Abolitionists,* ed. Lewis Perry and Michael Fellman (Baton Rouge, 1979), 195–218;
Ronald G. Walters, "The Boundaries of Abolitionism," in Perry and Fellman, eds.,
Anti-Slavery Reconsidered, 3–23.

From Bondage to Contract

eignty with particular ardor borne perhaps from knowing its denial. The narrative of one fugitive began, "A horse don't know that he's property, and a man does." The former slave Samuel Ringgold Ward made the point succinctly in an 1850 speech: "This is the question, Whether a man has a right to himself." To most abolitionists the conflict between fundamental rights and self dispossession was a guiding assumption.[46]

In exalting the inviolable right of self ownership, antislavery advocates did not simply argue on the abstract plane of natural law; they turned to the body's palpable torments and reasoned in sensual, empirical ways. They compiled excruciating evidence of physical suffering, which was meant to incite a visceral response and played upon the cult of feeling dominant in Victorian America. Abolitionists were by no means alone in deploying images of suffering bodies; the literature of antebellum humanitarian reform was stocked with them. Conceivably, even the most empathetic of white abolitionists might not have been able to exclude all traces of voyeurism from their representations of the suffering slave. For black abolitionists, however, these images may have represented not only the singular horrors of slavery but also the vulnerability to violence and coercion shared by all members of their race. Again and again, Frederick Douglass summoned his audience to feel the slave's pain as his back was "torn all to pieces . . . flesh . . . cut with the rugged lash . . . warm brine . . . poured into . . . bleeding wounds." And the crimes of the domestic slave trade came alive through an inventory of marketable body parts. "At these auction-stands," stated William Wells Brown, a leader of the black abolitionist movement, "bones, muscles, sinews, blood and nerves, of human beings, are sold."[47]

The bodily images reflect how seriously abolitionists took the cor-

---

[46] Walters, "Boundaries of Abolitionism," 9; Elizabeth Cady Stanton, Susan B. Anthony, and Matilda J. Gage, eds., *History of Woman Suffrage* (6 vols., Rochester, 1887), 1: 339; *A Narrative of the Life and Travels of Mrs. Nancy Prince. Written by Herself,* 2nd ed. (Boston, 1853) in *Collected Black Women's Narratives,* ed. Henry Louis Gates, Jr. (New York, 1988), 49–50; "Narrative by Lewis G. Clarke," in *The Black Abolitionist Papers,* ed. C. Peter Ripley (5 vols., Chapel Hill, 1991), 3: 393; Speech by Samuel Ringgold Ward in Ripley, ed., *Black Abolitionist Papers,* 4: 50.

[47] "Letter to William Lloyd Garrison," *Liberator,* November 18, 1842, in *The Life and Writings of Frederick Douglass: Early Years, 1817–1849,* ed. Philip S. Foner (5 vols, New York, 1950), 1: 108–9; William Wells Brown, "The American Slave-Trade," *Liberty Bell* (Boston, 1848), 235–36. See Karen Halttunen, "Humanitarianism and the Pornography of Pain in Anglo-American Culture," *American Historical Review,* 100 (April 1995), 303–34; Elizabeth B. Clark, " 'The Sacred Rights of the Weak': Pain, Sympathy, and the Culture of Individual Rights in Antebellum America," *Journal of American History,* 82 (September 1995), 463–93; Karen Halttunen, *Confidence Men and Painted Women: A Study of Middle-Class Culture in America, 1830–1870* (New Haven, 1982); Elizabeth Alexander, " 'Can You Be BLACK and Look at This?': Reading the Rodney King Video(s)," *Public Culture,* 7 (1994), 77–94.

poreal dimension of the formal right of self proprietorship, which they regarded as the only secure guarantee of personal autonomy. The obverse of the slave whose person was dismembered, through punishment and as a commodity, was the autonomous individual whose body was inviolate. Freedom, as Douglass curtly defined it, was "appropriating my own body to my use." Here abolitionism differed from other contemporary expressions of liberal thought, in which the attributes of individualism characteristically implied a renunciation of bodily experience and the irrationality and carnality long associated with matters of the flesh. Rather than being unintelligible in the terms of Enlightenment political theory, the body's claims were formulated by abolitionists in the classical, legal language of rights. To be sure, antislavery rendered freedom abstract by enshrining ownership of self, at the expense of an older republican emphasis on ownership of productive property. But by representing free individuals (in contrast to slaves) as unmistakably embodied bearers of rights, abolitionists rendered self ownership concrete while suggesting a new moral and ideological framework for thinking about the vicissitudes of human bodies. By their lights, soul and body were inseverable; spirit could not be emancipated where flesh was bound.[48]

Above all, abolitionists dwelled on the circumstances of the enslaved female body through evocations affirming the ideal of contract freedom. In their eyes, the two sexes suffered differently under slavery. They constantly stressed that the bondswoman alone endured sexual violence, as well as bloody punishment and the terror of the auction block. As one writer observed, only in regard to women chattel did the master's lust swell his sadism and greed, mingling "the effervescence of lewdness with the wantonness of ferocity." Such arguments countered southern apologetics about the slave-holding family, black and white, and attacked the analogy, so central to the southern worldview, of slavery and marriage.[49]

---

[48] "Letter to Garrison," 109. See Clark, " 'Sacred Rights of the Weak' "; Leonore Davidoff, " 'Adam Spoke First and Named the Orders of the World': Masculine and Feminine Domains in History and Sociology," in *Politics of Everyday Life: Continuity and Change in Work and Family*, ed. Helen Corr and Lynn Jamieson (London, 1990), 229–55; Karen Sanchez-Eppler, *Touching Liberty: Abolition, Feminism, and the Politics of the Body* (Berkeley, 1993), 1–49. For recent scholarship stressing the opposition between liberal theory and circumstances of human embodiment – an opposition that abolitionist rhetoric challenges – see Michel Foucault, *The History of Sexuality. Volume 1: An Introduction* (New York, 1978), esp. pp. 145–59; Pateman, *Sexual Contract*, esp. pp. 189–234; Lauren Berlant, "National Brands/National Body: Imitation of Life," in *The Phantom Public Sphere*, ed. Bruce Robbins (Minneapolis, 1993), 176–79.

[49] George Bourne, *Slavery Illustrated in Its Effects upon Woman and Domestic Society* (Freeport, N.Y., 1972; orig. pub. 1837), 59; See Eliza Lee Follen, "Women's Work,"

By the late 1830s antislavery literature focused on violation of the marriage contract, as abolitionists made a mission of revealing slavery's unspeakably private dimensions. According to one 1837 tract, "no part of the dark and hidden iniquities of slavery" demanded exposure more than its "odious lusts" and destruction of the "nuptial covenant." The African Methodist Episcopal Church declared that slavery was synonymous with "fornication, adultery, concubinage." No abolitionist argument proved more compelling than that testifying to the conflict between slavery and domesticity, as illustrated by Harriet Beecher Stowe's best-selling 1852 melodrama, *Uncle Tom's Cabin*. "Don't you know a slave can't be married?" asked one of Stowe's characters. "I can't hold you for my wife."[50] Family images pervaded antebellum public discussion, and abolitionism was not alone in defining marriage as a fundamental right. Yet the debate over slavery made marriage central as never before to the understanding of contract freedom. Domesticity supplied a language for sectional conflict, and marriage a measure for the morality of opposing social systems. The question was whether slavery or freedom constituted the bedrock of home life. While southerners equated master and slave with husband and wife, abolitionists linked the household's integrity to free contract relations. Frederick Douglass condemned the defense of slavery as a "domestic institution," protesting that this "soft and innocent term" hid the fact that slav-

---

Liberty Bell (Boston, 1842), 8; Eugene Genovese, " 'Our Family, White and Black': Family and Household in the Southern Slaveholders' World View," in *In Joy and in Sorrow: Women, Family, and Marriage in the Victorian South*, ed. Carol Bleser (New York, 1991), 69–87; Stephanie McCurry, "The Two Faces of Republicanism: Gender and Proslavery Politics in Antebellum South Carolina," *Journal of American History*, 78 (March 1992), 1245–64; Michael P. Johnson, "Planters and Patriarchy: Charleston, 1800–1860," *Journal of Southern History*, 46 (1980), 45–72; Margaret A. Burnham, "An Impossible Marriage: Slave Law and Family Law," *Law and Inequality*, 5 (1987), 187–225. On female slaves, see Jacqueline Jones, *Labor of Love, Labor of Sorrow: Black Women, Work, and the Family from Slavery to the Present* (New York, 1985); Deborah Gray White, *Ar'n't I a Woman: Female Slaves in the Plantation South* (New York, 1985); Elizabeth Fox-Genovese, *Within the Plantation Household: Black and White Women of the Old South* (Chapel Hill, 1988).

[50] Bourne, *Slavery Illustrated*, 13, 31, 29; Ripley, ed., *Black Abolitionist Papers* 4: 196; Harriet Beecher Stowe, *Uncle Tom's Cabin* (New York, 1952; orig. pub. 1852), 17. See also Lydia Maria Child, *Authentic Anecdotes of American Slavery* (Newburyport, Mass., 1838), 15, 6; Theodore W. Weld, *Slavery As It Is: Testimony of a Thousand Witnesses* (New York, 1839); Harriet Beecher Stowe, *The Key to Uncle Tom's Cabin* (London, 1853); Harriet A. Jacobs, *Incidents in the Life of a Slave Girl. Written by Herself*, ed. Jean Fagan Yellin (Cambridge, Mass., 1987), 18. On the violation of slave marriages and rape of slave women, see Ann P. Malone, *Sweet Chariot: Slave Family and Household Structure in Nineteenth-Century Louisiana* (Chapel Hill, 1992), 228; Robert W. Fogel, *Without Consent or Contract: The Rise and Fall of American Slavery* (New York, 1989), 167, 179, 183–84; Burnham, "Impossible Marriage," 195–202; Herbert G. Gutman, *The Black Family in Slavery and Freedom, 1750–1925* (New York, 1976), 318; Melton A. McClaurin, *Celia, A Slave* (Athens, Ga., 1991), 98.

ery's reality was "to sunder families for the convenience of purchasers" and subject female slaves to the "barbarous work" of debauched slave masters. Douglass wrote of the "hearts of husbands and wives" torn by slaveholders, "bleeding ligaments . . . which before constituted the twain one flesh."[51]

Abolitionists sought literally to bring home the conflict between slavery and marriage by asking free persons to imagine themselves as slaves. Appeals for empathetic projection must have had special effect when delivered by former slaves. "Go into a southern market and see men and women sold in lots," implored William Wells Brown. "Place your wife, daughter or child in their position." The fugitive slave Lewis Clarke toured the North calling on free men to put themselves in the position of the slave without rights to his womenfolk. "I can't tell these respectable people as much as I would like to, but think for a minute how you would like to have *your* sisters, and *your* wives, and *your* daughters, completely, teetotally, and altogether, in the power of a master. . . . If a husband dares to say a word . . . they tie him up." Scenes of women sold at auction and at the mercy of slaveholders were meant to stir men who were used to being masters at home.[52]

The flesh of female slaves thus took center stage in abolitionist propaganda. Within the antislavery repertoire of bodily metaphors, the predominant one was the scourged body of the bondswoman, an image that symbolized the slave's utter debasement. Even abolitionists left to private fantasy the master's rape of his female slave, but they did not flinch from depicting other abuses that were disturbingly full of sexual meaning. In his autobiography Frederick Douglass dwelled on the wounds of slave women, giving a detailed account of the punishment delivered by a jealous master on a female slave for daring to meet illicitly with her lover: "Esther's wrists were firmly tied. . . . Her back and shoulders were bare to the waist. Behind her stood old master, with cowskin in hand, preparing his barbarous work with all manner of harsh, coarse, and tantalizing epithets. The

---

[51] Douglass, "Address of Southern Delegates," 358; "Letter to Garrison." See also Kerber, "Paradox of Women's Citizenship," 354–55; Genovese, *The World the Slaveholders Made*, 195–202; Johnson, "Planters and Patriarchy"; Catherine Clinton and Nina Silber, eds., *Divided Houses: Gender and the Civil War* (New York, 1992); Ronald G. Walters, "The Erotic South: Civilization and Sexuality in American Abolitionism," *American Quarterly*, 25 (May 1973), 177–201; Elizabeth Fox-Genovese, "Family and Female Identity in the Antebellum South: Sarah Gayle and Her Family," in Bleser, ed., *In Joy and in Sorrow*, 15–31; Kristin Hoganson, "Garrisonian Abolitionists and the Rhetoric of Gender, 1850–1860," *American Quarterly*, 45 (December 1993), 558–95.
[52] Speech of William Wells Brown, October 23, 1854, in Ripley, ed., *Black Abolitionist Papers* 4: 247; "Narrative by Lewis G. Clarke," 393–94.

screams of his victim were most piercing. He was cruelly deliberate, and protracted the torture, as one who was delighted with the scene." Douglass recalled that he was first aroused to slavery's wickedness as a young boy, watching the whipping of his own cousin: "Her neck and shoulders were covered with scars . . . her face literally covered with blood."[53]

In accounts tinged with eroticism, abolitionists evoked a corporeal slave economy that was diametrically opposed to the sexual order of free society, in which female purity was valued as a priceless possession. Witness after witness divulged the slave masters' " 'habit not only of stripping their female slaves of their clothing . . . but of subjecting their naked persons to the most minute and revolting inspection.' " Horror at such lewdly intimate practices of calculating profit drew together diverse antislavery advocates – black and white, male and female, those born both slave and free. They joined in describing scenes that were all but pornographic, lingering particularly over the unclothed body of the female slave. Routinely, they testified, she was put up for exhibition as a commodity, entirely naked. The former slave Louisa Picquet spoke from personal experience, recounting the procedure of her own sale at a public auction: "whoever want to buy come and examine, and ask you whole lot of questions. They began to take the clothes off of me." According to Thomas Wentworth Higginson, when a female slave was for sale, slave traders bid buyers to "*strip her naked and examine every inch of her.*"[54]

Such representations were no less potent in abolitionist polemics against slavery as an immoral labor system and illegitimate exercise of power. Jehiel Beman, a free black, recounted journeying for the

[53] Frederick Douglass, *My Bondage and My Freedom* (New York, 1969; orig. pub. 1855), 87, 82. See also Jean Fagan Yellin, *Women and Sisters: The Antislavery Feminists in American Culture* (New Haven, 1989), 71–89; Margaret M. R. Kellow, "The Divided Mind of Antislavery Feminism: Lydia Maria Child and the Construction of African American Womanhood," in *Discovering the Women in Slavery*, ed. Patricia Morton (Athens, Ga., 1996), 107–26; Hazel V. Carby, *Reconstructing Womanhood: The Emergence of the Afro-American Woman Novelist* (New York, 1987), 35; Hortense J. Spillers, "Mama's Baby, Papa's Maybe: An American Grammar Book," *diacritics*, 17 (Summer 1987), 65–81; Walters, "The Erotic South"; Ann duCille, "The Occult of True Black Womanhood: Critical Demeanor and Black Feminist Studies," *Signs*, 19 (Spring 1994), 591–629, quote at p. 592. Not only female abolitionists dwelled on sexual matters, as has been suggested in recent scholarly assessments; see, for example, Sanchez-Eppler, *Touching Liberty*, 22–23.
[54] Weld, *Slavery As It Is*, 154; H. Mattison, *Louisa Picquet, The Octaroon: A Tale of Southern Slave Life, Or Inside Views of Southern Domestic Life* (New York, 1861), in Gates, ed., *Collected Black Women's Narratives*, 16; Higginson cited in Charles K. Whipple, *The Family Relation, as Affected by Slavery* (Cincinnati, 1858), 15. See also Halttunen, "Pornography of Pain"; Darlene C. Hine and Kate Wittenstein, "Female Slave Resistance: The Economics of Sex," in *Black Women Cross-Culturally*, ed. Filomina C. Steady (Cambridge, Mass., 1981), 290–96.

first time in the South and being stricken nearly speechless by the sight of "my sisters toiling, pitchfork and rake in hand, under the scorching rays of the sun ... but little on the body ... my feelings were such as I cannot describe. I tried to raise my cries to Heaven, but in this I was interrupted, for the flowing tear forced its way down my care-worn cheek." Matter-of-factly, the Yankee reformer Samuel Gridley Howe sought to touch a nerve in northern audiences by describing a public whipping at a New Orleans slave prison: "There lay a black girl, flat upon her face on a board ... a strap passed over the small of her back. ... Below the strap she was entirely naked."[55]

On the bodies of female slaves, therefore, abolitionists saw most spectacularly branded the crimes of slavery that accrued from treating human beings as property to be bought and sold. Just when blackface minstrel performances were fetishizing black bodies in a new form of commercial entertainment, antislavery reformers were calling public attention to the commodified bodies of female slaves for insurrectionary purposes.[56] Dishonored, stripped bare, the bondswoman literally embodied the denial of property in the self, which for abolitionists counted as the ultimate wrong. In antislavery literature she served as the symbol of the dispossessed self, someone without any rights, the paradigmatic chattel. Through her image abolitionists sanctified, by negation, the ideal of self ownership as the essence of freedom.

This method of reasoning had no precedent in the classical liberal thought of the seventeenth and eighteenth centuries from which American abolitionists derived central elements of their critique of slavery. Although contrasting freedom and bondage, Enlightenment writers certainly did not take the subjugation of slave women as a platform for asserting the fundamental rights of free men. It is doubtful they even considered women within the category of autonomous, self-owning individuals.[57] For abolitionists, however, there was obvious utility in attacking the slave system on behalf of the female sex; indeed, diverse battles had long been rhetorically waged in the name of violated womanhood.

But for antislavery thinkers to anchor visions of contract freedom in the negative symbolism of the bondswoman's body was something new, and the imagery was full of ambiguities. According to reigning

---

[55] Jehiel C. Beman to Joshua Leavitt, August 10, 1844, in Ripley, ed., *Black Abolitionist Papers* 3: 451; Samuel Gridley Howe, "Scene in a Slave Prison," *Liberty Bell* (Boston, 1843), 177.

[56] On the centrality of the black male body and sexuality in minstrelsy, see Eric Lott, *Love and Theft: Blackface Minstrelsy and the American Working Class* (New York, 1993), 111–22. For a differing interpretation, see Roediger, *Wages of Whiteness*, 115–31.

[57] See Pateman, *Sexual Contract*.

cultural beliefs, the body of a black woman exemplified both degenerate female sexuality and the alleged natural inferiority of her race.
Yet this abject icon became central to an antislavery politics of human emancipation. Since ancient times the idea of personal freedom
had entailed the right to an inviolate body – but only for men. By
defining freedom through the negative example of the female slave's
subjection, abolitionists opened to question the right of women to
own themselves. Thus the eroticized symbolism of antislavery held
the potential to challenge the categories of sex difference embedded
in classical liberalism and Victorian scientific theory as well as in
older intellectual traditions.[58]

For most abolitionists that was hardly the intended outcome of
their outcry against slavery. Virtually all of them looked to emancipation to transform chattels into self proprietors: "to restore the
slave to himself." But they differed over whether this form of deliv-
erance would abolish distinctions based on sex as well as on race. At
stake were opposing visions not only of self entitlement but of the
relationship between freedom and marriage.[59]

The dominant abolitionist position was that slave emancipation
would convert freedmen alone into sovereign, self-owning individuals. Property in women would simply be conveyed from slaveholders

[58] Recent scholarship suggests that the emphasis on the corporeal dimensions of individual sovereignty was newly fashioned in the nineteenth century by antislavery
feminists. See Sanchez-Eppler, *Touching Liberty*, 1–21; Ellen Carol DuBois, "Outgrowing the Compact of the Fathers: Equal Rights, Woman Suffrage, and the
United States Constitution, 1820–1878," *Journal of American History*, 74 (December
1987), 836–62, esp. p. 856; Eric Foner, "The Meaning of Freedom in the Age of
Emancipation," *Journal of American History*, 81 (September 1994), 435–60, at p. 450;
Elizabeth B. Clark, "Self-Ownership and the Political Theory of Elizabeth Cady
Stanton," *Connecticut Law Review*, 21 (1989), 905–41. In fact, this idea originated
among male political thinkers in ancient Greece. See David M. Halperin, "The
Democratic Body: Prostitution and Citizenship in Classical Athens," *differences: A
Journal of Feminist Cultural Studies*, 2 (1990), 1–28. On age-old corporeal rationales
for female subjection, see Lorraine Daston, "The Naturalized Female Intellect,"
Science in Context, 2 (1992), 209–35. On conventional constructions of the black
female body, see Sander Gilman, "Black Bodies, White Bodies: Toward an Iconography of Female Sexuality in Late Nineteenth-Century Art, Medicine, and Literature," in *"Race," Writing, and Difference*, ed. Henry Louis Gates, Jr. (Chicago, 1986),
223–61; Londa Schiebinger, *Nature's Body: Gender in the Making of Modern Science*
(Boston, 1993), 115–83. On the ambiguity of abolitionist iconography of the
chained female slave, see Yellin, *Women and Sisters*.
[59] Editorial by Thomas Hamilton in Ripley, ed., *Black Abolitionist Papers* 5: 41. Recent
studies focusing on the late nineteenth and twentieth centuries highlight the profound and complex ideological significance of marriage in the tradition of antislavery and African-American women's writing. See Ann duCille, *The Coupling Convention: Sex, Text, and Tradition in Black Women's Fiction* (Oxford, 1993); Claudia Tate,
Domestic Allegories of Political Desire: The Black Heroine's Text at the Turn of the Century
(New York, 1992); Hazel Carby, " 'On the Threshold of Woman's Era': Lynching,
Empire, and Sexuality in Black Feminist Theory," in Gates, ed., *"Race," Writing, and
Difference*, 301–16, at p. 315.

to husbands. This conception recapitulated the gender rules of classical liberal theory, which defined men as masters of the household with proprietary rights to their dependent wives. Upon the abolition of the slave master's "prior right," the former bondsman would gain the birthright of all free men: title not only to himself but to his wife – to her person, labor, and sexuality. In an argument inconsistent with his commitment to women's rights and his opposition to restrictive gender distinctions, William Lloyd Garrison affirmed the sovereignty of husbands as a fundamental aspect of freedom. The freedman, he declared unequivocally, would be "master of his own person, of his wife." As masters at home, former bondsmen could lay claim to the chastity of black women violated under slavery.[60]

So entrenched, so authoritative, was this definition of freedom that even female abolitionists who condemned patriarchal institutions employed its terms. In her 1836 *Appeal to the Christian Women of the South*, Angelina Grimké asserted the right of free women to combat slavery but rather contradictorily set forth only the manhood rights annulled by slavery. Slavery, she argued, "is a violation of the natural order of things." It *"robs the slave of all his rights* as a *man"*: slaves were "robbed of wages, wives, children." By the order of nature, therefore, the freedman's property in his wife would be as irrevocable as in his wages, while the freedwoman would become entitled to her husband's protection – a reciprocity of marriage rights denied to slaves. For the freedwoman, emancipation would lie not in rights of individual ownership but rather in coverture – what one antislavery writer termed *"woman's grand shield,* MATRIMONY."[61] Thus would freedom represent slavery's opposite, as interpreted by the binary rules of sex difference.

But this was not the only abolitionist construction of restoring the rights of the slave. A divergent strain of antislavery thought made subversive use of the figure of the bondswoman and of appeals grounded in the body to voice women's claim to contract freedom. Emancipation was prophesied in terms not of marriage bonds but of female self ownership. Here, the symbolic power of the debased female body established the logic of personal sovereignty as a universal right, unqualified by sex difference. Even though this remained a

[60] Bourne, *Slavery Illustrated,* 61, 121; "Free Laborers and Slaves," *Liberator,* December 7, 1855.
[61] Angelina E. Grimké, *Appeal to the Christian Women of the South* (New York, 1836), 24, 12; Bourne, *Slavery Illustrated,* 121. See also Kellow, "Divided Mind of Antislavery Feminism"; Pateman, *Sexual Contract;* Catherine Hall, *White, Male and Middle Class: Explorations in Feminism and History* (New York, 1992), 205–54; Catherine Hall, "In the Name of Which Father?" *International Labor and Working-Class History,* 41 (Spring 1992), 23–28; Hoganson, "Garrisonian Abolitionists."

recessive strain of abolitionism, it was not without highly articulate
and influential exponents, particularly in the black antislavery community.

Foremost among them was Frances Ellen Watkins Harper, the
most prominent black woman writer and orator of her generation.
Contemporaries called her the "bronze muse" and recognized her
as a "glorious speaker" – "one of the ablest advocates . . . of the
slave." In an address to the annual meeting of the American Anti-
Slavery Society in 1858, Harper set forth a heterodox vision of freedom. She invoked the accepted principle that the slave must be
granted "the rights of a man." But she argued that the right of a
man to himself must also belong to a woman.[62]

Eloquently fusing the rhetoric of possessive individualism with
that of radical Christianity, Harper extended the scope of natural
rights to guarantee women property in the self. She began by equating personal freedom with proprietary rights, as she pointed out that
the "bondman . . . does not own the humblest joint that does the
feeblest services . . . that the slave mother who clasps her child . . .
does not own it by right of possession." Then she spoke in the first
person of her own individual rights. Although freeborn, she pictured
herself as a fugitive slave brought to trial in the North. "[T]o prove –
what?" she demanded. "To prove whether I have a right to be a free
woman or am rightfully the chattel of another; whether I have the
right to possess all the faculties that God has given, or whether another has the right to buy and sell, exchange and barter that temple
in which God enshrined my human soul."[63] Harper's vision of emancipation powerfully demonstrated the multivalence of the symbol of
the female slave. For her, this symbol's antithesis was a freedwoman
fully endowed with rights, whose body was as sacred as a holy shrine.
Her argument did not simply controvert the racist association of

[62] Dorothy Sterling, ed., *We Are Your Sisters: Black Women in the Nineteenth Century* (New
York, 1984), 160; William Still, *The Underground Rail Road: A Record of Facts, Authentic
Narratives, Letters* (Philadelphia, 1872), 779, 158, and see pp. 758–61; Frances Smith
Foster, ed., *A Brighter Coming Day: A Frances Ellen Watkins Harper Reader* (New York,
1990), 5; "Twenty-Fifth Annual Meeting of the American Anti-Slavery Society.
Speech of Miss Frances Ellen Watkins, *National Anti-Slavery Standard*, May 22, 1858.
See Carby, *Reconstructing Womanhood*, 62–94; Bert J. Loewenberg and Ruth Bogin,
eds., *Black Women in Nineteenth-Century American Life: Their Words, Their Thoughts, Their
Feelings* (University Park, Md., 1976), 243–51; Shirley Yee, *Black Women Abolitionists:
A Study in Activism, 1828–1860* (Knoxville, 1992), 112–35; Julie Winch, " 'You Have
Talents – only Cultivate Them': Black Female Literary Societies and the Abolitionist
Crusade," and Anne M. Boylan, "Benevolence and Antislavery Activity among Afri-
can American Women in New York and Boston, 1820–1840," both in *The Abolition-
ist Sisterhood: Women's Political Culture in Antebellum America*, ed. Jean Fagan Yellin and
John C. Van Horne (Ithaca, 1994), 101–18, and 119–37.
[63] "Speech of Miss Frances Ellen Watkins."

black women with the body's most squalid habits and carnal passions. By counterposing religious and market metaphors, by linking soul and body, it also represented the freedwoman as a sovereign, self-owning individual, not as the object of her husband's contract rights.

Harper herself did acquire a husband. But throughout her life she challenged the theory of marriage as a property relationship based on male dominion and female dependence. Her poems and fiction writing repeatedly portrayed women who, as wives, lost neither economic independence nor independence of spirit. In a short story published in 1859 she assailed coverture in language echoing the attack on chattel slavery. The marriage contract should not "be a matter of bargain and sale," the heroine declares. But the villain regards it "as the title-deed that gave him possession of the woman."[64] For Harper, the husband's claim to property in his wife violated inalienable rights much as did the slave master's claim to his chattel property.

The pursuit of self entitlement was also the central drama of Harriet Jacobs's slave narrative, *Incidents in the Life of a Slave Girl, Written by Herself,* which was promoted by leaders of the abolition movement. Unlike Harper's work, however, Jacobs's story of her own passage from slavery to freedom directly confronted the problem of sexual property in women. For Jacobs, freedom entailed self ownership of a clearly sexual character. As a slave she chose to take a white lover rather than submitting to her master's claims. Idealizing relations of voluntary exchange, insisting on bodily autonomy, she defended her desperate resort to illicit sexual relations as a matter of free contract. "It seems less degrading to give one's self, than to submit to compulsion," she wrote. "There is something akin to freedom in having a lover who has no control over you, except that which he gains by kindness and attachment." Jacobs refused to recognize herself as property, even to the extent of having her freedom bought (though eventually it was) against her will. For she explained that the more she became used to the values of free society, the more intolerable

---

[64] Frances Ellen Watkins (Harper), "The Two Offers," *Anglo-African Magazine,* September/October 1859, 288, 290. By Harper, see, for example, *Sketches of Southern Life* (Philadelphia, 1890), 12–15, 19, 21; "John and Jacob – A Dialogue on Woman's Rights," in Foster, ed., *A Brighter Coming Day,* 240–42; *Iola Leroy; or, Shadows Uplifted* (2nd ed., Boston, 1987; orig. pub. 1893), 154–55, 172–73, 178, 205, 210, 242, 277. See also Carby, *Reconstructing Womanhood,* 79–80; Frances Smith Foster, *Written by Herself: Literary Production by African American Women, 1746–1892* (Bloomington, 1993), 88–93, 183–86; duCille, *Coupling Convention,* 3–12, 32–34, 44–47; Tate, *Domestic Allegories,* 147–49, 169–71; Barbara Christian, *Black Women Novelists: The Development of a Tradition, 1892–1976* (Westport, 1980), 3–29; Still, *Underground Rail Road,* 755–80.

she found even the most benevolent owner, implying that genuine
freedom meant owning herself. "The more my mind had become
enlightened, the more difficult it was for me to consider myself an
article of property. . . . [B]eing sold from one owner to another
seemed too much like slavery." Jacobs did not explicitly protest the
proprietary character of marriage, yet she hardly assumed that the
slaveholder's sexual rights should rightfully pass to a husband. Nor
did she see marriage and freedom as one and the same. Rather, she
counterposed them in a way suggesting their asymmetries, declaring
at her narrative's close, "my story ends with freedom; not in the
usual way, with marriage." Jacobs became a freedwoman, but not a
wife.[65]

Marriage had no place either in the contrast between freedom
and slavery formulated by Sarah Parker Remond, a popular abolitionist lecturer in both England and America. Speaking in London
in 1859, she put the plight of female slaves at the center of an appeal
that culminated in affirming women's rights as autonomous, propertied individuals. She called for the emancipation of her race but
also "pleaded especially on behalf of her own sex." Like other abolitionists, she began by explaining that words failed to express the
unique suffering of women on southern plantations: "the unspeaka-
ble horrors," the "depth of the infamy into which they were plunged
by the cruelty and licentiousness of their brutal masters."[66]

But the argument Remond went on to develop departed from
standard antislavery themes. She favorably compared the situation of
poor English needlewomen with the plight of American slaves. Evoking the misery of seamstresses made famous in Thomas Hood's
poem, "Song of the Shirt," she admitted "the trials and toils of the
women of England – how, in the language of Hood, they were made
to 'Stitch, stitch, stitch,' till weariness and exhaustion overtook
them." This was a common abolitionist ploy: granting the debasement of hirelings, only to assert their elevation above chattel slaves.
Yet to draw this contrast on the bondswoman's behalf radically altered the antislavery ideal of contract freedom. Regarding the seamstresses, Remond claimed, "there was this immeasurable difference

[65] Jacobs, *Incidents*, 55, 199, 201. On the subversive quality of Jacobs's narrative, see
    Carby, *Reconstructing Womanhood*, 36–61; Foster, *Written by Herself*, 95–116; duCille,
    Coupling Convention, 4–5; Yellin, *Women and Sisters*, 87–96; Beth Maclay Doriani,
    "Black Womanhood in Nineteenth-Century America: Subversion and Self-
    Construction in Two Women's Autobiographies," *American Quarterly*, 43 (June
    1991), 199–222; Sanchez-Eppler, *Touching Liberty*, 83–104. For an alternative inter-
    pretation, see Fox-Genovese, *Plantation Household*, 375–76.
[66] "Lectures on American Slavery," *Anti-Slavery Reporter*, July 1, 1859. See also Clare
    Midgley, *Women against Slavery: The British Campaigns, 1780–1870* (London, 1992),
    143–45.

between their condition and that of the slave-woman, that their persons were free and their progeny their own, while the slave-woman was the victim of the heartless lust of her master, and the children whom she bore were his property." Remond not only argued that women were entitled to themselves, she represented children, rather than wages, as the fruits of toil that also must belong to them. For her, property in the sexual body, as opposed to the laboring body, defined the essential difference between slavery and freedom.[67]

This argument circumvented the claims of marriage, treating the rules of coverture as a dead letter, depicting woman's freedom as greater than it actually was. Remond did not speak of the rights or duties of husbands and fathers. Nor did she see female virtue as an emblem of male honor. Rather, the needlewomen owned in themselves – fee simple – the same property possessed by slave masters in their women chattel. Though stamped with classical contract ideas of self proprietorship, this view of emancipation subverted the very tradition to which it was heir.

Thus the theory of female self ownership was a vital aspect of abolitionism. It is well known that women's rights advocates in this era adopted antislavery rhetoric – pairing women with slaves, and marriage with bondage – and that they viewed self entitlement as paramount. Elizabeth Cady Stanton unceasingly attacked the wife's status as "the property of another."[68] But among the antislavery vanguard it was black women who most unequivocally asserted a woman's right to herself. Some of them had directly known a slave master's dominion; most of them had never known dependence on a husband. Like other abolitionists, they assailed the female slave's subjection and defended free women's right to speak on her behalf. Yet in their hands the symbol of the bondswoman represented not only the terrors of slavery but the rights of freedom. Their black antislavery brethren neither expressly endorsed nor disowned the idea of the husband as master. But in disrupting any simple connection between emancipation and marriage – in affirming a slave

---

[67] "Lectures on American Slavery." See also Foner, *Politics and Ideology*, 57–76; Glickstein, " 'Poverty Is Not Slavery.' "

[68] Ellen Carol DuBois, ed., *Elizabeth Cady Stanton, Susan B. Anthony: Correspondence, Writings, Speeches* (New York, 1981), 48. See Clark, "Self-Ownership and the Political Theory of Elizabeth Cady Stanton"; Blanche G. Hersh, *The Slavery of Sex: Feminist-Abolitionists in America* (Urbana, 1978), 66; DuBois, "Outgrowing the Compact"; Ellen Carol DuBois, *Feminism and Suffrage: The Emergence of an Independent Women's Movement in America, 1848–1869* (Ithaca, 1978); Linda Gordon, *Woman's Body, Woman's Right: A Social History of Birth Control in America* (New York, 1976), esp. pp. 95–115; William Leach, *True Love and Perfect Union: The Feminist Reform of Sex and Society* (New York, 1980); Wai-chee Dimock, "Rightful Subjectivity," *Yale Journal of Criticism*, 4 (1990), 25–51.

woman's right to herself – black female thinkers transformed the meaning of contract freedom. As the ex-slave Bethany Veney claimed, in "my Northern home. . . . I had the same right to myself that any other women had. No jailor could . . . sell me at auction to the highest bidder. My boy was my own, and no one could take him from me." It has been argued that the Western ideal of personal freedom emerged in ancient times from the longing of female slaves to negate their condition (since women first underwent mass enslavement) but that this ideal was appropriated by male thinkers. If so, then black female abolitionists could be said to have reclaimed their rightful intellectual legacy.[69] Yet their vision differed from other images of propertied individualism, for the self-owning freedwoman would not be fenced off from the interdependencies of social relations but rather would be included in a community of rights-bearing individuals.[70]

Both abolitionism's dominant and recessive strains altered the traditional currents of contract thought. The dominant strain denied the symmetry between marriage and wage labor as relationships that each merged elements of autonomy and subordination. Whereas the hireling was now said to be wholly free, the wife was said to remain in the position of dependency she had occupied for centuries. But the recessive strain of abolitionism broke more fully with older intel-

---

[69] *The Narrative of Bethany Veney, a Slave Woman* (Worcester, 1889), in Gates, ed., *Collected Black Women's Narratives*, 38. See also Orlando Patterson, *Freedom*, Vol. 1 (New York, 1991), esp. pp. xv, 50–63, 78, 106–32; Gerda Lerner, *The Creation of Patriarchy* (New York, 1986), 77–100. On black female antislavery thought, see Foster, *Written by Herself*; Nell Irvin Painter, "Difference, Slavery, and Memory: Sojourner Truth in Feminist Abolitionism," in Yellin and Van Horne, ed., *Abolitionist Sisterhood*, 139–58; Nell Irvin Painter, *Sojourner Truth: A Life, a Symbol* (New York, 1996); Yee, *Black Women Abolitionists*, 136–54; Carby, *Reconstructing Womanhood*; Yellin, *Women and Sisters*, 77–96. On the ambiguities of black male abolitionists' perspectives on female self sovereignty, see James O. Horton, "Freedom's Yoke: Gender Conventions among Antebellum Free Blacks," *Feminist Studies*, 12 (Spring 1986), 51–76; bell hooks, *Ain't I a Woman: Black Women and Feminism* (Boston, 1981); Julie Winch, *Philadelphia's Black Elite: Activism, Accommodation, and the Struggle for Autonomy, 1787–1848* (Philadelphia, 1988), 86; Stanton et al., *History of Woman Suffrage* 1: 668; Rosalyn Terborg-Penn, "Black Male Perspectives on the Nineteenth-Century Woman," in *The Afro-American Woman: Struggles and Images*, ed. Sharon Harley and Rosalyn Terborg-Penn (Port Washington, N.Y., 1978), 28–42; Hoganson, "Garrisonian Abolitionists," 571.

[70] For a critique of possessive individualism as isolating rights holders from the larger political community, see Hendrik Hartog, "The Constitution of Aspiration and 'The Rights That Belong to Us All,'" *Journal of American History*, 74 (December 1987), 1013–34. But see also Eileen Boris, "Gender, Race, and Rights: Listening to Critical Race Theory," and "Response" by Melinda Chateauvert, both in *Journal of Women's History*, 6 (Summer 1994), 111–24 and 125–32; Ellen Carol DuBois, "Taking the Law into Our own Hands: *Bradwell, Minor*, and Suffrage Militance in the 1870s," in *Visible Women: New Essays in American Activism*, eds. Nancy A. Hewitt and Suzanne Lebsock (Urbana, 1993), 19–40.

lectual traditions by claiming that the freedwoman's condition must mirror what most abolitionists saw as the ideal of the emancipated slave: "He is free, and his own master, and can ask for no more."[71] In leaving bondage, chattel slaves of both sexes would be equally endowed with contract freedom.

The Civil War transposed the passage from slavery to contract from the realm of visionary politics to the terrain of actual experience. At the very outset of emancipation, the North began the project of establishing voluntary wage labor on southern soil and guarantying the marriage rights of former slaves, while Confederate defeat cleared the ground for securing the ascendance of contract that was the cornerstone of the abolitionist cause. Yet to transfer freedom to the South was "theoretically and practically," as a Boston lawyer wrote to Garrison late in 1865, "one of the most difficult problems ever presented to statesmen and philanthropists."[72] Emancipation brought Yankee ideals face to face with the aspirations of freed slaves as well as with the interests of former masters. Not the least of the difficulties presented was foreshadowed by antislavery doctrine – the encounter of rival understandings of free contract.

Even before the abolition of slavery the Union army had designated contract the instrument of freedom. Military decrees set fugitive slaves to work on plantations under contracts, required planters to pay wages, and enlisted soldiers to maintain discipline. Cotton cultivation in the South Carolina Sea Islands was the most famous wartime experiment with free labor; but throughout the South the advance of Union troops brought a new order founded on the rights and duties of contract.[73]

The principles of the new order were officially set forth by the American Freedmen's Inquiry Commission, which was appointed in 1863 by the U.S. War Department and staffed by abolitionist leaders. Urging that freedpeople should "stand alone" as soon as possible, relying simply on equal protection of the law, the commission favored temporary government oversight of the transition to freedom

---

[71] Statement of William Jay, quoted in Foner, "Abolitionism and the Labor Movement," 64.

[72] Letter of Samuel Sewall to William Lloyd Garrison, December 24, 1865, William Lloyd Garrison Collection, Boston Public Library, Boston, Mass.

[73] See Ira Berlin, Thavolia Glymph, Steven F. Miller, Joseph Reidy, Leslie Rowland, and Julie Saville, eds., *Freedom: A Documentary History of Emancipation 1861–1867.* Series 1, Volume 3: *The Wartime Genesis of Free Labor: The Lower South* (Cambridge, 1990); Willie Lee Rose, *Rehearsal for Reconstruction: The Port Royal Experiment* (London, 1964); Leon Litwack, *Been in the Storm So Long: The Aftermath of Slavery* (New York, 1979); Eric Foner, *Reconstruction: America's Unfinished Revolution 1863–1877* (New York, 1988), chs. 1–4.

but warned against perpetuating the dependencies of slavery. It underscored the value of free labor for the ex-slaves – "Working for wages, they soon get an idea of accumulating." It also claimed that ex-slaves regarded marriage "as a privilege appertaining to emancipation," but maintained that they were strangers to family life, that the wife must learn the "instinct of chastity" and the husband the "obligation to support his family." In the commission's blueprint for emancipation, work and marriage were mutually reinforcing contracts that would create economic and moral order and instill the ideal of self support.[74]

After the war the newly created Freedmen's Bureau enforced the regime of contract. Enjoining former slaves to obey the "solemn obligation of contracts," the bureau taught that freedom was inimical not just to coercion but to idleness and immorality. The bureau's chief, Gen. Oliver Otis Howard, explained the plan for dealing with the ex-slaves: "If they can be induced to enter into contracts, they are taught that there are duties as well as privileges of freedom." Howard defined sanctity of contract, self support, and equal justice under the law as the mainstays of the new social order, and he pledged to bar compulsory unpaid labor and protect domestic rights. According to bureau protocols, wage agreements had to be written and marriages officially registered to ensure that both were enforceable at law.[75]

Across the South bureau officers gathered together ex-slaves for "little talks" in which they inculcated contract rules by "partly persuading and partly threatening." Within the bureau there was disagreement about whether freed slaves should become a permanent hireling class or a landowning yeomanry but not about the link between freedom and contract. "This thing you must learn above all others: a contract must be sacredly observed," admonished Louisiana's conservative bureau chief, Gen. Joseph S. Fullerton, explaining

[74] *Preliminary Report Touching the Condition and Management of Emancipated Refugees, Made to the Secretary of War by the American Freedmen's Inquiry Commission, June 30, 1863,* and *Final Report of the American Freedmen's Inquiry Commission to the Secretary of War,* in *Report of the Secretary of War,* 38th Cong., 1st sess., Sen. Exec. Doc. 53 (1864), quotations at pp. 110, 8, 4, 3, 4. See James M. McPherson, *The Struggle for Equality: Abolitionists and the Negro in the Civil War and Reconstruction* (Princeton, 1964), 181–86.

[75] *Message from the President Communicating Reports of Assistant Commissioners of the Freedmen's Bureau,* 39th Cong., 1st sess., Sen. Exec. Doc. 27 (1865), 164; "Meeting at Augusta, Me., in Behalf of the Freedmen – Speech of Gen. Howard," *National Freedman,* August 1865, 233–39; "Circular, No. 5," July 1865, 200–201; *Orders Issued by the Commissioner and Assistant Commissioners of the Freedmen's Bureau,* 39th Cong., 1st sess., House Exec. Doc. 70 (1865), 102. See also William S. McFeely, *Yankee Stepfather: General O.O. Howard and the Freedmen* (New York, 1868), 150–61; Foner, *Reconstruction,* ch. 4.

that his staff would dispense neither land nor alms but only legal protection and lessons about free society. "If you do not renew your contracts and live up to them, you will have no means of living." The assistant bureau commissioner Rufus Saxton supported radical plans for converting former slaves into freeholders while also affirming that contract was intrinsic to freedom. "Keep in good faith all your contracts and agreements, remembering always that you are a slave no longer," he exhorted in the summer of 1865. "Your liberty is a great blessing. . . . Try to show, by your good conduct, that you are worthy." Like outward signs of religious salvation, fidelity to contract would demonstrate that ex-slaves were fit for freedom.[76]

Bureau agents were as exacting about marriage as about labor contracts. Requiring former slaves to marry by law, they performed weddings, formulated rules for legitimating slave unions, and adjudicated the complex claims arising from the forced separation of slave couples. "At each meeting," reported a Virginia agent, freedpeople in his charge learned "the duties and relations of the matrimonial state." This instruction often dealt with gender traits. The assistant commissioner in Tennessee taught that a wife must be her husband's "help meet" and "the charm of the household." She must not be "a slovenly woman who goes about with her heels out of her stockings, her dress unpinned, her hair uncombed, with dirt under her finger-nails." Likewise, the husband must "Be a MAN. Earn money and save it." The freedmen were told, "Your wives will not love you if you do not provide bread and clothes for them."[77]

Yankee schoolteachers and missionaries who worked among the

[76] James Davison to Davis Tillson, January 8, 1866, *Message from the President Communicating Reports of Assistant Commissioners of the Freedmen's Bureau,* 39th Cong., 1st sess., Sen. Exec. Doc. 27 (1865), 90; J.W. Sharp to Thaddeus Stevens, February 9, 1866, Thaddeus Stevens Papers, Library of Congress, Washington, D.C.; Fullerton address reprinted in the *National Anti-Slavery Standard,* November 11, 1865; *Report of the Joint Committee on Reconstruction, at the First Session of the Thirty-Ninth Congress* (Washington, D.C., 1866), 230–31. See also Herbert G. Gutman, "Mirrors of Hard Distorted Glass: An Examination of Some Influential Assumptions about the Afro-American Family and the Shaping of Public Policies: 1861–1965" in *Social History and Social Policy,* ed. David J. Rothman and Stanton Wheeler (New York, 1981), 239–73; Foner, *Reconstruction,* 134–70.

[77] Letter of Bureau Ass't. Sup't. to Cap't. James A. Bates, April 30, 1866, Records of the Assistant Commissioner (hereafter RAC), Virginia, Records of the Bureau of Refugees, Freedmen, and Abandoned Lands, Record Group 105, National Archives (hereafter BRFAL), M1048, reel no. 44; Fisk, *Plain Counsels,* 25, 27, 33–34, 23, 32; *Orders Issued by the Commissioner and Assistant Commissioners of the Freedmen's Bureau,* 39th Cong., 1st sess., House Exec. Doc. 70 (1865), 93. See Joel Williamson, *After Slavery: The Negro in South Carolina during Reconstruction, 1861–1877* (Chapel Hill, 1965), 306–10; Litwack, *Been in the Storm So Long,* 233–42. See also Nancy F. Cott, "Giving Character to Our Whole Civil Polity: Marriage and the Public Order in the Late Nineteenth Century," in Kerber et al., eds., *U.S. History as Women's History,* 107–21.

former slaves disseminated the same codes of contract. As a means
of persuasion they relied not on soldiers' bayonets but rather on
primers featuring didactic tales of emancipation, which replaced
slave narratives with black versions of *Pilgrim's Progress* charting freedpeople's trials and triumphs. The genre was typified by *John Freeman
and His Family*, a story published in 1864 by the American Tract
Society as the first volume of a new "Freedman's Library," which was
designed to offer "counsel to the colored people in their new circumstances, and also pleasant family reading." The story's hero had
once been a plantation slave, but even then he was a "sort of
prince," and when freed he "had the right idea of manhood and
liberty." He embodied emancipation, in contrast to abolitionist images of women in bondage. His transition from bondage to freedom
was told through three scenes of contract: a social contract, a labor
contract, and a marriage contract.[78]

In the first scene a Union army officer, who symbolized the national state, made an offer to a gathering of ex-slaves: " 'Now mind
your orders, do your work, and we will feed you, look after your
families, and teach your children. . . . Who among you will agree to
this?' " With John Freeman among them, the freedmen accepted:
" 'I will, I will, I will.' " No women were involved in this original
contract of emancipation that replaced the reciprocities of master
and slave. In later scenes John Freeman learned the rules of contract. He explained to other former slaves that free society was ordered by market exchange and voluntary labor: " 'That means, you
give me and I give you. . . . General Saxton has work to do, and he
says you give me your labor, I give you money. Very well. Ain't it all
beautiful and good, brethren?' " To his wife, he proposed that they
marry in " 'liberty fashion,' " like " '[w]hite folks,' " with " 'the
book and the minister and a heap of ceremony . . . and nothing can
ever separate them.' " Through contracts, and as both a hireling and
a husband, this freeman escaped "the clinging dust of slavery" and
the disabilities of race.[79]

For his wife, however, emancipation was more ambiguous; even
her name signified her uncertain status. Her husband took the title
"Freeman," rejecting his slave name, and was told to give it to his
family, like Adam in the creation story. But in choosing to marry, she
became "Mrs. Freeman," a name summing up the contradictions of
being both a freedperson and a wife. When first called this she was

---

[78] Advertisement for *John Freeman and His Family* in *National Freedman*, November 1864,
44; Helen E. Brown, *John Freeman and His Family* (New York, 1980; orig. pub. 1864),
7, 45.

[79] Brown, *John Freeman*, 18, 35, 50–51, 47.

confused, hardly knowing "what to do"; but her husband took readily to his new name, declaring, " 'That suits me a heap.' " Moreover,
unlike him, slavery had left her unfit for freedom. While he easily
assumed the duties of free labor and marriage, she lacked the faculty
for housekeeping considered natural to her sex. A female teacher
found the Freeman's home "completely littered and filthy": it reflected the "old, lazy, filthy habits of the slave-quarters," not the
"true idea of home. Women who had toiled all their lives in the
cotton-field . . . could not know much sweeping, washing, and cooking." In contrast to her husband, the freedwoman had been dena-
tured – a state symbolized by her filthy home – by slavery.[80]

The obvious message of *John Freeman* was that freedom was premised on work and family. More subtly it taught that emancipation's
most difficult task was accustoming not freedmen to free market
relations but freedwomen to home life – that slavery countermanded
the laws of sex difference even more than the rules of political economy. Notably, too, it told a story of contract freedom in which the
wife did not talk of rights but rather learned to keep house.

Parables such as *John Freeman* reflected a two century-old tradition
of liberal thought, translating into homespun language the contractual model of social relations constructed by political theory and
political economy, idealizing its principles of voluntary exchange
and sex difference. But how former slaves read such parables is less
clear than the doctrine their emancipators hoped to impart. The
language and values of former slaves bore the imprint of this doctrine but were distinguished by the experience of bondage and the
culture of slave life. And former slaves were not themselves of one
mind about contract's meaning for their new circumstances.

To at least some freedpeople, formal rights of contract matched
their understanding of emancipation. Using language very like that
of their emancipators, they insisted on untrammeled rights of self
ownership, free labor, and family security. A November 1865 convention of South Carolina blacks, headed by a former slave, proclaimed
the free man's "lawful title" to "his own body and mind," as well as
to "money and other property." The convention also gave voice to
market ideals of liberty of contract by demanding, among other
things, that the laborer be "as free to sell his labor as the merchant
his goods." Other freedpeople measured the distance between slavery and freedom by the rights to "belong to ourselves," to "change
places and work for different men," and to "git pay for my work."
They also counted the right to marry and the "sanctity of our family
relations" as badges of freedom. As one freedman averred, "The

---

[80] Ibid., 21, 22, 26, 21, 28, 31–32.

Marriage Covenant is at the foundation of all our rights. In slavery we could not have *legalized* marriage: *now* we have it." Affirming the intersection between the wage contract and marriage contract that the Freedmen's Bureau stressed as an incentive to industry, ex-slaves in North Carolina called on the state constitutional convention of 1865 to recognize their right to "just compensation" for their labor in order to maintain their families and secure their rights as husbands.[81]

From across the South, however, came conflicting accounts of freedpeople's response to the system of labor contracts instituted by the bureau. In South Carolina, for example, bureau agents in some districts reported that by the spring of 1866 most freedmen had "entered into Contracts willingly" and were fulfilling their terms. "That free labor is a success there can be no doubt," the head of the bureau in South Carolina wrote confidently to O.O. Howard in November 1866. But other bureau officials in the state portrayed a different situation. "Prominent men have advised the people not to Contract," stated a report from the Anderson District, where only half of the freedmen had signed annual labor contracts early in 1866. In Beaufort there was "little success . . . in persuading the freedmen to make Contracts." From elsewhere in the South came reports that some freedpeople associated wage relations with enslavement and refused to accept the distinction between the sale of labor and that of persons. A bureau official in Mississippi wrote that freedmen were "afraid to contract with their old masters for fear they would be brought into slavery again." Though pledging to prevent involuntary servitude and treat labor like other commodities in the "open market," the bureau often had to compel ex-slaves into wage work. As O.O. Howard admitted, many freedpeople viewed labor contracts with the "greatest aversion."[82]

---

[81] "A State Convention of the Colored People of South Carolina" and "A Memorial of the Colored People of South Carolina," both in *National Anti-Slavery Standard,* December 9, 1865; Litwack, *Been in the Storm So Long,* 226, 228; "Letter from L. Maria Child," *Independent,* April 5, 1866; "Address of the North Carolina Freedmen," *National Freedman,* October 1865, 302. See also Ira Berlin, Steven F. Miller, and Leslie S. Rowland, "Afro-American Families in the Transition from Slavery to Freedom," *Radical History Review,* 42 (1988), 89–201, quote at p. 97; "Address of the North Carolina Freedmen," 302; Laura F. Edwards, *Gendered Strife and Confusion: The Political Culture of Reconstruction* (Urbana, 1997), 18, 25, 45–54.

[82] Edgefield, Georgetown, and Pickens Districts in "Report of R.K. Scott to O.O. Howard," March 15, 1866, and Assistant Commissioner, Bureau Refugees, Freedmen & A. Lands to Maj. Gen'l. O. O. Howard, November 1, 1866, RAC, South Carolina, BRFAL, M869, reel 1. See Anderson and Beaufort Districts in "Report of R.K. Scott to O.O. Howard, March 15, 1866; *Report of the Joint Committee on Reconstruction* 3: 6; *Orders Issued by the Commissioner and Assistant Commissioners of the Freedmen's Bureau,*

The roots of that aversion lay deep, both in the aim of freedpeople to escape economic dependency on former masters and in the racial enmity created by slave relations. The greatest obstacle to transplanting wage labor in the New South was freedpeople's pursuit of independent land ownership. For many months after the war's end they clung to the hope that tracts of land would be distributed to them as initially promised by military proclamations and bureau decrees. These "injurious expectations," claimed the bureau chief in Alabama, led them to avoid selling their labor, despite market stimuli of "hunger and cold." Their desire to own land, noted another bureau official, amounted "almost to a passion" and was one of the "strongest motives preventing the making of contracts." In the eyes of many former slaves, land ownership represented the natural outcome of emancipation – a bounty of war, a recompense for unrequited toil, an entitlement due by the labor theory of property. As defined by Georgia freedmen, freedom did not mean substituting the impersonal discipline of wage contracts for slave masters' personal dominion but rather being independent and owning property other than the self: the right to "reap the fruit of our own labor," to "take care of ourselves," and to "have land, and turn it and till it by our own labor."[83]

The chasm of race difference also militated against the smooth transition to wage contracts. Though political economy held that contracts required trust between the parties, neither former masters nor former slaves put much faith in promises made by members of the other race. However much southerners might agree that contract obligations ranked among the "most important fruits of civilization," they were unwilling to bargain with free blacks as equals. "What? Contracts with those niggers?" a former slaveholder allegedly demanded of Carl Schurz during his tour of the southern states in 1865. "No nigger knew what a contract was and would keep one unless forced to." Convinced that freedpeople were racially unfit for

39th Cong., 1st sess., House Exec. Doc. 70 (1865), 59; Oliver Otis Howard, *Autobiography of Oliver Otis Howard. Major General, United States Army* (2 vols., New York, 1907), 2: 240.

[83] *Message from the President Communicating Reports of Assistant Commissioners of the Freedmen's Bureau*, 39th Cong., 1st sess., Sen. Exec. Doc. 27 (1865), 60; *Report of the Joint Committee on Reconstruction* 3: 36, 41; "The Freedman in Georgia," *Christian Recorder*, February 18, 1865. See *Message from the President Communicating Reports of Assistant Commissioners of the Freedmen's Bureau*, 39th Cong., 1st sess., Sen. Exec. Doc. 27 (1865), 25; Julie Saville, *The Work of Reconstruction* (New York, 1994); Barbara Fields and Leslie Rowland, "Free Labor Ideology and Its Exponents in the South during the Civil War and Reconstruction" (paper delivered at Organization of American Historians Annual Meeting, 1984); Foner, *Reconstruction*, 102–10, 158–65; McFeely, *Yankee Stepfather*, 150–61.

relations of voluntary exchange, planters sought to perpetuate slavery's compulsions through contracts containing what one bureau official called "tyrannical provisions" that controlled personal conduct and household affairs as well as labor. On their part, former slaves distrusted offers made by white employers. Suspicions arose not simply from the slave experience but also from broken wartime promises of wage payment that Union officials had made to freed slaves who had served as soldiers or as laborers on occupied lands. According to one northern observer, former slaves had been "so constantly cheated by white men that they do not care to trust strangers." And former slaves put little stock in their former owners' words. As one freedman described his first tense contract negotiations with his ex-master,

The white men read a paper to all of us colored people telling us that we were free and could go where we pleased and work for who we pleased. The man I belonged to told me it was best to stay with him. . . . and we could get protection from our old masters.

I told him I thought that every man, when he was free, could have his rights and protect themselves. He said, "The colored people could never protect themselves among the white people. So you had all better stay with the white people who raised you and make contracts with them to work for one-fifth of all you make. . . . We have contracts for you all to sign. . . ."

I told him I would not sign anything. I said, "I might sign to be killed. I believe the white people is trying to fool us."

Such negotiations did not conform to the rules of bargaining imposed by northern exponents of free labor: while the planter offered the wage contract as a paternal relation, the freedman refused to sign a document that he likened to a death warrant.[84]

In other cases, however, former slaves invoked their contract rights. Although they certainly did not always prevail, they generated extensive litigation in Freedmen's Bureau courts over unpaid wages, excessive discipline, and other violations of contract provisions. Through legal enforcement of contracts they aimed to secure a measure of autonomy and equity. In doing so, perhaps they were influ-

[84] C.G. Memminger (former Confederate secretary of the treasury) to Andrew Johnson, September 4, 1865, in *Documentary History of Reconstruction: Political, Military, Social, Religious, Education and Industrial, 1865 to the Present Time*, ed. Walter L. Fleming (2 vols., Cleveland, 1906), 1: 249; Carl Schurz, *The Reminiscences of Carl Schurz* (3 vols., New York, 1907–08), 3: 160; *Report of the Joint Committee on Reconstruction* 2: 240, and see pp. 177, 218–19; Berlin et al., eds., *Freedom* 3: 242; Dorothy Sterling, ed., *The Trouble They Seen* (Garden City, N.Y., 1976), 6. See also statement of Edward L. Pierce, in Berlin et al., eds., *Freedom* 3: 201; J.W. Alvord, *First Semi-Annual Report on Schools and Finances of Freedmen, January 1, 1866* (Washington, D.C., 1868), 15.

enced not simply by the counsel of bureau agents but also by the outlook of free blacks, such as those in New Orleans who declared in March 1865 that the right of free contract was "the unquestionable attribute of every freeman." They may also have transformed informal, customary notions of reciprocal rights and duties asserted under slavery – an unauthorized kind of contractualism rooted in slave resistance – into formal rights recognized by the state.[85]

The very act of litigating their labor grievances led former slaves to speak in contract language. A December 1865 complaint made by a Louisiana freedman Virgil Loyd suggests that some former slaves quickly learned the rules of the game. Speaking on behalf of eleven freedpeople, he charged that there had been a "gross violation of the rights of said Freedmen." Their employer "broke and Changed the Contract," and by "threats and artifices" they were "compelled and frightened" into signing a "Substituted Contract." Their pay was cut, and they were "robed of their labor." In the "spirit, of Fraud and injustice . . . without the Knowledge or consent of the Freedmen" the employer contrived to "rob these Freedmen of their rights under said contract."[86] Endowed by emancipation with new legal standing, former slaves asserted their rights against their former owners in the established language of contract.

Complaints such as Virgil Loyd's testify to the credence that at least some former slaves gave to freedom of contract. Few could have found contract rights a sufficient guarantee of liberty, given the stark asymmetries of social and economic power they confronted. Indeed, some freedmen wholly dissociated emancipation and contract. As one freedman wrote in 1866 from the Sea Islands of South Carolina, where he had been sent, as a soldier, to drive away ex-slaves who refused to perform wage work, "I hope soon to . . . have the rights of a citizen. I am opposed myself to work under a contract." Nevertheless, for other ex-slaves the rules of contract held possibilities not unlike the broader promise of equal rights. In the imperfect world of the South after emancipation the forms and language of contract validated social relations that in certain ways resembled slavery, but

[85] Berlin et al., eds., *Freedom* 3: 595. See Sara Rapport, "The Freedmen's Bureau as a Legal Agent for Black Men and Women in Georgia: 1865–1868," *Georgia Historical Quarterly*, 73 (Spring 1989), 26–53; Donald G. Nieman, *To Set the Law in Motion: The Freedmen's Bureau and the Legal Rights of Blacks, 1865–1868* (Millwood, N.Y., 1979); Edwards, *Gendered Strife*; Emilia Viotti da Costa, "From All According to Their Abilities, to All According to Their Needs: Day-to-Day Resistance and Slaves' Notions of Rights in Guiana, 1823–1832" (unpublished paper prepared for the Conference on Slavery and Freedom in Comparative Perspective, University of California, San Diego, October 4–6, 1991).
[86] Berlin et al., eds., *Freedom* 3: 614–15.

they also inhibited the dominion of former masters over freed slaves.[87]

The meaning of the marriage contract was, if anything, more full of complexity for former slaves; for this contract not only negated the bonds of slavery, it also created new bonds between freedmen and freedwomen. Whereas the wage contract reconstituted the relationship between former slaves and former masters, the marriage contract gave new legal force to the rights and duties of husbands and wives, thereby removing family relations from the direct control of former masters and instead interposing the state's authority. It secured the formal freedom of the household, a collective right as central to ex-slaves' understanding of emancipation as were individual entitlements.[88]

Just a few months after the Emancipation Proclamation, one freedman attested that there were "more married than ever I knew before." Former slaves heralded the marriage contract as they did not the right to sell their labor. After the war multitudes rushed to marry, often in mass ceremonies. "The marriage law gives general satisfaction among the Freedmen and their wives," reported a Virginia agent of the Freedmen's Bureau in 1866. Neither the bureau nor the legal codes of most southern states legitimated slave marriages simply as an incident of emancipation; instead they required freedpeople to renew old vows or exchange new ones in proper wedding ceremonies or else to be punished for fornication and adultery. As another Virginia agent explained, "I carefully read the law to them and take pains in explaining it to them so that they may fully understand it and its penalties."[89] In complying with the law, husbands and wives transmuted the nonbinding rites of slavery into the rights of freedom.

Yet former slaves were not unambivalent about putting their marriages into official contractual form. Nor, once married, did they

---

[87] Letter of Melton R. Linton to *South Carolina Leader*, March 31, 1866, quoted in Sterling, ed., *Trouble They Seen*, 43.

[88] See Gutman, *Black Family*; Brenda Stevenson, "Distress and Discord in Virginia Slave Families, 1830–1860," in Bleser, ed., *In Joy and in Sorrow*, 103–24; Jones, *Labor of Love*; Berlin et al., "Afro-American Families"; Edwards, *Gendered Strife*, 45–54; Tera W. Hunter, *To 'Joy My Freedom: Southern Black Women's Lives and Labors after the Civil War* (Cambridge, Mass., 1997), 35–40.

[89] Berlin et al., eds., *Freedom* 3: 252; Letter of Ass't. Sup't., J.W. Barnes to Captain L.F.P. Crandon, April 30, 1866, RAC, Virginia, BRFAL, M1048, reel 44; Letter of Ass't. Sup't. J. M. Tracy to Cap't. [illegible] of Petersburgh, Va., April 30, 1866, RAC, Virginia, BRFAL, M1048, reel 44. See Litwack, *Been in the Storm So Long*, 239–41; Gutman, *Black Family*, 412–26; *Orders Issued by the Commissioner and Assistant Commissioners of the Freedmen's Bureau*, 39th Cong., 1st sess., House Exec. Doc. 70 (1865), 108–11; *Laws In Relation to Freeman*, 39th Cong., 2nd sess., Sen. Exec Doc. 6 (1866).

always obey the letter of the law. Despite their ambition of protecting family unity, many reportedly ignored both legal procedures and moral norms. One exasperated bureau agent claimed that former slaves had an antinomian approach to marriage, "The marriage law is not understood, and a decided aversion shown towards understanding it. They prefer 'God Almighty! Marriage' and appeal to the same authority for divorce." Reports circulated throughout the South that freed slaves cohabited simply by mutual consent and deserted each other at will. In South Carolina bureau agents complained that wives were "put away at pleasure" and couples separated "on the slightest cause. . . . [T]he freedmen readily promise to do better, but fail." Schoolteachers for the freedpeople also despaired about their private lives while attributing their moral lapses to the slave system. From her post in Alexandria, Virginia, the famous fugitive slave Harriet Jacobs wrote in 1863 that the "marriage law has been disregarded, from old habits formed in slavery." An 1866 account written by a young black woman who worked with the freedpeople in Lafayette Parish was more explicit. "They are given greatly to the sin of adultery. Out of three hundred I found but three couples legally married. This fault was largely the masters and it has grown upon the people till they cease to see the wickedness of it." A teacher in the Sea Islands reported that many freedmen readily admitted, " 'No, not married . . . but I just tuck [took] her and brought her home.' "[90]

When persuasion failed, freed slaves were sometimes forced into marriage contracts against their will. They were subjected to threats and even criminal punishment, the same coercions they faced when refusing to enter into and fulfill work contracts. One Yankee teacher described in detail how he punished a South Carolina freedman for illicit cohabitation and ordered the contracting of a forcible marriage:

I called him up to me one afternoon . . . and told him he must go to church and be married by the minister according to law. He flatly refused. . . . I thereupon told him he must go home with me, showing him I had a pistol, which I put in my outside pocket. He came along, swearing all the way and

---

[90] Letter of Ass't. Sup't. Edward Lyon to Col. O. Brown, April 30, 1866, RAC, Virginia, BRFAL, M1048, reel 44; Report of R.K. Scott to O.O. Howard, May 23, 1867, RAC, South Carolina, BRFAL, M869, reel 1; Report of [illegible], May 15, 1866, RAC, South Carolina, BRFAL, M869, reel 1; Report of R.K. Scott to O.O. Howard, July 20, 1867, RAC, South Carolina, BRFAL, M869, reel 1; Harriet A. Jacobs to Lydia Maria Child, March 18, 1863, in Ripley, ed., *Black Abolitionist Papers* 5: 194; Letter of Edmonia G. Highgate to the American Missionary Association, in Sterling, ed., *The Trouble They Seen*, 20; *Letters and Diary of Laura M. Towne: Written from the Sea Islands of South Carolina 1862–1884*, ed. Rupert S. Holland (New York, 1969; orig. pub. 1912), 24. See Stevenson, "Distress and Discord," 118–20.

muttering his determination not to comply. I gave him lodging in the dark hole under the stairs, with nothing to eat. . . . He finally gave up and promised to go. So I let him off with an apology.

Bureau agents used similar measures; as a South Carolina agent stated in 1867, many ex-slaves disobeyed the marriage law unless they "had a Bayonet at their backs all the time."[91] These disapproving accounts implicitly justified the continuing presence of the bureau and missionaries of uplift in the South, but so too did favorable reports that former slaves had learned respect for morals under Yankee influence. The contrasting representations alike merit both credit and skepticism. The ambiguities of former slaves' views of the marriage contract appear as well in their own accounts, such as a letter that a North Carolina freedman wrote to the bureau in 1867 describing the conflict that had broken out in Bladen County over the right to marry. "The Colored people of this place are trying to make their colored brethren pay some respect to themselves and the laws of the country by making them pay some respect to the marriage bond and stop the slave style of living to gather without being married." He reported an especially troublesome case: "A colored man has been promising to marry a girl for the last year has been bedding with her most of the time. . . . The colored men of this place appointed a committee to wait on him and see if they could not influence him to do better but no satisfaction could be obtained." Along with their liberators, former slaves enforced marriage "by law," though without always succeeding. Compulsion to obey the rules of free society and desire to negate slavery shaped the decision to marry. If for many ex-slaves marriage meant freedom, for others it meant constraint.[92]

Ambiguities were also evident in the way in which former slaves construed the reciprocal rights and duties of husband and wife. In freedom, as under slavery, they endeavored to make marriage a relationship of mutual dependency, with spouses relying on each other to fulfill both material and emotional needs. The ideal of mutuality emanated from traditional notions of kinship obligation that were prevalent in Africa and persisted in American slave culture, and that associated freedom with communal ties rather than with modern ideas of individual autonomy. Yet bonds of mutual obligation have

---

[91] Elizabeth Ware Pearson, ed., *Letters from Port Royal Written at the Time of the Civil War* (Boston, 1906), 95; Report of R.K. Scott to O.O. Howard, May 23, 1867, RAC, South Carolina, BRFAL, M869, reel 1.

[92] Letter of J.E. Eldredge, July 29, 1867, in Berlin et al., "Afro-American Families," 98–99. For conflicting assessments of freed slaves' inclination to enter into formal marriage contracts, see Gutman, *The Black Family*; Ripley, ed., *Black Abolitionist Papers* 5: 196; Edwards, *Gendered Strife*, 54–60.

never precluded relations of personal dominion and dependency or
conflicts over power, and they did not do so in the marriages of
former slaves. Furthermore, former slaves fused ideals of mutuality
with assertions of individual contract rights of sovereignty and proprietorship.[93]

The ideal of reciprocity in marriage was summed up by a Texas
freedman in an 1867 letter that he wrote to his sister. Affection plus
duties of labor that were thought appropriate to each sex were the
essential components. "She and I talked the matter over and she
told me she liked me well enough to try to take care of me, and I
promised to do the same for her," he confided. "She is industrious.
. . . I was lonely, wanted some kind hand to smooth my pillow. . . . I
am able to do good work yet, stock plows, make wheels, reels and
such things." Emancipation brought freedwomen's withdrawal from
the fields; husbands valued their wives' housework and wives valued
their husbands' wages and the relatively greater access to economic
resources that freedmen possessed as newfound heads of households. "I didn't have no money nor no home neither," one freedwoman explained, "he bought me some shoes and handkerchiefs and
a pretty string of beads. . . . I was might glad to marry him to get a
place to stay." There was also far more chance of "marrying for
love," as one South Carolina freedman explained, than in "secesh
times."[94]

But in freedom, as under slavery, the problem of mastery was
never far from the minds of husbands and wives. It was central not
only to the opposition they mounted against their former owners'
authority over their households but also to their private relations
with each other. According to most observers, both northern and
southern, freedmen claimed to be the rightful successors to the
slaveholder's domestic dominion, which they sometimes exercised as
brutally as former masters. Frances Ellen Watkins Harper reported
in outrage from the South that freedmen "positively beat their
wives." Of freedwomen, she wrote, "their subjection has not ceased
in freedom." Planters contended that "men have tied their wives up
to the house & whipped them," allegations borne out by court records. Like the cruelty of other men in their own households, these

[93] See David Brion Davis, *Slavery and Human Progress* (New York, 1984), 15–16; Patterson, *Freedom*, 55; Malone, *Sweet Chariot*; White, *Ar'n't I a Woman*, 142–60; Stevenson,
"Distress and Discord"; Jones, *Labor of Love*.

[94] Sterling, ed., *Trouble They Seen*, 218; Sterling, ed., *We Are Your Sisters*, 309; Berlin et
al., eds., *Freedom* 3: 252. See Susan A. Mann, "Slavery, Sharecropping, and Sexual
Inequality," *Signs*, 14 (Summer 1989), 774–98; Litwack, *Been in the Storm So Long*,
244–45; Jones, *Labor of Love*, 11– 63; Jim Cullen, " 'I's a Man Now': Gender and
African American Men," in Clinton and Silber, eds., *Divided Houses*, 76–91.

acts were extreme manifestations of the sovereignty many freedmen
claimed at home. As the same Texas freedman whose marriage involved mutual dependency wrote approvingly of his wife, "She does
as I direct. What is my pleasure seems to be hers." Reciprocal obligations were closely wedded to supremacy and subjugation.[95]

The marriages of freed slaves thus in certain ways resembled the
relations of bondage. Yet some freedmen reputedly believed that the
subjection of their wives affirmed their own emancipation. For freedmen, observed a teacher in the Sea Islands in 1867, "domestic freedom – the right, just found, to have their own way in their families
and rule their wives – that is an inestimable privilege!" In claiming
the right to rule their wives, freedmen expressed the entrenched
southern view that governing a household of dependent persons was
a birthright of free men; and it is scarcely surprising that they sometimes exercised that right with violence. For, as Frederick Douglass
explained, brutality was the custom in the extended plantation
households of the Old South: "The whip is all in all. It is supposed
to secure obedience to the slaveholder, and is held as a sovereign
remedy among the slaves themselves. . . . Slaves, as well as slaveholders, use it with an unsparing hand." The claim of slaveholders was
that southern domestic relations were inseparable from slavery, and
this legacy endured in the marriages of former slaves.[96]

But freedmen's ideas of husbandly sovereignty undoubtedly reflected Yankee influence as well. The precept that men were masters
at home was as established in the North as in the South, for it was
set forth in biblical and common law codes that were honored across
the sectional divide. The schoolbooks handed out by northern teachers to former slaves quoted the Bible on marriage – for example, *The
Freedman's Spelling-Book* taught passages from Ephesians, declaring
"The Bi-ble con-tains ma-ny di-rec-tions to hus-bands, wives. . . .
Wives, sub-mit your-selves un-to your own hus-bands." One teacher
noted that ex-slaves "had profound respect for quotations from the
Bible" and that freedmen recited the rule from Ephesians. The

---

95 Sterling, ed., *We Are Your Sisters*, 340; Foster, ed., *A Brighter Coming Day*, 134; Berlin
    et al., eds., *Freedom* 3: 602; Sterling, ed., *The Trouble They Seen*, 218. See also Victoria
    Bynum, "Reshaping the Bonds of Womanhood: Divorce in Reconstruction North
    Carolina," in Clinton and Silber, eds., *Divided Houses*, 320–33; Catherine Clinton,
    "Reconstructing Freedwomen," in Clinton and Silber, eds., *Divided Houses*, 306–19;
    Foner, *Reconstruction*, 87; Jones, *Labor of Love*, 62–68; Litwack, *Been in the Storm So
    Long*, 244–45.
96 Holland, ed., *Letters and Diary of Laura M. Towne*, 184; Douglass, *My Bondage and My
    Freedom*, 72. See also McCurry, "The Two Faces of Republicanism"; White, *Ar'n't I a
    Woman*, 151–53; Malone, *Sweet Chariot*, 228–29; Stevenson, "Distress and Discord";
    Mann, "Slavery, Sharecropping, and Sexual Inequality."

Freedmen's Bureau institutionalized the husband's supremacy, instructing freedmen to keep their wives "in subjection," authorizing them to sign labor contracts for their wives, and charging them with the responsibility to "make the Female Members of their families work in the crops." In bureau courts it was freedmen who, obeying the law of coverture, sued on their wives' behalf. Meanwhile, missionaries from northern black churches also taught traditional marriage doctrine. The " 'ruling power' is unquestionably lodged in the husband," declared the African Methodist Episcopal Church, and its pastors in the South sympathized with freedmen that the "difficulty has heretofore been, *our ladies were not always at our own disposal.*"[97]

Many freedmen therefore understood the right to have a wife at their own disposal as a bequest of emancipation. As they saw it, freedom deeded them property in her person and labor; in stating exclusive claim to her, they declared themselves slaves no more. Accordingly, between freedmen and former masters there was deep conflict over the ownership of freedwomen's labor. "When I married my wife," claimed a Tennessee freedman, "I married her to wait on me." An inheritance from the days of slavery, when forcible female fieldwork had gone hand-in-hand with forcible female sex, this antagonism burst into the open after emancipation, when husbands asserted their rights by trying to keep their wives from serving two masters. As one freedman reported, "I seen on some plantations . . . where the white men would drive the colored women out in the fields to work, when the husbands would be absent from their home, and would tell the colored men that their wives and children could not live on their places unless they work in the fields. The colored men would tell them . . . whenever they wanted their wives to work they would tell them themselves; and if he could not rule his own domestic affairs on that place he would leave it and go somewhere else." Opposing the claims of ex-masters, freedmen asserted title to their wives. "I consider her my property," announced a North Car-

---

97 *The Freedman's Spelling-Book* (Boston, 1865–66), 127; Elizabeth H. Botume, *First Days amongst the Contrabands* (Boston, 1893), 122, 96, 166; Jones, *Labor of Love*, 62; Letter of Bureau Ass't. Sup't., Mecklenburg County, Va., to Gen'l. O. Brown, August 31, 1866, RAC, Virginia, BRFAL, M1048, reel 45; "Matrimonial Happiness," *Christian Recorder*, July 9, 1864; *Respect Black: The Writings and Speeches of Henry McNeal Turner*, ed. Edwin S. Redkey (New York, 1971), 10. On freedmen's suits on their wives' behalf, see, for example, *Peter Davis v. Lucy Bearly, Jim Daniel v. John Smith, Dick Denton v. William Wyme, Ruben Brooks v. William Gordon*, all in RAC, Virginia, BRFAL, reel 62. On the gender ideology of the black church, see Daniel A. Payne, *History of the African Methodist Episcopal Church* (Nashville, 1891); Evelyn Brooks Higginbotham, *Righteous Discontent: The Woman's Movement in the Black Baptist Church, 1880–1920* (Cambridge, Mass., 1993). See Mann, "Slavery, Sharecropping, and Sexual Inequality."

olina freedman, who sought his wife's return from her white employer's home (in this case, against her own will). Here, household autonomy meant the freedman's ownership of his wife.[98]

Yet not all freedwomen reckoned themselves tokens of their husbands' emancipation. Clearly, most shared the ambitions of their menfolk more than their ex-masters' interests. But many also appeared to value their own personal autonomy as a right of emancipation. Though embracing kinship bonds and seeking collective freedom, they did not always consent to a husband's assuming the master's authority. No less than freedmen, they viewed themselves not simply as family members but also as rights-bearing individuals – with rights premised on possession of the self.[99]

Supposedly, some freedwomen were so intent on self entitlement that they would not marry. "When acting for the Freedman's Aid Society, the orders came to us to compel marriage, or to separate families," reported the antislavery feminist Frances Gage, who worked among ex-slaves in South Carolina and Mississippi under Rufus Saxton's command. "But the women came to me and said, 'We don't want to be married.'" Gage claimed that the freedwomen said, "'You give us a nominal freedom, but you leave us under the heel of our husbands, who are tyrants almost equal to our masters.'" In this 1867 speech to a meeting of the American Equal Rights Association in New York City, where abolitionists and feminists had gathered to promote emancipation, Gage may well have put her own beliefs into the mouths of freedwomen. Yet she also may have captured the gist of their ideas, if not their exact words. According to an Alabama freedwoman, emancipation sometimes did mean escaping marriage. "I have lived a life of trouble with him," she wrote in December 1865, "& a white man has ever had to Judge between us, & now to be turned loose from under a mas-

---

[98] Quoted in Litwack, *Been in the Storm So Long*, 245; Sterling, ed., *We Are Your Sisters*, 322; Victoria Bynum, "Reshaping the Bonds of Womanhood," 331. See also Paula Giddings, *Where and When I Enter: The Impact of Black Women on Race and Sex in America* (New York, 1984), 58–64; Clinton, "Reconstructing Freedwomen"; Horton, "Freedom's Yoke"; hooks, *Ain't I a Woman*.

[99] For the prevailing scholarly view that black women in nineteenth-century America did not conceptualize freedom in terms of individual autonomy, see, for example, Jones, *Labor of Love*, 58; Elsa Barkley Brown, "Negotiating and Transforming the Public Sphere: African American Political Life in the Transition from Slavery to Freedom," *Public Culture*, 7 (1994), 107–46; Laura Edwards, "Sexual Violence, Gender, Reconstruction, and the Extension of Patriarchy in Granville County, North Carolina," *North Carolina History Review*, 68 (July 1991), 237–60; Fox-Genovese, *Within the Plantation Household*. But other recent work suggests the need for further study of freedwomen's rights consciousness. See Patricia Williams, *The Alchemy of Race and Rights* (Cambridge, Mass., 1991); Boris, "Listening to Critical Race Theory."

ter, I know that I could not live with him in no peace, therefore I left him."[100]

Most freedwomen chose to marry, but even then many refused to yield their rights as individuals. Seeking to exercise the contract rights denied by coverture, some freedwomen opposed their husbands signing labor agreements for them and claimed title to their own wages. Others opposed their husbands' authority over persons and property at home. Often the conflict came before the Freedmen's Bureau. For instance, a Virginia freedman charged that his wife had left him and "taken most of his things with her and threatened that if she was forced to live with him she would kill him when asleep by pouring melted lead in his ear." She testified, "there is no standing [him] . . . he seems full of the devil, abuses and annoys . . . every way he can think of." But the bureau ordered this fugitive home.[101]

Other freedwomen invoked their legal rights within marriage by suing their husbands to oblige them to fulfill their half of the domestic bargain. They displayed an awareness not simply of contract, but of the exchange value of their own labor and persons. As chattels, they had no right to exact a quid pro quo from the slave master. Yet as freedpersons, they claimed from a husband what the law paternalistically termed "support," but what also might have been defined as wage payment for keeping house, growing crops, and sharing his bed. Sometimes, noted a bureau agent in 1866, marriage law was not satisfactory to freedmen, who "think their liberties much curtailed. . . . But the women, many of whom have been abandoned . . . are delighted with the protection it affords." Still other freedwomen had their husbands arrested for whipping them. In 1866 a Georgia freedwoman, who had been married for less than a year, had her husband brought before the bureau several times to stop him both from being violent and from getting something for nothing. "He has abused me," she claimed, "& refuses to pay for the rent of my room & has not furnished me with any money, food or clothing." Allegedly, he finally went to her room, took his belongings and some of her sheets and underwear, and tore up two of her dresses, declaring that " 'he would rather Keep a woman than be married – because she could not carry him to law & I could.' " Ironically, the name of the plaintiff was Rose

[100] Stanton et al., *History of Woman Suffrage* 2: 197; Sterling, ed., *We Are Your Sisters,* 310. See also Painter, *Sojourner Truth,* 164–78.
[101] *Thomas Carey v. Nancy Carey* (1866), RAC, Virginia, BRFAL, M1048, reel 62. See also Brown, "Negotiating and Transforming"; Bynum, "Reshaping the Bonds of Womanhood"; Gutman, *The Black Family,* 493; Foner, *Reconstruction,* 88; Jones, *Labor of Love,* 332.

Freeman, but she was a wife who claimed the rights of emancipation.[102]

That virtually no freedwomen possessed an education in classical
contract theory is obvious. Yet their views in some cases had much in
common with liberal precepts. They strove to control their own bodies, to possess their labor and its proceeds, and to enforce voluntary
relations of exchange. Even as wives, many saw themselves, at some
level, as autonomous individuals vested with contract rights – a self
image that stood in contrast to the domestic bonds that constituted
chattel slavery and marriage as similar, though not identical, property relationships. Mostly, as the legal documents attest, their rene-
gade views were expressed by acts rather than by words, and by ne-
gations of their husbands' claims rather than by explicit assertions of
positive individual rights. Perhaps this was why Yankee observers
thought they more dimly understood "they had rights" than did
freedmen who had gone to war for emancipation.[103]

But there were other sources of rights consciousness than contract
treatises and warfare. In the early years of emancipation freedwomen
participated in the mass politics of black communities, a form of
public franchise that may have highlighted the private contradictions
of wifely submission. At the same time they may also have been influenced by encountering female abolitionists who spoke of women's
rights. For ex-slaves, marveled the black antislavery advocate Charlotte Forten, who went south to teach in the Sea Islands, "It must
have been something very novel and strange . . . to hear a woman
speak in public." They "seemed much moved," she remarked, by a
speech on freedom that Frances Gage gave on Thanksgiving Day in
1862. For freedwomen it must have been even more agitating to
hear women of their own race speak out.[104]

No figure more famously symbolized the merger of abolitionism
and feminism than the fugitive slave Sojourner Truth; and Truth
exemplified as well the process by which the antislavery ideas of free
black women in the North were transmitted to former slaves in the
South. While working as an agent of the National Freedmen's Relief
Association, she broadcast her beliefs to ex-slaves. "I . . . go around
among the Freedmen's camps," she stated in 1864. "They are all

---

[102] Letter of Ass't. Sup't., Sub-district of Middlesex, Va., to Capt. James A. Bates, April
30, 1866, RAC, Virginia, BRFAL, M1048, reel 44; Berlin et al., "Afro-American
Families," 99–100. See also Edwards, "Sexual Violence, Gender, Reconstruction";
Hunter, *To 'Joy My Freedom*, 40; Michael Grossberg, *Governing the Hearth: Law and
the Family in Nineteenth-Century America* (Chapel Hill, 1985), 300–302.

[103] Botume, *First Days amongst the Contrabands*, 152. See Cullen, " 'I's a Man Now.' "

[104] *The Journal of Charlotte Forten: A Free Negro in the Slave Era,* ed. Ray Allen Billington
(London, 1953), 156.

delighted to hear me talk.'' Something she might have talked about was her apprehension that freedom would remain unrealized: "colored men will be masters over the women, and it will be just as bad as it was before. . . . I want women to have their rights.'' Perhaps she sounded the themes of her famous speeches to northern reformers. "If I have to answer for the deeds done in my body just as much as a man, I have a right to have just as much as a man. . . . You [men] . . . think that, like a slave-holder, that you own us. . . . I have plead with all the force I had that the day might come that the colored people might own their soul and body. Well, the day has come, although it came through blood. . . . We are now trying for liberty that requires no blood – that women shall have their rights.'' Precisely what Truth said in the freedpeople's camps went unrecorded, but it is plausible that she spoke there, as elsewhere, on women's right of self ownership.[105]

In the wake of slave emancipation, scores of other black female abolitionists besides Truth acted as ambassadors of freedom, traveling south to work as teachers and missionaries among the former slaves. Along with Bibles, clothing, and spelling books, they no doubt dispensed their views on female emancipation.

Frances Ellen Watkins Harper crisscrossed the South between 1867 and 1871, giving public lectures to former slaves, staying in their cabins. "How busy I am,'' she wrote from South Carolina in May 1867. "Traveling, conversing, addressing day and Sunday-schools.'' In some ways her efforts resembled those of Elizabeth Cady Stanton, who traversed the country during the same years while campaigning for women's emancipation. Stanton met separately with small groups of white women to discuss marriage and sexual matters. Harper met alone with freedwomen, speaking out on the same issues. "Sometimes I speak twice a day,'' she wrote from rural Georgia. "Part of my lectures are given privately to women, and for them I never make any charge.''[106]

The lectures expressed the complexities of Harper's understanding of freedom and marriage. On the one hand, she urged fidelity to the marriage contract as a mark of racial progress: "the colored man needs something more than a vote in his hand: he needs to know the value of home life; to rightly appreciate and value the marriage relation . . . to leave behind him the old shards and shells of slavery.'' But, on the other hand, she taught that female subjec-

---

[105] Sterling, ed., *We Are Your Sisters*, 253; Stanton et al., *History of Woman Suffrage* 2: 193–94, 224–25. See also Painter, "Difference, Slavery, and Memory''; Painter, *Sojourner Truth*; Giddings, *Where and When I Enter*, 65–71.
[106] Still, *Underground Rail Road*, 767, 772.

tion ran counter to a right valuing of marriage as a form of emancipation. "Part of the time I am preaching against men ill-treating
their wives," she stated. "The condition of the women is not very
enviable in some cases. They have had some of them a terribly hard
time in slavery, and their subjection has not ceased in freedom. . . .
One man said of some women, that a man must leave them or whip
them." By this time, Harper had attended women's rights conventions and doubtless aimed to promote freedwomen's sense of their
personal autonomy. Hearing such talk, meeting apart from their
menfolk, some freedwomen might well have reached a greater consciousness of their right to themselves, a sense of self antagonistic to
the doctrine of freedmen's masterhood.[107]

More cryptic were Charlotte Forten's remarks. On witnessing the
marriage ceremonies of former slaves in the Sea Islands, she wrote
in her diary that she was "*truly* glad that the poor creatures are trying
to live right and virtuous lives." But for herself, she confided in a
later entry, "Think *I* sh'ld dread a funeral much less."[108] Was she
thinking of the rule of coverture that rendered the wife dead in the
eyes of the law? Perhaps her ambivalence (inadvertently) colored the
perceptions of the former slaves whom she taught.

The possibility that resonances may have existed between the
ideas of reformers such as Forten, Harper, and Truth and the aspirations of freedwomen does not imply that freedwomen were akin to
blank tablets on which their Yankee sisters wrote their own worldview
wholesale. Rather, the point is that in the shaping of freedwomen's
consciousness of their contract rights, one potent source may have
been the encounter with female abolitionists, particularly of their
own race, who were also apostles of feminism.[109]

Paradoxically, at the very moment many freedmen were collectively invalidating self ownership as a sufficient material basis for
freedom, some of their wives were claiming a right to own themselves. Whether or not its antebellum exponents planted it there,
antislavery's recessive strain lived on in the minds of some freedwomen. Thus a Georgia freedman in an 1876 divorce petition alleged that his wife had defiantly declared, "I am my own woman and
will do as I please." Perhaps this freedwoman translated unarticu-
lated notions of personal autonomy into a full-fledged assertion of
self entitlement. Or perhaps this was a stock complaint, formulaically

[107] Ibid., 770, 773, 777; Stanton et al., *History of Woman Suffrage* 2: 178, 182–83. See
also Foster, ed., *A Brighter Coming Day*, 126–27; duCille, *Coupling Convention*; Tate,
Domestic Allegories.

[108] Billington, ed., *Journal of Charlotte Forten*, 153, 207.

[109] See Patricia Hill Collins, "The Social Construction of Black Feminist Thought,"
Signs, 14 (Summer 1989), 745–73, quote at p. 750.

invoked by husbands against wives, for the same phrase appeared in another divorce suit filed the same year in the same county.[110] Even if a formula, the complaint suggests that freedwomen transgressed by staking a claim to property in the self.

The ideal of contract freedom was inscribed into national law by the Civil Rights Act of 1866. But in debating this central enactment of Reconstruction, Congress set its imprimatur as well on the link between contract rights and the dependencies of marriage. The act was intended to elaborate the Thirteenth Amendment – to convert the "abstract truths" of abolition into "practical freedom" – explained its author, Senator Lyman Trumbull. It was meant "to draw the precise line, to say where freedom ceases and slavery begins."[111] The effort to establish this boundary, to specify the essential rights of emancipation, simultaneously enshrined the anomalies of the wife's status in a free society based on contract.

As Congress convened in the winter of 1865–1866, it confronted reports that southerners were aiming to recreate the conditions of slavery. This goal was manifest in the Black Codes passed by southern legislatures, which restricted the liberties of freedpeople. Even a former slaveholder warned Representative Thaddeus Stevens that "the feeling is becoming general here that slavery will be re-established." Union army men pressed congressional Republicans to enact federal law defining the Thirteenth Amendment's "true intent" and guarantying "equal rights." The outcome was the 1866 Civil Rights Act, thereafter given constitutional sanction by the Fourteenth Amendment.[112]

Principles of contract rang through the halls of Congress during the debate over the Civil Rights Act. The act asserted the principle of equality before the law and the authority of the national government to guarantee the irrevocable rights of citizens, which it enumerated as those of contract, property, and personal liberty. But its immediate purpose was to nullify the Black Codes, and the equal right of contract was the nub of the legislation. One congressman expostulated, "there are certain rights which belong to a freedman. He has a right to contract. He has a right to support himself." To an Ohio legislator, it was "mockery" to grant a citizen the right to live

---

[110] Quoted in Bynum, "Reshaping the Bonds of Womanhood," 330, and in Edwards, "Sexual Violence, Gender, Reconstruction," 255.
[111] *Congressional Globe*, 39th Cong., 1st sess. (1866), 474, 475.
[112] R.W. Flourney to Thaddeus Stevens, November 20, 1865, Thaddeus Stevens Papers, Library of Congress, Washington, D.C.; Benjamin F. Butler to Thaddeus Stevens, November 20, 1865, Stevens Papers; M.S. Littlefield to Lyman Trumbull, August 5, 1865, Lyman Trumbull Papers, Library of Congress, Washington, D.C.

"yet deny him the right to make a contract to secure the privilege and the rewards of labor." Republican lawmakers affirmed that freedom did not simply mean that slaves "should no longer be bought and sold like beasts in the shambles," it meant "the right to contract."[113]

The legislation was intended to ensure that both marriage rights and free labor would be inviolable. Proponents of the Civil Rights Act declared that it would afford the freedman the "right to become a husband or a father" as well as the "right to buy and sell." In a double sense the act ratified free contract by upholding hirelings' rights in the market and former bondsmen's rights at home. As Senator John Sherman stated, citizens were entitled to earn the "fruits of their own labor" and to be "protected in their homes and family."[114]

Perhaps the only feature of freedom not in dispute among members of Congress was the ex-slave's right to enter into contracts. Some conceded the point only grudgingly, yet it was generally acknowledged that emancipation had made freedmen into proprietors of their own persons and labor, giving them the legal capacity to participate in voluntary exchange relations and abolishing the system, as one Delaware senator admitted, "in which one man belongs to another." Slavery's antithesis, agreed legislators from both sides of the Mason–Dixon line, was free contract – the right of self-owning freedmen to sell their labor for wages and to marry and maintain a household.[115]

What members of Congress could not agree on, however, was the authority of the national government to guarantee contract rights, or any other right of citizenship. The existing rule was that contract relations, whether of the household or the market, fell under the states' jurisdiction. But the Civil Rights Act linked equal contract rights to the sovereignty of the national state. Trumbull justified this transformation by claiming that the freed slave could not be left "at the mercy of the State to be deprived of his civil rights." But defenders of states' rights denied that contract freedom justified federal interference with local law. This was "centralizing with a vengeance and by wholesale," argued the Kentucky senator, Garrett Davis. "One short bill breaks down all the domestic systems of law."[116]

---

[113] *Congressional Globe,* 39th Cong., 1st sess. (1866), 768, 1833, 903.
[114] Ibid., 502, 599, 42. See also Cott, "Giving Character to Our Whole Civil Polity."
[115] *Congressional Globe,* 39th Cong., 1st sess. (1866), 476, and see pp. 1268, 936, 1156, 363, 576, 628.
[116] Ibid., 39th Cong., 1st sess. (1866), 322, 598. See also Harold Hyman, *A More Perfect Union: The Impact of Civil War and Reconstruction on the Constitution* (New York, 1973); Robert Kaczorowski, "To Begin the Nation Anew: Congress, Citizenship, and Civil

The states' rights argument exploited the legal parallels between slavery and marriage as household institutions, and thereby threw into relief the conflict between contract freedom and marriage bonds. As "domestic relations," the argument went, both slavery and marriage had been governed exclusively by state law, just as contracts had "ordinarily been regulated by the States." The Civil Rights Act threatened to establish absolute individual rights and encroached on state codes that set the terms of marriage as well as of race relations.[117] Suddenly, the debate shifted from the transactions between former slaves and former masters to the commerce between husband and wife. The guarantee of equal contract rights, as Senator Edgar Cowan objected, raised the specter of wives set free from their husbands.

A married woman in no State that I know of has a right to make contracts generally. . . . Now, I ask Senators . . . whether they are willing . . . to interfere with regard to the contracts of married women. . . . I say that this bill . . . confers upon married women, upon minors, upon idiots, upon lunatics . . . the right to make and enforce contracts.[118]

If only for argument's sake, states' rights men pushed the logic of emancipation to its extreme conclusion, demonstrating that its crowning legal achievement – contract freedom – extended beyond slavery to the paternal bond between husband and wife. Cowan assailed an interpretation of the Thirteenth Amendment that would allegedly end up subverting the wife's "*quasi* servitude" by safeguarding the freedman's contract rights in federal law. "What was the slavery mentioned there?" he asked.

What was the involuntary servitude mentioned there. . . . Was it the right the husband had to the service of his wife? Nobody can pretend that those things were within the purview of that Amendment; nobody believes it.[119]

Congress had become a forum for debating the meaning of antislavery contract principles for relations between the sexes.

The response of Republican lawmakers was to dissociate emancipation from any household relation but slavery. Limiting the scope of freedom, they denied that it altered either the marriage contract or the wife's status. Rather, they drew a sharp line between race and sex distinctions at law and qualified the guarantee of "civil rights" to bar only discrimination based on "race, color or previous condi-

---

Rights after the Civil War," *American Historical Review*, 92 (February 1987), 45–68; Morton Keller, *Affairs of State: Public Life in Late Nineteenth Century America* (Cambridge, 1977), 37–84.
[117] *Congressional Globe*, 39th Cong., 1st sess. (1866), 318, and see p. 599.
[118] Ibid., 1781–82.   [119] Ibid., 499, 1784.

tion of slavery.'' The right of contract, one radical Republican
blithely assured Congress, conferred no rights whatsoever on wives.

It makes no law as to this. . . . Your State may deprive women of the right to
. . . contract. . . . But if you do so, or do not so as to one race, you shall treat
the other likewise. . . . If you do discriminate, it must not be on account of
race, color, or former condition of slavery.[120]

When confronted with the legal analogy between marriage and slavery, Republicans recast emancipation's achievement as a matter simply of race. Only a "distinction" between two wives or between two
single women was "unequal," claimed Thaddeus Stevens, "but
where all of the same class are dealt with in the same way then there
is no pretence of inequality."[121] Pressed to state their beliefs about
inequalities based on sex, radicals interpreted equal rights in a limited and formal way that barred only legal distinctions based on race.
This was not written into law, yet the idea that contract freedom
disallowed race difference but assumed sex difference won explicit
congressional sanction.

The Republican program did not merely refrain from tampering
with the marriage contract, it recognized freedmen as having a property right in their families. "Is a freeman," one senator demanded,
to be deprived of the right of "earning and purchasing property; of
having a home . . . a wife and family, or of eating the bread he
earns?"[122] This inventory supposed that a man's right to his wife was
equivalent to his title to material things or the means to acquire
them. It rested on a conception of the family as an indivisible unit
based on male authority and female dependence, a unity that precluded a wife's contract rights. Unlike freed slaves, explained one
congressman, women were a "part of the family" and therefore
needed no individual entitlements:

inasmuch as the negro is not even of the white family, is of a different race
and so treated . . . you have no right to strip him of every attribute of manhood. . . . You do not associate with him; you do not affiliate with him. . . .
None of these causes operate in regard to the family.[123]

In this view, freedmen's rights issued from the social distance between the races, while women remained within households bound

---

[120] Ibid., 1118, 1293.
[121] Ibid., 1064, and see p. 1782. See also Barbara J. Fields, "Ideology and Race in
American History," in *Region, Race, and Reconstruction: Essays in Honor of C. Vann
Woodward*, ed. J. Morgan Kousser and James M. McPherson (Oxford, 1982), 143–
77; DuBois, *Feminism and Suffrage*, 53–78, 162–202.
[122] *Congressional Globe*, 39th Cong., 1st sess. (1866), 504. See also Foner, "The Meaning of Freedom in the Age of Emancipation," 455.
[123] *Congressional Globe*, 39th Cong., 1st sess. (1866), 410.

together by ties of affection. Converting the wife into an autonomous, contracting individual would have stripped a free man of the
right to be master of a family.

The congressional authors of emancipation thus elevated contract
into a sovereign right of citizenship. Yet they simply extended free
men's established contract rights to former bondsmen, leaving wives
of both races to the protections offered by the marriage contract.
Indeed, the subject of marriage arose only as a reductio ad absur-
dum. But the undeniable logic of that argument provoked a reinter-
pretation of emancipation that emphasized themes of race rather
than portraying a transition from dominion and dependence to self
ownership and voluntary exchange. At law, only freedmen fully made
the exodus from slavery to contract. Emancipation turned the slaveholders' world upside down, but the bonds of marriage remained
intact.[124]

The ideal of a society ordered by contract that inspired the Puritan
errand to America was made ascendant throughout the nation by
the abolition of slavery. Yet this ideal was transformed between the
Puritan era and the era of emancipation. Almost invariably, contract
was contrasted with bondage. But from an ideal of voluntary political
submission, it became first an image of free market relations and
then was recast as the embodiment of citizens' freedom in a republic
purged of chattel slavery.

Always, however, the contracts of wage labor and marriage stood
for the fundamental freedom denied to slaves. Always, according to
the dominant worldview, contract freedom assured men property
not only in themselves but in their wives. And always, contract served
as a legitimating symbol for social relations in which inequality was
either cloaked by exchange or said to arise from consent. This symbolism had always been subject to conflicting representations. But
with the downfall of slavery its ambiguities became more evident
than ever before, as public debate turned from the problem of chattel slavery to the contracts of wage labor and marriage guaranteed
by emancipation.

[124] For parallels in the era of the American Revolution, see Kerber, "The Paradox of
Women's Citizenship in the Early Republic."

2

The Labor Question and the Sale of Self

Throughout the Western capitalist world the late nineteenth century was the age of the labor question. Industrial wage work and the conditions of proletarian life had come to represent distinct social problems – objects of scientific investigation, social reform, and political debate. In the United States, as in England and on the Continent, the labor question reflected the upheavals of the industrial revolution and the rise of working-class activism. Both labor protest and the study of laboring life had burgeoned earlier with industrial transformation; but in the late nineteenth century the scale of concern was as new as the scale of mass insurgency that was evident in proliferating strikes, expanding labor associations, and mounting political agitation often influenced by socialism. Everywhere, the labor question encompassed issues ranging from wages, work relations, factory laws, and the legality of collective action to metropolitan poverty, plebeian home life, housing, and crime; and everywhere, the participants in the debate included a broad range of labor advocates, state officials, moralists, jurists, and social scientists.[1]

The American labor question was profoundly marked by the problem of slavery and emancipation. Only in the United States did full-scale industrial capitalism develop simultaneously with, and literally alongside, the consolidation and overthrow of chattel slavery. And when Americans turned to the labor question in the wake of abolition, they claimed that it followed inevitably from the slavery ques-

[1] See Michael J. Lacey and Mary O. Furner, eds., *The State and Social Investigation in Britain and the United States* (New York, 1993), esp. chs. 1–6; Martin Bulmer, Kevin Bales, and Kathryn Kish Sklar, eds., *The Social Survey in Historical Perspective 1880–1940* (New York, 1991); Dorothy Ross, *The Origins of American Social Science* (New York, 1991), chs. 3–4; James Leiby, *Carroll Wright and Labor Reform: The Origin of Labor Statistics* (Cambridge, Mass., 1960); Joan Wallach Scott, *Gender and the Politics of History* (New York, 1988), chs. 5–7; Judith G. Coffin, *The Politics of Women's Work: The Paris Garment Trades, 1750–1915* (Princeton, 1996); Kathleen Canning, " 'The Man Transformed into a Maiden'? Languages of Grievance and the Politics of Class in Germany, 1850–1914," *International Labor and Working-Class History*, 49 (Spring 1996), 47–72; Kathryn Kish Sklar, *Florence Kelley and the Nation's Work: The Rise of Women's Political Culture* (New Haven, 1995).

tion. Labor spokesmen argued that now was the time for the country
to be "interrogated" by the needs of Yankee hirelings. Republican
congressmen called the labor question the "logical sequence of the
slavery question." Ministers claimed, "Now that slavery is out of the
way, the questions that concern the welfare of our free laborers are
coming forward." Indeed, abolitionist reformers who had rejected
the wage–slavery argument now saw the issue of free wage work in
the North as an outcome of emancipation. Speaking on labor reform
at Boston's Faneuil Hall in November 1865, Wendell Phillips recalled how he had first appeared there – "speaking for labor" – on
the slave's behalf. "Twenty-eight years have been spent in pleading
for a race which individuals assumed to own, to buy and sell. . . . That
struggle for the ownership of labor is now somewhat near its end;
and we fitly commence a struggle to define and to arrange the true
relations of labor and capital." From the slave's condition as property, the question had become the terms by which free labor would
be exchanged in the market.[2]

Thus the labor questions in the postbellum North and South were
in some ways understood as one. Both were ideologically framed by
the antithesis of slavery and freedom – the opposition between the
principle of human chattel and the ideal of contract freedom. Both
centered on the material, moral, and legal differences between unfree and free commodity relations. Insofar as the debate over northern arrangements explored the equities of the wage bargain, house-

[2] "Labor Reform in New England," *Workingman's Advocate*, January 16, 1869; Speech
of George W. Julian in the House of Representatives, *Workingman's Advocate*, April l,
1871; Washington Gladden, *Working People and Their Employers* (Boston, 1876), 3;
Wendell Phillips, *Remarks of Wendell Phillips at the Mass Meeting of Workingmen in Faneuil Hall, Nov. 2, 1865* (Boston, 1865), 3; "Wendell Phillips on the Eight-Hour
Question," *National Anti-Slavery Standard*, November 18, 1865; and see also Charles
Sumner's argument, quoted in Phillips's speech of April 1872, in Wendell Phillips,
The Labor Question (Boston, 1884), 33. See David Brion Davis, *The Problem of Slavery
in the Age of Revolution 1770–1823* (Ithaca, 1975); David Montgomery, *Beyond Equality: Labor and the Radical Republicans 1862–1872* (New York, 1967); David Montgomery, *Citizen Worker: The Experience of Workers in the United States with Democracy and the
Free Market during the Nineteenth Century* (New Haven, 1993); Barbara Fields, *Slavery
and Freedom on the Middle Ground: Maryland during the Nineteenth Century* (New Haven,
1985); Eric Foner, *Reconstruction: America's Unfinished Revolution 1863–1877* (New
York, 1988); David Roediger, *The Wages of Whiteness: Race and the Making of the American Working Class* (New York, 1991); Eric Foner, "The Meaning of Freedom in the
Age of Emancipation," *Journal of American History*, 81 (September 1994), 435–60;
Jonathan A. Glickstein, *Concepts of Free Labor in Antebellum America* (New Haven,
1991); William E. Forbath, "The Ambiguities of Free Labor: Labor and the Law in
the Gilded Age," *Wisconsin Law Review*, no. 4 (1985), 767–817; Thomas C. Holt, *The
Problem of Freedom: Race, Labor, and Politics in Jamaica and Britain, 1832–1938* (Baltimore, 1992); Patricia Hollis, "Anti-Slavery and British Working-Class Radicalism in
the Years of Reform," in *Anti-Slavery, Religion, and Reform: Essays in Memory of Roger
Anstey*, ed. Christine Bolt and Seymour Drescher (Hamden, Conn., 1980), 294–315.

hold relations, or economic authority and dependence, it dealt with laboring women and children as well as with men.[3] But the fundamental question of self ownership concerned hireling men: whether the buying and selling of their labor as a market commodity rendered them like or unlike chattel slaves. At stake was the very legitimacy of contract as the organizing principle of free society. Although in the agrarian South the question of labor and self entitlement remained yoked to the issue of landowning, in the industrial North this question became principally about the sale of time.[4]

By the end of Reconstruction the free wage system was ascendant throughout the country; chattel slaves in the South and independent commodity producers in the North had been transformed into a class of hirelings. This was a permanent condition for the vast majority, who could only dream of becoming independent property owners. Postbellum census data revealed that for the first time in the nation's history wage earners had come to outnumber the self-employed, a situation contradicting ideals of economic independence; and the disproportion grew larger over time. As the Massachusetts Bureau of Statistics of Labor declared in 1873, wage labor was universal, "a system more widely diffused than any form of religion, or of government, or indeed, of any language."[5]

---

[3] See this volume, Chapters 4, 5, and 6.

[4] On the significance of time in the age of the industrial revolution, see E.P. Thompson, "Time, Work-Discipline, and Industrial Capitalism," *Past and Present*, 38 (December 1967), 56–97; Michael O'Malley, *Keeping Watch: A History of American Time* (New York, 1990). On conflict over the workday on postbellum southern plantations and in northern workshops, see, respectively, Julie Saville, *The Work of Reconstruction: From Slave to Wage Laborer in South Carolina, 1860–1870* (New York, 1994); Montgomery, *Beyond Equality*; Herbert G. Gutman, *Work, Culture and Society in Industrializing America: Essays in American Working-Class and Social History* (New York, 1977), 3–78; David Roediger, "Ira Steward and the Anti-Slavery Origins of American Eight-Hour Theory," *Labor History*, 27 (Summer 1986), 410–26. My interpretation differs substantially from that of Lawrence Glickman, for it contends that in arguing in terms of time, hirelings challenged the fundamental legitimacy of wage labor whereas Glickman maintains that leaders of the eight-hour movement "legitimated wages" by focusing on consumption. See Lawrence Glickman, *A Living Wage: American Workers and the Making of Consumer Society* (Ithaca, 1997), 99–107, quote at 103.

[5] Massachusetts Bureau of Statistics of Labor, *Fourth Annual Report* (Boston, 1873), 440. See U.S. Industrial Commission *Report of the Industrial Commission on the Relations and Conditions of Capital and Labor Employed in Manufactures and General Business* (19 vols., Washington, D.C., 1901), 7: 7; Sean Wilentz, *Chants Democratic: New York City and the Rise of the American Working Class, 1788–1850* (New York, 1984); Bruce Laurie, *Working People of Philadelphia, 1800–1850* (Philadelphia, 1980); Montgomery, *Beyond Equality*, 3–44; David Montgomery, *The Fall of the House of Labor: The Workplace, The State, and American Labor Activism, 1865–1925* (New York, 1987), 46–51; Daniel T. Rodgers, *The Work Ethic in Industrial America, 1850–1920* (Chicago, 1974), ch. 2;

Like religion, government, and language, the wage system also reflected a complicated fusion of law and custom, for it rested on contract rules that were written and unwritten, spoken and unspoken, and formal and informal – rules that were interpreted in many differing ways. These rules governed the buying and selling of free labor: the procedures for entering and exiting a wage contract and the rights and duties created by the contract. These contract rules therefore represented a starting point of the labor question.

When agents of the Freedmen's Bureau tried, at the war's end, to induce former slaves to enter into yearlong written labor contracts, they claimed that this was "the system adopted by free laborers everywhere." But, in fact, putting wage contracts on paper was not the rule at the time. "Contracts of hiring," explained an 1886 treatise entitled *A Plain Statement of the Laws Relating to Labor*, "are generally made verbally, and . . . but few words are used. The rest is left to the custom of the trade, and the parties are bound by it." However, customs of the trades and contracts of hiring were full of idiosyncracies and inconsistencies that legal treatises did not examine.[6]

The rise of the wage system transformed northern craft trades in dissimilar ways. By the late nineteenth century, as the scale of industrial production expanded, the factory system came to prevail: rival firms united into single enterprises, and increasing use of machinery and division of tasks reduced the ratio of skilled laborers to the unskilled. At least four-fifths of the three million Americans who were employed in mechanical industries worked in factories, the labor statistician Carroll Wright reported in 1880. Yet concentrated ownership and task work also fractured production into small workshops and intensified the use of sweated home labor, most notably in the manufacture of cigars and clothing; tenement-house shops countered the trend toward factory work. In 1895 Florence Kelley, as state factory inspector of Illinois, stressed how unevenly capitalist industry had developed: "the shoemaker's shop, with its little group of workers, has become the shoemaking town, with a vast organization, both of capital and of labor. . . . The garment worker, on the contrary, still works in his kitchen." Factories were also diverse. Some were enormous, massing together thousands of workers, as in textiles, metals, and machinery. But these were the exceptions. In Boston, for example, over half of all manufacturing firms employed

Eric Foner, *Free Soil, Free Labor, Free Men: The Ideology of the Republican Party before the Civil War* (New York, 1970), ch. 1.

[6] *Orders Issued by the Commissioners and Assistant Commissioner of the Freedmen's Bureau*, 39th Cong., 1st sess., House Exec. Doc. 70 (1865), Henry A. Haigh, *A Plain Statement of the Laws Relating to Labor* (Detroit, 1886), 2.

fewer than six persons in the late 1870s, while over a third of all workers toiled in shops with twenty persons or less. There, as in other cities, the most common jobs were unskilled day labor and domestic work. Especially in the building and machine trades, however, skilled craftsmen remained central to industry.[7]

Both factories and tenement workrooms brought together immigrant and nativeborn laborers, as well as men, women, and children. Common labor assembled both black men and white men. Immigrants from Ireland, Britain, Germany, and, increasingly by the century's end, from southern and eastern Europe worked mainly in the consumer-finishing industries or as operatives and common laborers in textiles, mining, and the metal trades. Women were concentrated in clothing manufacture and textiles. Descriptions of tenement streets illustrated in microcosm the array of hirelings and their labor. On a New York City block where three hundred families lived, the men worked in seventy-two different trades: a quarter were tailors, but cigar makers, peddlers, painters, butchers, and shoemakers were also numerous. These men were mostly German, but their neighbors included Americans, Hungarians, Irish, Poles, Russians, Bohemians, and Chinese. On a Boston tenement street where a hundred families lived, the Irish predominated, but there was also a scattering of German, English, Italian, Hebrew, French, and African-Americans. Most of the men in these families were common laborers; six were carpenters, and one each worked as a lather, cobbler, sailor, piano maker, lineman, machinist, carriage washer, bridge builder, and organ varnisher.[8]

[7] Samuel Lane Loomis, *Modern Cities and Their Religious Problems* (New York, 1887), 55; Samuel Sewell Greeley, *Hullhouse Maps and Papers: A Presentation of Nationalities and Wages in a Congested District of Chicago, Together with Comments and Essays on Problems Growing out of the Social Conditions* (New York, 1970; orig. pub. 1895), 39; see also pp. 27–31; Massachusetts Bureau of Statistics of Labor, *Eighth Annual Report* (Boston, 1877), 249. See also John R. Commons, *Trade Unionism and Labor Problems* (New York, 1967; orig. pub. 1905), 316–35; Bruce Laurie and Mark Schmitz, "Manufacture and Productivity: The Making of an Industrial Base, Philadelphia, 1850–1880," in *Philadelphia: Work, Space, Family, and Group Experience in the Nineteenth Century,* ed. Theodore Hershberg (New York, 1981), 43–92; Alan Dawley, *Class and Community: The Industrial Revolution in Lynn* (Cambridge, Mass., 1976); Wilentz, *Chants Democratic;* Daniel Nelson, *Managers and Workers: Origins of the New Factory System in the United States 1880–1920* (Madison, 1975); Daniel J. Walkowitz, *Worker City, Company Town: Iron and Cotton-Worker Protest in Troy and Cohoes, New York, 1855–84* (Urbana, 1981); David Brody, *Steelworkers in America: The Nonunion Era* (New York, 1960), 1–95; David M. Gordon, Richard Edwards, and Michael Reich, *Segmented Work, Divided Workers: The Historical Transformation of Labor in the United States* (New York, 1982), 48–164; Montgomery, *House of Labor;* Christine Stansell, *City of Women: Sex and Class in New York, 1789–1860* (New York, 1986), 105–29; Eileen Boris, *Home to Work: Motherhood and the Politics of Industrial Homework in the United States* (New York, 1994).
[8] William T. Elsing, "Life in New York Tenement-Houses as Seen by a City Missionary," *Scribner's Magazine,* 11 (June 1892), 697–721; Alvan Francis Sanborn, *Moody's*

Evidence is sparse of the contract practices in all of these trades. By law, every contract presumed an offer and acceptance, but except in cases of well-documented strikes, it is unclear how hirelings came to terms with their employers. The sale of chattel slaves had been by written deed, and obsolete indenture contracts, entailing long years of unpaid work for bound laborers and apprentices, had also been in writing (on papers with torn, or "indented," edges). In oral agreements, the antebellum jurist Tapping Reeve had explained, "room is left for controversy." Because apprenticeship, for example, was a "personal trust" – a paternal relation of personal authority and submission rather than a mere commercial bargain – it was "very reasonable" to require this "contract of so much importance" to be in writing. Unlike provisions for unfree labor, however, wage contracts in the postbellum North denoted more limited duties and therefore were made informally. To be enforceable as law, labor contracts extending beyond a year had to be written: otherwise, neither statutes nor common law required any special kind of legal instrument. Throughout the century contracts usually ran for several months in farm labor, until a crop was harvested, but in most manufacturing trades the hiring was day-to-day, not for a definite time. Either party could end the contract at will, and their duties and rights were usually left implicit. Moreover, common law bound employers only to use "reasonable care" in hiring labor and in maintaining the workplace, while holding that workers assumed all risk not due directly to the employer's negligence. The wage bargain simply constituted a promise (express or implied), stated Theophilus Parsons's influential *Law of Contracts*, "that the party employing will pay for the service rendered; and . . . the party employed will use due care and diligence, and have and exercise the skill and knowledge requisite for the employment undertaken." Most free labor contracts were simple, oral agreements.[9]

Lodging Home and Other Tenement Sketches (Boston, 1895), 100–103. See Herbert Gutman, "Social and Economic Structure and Depression: American Labor in 1873 and 1874" (Ph.D. Dissertation, University of Wisconsin, Madison, 1959), 241–75; Alice Kessler-Harris, *Out to Work: A History of Wage-Earning Women in the United States* (New York, 1982), 75–141; Gordon et al., *Segmented Work*, 92–93; Montgomery, *House of Labor*, 48–49, 65–87, 112, 122–27.

9 Tapping Reeve, *The Law of Baron and Femme, of Parent and Child, Guardian and Ward, Master and Servant and of the Powers of the Courts of Chancery* (Albany, 1862), 485; Theophilus Parsons, *The Law of Contracts* (3 vols., Boston, 1873), 2: 57; see also pp. 43–47. See also J. Chitty, *A Practical Treatise on the Law Relative to Apprentices and Journeymen and to Exercising Trades* (London, 1812), 64–75; John C. Hurd, *Law of Freedom and Bondage in the United States* (2 vols., Boston, 1858), 1: 93–98, 158–66, 218–20, 283, 326–27, 2: 672–914; Horace G. Wood, *A Treatise on the Law of Master and Servant Covering the Relations, Duties and Liabilities of Employers and Employees* (Albany, 1886), 44–69; Irving Browne, *Elements of the Law of Domestic Relations and of*

Sometimes, not simply a few words, but no words at all could seal
the buying and selling of free labor. In an 1876 ruling on claims to
wages arising in a textile factory, the Massachusetts Supreme Judicial
Court recognized the subtleties of contract practice: "Assent may be
by acts as well as words, and by silence, where a party is fairly bound
to speak, if he dissents." In some employments, especially the
sweated trades, hirelings had little choice other than to assent silently. Where trade unions were powerful, they might have considerable say in deciding wages, hours, and work rules as well as the
conditions of hiring and discharge. But where no unions existed,
employers often unilaterally set the terms. According to the law,
workers silently signified their consent by simply taking a job. This
was freedom of contract.[10]

Nor was it always the custom for laborers to deal directly with
employers. Often they were selected by foremen, hiring agents, or
subcontractors. In the Rhode Island textile mills the rule was not
"for the manufacturer personally to hire or discharge help. . . . Overseers are tenacious of their prerogatives in this respect." Sometimes
craftsmen in the metal industry "came directly into the shop," one
machinist explained, "and asked the foreman for a job." But in most
trades crowds usually waited outside factory gates, responding to employment notices posted about town or in newspapers, or having
learned of the work by word of mouth. Employment agents "would
look over the group generally," said a worker in the Chicago meat-
packing plants. "So far as I could see there was no bargaining and
discussion about wages, terms of employment, or anything of that
sort. Just the employment agent would tap the one he wanted on the
shoulder and say, 'Come along.' " Similarly, authorities on female

Employers and Employed (Boston, 1883), 122–35; Christopher G. Tiedeman, *A Treatise on State and Federal Control of Persons and Property in the United States Considered from Both a Civil and Criminal Standpoint* (New York, 1900), 340–44, 425; *Farwell v. Boston and Worcester Rail Road Corp.*, 45 Mass. (4 Metc.) 49 (1842); *Hansell v. Erickson*, 28 Ill. 257 (1862); *Thrift v. Payne*, 71 Ill. 408 (1874); *Hofstetter v. Gash*, 104 Ill. App. 455 (2d Dist. 1902); Illinois Bureau of Labor Statistics, *Second Biennial Report* (Springfield, 1883), 298–345; Richard B. Morris, *Government and Labor in Early America* (New York, 1946); Robert J. Steinfeld, *The Invention of Free Labor: The Employment Relation in English and American Law and Culture, 1350–1870* (Chapel Hill, 1991); Sharon Salinger, "Colonial Labor in Transition: The Decline of Indentured Servitude in Late Nineteenth Century Philadelphia," *Labor History*, 22 (1981), 165–91; Christopher Tomlins, *Law, Labor, and Ideology in the Early American Republic* (New York, 1993); Montgomery, *Citizen Worker*, 13–51; Christopher L. Tomlins, *The State and the Unions: Labor Relations, Law, and the Organized Labor Movement in America, 1880–1960* (Cambridge, 1985), 72–73.
[10] *Preston v. American Linen Co.*, 119 Mass. 400, 404 (1876). See also Gutman, "Social and Economic Structure," 313–16; Montgomery, *Beyond Equality*, 138–56; and Montgomery, *House of Labor*, 9–17, 107, 152–62; Montgomery, *Citizen Worker*, 41–44.

employment observed that the "swarming crowd" was "absolutely at the mercy of the manager or foreman, who . . . makes the selections according to fancy, youth and any gleam of prettiness." The asymmetries of this practice and the absence of bargaining were epitomized by the sweated clothing trades, where subcontractors preferred to hire immigrants "just landed" and "ignorant of the customs . . . of the country . . . who cannot speak a word of English." In New York City tenement bosses would "go to Castle Garden, pick up the green hands from Poland or Germany, and promise them work right away." Here, the customs of the trade were irrelevant.[11]

When wage contracts had been left vague at inception, it was customary for employers to post up shop rules and claim them as part of the original bargain. The stipulations took varied forms and, again, the law inferred workers' consent unless they dissented immediately or quit. A Pennsylvania nail manufacturer posted wage rates for puddling in a "conspicuous part of the mill," claiming that this system of establishing "rules for the government of the work" was the "universal custom" in metal shops and that the "rules became part of the contract between the employer and employee." At a Massachusetts cotton textile factory the back of each operative's monthly pay envelope stated that two weeks notice must be given before quitting the job or else wages would be forfeited. The Massachusetts Supreme Judicial Court agreed that once a worker knew the rule, even though unstated at the time of hiring, it became part of the "contract binding upon him." Even if rules were not made explicit, hirelings presumably "entered into the contract with knowledge of the established usages of the employment," a New York court of appeals held in a dispute over a scowman's wages. In this case unspoken tradition on the docks requiring a ten-hour day overruled an 1867 state law declaring that eight hours was a legal day's work.[12]

It was also the custom in many trades for foremen to set the terms of contracts, which often varied even among workers performing the same tasks. In textile factories the scope of the foreman's personal discretion reputedly led to "favoritism, jealousy, spite, revenge." Foremen also controlled the tenement shops. In New York City cigar

---

[11] Lillie B. Chace Wyman, "Studies of Factory Life: The Village System," *Atlantic Monthly*, 62 (July 1888), 16–29, 25; "The New Man in the Shop," *Iron Trade Review*, December 13, 1884; Nelson, *Managers and Workers*, 81; Helen Campbell, *Prisoners of Poverty* (Boston, 1970; orig. pub. 1887), 34; *Some Facts of Interest to Boston Clothing Merchants* (Boston, 1889), Pamphlet Collection, Wisconsin State Historical Society, Madison, Wisc., 10, 11, 14. See also Nelson, *Managers and Workers*, 34–54.

[12] *Godcharles v. Wigeman*, 113 Pa. 431, 432–33 (1886); *Preston v. American Linen Co.*, 119 Mass. 400, 402 (1876); *McCarthy v. Mayor, Aldermen and Commonality of the City of New York*, 96 N.Y. 1, 7 (1884). See also Montgomery, *Citizen Worker*, 43.

makers picked up tobacco from foremen and brought it to their
tenement homes, where the whole family stripped, bunched, and
rolled it into several thousand cigars, which were returned to the
foremen in exchange for wages. The wage rates were "very arbitrary," claimed the labor leader Samuel Gompers, but if "people
object to this they are told they will be paid the whole wage only
when they deliver 'good work.' " Under the sweating system, subcontractors took the foreman's place, negotiating with manufacturers
who owned the materials and then hiring workers to stitch clothing
in tenement shops. In sweatshops there was no single standard for
wages or hours. Observing the workings of free contract, Florence
Kelley noted that "as individuals," employers of sweated labor bar-
gained with manufacturers – "undercutting each other, and calculating upon their power to reduce the pay of their employees below
any point to which the manufacturers may reduce theirs" – and "as
individuals," they also "tyrannize over the victims who have the misfortune to work in their shops." The sweated laborer, stated the
economist John Commons, was the most "isolated and unknown" of
all hirelings.[13]

Trade unions stood opposed to the unruly system of contracting
and asserted labor's right to establish collectively the terms of work.
Their efforts altered the wage contract's form from an oral promise
full of ambiguity to a precisely worded, written document. Conflict
centered not only on clauses regarding wages, hours, and work rules,
but also on whether written contracts should represent individual or
collective bargains. The first written collective agreements were usually entered into when a strike was imminent or just had been won,
as labor aimed to oblige capital to accept its demands through the
legal instrument of a written contract. Only a minority of workers
belonged to unions and fewer were protected by trade agreements,
but in skilled crafts such as machinery and metals, unions did win
written contracts recognizing collective action. Likewise, employers
saw the value of formalizing rules through written contracts. The
most infamous were "iron-clad" contracts, which were made with
individual workers and which banned joining unions or striking. An
1875 contract offered by an Ohio coal company bound workers not
to "enter into or in any way aid or sanction any strike or combination." These agreements grew more common from the 1870s on,
and the restrictions on liberty became more explicit. An 1885 min-

[13] Wyman, "Studies of Factory Life," 25, 23; New York Bureau of Statistics of Labor,
   Second Annual Report (New York, 1885), 149; Stuart Kaufman, ed., *The Samuel Gom-
   pers Papers* (6 vols., Urbana, 1986), 1: 190; Greeley, *Hullhouse Maps*, 31; Commons,
   Trade Unionism, 317. See also Nelson, *Managers and Workers*, 43–45; Montgomery,
   House of Labor, 118–22.

ing contract required a yearlong term of service, forbade workers to hold any labor meetings or go on strike, and stated that the firm would only "deal directly and individually with each of its employees," and not with "any committee purporting to represent any . . . combination of workmen." For violating their individual contracts in concert, workers were fired, blacklisted, and forced to forfeit wages.[14]

Though iron-clad agreements formally complied with contract rules of voluntary exchange by involving economic reciprocity but no physical or legal coercion, labor advocates claimed that they embodied an unfree sale of labor. Just as freedpeople refused to sign plantation wage contracts, which appeared to them as a new form of bondage, northern workers argued that contracts barring collective acts were enslaving. "We look back in pride to the days when the independent Barons compelled King John to give the oppressed people of England their *Magna Charta,* and yet to-day we are threatened with a slavery which would make even King John blush for shame," the *National Labor Tribune* declared in 1875. "Look, ye silk fingered gentry at the . . . cursed articles of agreement, wherein it is provided that every vestige of liberty, of thought or action is signed away." Workingmen protested that they were becoming "a race of iron-clad slaves." An 1884 article in the *Carpenter* called such slavery more coercive than in "olden times," precisely because it had the guise of consent and contract. The "master of today" did not punish labor "at the whipping post," but simply required that "the slave has signed away his liberty and consented to be fleeced."[15]

Thus, for many hirelings, the blunt terms of free contracts were expressions of wage slavery rather than their own ideals of trade custom. The ironclad agreement exemplified in extreme the features of contract making that they found objectionable: the inequality of power underlying the voluntary rituals of offer and acceptance

---

[14] "Article of Agreement," issued by the Mercer Mining and Manufacturing Company of Ohio, reprinted in *National Labor Tribune,* May 8, 1875; "Hocking Valley Miner's Annual Contract," *Journal of United Labor,* January 25, 1885. See also U.S. Congress, *Report of the Committee of the Senate upon the Relations between Labor and Capital, and Testimony Taken by the Committee* (4 vols., Washington, D.C., 1885), 1: 198–200, 1120; *Ramsey v. People of the State of Illinois,* 142 Ill. 380 (1892); *Braceville Coal Co. v. People of the State of Illinois,* 147 Ill. 66 (1893); *Journal of United Labor,* February 1883; Montgomery, *Beyond Equality,* 136–58; Montgomery, *House of Labor,* 9–31, 115, 151, 162–63, 180–93; Dawley, *Class and Community,* 184–92; Brody, *Steelworkers in America,* 50–79; Nelson, *Managers and Workers,* 38–39, 46–47; Tomlins, *The State and the Unions,* 72–73.
[15] "The Coming Struggle," *National Labor Tribune,* May 22, 1875; "Are We to Be Made Iron-Clad Slaves," *Carpenter,* March 1884. See also "Hocking Valley Miner's Annual Contract"; "Serfdom Threatened," *National Labor Tribune,* May 8, 1875; "The Crisis of Labor," *National Labor Tribune,* April 18, 1874.

and the exchange of labor for a wage. Strikes – the withholding of labor from sale – had long been the custom by which workers wholly negated unacceptable contracts. If employers imposed wage cuts or unwanted work rules or posted up other kinds of "obnoxious notice," labor ultimately countered by striking. As one carpenter explained this practice in 1885, a mass meeting would be held to vote on "whether there shall be a strike or what shall be the demand for the coming season." Then, "we get circulars printed and send them around to the employers, giving them a certain time, say a week or two, to make up their minds to comply with the demands; if not, we fix a certain day, and there will be a strike upon that day." In the postbellum era these tactics became more the custom than ever before. Against a backdrop of recurring economic depression, intense competition, and growing concentration of industry, a rising tide of strikes swept the country, sometimes spreading from single workshops to entire cities and trades.[16]

The mounting conflict over contracts of hiring led many Americans to views on the labor question summed up by the economist John Bates Clark in 1886: "A contest is here in process on a scale of magnitude impossible in earlier times, a battle in which organized classes act as units."[17] The labor question was understood as joining contract relations with relations of class. In question was not simply the wage contract's form, whether it was written or unwritten, individual or collective, or even the terms on which free labor would be sold. Also momentous were less concrete questions – whether contract represented a principle of social order or disorder, and whether commodity exchange was a morally defensible model of rights and duties among free persons.

The political prominence of the Gilded Age labor question was nowhere more evident than in an 1883 congressional investigation into the relations between labor and capital. A committee of the Senate convened hearings across the country, taking testimony from a wide

[16] Illinois Bureau of Labor Statistics, *Second Biennial Report* (1883), 260–64, 267–83; New York Bureau of Statistics of Labor, *Third Annual Report* (New York, 1886), 237, 219. See also David Montgomery, "Strikes in Nineteenth-Century America," *Social Science History*, 4 (February 1980), 81–104; Leon Fink, *Workingmen's Democracy: The Knights of Labor and American Politics* (Urbana, 1983); Nell Irvin Painter, *Standing at Armageddon: The United States, 1877–1919* (New York, 1987), 1–35; James Livingston, "The Social Analysis of Economic History and Theory: Conjectures on Late Nineteenth-Century American Development," *American Historical Review*, 92 (February 1987), 69–95; Martin J. Sklar, *The Corporate Reconstruction of American Capitalism, 1890–1916: The Market, The Law, and Politics* (New York, 1988).

[17] John Bates Clark, *Philosophy of Wealth: Economic Principles Newly Formulated* (Boston, 1886), 66.

range of witnesses – laboring men, employers, reformers, social scientists, ministers, journalists, and state officials – who offered an array of views on the free labor system. This was not the first time that
Congress had held major public hearings on social problems; it had
investigated affairs in the South in the 1871 Ku Klux Klan hearings,
and also the economic depression of the 1870s. But it had never
before examined work and living conditions under industrial capitalism. "We want to get all the light we can from every source, and
especially from men who have personal practical knowledge of the
workingmen, their condition, their views, their feelings, and their
desires," explained one congressman. The object was to study "the
whole question of the relations between labor and capital and the
troubles between them." For the national state, wage labor had become a problem as serious as economic crisis or the relations between former slaves and former masters. And the hearings revealed
that relations of free contract were producing conflict in the North
to an extent unforseen when slavery was destroyed.[18]

At the turn of the century the labor reformer George McNeill
recalled that concern with the wage system corresponded directly to
the intensity of labor unrest. He claimed that it was not until the
1877 railroad strikes that "you could get an article upon the labor
question into a magazine." Thereafter, since "property was frightened," the nation was transfixed by the "whole wage question." But
other contemporaries offered a somewhat different chronology. According to E.L. Godkin, the editor of the *Nation,* the labor question
became central just after the Civil War. In an 1867 essay on "The
Labor Crisis" he stressed the political importance of this issue in the
North as well as in the South. Taking note of expanding trade unions
and the rise of eight-hour reform, he observed sardonically that Yankee workingmen had "brought the political leaders to their feet"
and that "now no convention ever draws up a platform without in-
serting in it a small parcel of twaddle on the 'rights of labor.' "
Though Godkin exaggerated, many journals of opinion expressed
anxiety about the political consequences of rising labor conflict. During the hard times of the 1870s, trade unionism slowed, but not
strikes and lockouts. As a religious journal warned in 1875, there

---

[18] U.S. Congress, Senate, *Relations between Labor and Capital,* 1: 565; see also pp. 7, 213,
216, 566. See also *Congressional Record,* 47th Cong., lst sess., 1882, 4934, 5161, 5430,
6696; Mary O. Furner, "The Republican Tradition and the New Liberalism: Social
Investigation, State Building, and Social Learning in the Gilded Age," in Lacey and
Forner, eds., *The State and Social Investigation; U.S. Congress, The Ku-Klux Conspiracy:
Testimony Taken by the Joint Select Committee to Inquire into the Condition of Affairs in the
Late Insurrectionary States* (3 vols., Washington, D.C., 1872); U.S. Congress, *Investiga-
tion by a Select Committee Relative to the Causes of the General Depression in Labor and
Business,* 46th Cong., 2nd sess., House Misc. Doc. 5 (1879).

had not yet been found "any contrivance which might establish harmonious relations." Subjects such as "How to Deal with Communism" were a commonplace for postbellum men of letters.[19]

By the 1880s, debate over what some termed the "white-labor question" had become far-reaching. The settings varied from labor meetings and church services to conferences of social scientists. "Lectures had been delivered and . . . agitation meetings held at frequent intervals. The press was filled with labor news. The clergy opened the doors of their associations to labor men for the discussion of labor measures or methods," wrote McNeill in 1887. Spokesmen for manufacturers reported that "unsatisfactory and strained" labor relations had "pushed the so-called labor question into unpleasant prominence." Ministers preached on the "labor troubles," warning of "pain and disaster, even as the overthrow of slavery was accomplished, only by a bloody war." At its 1885 founding the American Economics Association declared that state, church, and social science must collaborate in mediating the antagonism between labor and capital. Scholarly symposiums on the "Labor Problem" proposed measures ranging from collective bargaining and arbitration to profit sharing and industrial partnership, while some professors insisted that the answer was technical expertise and that engineers must "manage the great world of labor." In the view of the economist Henry Carter Adams, the labor question would "give color to the history of the last quarter of the nineteenth century"; there was "no subject of greater interest to the public."[20]

Thus the 1883 congressional investigation exemplified forms of social inquiry that crossed class lines as well as the boundaries of labor reform, moral reform, and professional social science. It also drew on the methods and conceptual categories of surveys conducted by state boards of labor statistics, which were established in leading industrial states in the postbellum era. The practical results of the 1883 investigation were modest; though labor failed to secure the enforcement of an eight-hour law, Congress enacted legislation

[19] U.S. Industrial Commission, *Report of the Industrial Commission* 7: 115–16; E.L. Godkin, "The Labor Crisis," *Nation*, 4 (April 15, 1867), 335; "The Labor Question," reprinted from *New Age* in *Workingman's Advocate*, November 15, 1875; John Bates Clark, "How to Deal with Communism," *New Englander*, 37 (July 1878), 533–42.
[20] U.S. Congress, Senate, *Relations between Labor and Capital* 1: 1095; George E. McNeill, ed., *The Labor Movement: The Problem of To-Day* (Boston, 1887), 171; William E. Barns, ed., *The Labor Problem: Plain Questions and Practical Answers* (New York, 1886), 52; Charles Oliver Brown, *Talks on the Labor Troubles* (Chicago, 1886), 5; Richard T. Ely, "Report of the Organization of the American Economic Association," *Publications of the American Economic Association*, 1 (1887), 7; Henry C. Adams et al., "The Labor Problem," *Scientific American Supplement*, 22 (August 21, 1886), 8861–62. See also "A Symposium on Several Phases of the Labor Question," *Age of Steel*, January 2, 1886, 15–24; Rodgers, *The Work Ethic*.

that established a national bureau of labor, prohibited contract immigration, and allowed the incorporation of unions.[21]

But the congressional hearings turned up masses of evidence that the wage contract positioned buyers and sellers of free labor like "two pugilists contending in a ring." This evidence controverted reigning beliefs about the mutuality of labor and capital in free society and the natural harmonies of the unregulated market.[22] The very year of the hearings, William Graham Sumner had identified contract – a contract modeled on market exchange – as the paradigm of free social relations. Meanwhile, testimony was being taken that clashed with assumptions about the virtues of a social order based on contract. The state of labor documented by government investigation did not embody the antislavery ideal of contract freedom invoked to legitimate the commerce in free labor and wage dependence in both the North and South.

Even as the nation turned to the labor question, idealized representations of the wage system retained great cultural and legal power. There was a marked dissonance between empirical studies and theoretical statements of free labor and free contract principles, a dissonance that would contribute to the rise of realism in jurisprudence and the social sciences at the turn of the century.[23] But in the era immediately after the Civil War, wage labor still figured as the quintessential free contract relation in accounts of law and political economy that celebrated the downfall of slavery.

This was the vision presented by a committee of the Massachusetts legislature in an 1866 report recommending against labor's demand for a law limiting the length of the workday to eight hours. Presaging the courts' laissez-faire constitutionalism on wage relations, the report opposed all state interference with freedom of contract in the sale of labor. "The long struggle for the abolition of slavery, on which all the old civilizations rested, consisted in nothing but setting up the principle that it shall take two to make a bargain," the committee affirmed. "It is for the *man,* not the *State,* to say how many, or

[21] See P.J. McGuire, "The American Federation of Labor – Its History and Aims," appendix to William Trant, *Trade Unions: Their Origin and Objects, Influence and Efficacy* (New York, 1888), 40; Leiby, *Carroll Wright;* Furner, "The Republican Tradition and the New Liberalism."

[22] U.S. Congress, Senate, *Relations between Labor and Capital* 1: 562. See Morton Keller, *Affairs of State: Public Life in Late Nineteenth Century America* (Cambridge, Mass., 1977), 162–96; Sidney Fine, *Laissez-Faire and the General Welfare State, A Study of Conflict in American Thought, 1865–1901* (Ann Arbor, 1956), 29–164; John G. Sproat, *"The Best Men": Liberal Reformers in the Gilded Age* (New York, 1968), 142–68.

[23] Edward A. Purcell, *Crisis of Democratic Theory: Scientific Naturalism and the Problem of Value* (Lexington, Ky., 1973); Morton G. White, *Social Thought in America: The Revolt Against Formalism* (New York, 1949).

how few hours in the day he will use hand or brain" and that "it was not till the capitalist was left as free as the laborer, that labor was really emancipated." The report also found that labor and capital were not inevitably antagonistic, "not natural enemies but real friends."[24]

Law treatises of the late nineteenth century parsed the meaning of the wage contract in antislavery language. Echoing judicial rhetoric as well as the principles articulated during the debate over the 1866 Civil Rights Act, Christopher Tiedeman's authoritative statement on the limitations of state power declared that "liberty of contract" was the "badge of a freeman." Treatises on employment law posited that abolitionist ideals of free labor had been realized throughout the country. "To-day the labor contract is perfectly free," wrote Frederic J. Stimson in *Labor in Its Relation to Law.* "The recognition of the laborer as a free citizen, free to contract, capable of acquiring contractual rights, has been his great emancipation of the past." For jurists the wage contract distilled the rights of freedom.[25]

Accounts of the demise of unfree labor and the triumph of the wage contract also dominated postbellum texts on political economy. Even professors who anxiously studied the "labor problem," disclosing the inequalities of capital and labor and the harsh conditions of factory work, extolled labor's passage from status to contract and the wage system as the fruits of the long contest against slavery and serfdom. As Edmund J. James, an economics professor at the Wharton School of the University of Pennsylvania, described the transformation, "a steadily progressing emancipation" had occurred over the centuries, from "absolute slavery" through "intermediate stages" of villenage and other forms of bound labor, "until slavery gave way to personal freedom of the present century," when the bond between master and laborer became a "relation of contract pure and simple." In an 1887 essay that was among the first to be published under the auspices of the American Economics Association, Henry

[24] Massachusetts House of Representatives, "Report of the Special Commission on the Hours of Labor and the Condition and Prospects of the Industrial Classes," Doc. 98, (1866), 31, 25, 35. See Charles McCurdy, "The Roots of 'Liberty of Contract' Reconsidered: Major Premises in the Law of Employment, 1867–1937," *Supreme Court Historical Society Yearbook* (1984), 20. 33; Forbath, "Ambiguities of Free Labor."

[25] Tiedeman, *State and Federal Control,* 315; Frederic J. Stimson, *Labor in Its Relations to Law* (Freeport, N.Y., 1972; orig. pub. 1895), 51, 77. See also William Nelson, "The Impact of the Antislavery Movement upon Styles of Judicial Reasoning in Nineteenth Century America," *Harvard Law Review,* 87 (1974), 513–66; Forbath, "Ambiguities of Free Labor." But see also James Schouler, *A Treatise on the Law of the Domestic Relations; Embracing Husband and Wife, Parent and Child, Guardian and Ward, Infancy, and Master and Servant* (Boston, 1870).

Carter Adams postulated that modern industry rested on four essential "legal facts": private property in land, capital, and labor, and the "right of contract for all alike."[26]

The overarching theme of the labor history written in this era was the transition from bondage to free contract. The ascendance of contract allegedly had transformed labor from a relation of personal dominion and dependence to a commodity exchange in which buyers and sellers were formally equal and free, yet also mutually dependent on one other. No longer was the laborer human property, a commodity possessed by a slave master; rather, the self-owning hireling brought labor – something abstracted from self – into the free market to sell as a commodity in exchange for a wage. By the late nineteenth century, the abolitionist view of wage labor, which constituted the official ideological framework of emancipation, had become a conceptual foundation for the social sciences as well as for the law. Writing on the history of "Mechanical Labor" and the "Modern Laborer," Edmund James of the Wharton School explicated this body of thought. "Until very recent times the great majority of men were in a condition of personal dependence, which, although varying much in different countries and at different times, may be fairly termed personal slavery. The many have been compelled to labor for the few, who, in the light of law and custom, were alone entitled to the fruits of the labor." But with the rise of the "freedom of the laborer" and "freedom of contract" came "the conversion of the laborer into a free merchant of the commodity, labor." The "subordination of the laborer" gave way to his "equality with the master as the seller of a commodity":

finally, in the nineteenth century, the old relation is abolished entirely and the status is converted into a contract. This mode of treatment converts the laborer into an independent human being on the same footing exactly as the master, and secures to him, nominally at least, perfect freedom in the disposition of his time and labor, which form the commodities which he has for sale.

The era of bondage was past, wrote the economist Edward Atkinson, "men have become sorted as capitalists and laborers . . . wage-payers and wage-receivers," whose "method is to exchange." The jurist Christopher Tiedeman explained in 1886 that the traffic in labor

---

26 Edmund J. James, "The Rise of the Modern Laborer," and Edmund J. James, "History of Mechanical Labor," both in McNeill, ed., *Labor Movement*, 5, 43; Henry Carter Adams, "Relation of the State to Industrial Action," *Publications of the American Economic Association*, 1 (January 1887), 499. See also Carroll D. Wright, "The Factory System as an Element in Civilization," *Journal of Social Science Containing the Transactions of the American Association*, 16 (December 1882), 109.

was no longer an exchange in which master and labor stood on an
"unequal footing in their mutual dealings."[27]

Yankee clergymen lent moral authority to this antislavery construction of the wage contract, adopting the vocabulary of the marketplace. The Boston minister Edward Everett Hale, who sympathized with labor's demands, maintained that reform must be
premised on securing "complete freedom" for every man in "the
sale" of his "prime commodity, his labor." Other preachers affirmed that free labor was simply "a matter of barter and sale," and
that for those with "labor to sell, and nothing else" and for those
seeking to purchase it, the only questions were, "Will you buy? . . .
Will you sell?" The understanding was that the legitimacy of the
commerce lay in the legal equality of employers and workers and the
likeness of labor to other commodities. In a tract entitled *Employers
and Employed: Their Relations and Duties to Each Other*, a New York
minister averred that workers were "no longer slaves or serfs or servants, but free men, entering the market with their labor, the equals
in prerogatives with the capitalists who bring in their money. They
stand as much on a par with those who buy their services, as do the
vendors of any commodity with those who purchase it." In hiring
"the carpenter or mason, the tailor or shoemaker," paying a wage
"liquidates his claim upon us."[28]

The cash nexus was thereby thought to define the obligation between buyers and sellers of free labor, to dissolve all other ties. The
exchange was reckoned commercial – antithetical not only to involuntary servitude but also to paternalistic bonds between master and
laborer. This was a core principle of the theory that labor represented a commodity, and the wage relation a contract, pure and
simple. It presupposed that labor no longer belonged to the dependent relations of the household sphere, but solely to the sphere of

[27] McNeill, ed., *Labor Movement*, 3, 41, 44; Edward Atkinson, "What Makes the Rate of
Wages?" *Journal of Social Science Containing the Transactions of the American Association*,
19 (December 1884), 47–116, quote at p. 57; Christopher Tiedeman, *A Treatise on
the Limitations of Police Power in the United States Considered from both a Civil and Criminal
Standpoint* (St. Louis, 1886), 567. This legal understanding marks a shift from earlier nineteenth-century definitions. See Schouler, *Law of the Domestic Relations*; Tomlins, *Law, Labor, and Ideology*. On the development of the concept of labor as an
entity distinct from the self, see C.B. Macpherson, *The Political Theory of Possessive
Individualism: Hobbes to Locke* (New York, 1962), 153; Karl Polanyi, *The Great Transformation* (New York, 1944); Anson Rabinbach, *The Human Motor: Energy, Fatigue,
and the Origins of Modernity* (Berkeley, 1992), 1–18, 52–83.

[28] Edward Everett Hale to Edward H. Rogers, December 20, 1866, Edward H. Rogers
Papers, Wisconsin State Historical Society; Fine, *Laissez-Faire*, 122; Philemon H.
Fowler, *Employers and the Employed: Their Relation and Duties to Each Other* (Utica, N.Y.,
1865), 40, 46–47. See also Samuel T. Spear, "Co-Operation vs. Wages," *Independent*,
September 2, 1869; Samuel T. Spear, "The Law of Wages," *Independent*, October
21, 1869.

the market, where "men met as strangers" and "hard bargaining" was the rule. The older domestic analogy of marriage and wage work, which abolitionists had renounced in asserting the hireling man's independence, was displaced by images of competitive commodity exchange between capital and labor.[29]

Postbellum economic theory denied the traditional location of wage labor within domestic relations. Explaining exchange as a "double transfer of commodities," economists held that the bargain between labor and capital – their trading of values, work for money – was strictly a case of market reciprocity. As Arthur Latham Perry wrote in his 1868 treatise, *Elements of Political Economy*, "the transaction between employers and employed is a case of pure exchange, a simple bargain," in which they "exchange to the mutual advantage of both, and one is as independent as the other." Francis Amasa Walker, a dean of American political economy, underscored the demise of household relations of labor and the disappearance of personal ties. Under the old order, he wrote, feudal lords and laborers had been bound by "mutual obligations . . . of service and protection," and masters, journeymen, and apprentices had also been "bound together . . . often in one family, under one roof." But under the modern wage system, "throngs of operatives" worked in factories for "strange masters." The employer viewed laborers like "the materials and supplies brought into his mill. These men came, he knew not whence; they might go to-morrow, he would know not whither. One thing they had to do for him: to work, upon what he pleased. . . . One thing he had to do for them: to pay their wages. That done, all was done." It was widely agreed, as a contributor to an 1886 collection on the *Labor Problem* observed, that "other than *wages*," no "human bond" joined labor and capital.[30]

But it was also widely agreed that the extinction of human bonds under the wage system was a main cause of the labor problem. What defined the wage contract as a token of freedom and equality – its embodiment of commodity exchange – was seen as the source of class antagonism. The perception was that because sympathy and

---

[29] Richard T. Ely, *An Introduction to Political Economy* (New York, 1889), 67. See also Amy Dru Stanley, "Home Life and the Morality of the Market," in *The Market Revolution in America: Social, Political, and Religious Expressions, 1800–1880*, ed. Melvyn Stokes and Stephen Conway (Charlottesville, 1996), 74–96. On the older domestic analogy, see Chistopher Tomlins, "Subordination, Authority, Law: Subjects in Labor History," *International Labor and Working-Class History*, 47 (Spring 1995), 56–90.

[30] Clark, *Philosophy of Wealth*, 62; Arthur Latham Perry, *Elements of Political Economy* (New York, 1868), 132, 146; Francis Amasa Walker, *Discussions in Economics and Statistics* (2 vols., New York, 1899), 2: 279; James A. Waterworth, "The Conflict Historically Considered," in Barns, ed., *Labor Problem*, 22.

benevolence no longer mediated the sale of free labor, the habit of
hard bargaining had become warfare between massed capital and
labor, a situation belying the classical economic precept that the free
market led naturally to social order and that competition and mutuality could coexist. Francis Amasa Walker's writings expressed the
conflict between abstract precept and new perceptions of the wage
relation. He termed hard bargaining the "order of the economical
universe," just as "gravity" was of the "physical universe . . . not less
harmonious and beneficent in its operation." But he found it "idle
to talk . . . of the 'harmony of labor and capital' " and saw "unceas-
ing struggle" as the outcome of contract freedom created by the
"breaking down of the old feudalistic barriers." Drawing on the ev-
olutionary social theory then in vogue, he claimed, "Struggle and
strife have to-day become the law of industry." Other economists
openly mourned that the root of the labor question lay in the absence of a "feeling of brotherhood," as Richard Ely wrote. This was
the view of the new school of "ethical economists" who were
grouped around the American Economics Association. But economists were not alone in ascribing enmity over work and wages to the
commodity relationship itself. So widespread was this idea that the
New York Times commented in 1874 on the "unavoidable" conflict
over wage labor: "The matter . . . has come to one of buying and
selling. . . . The object of trade is to get as much as you may and give
as little as you can."[31]

Labor spokesmen were the most explicit in attributing conflict in
the workplace to the logic of commodity relations and free contract.
Echoing antebellum critics of the wage system, they unceasingly
warned that when labor was for sale in a "speculative market" there
could be "no harmony between capital and labor," which instead
existed in "war relations." In the words of Terence Powderly, the
leader of the Knights of Labor,

So long as it is to the interest of one kind of men to purchase labor at the
lowest possible figure, and so long as it is to the interest of another kind of
men to sell labor to the highest possible bidder, just so long will there exist
an antagonism between the two which all the speakers and writers upon
labor cannot remove.

[31] Francis Amasa Walker, *Political Economy* (New York, 1883), 273; Francis Amasa Walker, *First Lessons in Political Economy* (New York, 1889), 11; Walker, *Discussions* 2:
281, 341; Ely, *Political Economy*, 67; *New York Times*, November 20, 1874, quoted in
Gutman, "Social and Economic Structure," 33. See also James, "History of Mechanical Labor," 45–47; Adams et al., "Labor Problem," 8877; Tiedeman, *Police Power*,
570–71; E.L. Godkin, "Labor Crisis," *North American Review*, 105 (July 1867), 192;
Barns, *Labor Problem*, 229–30; Gladden, *Working People*, 42, 34, 166, 168; Ross, *Origins of American Social Science*, 77–85, 98–122.

Labor spokesmen also were explicit in using the language of class to describe the differences between buyers and sellers of labor. Countering the assumption of classical political economy that "in exchange" men transacted their affairs like "particles of some fine dry powder absolutely destitute of cohesion," they argued that labor and capital had come to constitute "two distinct classes, whose interests are as widely separated as the poles."[32]

The labor question was directly joined in a debate staged by Boston's Central Labor Union on May 1, 1887. The debate pitted free labor ideals against protests about the social disorder arising from the wage contract; workers encountered economic orthodoxy in the person of Edward Atkinson. Atkinson defended the wage system's integrity and asserted the mutuality of labor and capital, arguing the workingman "will find out that the capitalist is your friend and not your enemy." But speaking for labor, E.M. Chamberlain insisted that irreconcilable class division was created by commodity relations:

No classes! Let us settle that point right here. . . . [T]here are two very well-defined classes at least; those who pay wages, and those who receive them. . . . [I]t is no use to prevaricate or to deny this. . . . The two parties – classes – in the contest stand out clear and bold against the background of events. . . . [T]here is no intermingling of the elements. Life is a death-struggle.[33]

What labor spokesmen did not question was the view that the transformation of the bond between master and servant into a purely contractual relation – a simple bargain – distanced wage work from the household sphere. But they did dispute the benefit said to be derived from designating individuals merchants and free labor a market commodity. They raised this issue again and again in tracts, journals, and declarations of principles and at lectures and mass meetings. As a writer in the *Workingman's Advocate* argued in 1877, assessing the changes from slavery to freedom and from household to modern capitalist industry, "The slave and the workman were in some measure members of the family. There were no lordly corporations, with their hundreds of labor retainers. . . . But how changed. . . . The two classes are necessarily antagonistic, for the gains of cap-

[32] "Declaration of Principles of the Central Labor Union of New York City," *John Swinton's Paper*, October 14, 1883; McNeill, ed., *Labor Movement*, 461; Knights of Labor, *Proceedings of the Fourth General Assembly* (Minneapolis, 1880), 169; Walker, *Political Economy*, 96–97, 202; "Can There Be Harmony," *Carpenter*, May 1881. See also Ira Steward, "Rights of Capitalists," "The Power of the Cheaper over the Dearer" (both unpublished manuscripts, circa 1875), Ira Steward Papers, Wisconsin State Historical Society.

[33] Edward Atkinson, *The Margin of Profits: How It Is Now Divided, What Part of the Present Hours of Labor Can Now Be Spared; Address to the Central Labor Lyceum, Boston, May 1, 1887* (New York, 1887), 42, 58.

ital are the losses of labor."[34] According to this argument, the inti-
macies and unfreedoms of household relations of labor had been
replaced by the class antagonisms and impersonal hierarchies of the
free market.

It was precisely the question of whether the wage contract retained any trace of household mutuality or was simply an exchange
between inimical classes that pervaded the 1883 congressional labor
hearings. The investigation was broad, covering work conditions,
wage levels, housing, family life, poverty, and political beliefs. But
the inquiry repeatedly returned to the issue, as one congressman put
it, of the "social relations between the wage-payers and the wage-
receivers." The congressional committee interrogated witnesses to
discover if harmony existed between labor and capital and how it
could be fostered. Rare was the testimony offered by the railroad
magnate Jay Gould, who voiced the implacable faith in the free market typical of a captain of industry. There was, he thought, "no disagreement" between labor and capital when they were "let alone"
to "regulate their relations." Most witnesses spoke instead of growing antagonism. As the New York City minister R. Heber Newton
attested, "The old common feeling is disappearing."[35]

The committee adhered to the family analogy, asking if hirelings
and employers "generally got along about as well together as men
do in their domestic relations." But the answer was that labor had
become "simply a commercial relationship," and therefore mistrust
and enmity were the rule. Drawing on images of commerce rather
than those of the household, Samuel Gompers said that capital per-
ceived labor "as the stock speculator looks at the ticking of the indi-
cator to see whether he cannot take advantage of those with whom
he is dealing." Other workingmen testified that this was especially
evident in situations of mass factory labor, where no aspect remained
of the artisan workshop. Employers did not "assert their human feelings over and above their commercial relations." Although once
"the workmen and the foremen and the boss were all as one family,"
they were now so estranged that the "average hand . . . would not
think of speaking to the boss." A spokesman for carpenters claimed,
"They do not know each other on the street."[36]

Testimony revealed the depth of estrangement between labor and
capital. The "belief is almost universal," a Chicago printer reported;
"all the employed believe that capital takes every effort to crush

---

[34] *Workingman's Advocate*, April 21, 1877. See also Ira Steward, "Philosophic Inquiry
into the Condition of the Laboring Classes" (address delivered to the Boston trade
unions at Faneuil Hall, n.d.), Wisconsin State Historical Society.

[35] U.S. Congress, Senate, *Relations between Labor and Capital* 1: 358, 1085, 1088, 552.

[36] Ibid., 256, 682, 376, 350, 743, 358.

down labor and to get it just as cheaply as it possibly can." A tailor in New York City noted that workers "hate the bosses . . . and that feeling is deep." Seeking to explain the parameters of the strife to the congressional committee, an editor of a manufacturers' trade journal pointed out, "The men do not hate the employer as an individual, but only as a member of a class." The evidence was not of contracts conducing to mutuality, but rather of commerce between opposing classes.[37]

The question of strikes crystallized the deeper social crisis brought to light during the hearings. Spokesmen for capital testified that collective labor activity was intrinsically coercive and that bargains were truly free only if made between individuals, which was the classical economic doctrine. But labor spokesmen claimed that both strikes and trade unions were direct and legitimate – indeed inevitable – expressions of labor's status as a commodity. Using the language of the market, one printer reasoned, "Even accepting the doctrine of the orthodox school of political economy, that labor is in large measure a commodity," workers had "a right to regulate the supply of labor," just like "dealers in other commodities." Nothing in a strike was "inconsistent with the doctrines of political economy," laboring men said. It was simply hard bargaining, withholding labor to sell at a higher price: "a rough-and-ready way of recognizing the market" that reflected the conflict "all the time going on." In this view, strikes and unions were as valid as the wage contract. By collectively ensuring free and equal exchange between individual sellers of labor and buyers representing concentrated capital, they were the "means to secure the liberty of workingmen."[38]

Both inside and outside the halls of the congressional hearings, therefore, the debate over the labor question focused on the social meaning of treating free men's labor as an impersonal market commodity and the implications of this commerce for relations of contract and class. And others joined laboring men in linking the outbreak of strikes to the ways of the market as well as to aspirations for contract freedom under the wage system. It was an issue, maintained a congressional examiner versed in classical economics, "as Mr. Smith said, of higgling in the market, and success in the higgling depends upon the intelligence and power which each higgler has to make his higgling successful." To the minister R. Heber Newton, strikes were "in our present stage of the 'free contract' system en-

[37] Ibid., 577, 416, 256. See also Gladden, *Working People*, 169–72; Barns, *Labor Problem*, 85–89.
[38] U.S. Congress, Senate, *Relations between Labor and Capital* 1: 668, 560, 859. See *Workingman's Advocate*, June 6, 1868, May 27, 1871, April 5, 1873, January 30, 1875; *Carpenter*, May 1881; Trant, *Trade Unions*.

tirely justifiable." By the 1880s this was hardly an unusual vantage
on the labor question, despite the anxiety generated by strikes. Two
decades earlier, in studying the "labor crisis," E.L. Godkin had
stressed the gap between economic doctrine and "daily life," and
had argued that collective activity placed "the workman on an equality with his master in the matter of contracts, so as to enable him to
contract freely," and to render labor "a commodity, sold like any
other commodity in open market for a price fixed by general competition." In the years after the hearings, the founders of the American Economics Association affirmed workers' right to join together
in selling their labor and withdrawing it from sale. Otherwise, wrote
Henry Carter Adams, men who owned nothing besides their labor,
"without property in tools or shop . . . will surely get the worst of any
bargain." Writers of legal treatises reasoned in the same vein. In his
leading study of the constitutional limits of state power, Christopher
Tiedeman held that free men – whose badge was "liberty of contract" – must either act in concert or be "at the mercy of the employer," a view that the courts, applying common law principles of
individual free contract, still did not fully accept.[39]

But even among those who defended strikes and other collective
acts, there were limits to the consensus on the labor question.
Though using a common language of the market and contract and
though agreeing that wage work no longer belonged to the domestic
realm, not all participants in the debate deduced from labor's commodity status a relation of equality between buyers and sellers that
would afford them equivalent freedom in the workplace. The ruling
theory of wage labor defined the marketplace as the arbiter of the
wage contract but the employer as the final arbiter of daily relations
at work. It vested authority in ownership – ownership arising not
from caste or status but from voluntary commodity exchange,
namely the employer's property rights in his shop and tools as well
as in the labor purchased for a wage. This theory recognized workers' right to set a common price on their labor, but not to decide its
use once sold. The congressional committee was troubled that strikes

[39] U.S. Congress, Senate, *Relations between Labor and Capital* 1: 491, 2: 538; E.L. Godkin,
"The Labor Crisis," *North American Review,* 105 (July 1867), 186, 179; E.L. Godkin,
"Wages against Cooperation," *Nation,* August 8, 1867, 111; E.L. Godkin, "Co-
Operation," *North American Review,* 106 (January 1868), 155; Adams et al., "Labor
Problem," 8862; Tiedeman, *State and Federal Control,* 424. See also Massachusetts
Bureau of Statistics of Labor, *Second Annual Report* (Boston, 1871), 39–42, 536–37;
Gladden, *Working People,* 137; Clark, *Philosophy of Wealth,* 65–76, 108–23, 132–36;
Walker, *Political Economy,* 368–71; Charles A. Ray, *Contractual Limitations, Including
Trade Strikes and Conspiracies and Corporate Trusts and Combinations* (New York, 1892);
Tomlins, *State and the Unions,* 10–95; William E. Forbath, *Law and the Shaping of the
American Labor Movement* (Cambridge, Mass., 1989).

trespassed on employers' rights. In the eyes of economists, there were both "evil liabilities" and virtues in labor's aim for equality and autonomy under the wage contract. Francis Amasa Walker denounced workingmen for "seeking to legislate concerning the ways in which industry shall be carried on" and the "spirit which delighted in humiliating and harassing the employer." He was thankful that labor was not "able to overbear the rightful authority of the employer, to interfere with his necessary control of his own business, to render it unsafe to undertake contracts." Giving exaggerated voice to the ruling wisdom, the minister Washington Gladden claimed, in a tract on *Working People and Their Employers,* that labor's collective efforts often violated freedom much as had the system of "the lords of the lash on the Southern plantations." Strikes appeared not as acts of free contract but as arrogations of illegitimate power; nor did wage work exclude dominion and subjection.[40]

The law emphatically reinforced this viewpoint. Like political economy, the labor law of the late nineteenth century no longer located the wage contract's unfreedoms in household relations of personal dependency, but simply in the sale of labor. A central common law precept was that a free man's labor formed "his stock in trade" to dispose of "as he pleases." Yet just as well established was the legal understanding of wage labor as both a free contract and a relation of authority and subordination. Both doctrines were set forth in an 1886 *Plain Statement* on labor law. Alluding to the abolition of involuntary servitude, this treatise explained that entitlement to service "arises now only by contract" – "in this country there is now no way in which one party can make another work for him except by the free will and consent of the person doing the work." But it also enunciated the "modern legal definition" of a hireling as "one who, by reason of some contract . . . becomes subject to the authority and control of another in some trade." This modern definition echoed antebellum law treatises, which drew on Enlightenment contract tenets of voluntary subjection in spelling out the laborer's duty to submit and the master's "power of directing." At the end of the century, law writers still held that the hireling must "yield his will" and that the wage contract entailed "the right of the master to direct and control the servant." They used the new language of employer and employee interchangeably with the older one of master and servant. What had changed was the notion of wage labor as

[40] U.S. Congress, Senate, *Relations between Labor and Capital* 1: 201; Walker, *First Lessons,* 278; Walker, *Discussions* 2: 335; Gladden, *Working People,* 141. See also Godkin, "The Labor Crisis," *Nation,* April 15, 1867, 335; " 'Free,' But Outlawed," *Carpenter,* April 1885.

literally lodged in the household. Domestic mastery had ceased to be at issue in the new compendiums of labor law, which did not represent employers as masters of a family, hirelings as dependent persons, or their exchange as paternalistic. Instead treatises had come to underscore the clumsy fit between new market relations and long-standing legal taxonomy that classed together marriage, wage labor, and slavery as "domestic relations."[41]

Thus the 1883 hearings on the labor question registered the wider concerns of public debate and social inquiry. The congressional investigation offered evidence not only of the disorder produced by wage labor and the disharmonies of the marketplace, but also of the enduring ambiguities of the wage contract in free society. The testimony evoked labor's peculiarity as a commodity, the contradiction of defining wage work as a market relation that represented chattel slavery's obverse but that nonetheless involved dominion and subjection. And it reflected the ideological power of both ideals of contract freedom and images of wage slavery. "There is not, then, in your opinion, a feeling of confidence, harmony, and good-will existing between the employers and the employed in this country?" the congressional committee asked witness after witness. "Directly the reverse," testified a member of the Knights of Labor. "The working people feel they are under a system of forced slavery."[42]

For many northern hirelings the idea of wage slavery was indeed inseparable from the postbellum labor question. The wage slave symbolized selling oneself, evoking fears that the self entitlement at the heart of contract freedom had been lost. Slave emancipation had not stilled antebellum arguments over the similarity between wage work and chattel bondage; to the contrary, it gave new force both to Yankee workingmen's outcry against the traffic in free labor and to the symbolism of wage slavery.[43] This symbolism cast doubt on the idea that freedom meant being a merchant of one's own labor, raising questions that were metaphysical as well as moral and economic – about the nature of the human essence, about autonomy and alienation, about the relation of self ownership, labor, and time.

---

[41] Wood, *Master and Servant*, 463; Haigh, *Plain Statement* 1: 184; Parsons, *Law of Contracts* 1: 114; Wood, *Master and Servant*, 229; Browne, *Law of Domestic Relations*, 121–22. See also chapter 1; John R. Commons, *The Legal Foundations of Capitalism* (New York, 1924), 314, 284; Karen Orren, *Belated Feudalism: Labor, the Law, and Liberal Development in the United States* (New York, 1991); Steinfeld, *Invention of Free Labor*; Arthur Linton Corbin, *Corbin on Contracts* (8 vols., St. Paul, 1960), 3A: 205. My understanding of the law's usage of the household paradigm differs somewhat from Tomlins's "Subordination, Authority, Law" and *Law, Labor, and Ideology*, 223–92.

[42] U.S. Congress, Senate, *Relations between Labor and Capital* 1: 219.

[43] See David R. Roediger, *The Wages of Whiteness: Race and the Making of the American Working Class* (New York, 1991), 87, 173–81.

In his 1872 study, *The Dangerous Classes of New York*, the city missionary Charles Loring Brace complained that the many could not comprehend the economic truths taught by the few. "It is one of the most unpleasant experiences of the student of political economy, that the axioms of his science can so seldom be understood by the masses, though their interests be vitally affected by them." What Brace left unsaid was that many plebeian readers of classical economic treatises openly disagreed with the axioms formulated there. Spokesmen for every kind of labor reform – whether factory laws or collective bargaining, state ownership or the cooperative commonwealth – criticized "the sophisms of Mill, Ricardo, McCulloch, Sumner" as the "silliest swash." They also inveighed against the "lawyers, parsons, and political economists" disseminating this theory, those who "constitute themselves the nursemaids of labor, and receive their fees for watching us." An 1871 labor procession through the streets of lower Manhattan represented the views of the masses. Some twenty-five thousand workingmen, including tailors, shoemakers, carpenters, plumbers, stonecutters, bricklayers, a brigade of black workers, and sections of the First International, gathered to advocate the eight-hour day. They marched from Fourteenth Street to the Bowery and then circled back up along Broadway to the Cooper Institute, where they read aloud resolutions decrying their "serfdom" and rejecting the "political economies in vogue" as "frauds upon the working classes."[44]

Such dissenting views were nourished in labor journals, reform leagues, and trade unions. As the Massachusetts Bureau of Labor Statistics reported in 1873, there were "Eight-Hour Leagues, Internationals, Labor Reform Leagues, Ten-Hour Associations, Councils, Conferences and Conventions. . . . Every night in the week, societies of workingmen are holding meetings and discussing their grievances."[45] The fruits of these discussions were strikes, political activism, and nuanced critiques of contract freedom that drew on the symbolism of wage slavery.

Postbellum images of the wage slave called into question not only

[44] Charles Loring Brace, *The Dangerous Classes of New York, and Twenty Years' Work among Them* (Montclair, N.J., 1967; orig. pub. 1872), 52; "Labor Union Social Science," *Workingman's Advocate*, April 17, 1869; "From New York," *Workingman's Advocate*, May 16, 1868; Joseph Labadie, "Labor Is Not a Commodity," *Carpenter*, April 1885; "Labor As a Commodity," *Journal of United Labor*, January 1884; "Idleness and Starvation," *Workingman's Advocate*, December 20, 1873; "Working People and Their Employers," *Workingman's Advocate*, August 26, 1876. On the workers' study of political economy and repudiation of classical economic doctrine, see also U.S Congress, Senate, *Relations between Labor and Capital* 1: 216, 870; "Who Shall Fix the Price of Labor?" *Workingman's Advocate*, July 19, 1873; "Capital," *Carpenter*, July 1881; Fink, *Workingmen's Democracy*, 11.

[45] Massachusetts Bureau of Statistics of Labor, *Fourth Annual Report* (1873), 248. See also Atkinson, *Margin of Profits*, 60; McNeill, ed., *Labor Movement*, 139.

free market doctrine, but also triumphant narratives of emancipation. The imagery was not very different from that deployed before
the war, but it was propagated more widely by constituencies ranging
from pragmatic craft unionists to socialist reformers, all of whom
advanced objections to the existing commerce in free labor. Sometimes race figured in the imagery. A member of the Knights of Labor
spoke for many in an 1886 essay entitled "Thoughts of a Workingman" and published in the *Journal of United Labor*. "They say slavery
is abolished in the United States now, but I say no. True, the colored
people are free, but how many thousands of white slaves are there
all over the country? What do you call men, women, and children
that work in a mill or factory fourteen and fifteen hours a day. . . .
Are they not slaves?" However, the dominant metaphor was not *white*
slavery but *wage* slavery. As one trade unionist concisely set forward
the argument at an 1871 labor reform convention in New York City,
"In the earliest historical period it was total slavery. . . . [A]nd then
from serfdom into villenage, and now at last we have another form
of slavery, which is the wages slavery." This argument countered
conventional portraits of labor's progress from slavery to freedom by
describing the reverse movement: a demise of independent commodity production, a transition from freedom to dependence. "Fifty
years ago we had millions of artisans working at their own homes, on
their own account," claimed labor spokesmen, but now the "majority are in the factories of the capitalists working as their wage-slaves.
From being their own masters . . . they work for other masters."[46]

Nevertheless, the transformative effect of abolition and the difference between contract relations and bound labor were not lost on
the northerners who pronounced themselves wage slaves. They did
not fail to recognize the distinction between the slave master's personal dominion and the impersonal discipline of the free market –
between brutal physical coercion and formal rights of voluntary
exchange. In some instances the equation of wage work with bondage was not finely qualified, especially when the claim was that capitalist industry was worse than the old plantation system. "The slavery
that died . . . was terrible, but, bad as it was," Terence Powderly insisted, "the new slavery . . . now reaches out with a far stronger hand
than the old," since a single stroke of the "lash of gold" fell not on
"one slave alone," but on "the backs of millions." More often,
though, hirelings distinguished between different kinds of unfree-

---

[46] John B. Kelly, "Thoughts of a Workingman," *Journal of United Labor*, September 25,
1886; Transcript of Speech at the New England Labor Reform Convention in New
York City, *Workingman's Advocate*, May 27, 1871; "Chapters on Labor," *Journal of
United Labor*, March 25, 1886; "Industrial Ideas," *Journal of United Labor*, August 10,
1886. For a discussion of postbellum imagery of the wage slave stressing themes of
consumption, see Glickman, *A Living Wage*, 17–34.

dom, thoughtfully noting the complexities of their own status as they argued that chattel slavery was in some ways commensurate with the dependency relations embedded in ostensibly free contracts. "In considering the word slave, we are too apt to take up that form of it, as we knew it to exist in the South," they reasoned. Admittedly, the wage worker had "personal liberty" and was "free in his movements to *seek* employment and just remuneration." Still, he was "far from being free" for he could not "produce without placing himself under a monster," toiling instead at the "beck and call of a 'master' " to whom he gave "tacit consent." He was neither chattel nor master of himself. "It must not be supposed that the proclamation of emancipation liberated mankind from slavery," declared workingmen; "the most subtle form of slavery – wages slavery – remains to be abolished."[47]

The wage slave thus stood for the illusions of contract freedom. Labor spokesmen agreed with the axiom that the exchange between capitalists and workers was not paternalistic, but purely commercial. But, to their way of thinking, market relations and dependence were not mutually exclusive – if labor was for sale. They emphasized the difference between the domestic dependencies of slavery and subjugation under the wage system. In the households of the Old South "the proprietor had absolute right over . . . his wife, his children, his slaves," but in northern factories the master was the property owner who possessed authority over "work, wages, and everything else" and "at whose nod or beck the poor unrequited slave who labors must bow the head and bend the knee in humble suppliance." The point was that there could be no such thing as a pure and simple bargain, a free contract, involving labor. As George McNeill wrote in his 1887 study, *The Labor Movement: The Problem of To-Day,* "A contract supposes *two* parties, – one with something to sell, and one wishing to buy. Whatever tends to put one of these parties under the power of the other, destroys the freedom of the act."[48]

This way of thinking discredited the legitimacy of labor's status as

---

[47] Knights of Labor, *Proceedings of the Tenth General Assembly* (Minneapolis, 1886), 10; "Letter from J.H. Bray," *National Labor Tribune,* May 1, 1876; "Industrial Ideas," *Journal of United Labor,* August 10, 1886; "Wage Slaves," *Journal of United Labor,* August 1883; "Industrial Ideas," *Journal of United Labor,* June 25, 1886. For similar formulations voiced by differing factions of the labor movement, see also "Labor, The Basis of Value," *National Labor Tribune,* April 15, 1876; "Slavery," *Workingman's Advocate,* August 25, 1866; "Workingmen Must Aid Themselves," *Workingman's Advocate,* May 30, 1868; "The Present Slavery," *John Swinton's Paper,* August 31, 1884; "Wages Slavery and Chattel Slavery," *Journal of United Labor,* May 25, 1884; "The Attempted Black List Degradation of Employees," *Locomotive Firemen's Magazine,* March 1885, 157; Massachusetts Bureau of Statistics of Labor, *First Annual Report* (Boston, 1870), 158–59; Speech of Uriah Stephens, in McNeill, ed., *Labor Movement,* 402.
[48] "Industrial Ideas"; "Wage Slaves"; "Industrial Ideas"; Knights of Labor, *Proceedings of the Fourth General Assembly* (1880), 169; McNeill, ed., *Labor Movement,* 479.

a commodity. It stood opposed to both classical economic theory
and abolitionist belief, which validated the buying and selling of free
labor. Yet it was also indebted to both, for the figure of the wage
slave denoted by negation a concept of freedom presupposing the
liberal right of property in the self, but not hinging on this entitlement alone. The crux of the disagreement concerned the meaning
of emancipating all men to sell their own labor – whether this transformation established self ownership or self dispossession, contract
freedom or wage slavery.

The opposing perspectives were reflected in the words of Adam
Smith, Wendell Phillips, and George McNeill. According to Smith,
all men were merchants in a market society. "Every man," he observed, "lives by exchanging, or becomes in some measure a merchant." Smith was explaining how men traded surplus produce – as
when a "butcher has more meat in his shop than he himself can
consume, and the brewer and the baker would each of them be
willing to purchase a part of it" – and the origin and use of money
in such exchange. He was not speaking of the circumstance where
men sold their own labor, rather than products, or of the payment
of money in exchange. Yet when Smith explained wages (and the
difference between natural and market prices) he equated human
labor with "any other commodity." In recognizing men as merchants, political economy drew no distinction between selling labor
and selling its fruits.[49]

A century later, when lecturing on capital and labor, Wendell
Phillips conflated these two elements of production. Drawing on
Smith's legacy, he saw no difference between merchants of labor and
merchants of other commodities. "Capital and Labor are . . . twins;
more than this, Siamese twins," Phillips affirmed.

Capital is only the labor of yesterday which has not been consumed, and
Labor is only the capital of to-day that has not been refunded. Capital is but
frozen, crystallized labor, and labor is but capital dissolved and become ac-
tive. . . . Capital is the means which the rich man has to work with. . . . Labor
is a man's time, a man's capital, a man's means of working. It is only a
different name for the same thing.

In declaring labor and capital one and the same, Phillips's aim was
to show that they were not necessarily antagonistic but instead naturally harmonious. "The forces of society are only two. There is the
man that sells money, and the man that sells time – just two. Together they are a pair of scissors. . . . Separate them, and they are not

---

[49] Adam Smith, *An Inquiry into the Nature and Causes of the Wealth of Nations,* ed. Edwin
Cannan (New York, 1937; orig. pub. 1776), 22, 80; see also pp. 55–86.

worth chips." This was a far cry from abolitionist arguments about the evils of the commerce in slaves. There was no mention of flesh and blood, of human bodies and souls, the terms by which abolitionists had deplored treating chattel slaves as market commodities and denying them self ownership. Rather, the metaphors were of the marketplace and chemistry, of refunds and crystallization. Phillips defined labor not as a human endeavor but as "dissolved capital." It was tantamount to money – something abstract, insensate, wholly detached from the self – which was why he could assure Yankee hirelings that slave emancipation had ended the selling and owning of human beings. Phillips represented wage labor as freedom because he believed that only "a man's time" was for sale, a thing without form or substance, a disembodied value.[50]

But for George McNeill, to be a merchant of time was to sell oneself, to be a wage slave. He echoed Adam Smith's language, even as he attacked the principle that labor was like other commodities and that time was impalpable. "Men who are compelled to sell their labor," he wrote, "are merchants of their time. It is their only available capital." But in owning nothing else, having only labor time to sell, they lost title to themselves. "He who sells his labor sells himself," McNeill claimed. "Man should sell the product of his labor . . . the product of his time. . . . The truth is, when a man lost the power to sell the product of his labor he lost his liberty." In McNeill's view, labor – unlike its fruits – could not be severed from self; in the marketplace, a free man's time was not equivalent to money but rather to the person of a slave.[51]

What made time so central to the question of labor, freedom, and slavery were transformations in the work process that had occurred since the age of Adam Smith. Where wage relations were grafted onto traditional methods of work, the difference between selling products and selling time – between butchers with surplus meat and men with labor for sale – was blurred by the fact that hirelings often remained skilled craftsmen who produced entire commodities. The labor time they sold was still directly reflected in a coat, a chair, or a pair of shoes. By the late nineteenth century, however, as unskilled piecework in both factories and sweatshops displaced artisanal manufacturing, virtually all labor, as one shoemaker remarked, was "simplified and divided."[52] As the act of laboring was dissociated from a

---

[50] "Wendell Phillips on Labor and Capital," *Workingman's Advocate*, March 25, 1865; "Wendell Phillips on the Labor Party," *Workingman's Advocate*, May 13, 1871.

[51] McNeill, ed., *Labor Movement*, 470; U.S. Industrial Commission, *Report of the Industrial Commission* 7: 114–15. For a contrasting interpretation of McNeill's thought, which does not focus on the theme of wage slavery, see Glickman, *A Living Wage*, 99–107.

[52] Thomas Phillips to Ira Steward, n.d., Steward Papers, Wisconsin State Historical Society, Madison, Wisconsin. See also "Biography of Thomas Phillips," Thomas

finished, useful commodity, it became plain that time was for sale under the wage contract. The question was whether time was a property that could be alienated from the self.

As defined by political economy in the nineteenth century, a commodity was a thing that could be detached from its owner or creator and made the object of a valuable exchange. The distinguishing trait of a commodity was that it could be "alienated and transferred to new ownership," explained John Bates Clark in his 1886 treatise, *The Philosophy of Wealth.* An exchange "reduces itself to a double alienation and a double acquisition of concrete commodities." Therefore, the classical economic doctrine, "Labour is bought and sold like other articles," rested on the premise that labor could be alienated and transferred to a new owner no differently than any other commodity. Clark was among the leaders of the new school of economists who came to dispute this doctrine. But it had already been questioned by labor spokesmen, who argued that labor was not an alienable commodity that could be separated from its original owner. Their claim was that labor was part of the human essence; and thus if labor was transferred to a new owner, so was the laborer to whom it remained attached, which was slavery. "Labor cannot be transferred . . . it is not a substance that can be separated and carried away," wrote Edward Rogers, one of McNeill's fellow Boston reformers, in an 1867 report to the Massachusetts legislature. "A thing may be bought and sold, because it is a thing; but a man with his labor cannot be bought and sold, without recognizing slavery as a right."[53]

Boston was the center of this strain of labor thought, which drew strength from the city's vibrant movement for the eight-hour day. In an 1876 set of resolutions the Boston Eight Hour League enunciated the dissenting doctrine: "the Laborer [has] nothing of his own that he can sell, but his labor, – which is his *personality* or *himself,* for the time during which his services are bought." McNeill, together with his collaborator Ira Steward, led the Boston Eight Hour League. Steward called McNeill the "prince of organizers" and "a walking convention . . . when you hear him talk, you can be sure that he

Phillips Papers, Wisconsin State Historical Society; Norman Ware, *The Industrial Worker 1840–1860* (Chicago, 1964), xiv–iv.

[53] Clark, *Philosophy of Wealth,* 6, 63; Theodore Sedgewick, *Public and Private Economy* (New York, 1971; orig. pub. 1836), 38; Massachusetts House of Representatives, "Report of Commissioners on the Hours of Labor," Doc. 44 (1867), 137. See also Francis Wayland, *The Elements of Political Economy* (Boston, 1852), 160; Walker, *First Lessons,* 7; John Stuart Mill, *Principles of Political Economy with Some of their Applications to Social Philosophy,* ed. W. J. Ashley (New York, 1965; orig. pub. 1848), 450; Ely, *Political Economy,* 161; Edward Rogers, "Autobiography" (handwritten manuscript), Edward Rogers Papers, Wisconsin State Historical Society; McNeill, ed., *Labor Movement,* 127–28. See also Macpherson, *Possessive Individualism,* 153.

represents a number of us in one." But if McNeill was the spokesman, Steward was the main theorist. A machinist by trade, he expounded Yankee labor reform precepts in letters, speeches, and published and unpublished essays, shaping the protest against wage
work. He corresponded with American economists as well as with
members of the First International. He studied not only liberal political economy but Karl Marx's writings, and he was especially influenced by the passages in *Capital* on the workday.[54]

Steward dwelled on the difference between selling labor and selling its fruits, between time and concrete goods – what he termed
"days works" and the "products of days works." He did not condemn the principle of commodity exchange, only its extension to
human labor. Knowingly or not, in his ideas of how time and self
ownership were linked to the problem of freedom and bondage, he
echoed aspects of Hegel's philosophy. "Single products of my particular physical and mental skill . . . I can alienate to someone else,"
wrote Hegel. "By alienating the whole of my time, as crystallized in
my work, and everything I produced, I would be making into another's property the substance of my being, my universal activity and
actuality, my personality." Yet, in spirit, Steward's views were closer
to Marx's materialism than to Hegel's idealism, for he claimed that
market relations and formal rights of personal autonomy masked the
fact that free men could not be self owning if they owned nothing
but themselves. Steward averred that a capitalist might well say to a
hireling, "I can get along without your person if I can have all you
can do," but when the "only thing that most men sell, is Labor,"
their sustenance rested "on a life thus bought." For a laborer to lose
his power to sell something besides time was to "surrender himself."
Hewing to the tenet that freedom required title to productive property, Steward argued that the critical question was whether "a man
should own himself, or whether he should own enough else to supply his natural wants." How much was "a human being worth to
himself . . . who can call nothing his own but his body?" To Steward,
there were degrees of slavery and freedom, and self proprietorship
counted for very little when necessity led men to sell most of their
waking hours to other men. "Giving a man himself but taking away

---

[54] "Resolutions of the Boston Eight Hour League, May 31, 1876," *Workingman's Advocate,* June 10, 1876; Ira Steward to F.A. Sorge, March 13, 1876, and December 4,
1876, undated letters, Steward Papers. See McNeill testimony, U.S. Industrial Commission, *Report of the Industrial Commission* 7: 113; U.S. Congress, Senate (Testimony
of Samuel Gompers), *Relations between Labor and Capital* 1: 293; John R. Commons,
ed., *A Documentary History of American Industrial Society* (11 vols., Cleveland, 1910), 9:
24–33, 277–329; Montgomery, *Beyond Equality,* 249–60; Roediger, "American Eight-
Hour Theory."

all he does means an abstraction amounting to death. His life is abstracted; and without life there can be no freedom nor self ownership.''[55]

In explaining labor's peculiarity as an object of sale, Steward fleshed out the meaning of wage slavery. His analysis was far from original, for it merged republican traditions of American labor reform with Continental critiques of political economy. Rather, his contribution was to give systematic statement to this hybrid doctrine, to elaborate the notion of commodity exchange underlying hirelings' sense of the limits of contract freedom. There were many other exponents of this point of view, which led Francis Amasa Walker to realize that because political economy defined labor and commodities as "one and the same thing in exchange," there was little "respect and sympathy" for the science "on the part of the working classes." That was the lesson of the 1887 colloquy in Boston between the labor reformer E.M. Chamberlain and the economist Edward Atkinson. "You can control your own time, brains, and hands," Atkinson declared, denying that to sell labor was to "sell yourself at all." But Chamberlain replied that laborers were "not masters of themselves" for much of "the time from Monday morning to Saturday night." He measured a man's freedom by his right to keep his labor, not to sell it: "by the time he does not work for another, not by the time he does."[56]

These heresies circulated beyond Boston. Just as abolitionists had assailed slavery in both sensual and moral terms, so hirelings across the country portrayed the wage contract as a sale of body and soul. Arguing that labor was unlike money and products but was rather the basis of selfhood, they illuminated the properties distinguishing it from other commodities. A Philadelphia Knights of Labor journal contended that though the laborer was connected to his product under the labor theory of property, he was still more closely attached as a "proprietor" – in the "etymological sense of property" – to all which was "inseparable from his being, his senses, organs and faculties." According to the Principles of the Central Labor Union of New York City, a laborer owning "neither the land nor the means of production" was "compelled to sell his arms [and] brains." As one

---

[55] *Hegel's Philosophy of Right*, T.M. Knox, trans. (London, 1952), 54; Ira Steward, "Less Hours," "Notes on Freedom," and "Unemployment" (circa 1875) and "Freedom and Wealth" (circa 1875–79), (unpublished manuscripts), Steward Papers; Steward, "Poverty," in Massachusetts Bureau of Statistics of Labor, *Fourth Annual Report* (Boston, 1873), 411–12. For a contrasting interpretation of Steward's thought, which focuses on themes of wage levels and consumption rather than of commodity relations and bondage, see Glickman, *A Living Wage*, 99–107.

[56] Walker, *Discussions* 1: 317; Atkinson, *Margin of Profits*, 104, 55, 74.

of its members explained, a poor man "has nothing but his labor to sell, and that labor is attached to his personality." But all other sales involved a "simple transfer of some specific thing," not the "entire existence of the workman." The "contract to *sell* something" differed from "a contract to *do* something. . . . It has been well said that you can buy $50 worth of pig-iron, but you cannot buy $50 worth of puddling without a puddler." In Terre Haute, Indiana, the *Locomotive Firemen's Magazine* declared, "Labor is not tangible. . . . To buy labor is to buy the laborer; to sell labor is to sell the laborer." The outcry was over the right of men to property in themselves.[57]

In multiple ways, labor spokesmen used the issue of time to argue that there was no real difference between the commodity relations of freedom and of slavery. They claimed not only that wage slaves were unable to sell labor time apart from their persons, but that the sale – to one master or another – lasted for the entire length of their lives. As the long hours of single days stretched on for weeks and years, in perpetuity, the hireling's status edged closer to the slave's. Yet the rule of free labor, as McNeill objected, was that a man could not enter a wage contract "for the full time of his life; for that would be the reestablishment of slavery." Temporal distinctions were indeed central to legal understandings of free and slave labor. Although recognizing that wage work entailed submission, the common law forbade perpetual submission. Contracts for service were only lawful for a "limited period," not for a laborer's lifetime, and free laborers, unlike slaves, were entitled to end the exchange and to find other buyers whenever they chose. To laboring men, however, what mattered was not how long a single contract lasted, but the "continuous repetition of the transaction" throughout their lives. In exchange for the "necessaries of life," they asserted, a propertyless man was "required to keep up the repetition of the same bargain every day." He was "chained to his daily toil." Selling himself over and over, he confronted bondage as permanent as chattel status.[58]

[57] "Industrial Ideas," *Journal of United Labor,* August 10, 1886; "Declaration of Principles of the Central Labor Union," October 14, 1883; U.S. Congress, Senate, *Relations between Labor and Capital* 1: 705, 2: 870; "Labor and Capital," *Locomotive Firemen's Magazine,* February 1886. And see, "The Workingman a Chattel," *National Labor Tribune,* July 10, 1875; John Ehmann, "Is Not Labor a Commodity," *Carpenter,* October 1885. See Laurence Gronlund, *Cooperative Commonwealth in Its Outlines. An Exposition of Modern Socialism* (Boston, 1884), 134–35.
[58] George E. McNeill, *An Argument in Favor of a Legislative Enactment to Abolish the Tenement-House Cigar Factories in New York and Brooklyn* (New York, 1882), 19–20, Pamphlet Collection, Wisconsin State Historical Society; Tiedeman, *State and Federal Control,* 340–41; Wood, *Master and Servant,* 96, 2; "A Fair Day's Work for a Fair Day's Wages," *Carpenter,* September 1884; "A Sketch of Political Economy," *Journal of United Labor,* May 25, 1884.

Again, it was labor's peculiar traits as a commodity that allegedly annulled the temporal difference between wage work and slavery. In principle, explained hirelings, they were as free as other men to bide their time, save their time, and spend their time, but unless they owned other property, they could not live off their own time except by constantly selling it, by transferring it to new ownership. Labor and self were inseparable, but unsold labor did not provide a living. As eight-hour reformers in Philadelphia declared, time was unique in the marketplace in having "no fixed standard, its length being determined by the necessities of the seller." Labor time could be neither eaten nor worn; nor could it be stored up and sold later. "Days works must be sold each day, or their sale is lost forever," reasoned Ira Steward in one of his unpublished fragments. But others – speaking of "stomach-wants" – put this idea in print. "The laborer is compelled under the wage-system to sell his commodity today, or not sell it at all," wrote McNeill in *The Labor Movement*. And an essayist in the *National Labor Tribune*, who called himself Robert Meddlesome, argued that "the laborer's merchandise" was not "ordinary merchandise. Bodily necessities control it, and 'day's work is both uncertain and perishable.' . . . [F]or each day lost is withheld – is forever lost." Equating the ambiguities of emancipation in the South and the North, Meddlesome claimed that just as "unrepentant rebels" aimed to "make the freedom of the negro one of seeming only," so also for Yankee hirelings, "freedom of contract is not free, but only seemingly free."[59]

The merchant of time, then, was a man who sold himself for the entirety of his life. Permanent self dispossession was the essence of wage slavery, as this symbolism was used in the postbellum era. But at least some labor spokesmen also returned to the imagery of the household to denounce the traffic in free men. Testifying at the 1883 congressional hearings, a typefounder from New York City maintained that both the perpetuity of the wage contract and the transfer of human property that it involved made the labor bargain more like marriage than a simple market transaction.

When buyer and seller meet in the market the price is paid, the goods change hands, the men part; the transaction is complete. That has no resem-

---

[59] "Address to the Workingmen of America" (undated circular), Thomas Phillips Papers, Wisconsin State Historical Society; Steward, "Less Hours"; McNeill, ed., *Labor Movement*, 482; "Poverty," *National Labor Tribune*, January 30, 1875; "The Workingman a Chattel"; "The Coming Struggle." See also "A Sketch of Political Economy," *Journal of United Labor*, May 25, 1884; "Industrial Ideas," *Journal of United Labor*, June 25, 1886; McNeill, ed., *Labor Movement*, 561–74; U.S. Congress, Senate, *Relations between Labor and Capital* 1: 784–86, 801, 2: 707; Gronlund, *Cooperative Commonwealth*, 31, 51; Trant, *Trade Unions*, 22.

blance to the case of the workman and the employer, which is really the formation of a continuous relationship, which for the workman arranges, perhaps, the whole of his life. . . . If one wants $500 worth of fish he goes to the market and buys it; but if he wants $500 worth of wife the whole matter is changed. . . . He is not purchasing a mere *thing*.

To the typefounder, the model of a contract of sale was as illegitimate for labor as for marriage. Using the old-fashioned analogy of the wife and the hireling, he attacked "the idea that labor is or can be rationally dealt with as a commodity." Rather than a mere commodity exchange, the wage contract consumed all of the laborer and all of his lifetime, rendering him similar to both a wife and a slave. Capital, he attested, "purchases a man."[60]

The typefounder told the congressional committee that his views were those of "nearly all the speakers representing workingmen" – that the denial of the moral legitimacy of buying and selling free labor was "a fundamental proposition underlying all the demands of the labor movement of to-day." Certainly, he observed, "there may be various degrees of difference of opinion . . . but that is a position common to all." He rightly noted the differences, for while some labor groups called for reforming the wage system, others envisioned its demise. Yet he also rightly testified to hirelings' common belief that labor should not be designated a commodity or governed by the laws of market. Spokesmen for every type of labor reform protested against extending the principles of commerce to work and insisted on the "difference between a human being and a machine or an animal, in the market." Labor journals were filled with essays arguing that "as long as it exists under the wages-system, human labor is a commodity" but that "labor *ought not* to be classed as a commodity." Stressing the power of language to validate abhorrent practices, the *Locomotive Firemen's Magazine* vividly stated the gist of labor's position,

Labor combines muscle and mind, brain and brawn, heart and hand – aye, it is life itself! It is not a commodity. . . . Such terms had better be discontinued. Capitalists may prefer them – they like the idea of *buying* labor – but when working men discuss such topics, they will do well to choose words which, as the signs of ideas, do not place labor and laborers in a false position.

Sometimes the argument relied on Christian rhetoric, expressing older spiritualized conceptions of human labor that had been displaced by liberal political economy. As one carpenter announced, "Labor organizations come to-day to preach a holier gospel than was

[60] U.S. Congress, Senate, *Relations between Labor and Capital* 2: 869–70.

ever taught by the economists, they say it is wrong, unjust and immoral to make labor a mere commodity in the market . . . to put out
labor like a slave into the market, to be knocked down to any bidder." McNeill contrasted commodity relations to "the law of brotherhood taught by Christ." Especially by justifying wage slavery,
claimed hirelings, free market doctrine contradicted the Golden
Rule.[61]

It was but a short step from denying that time was like other
commodities, and wage labor a pure and simple market exchange,
to disowning the ideal of contract freedom made ascendant by slave
emancipation. For laboring men, the wage slave symbolized the conflict between commodity exchange and contract freedom produced
by the sale of their time. Yet it also reflected their own sense that the
contract right of self proprietorship distinguished free men from
slaves, however much they questioned the creed that men who possessed only labor to sell could fully own themselves. "If laborers were
sufficiently free to make contracts," wrote Ira Steward, "they would
be too free to need contracts." At the same time, laboring men who
declared themselves unfree continued to invoke contract as a model
of exchange among self-owning individuals. Against the image of
society as a vast marketplace and contract as a relation of buying and
selling, they counterposed not only biblical rules but also secular
images of the social contract. As one writer claimed, the commerce
in labor transformed the "contract of society into a contract of
sale."[62]

At the core of the labor conflict of the late nineteenth century lay
the question that most Americans believed had been resolved by
slave emancipation – the question of buying, selling, and owning
human property. For Yankee hirelings this remained the essential

[61] Ibid., 2: 870; Ehmann, "Is Not Labor a Commodity"; Labadie, "Labor Is Not a
Commodity," *Carpenter*, April 1885; "Labor As a Commodity," *Journal of United
Labor*, January 1884; "The Workingman a Chattel"; "Labor and Capital"; *Locomo-
tive Firemen's Magazine*, February 1886; Lecture of P.J. McGuire in "The Working
Class – Its History and Struggles," *Carpenter*, April 1884; George E. McNeill, *The
Eight Hour Primer. The Fact, Theory and the Argument* (New York, 1889), 6. See also
U.S. Congress, Senate, *Relations between Labor and Capital* 1: 688; McNeill ed., *Labor
Movement*, 468–69; Herbert Gutman, "Protestantism and the American Labor Movement: The Christian Spirit in the Gilded Age," in *Work, Culture and Society in Industrializing America: Essays in American Working-Class and Social History* (New York,
1977), 79–117; Rabinbach, *Human Motor*, 1–18. On the ethical economists' formulation of the clash between Christian doctrine and free market precepts, see, for
example, Richard T. Ely, *Social Aspects of Christianity, and Other Essays* (New York,
1889).

[62] Steward, "Less Hours"; "Chapters on Labor," *Journal of United Labor*, September
10, 1885.

labor question, just as abolitionists had defined it as the essential question of slavery. As the *Workingman's Advocate* explained in 1867, "Labor Reform aimed to restore this lost ownership of self."[63] This aspiration echoed the understanding of emancipation as entitling the bondsman to himself. Yet like the aspirations of many former slaves in the South, it dissociated the wage contract and freedom.

The consequences of the postbellum debate on the labor question were hardly insignificant. The debate heightened public concern over industrial work conditions, and by the turn of the century many leading social scientists and jurists had come not only to promote state intervention into the marketplace, but to agree that free contract was a fiction between individual laborers and corporate capital. Labor agitation and social scientific study together gave rise to legislation on issues ranging from tenement sweatshops to the right to join unions and the hours of work – legislation that gained full constitutional sanction only during the New Deal, for the courts were among the last to uphold the theory that the wage contract differed from other bargains. The debate of the postbellum era thereby contributed directly to the reshaping of liberalism.[64] Yet it left intact the classical economic tenet that labor was distinct from the self, a tenet enshrined by slave emancipation. This debate did not validate hirelings' claim that the sale of free labor resembled the traffic in slaves – that merchants of time sold themselves. On the contrary, in this era unfreedom would come to be defined as the condition of unpropertied men who did not sell their labor.

[63] "The Labor Reform Party," *Workingman's Advocate,* May 20, 1871.
[64] See Roscoe Pound, "Liberty of Contract," *Yale Law Journal,* 18 (May 1909), 454–87; Furner, "Republican Tradition and the New Liberalism"; Alice Kessler-Harris, *A Woman's Wage: Historical Meanings and Social Consequences* (Lexington, Ky., 1990), 33–56; Forbath, *Law and the Shaping.*

3

Beggars Can't Be Choosers

In the late nineteenth century anyone traveling on foot in an American city was likely to be accosted by a beggar asking for alms. Beggars had long been a familiar metropolitan sight, even in the New World. But, according to contemporaries, they were more commonplace in the years after the Civil War than ever before. With hands outstretched, they lined the streets, roved the parks, lingered on stoops.

By all accounts, the most vexing specimen was the sturdy beggar, a man in the prime of life telling a pitiful tale of need. He would be likely to say that he had no work and his family was starving. Should he be believed? Would alms help him or sink him deeper in pauperism by teaching him that he need not labor to live? Puzzling over the subject, the writer William Dean Howells described his own encounter with a street beggar in New York City. In the urban sketch, "Tribulations of a Cheerful Giver," he recounted being torn between the pulls of "conscience" and of "political economy." In the "presence of want," Howells observed, "there is something that says to me 'Give to him that asketh.' " But the question of alms was not so simple:

I have been taught that street beggary is wrong, and when I have to unbutton two coats and go through three or four pockets before I can reach the small coin I mean to give . . . I certainly feel it to be wrong.

In the end, Howells confessed, he gave the beggar fifteen cents without getting so much as a lead pencil in exchange.[1]

In following his conscience, Howells breached the code of contract. Charity belonged to the antiquated world of paternal relations that were based on protection and dependence rather than market exchange – a world Americans believed that had been doomed by slave emancipation. For his lapse, Howells suffered only misgivings. But if an officer of the law had witnessed the transaction, the beggar

---

[1] William Dean Howells, "Tribulations of a Cheerful Giver," in *Impressions and Experiences* (New York, 1972; orig. pub. 1896), 151–52, 160, 167.

would have been subject to arrest and forced to labor in a jail or workhouse.

In itself, the problem of the beggar was nothing new. Tales of encounters with needy strangers reached back to the Bible, and tracts on the most economical way to deal with dependence appeared during the seventeenth century, along with the first systematic texts on the acquisition of wealth and discipline of labor. Yet in postbellum America beggary did not only symbolize ancient problems of improvidence and misfortune, it marked the new prevalence of wage dependence and the effect of prolonged economic depression.[2]

Involuntary pauper labor had a long lineage as well. Early modern English law defined masterless persons subsisting outside wage contracts as criminally dependent and compelled them to work as punishment, spurring the transition from villenage to a market in free labor. American law drew on this inheritance; proscriptions against begging, vagabondage, and idleness were written into colonial codes and remained on the statute books of the states.[3] In the aftermath of slave emancipation, however, state legislatures throughout the North augmented the older codes by passing harsh new vagrancy laws, which punished persons who wandered about lacking work and asking for alms with imprisonment and forced labor. In an era of free labor's ascendance lawmakers shored up the tradition of involuntary labor for beggars.

The postbellum enactments against begging did not simply give new force to an English legal inheritance; they also expressed the indigenous and contradictory legacy of slave emancipation. Yankee liberators in the South imposed penal sanctions against idleness and vagrancy, obliging former slaves to enter into wage contracts, forcibly inculcating the habits of free labor. In the North a similar conjunction of coercion and contract swiftly appeared in rules against beggars. From Port Royal to Boston it became a crime for propertyless

---

[2] See C.J. Ribton-Turner, *A History of Vagrants and Vagrancy and Beggars and Begging* (Montclair, N.J., 1972, orig. pub. 1887); Edgar S. Furniss, *The Position of the Laborer in a System of Nationalism: A Study in the Labor Theories of the Later English Mercantilists* (Boston, 1920); Michael T. Wermel, *The Evolution of the Classical Wage Theory* (New York, 1939); Paul J. McNulty, *The Origins and Development of Labor Economics: A Chapter in the History of Social Thought* (Cambridge, Mass., 1980); David M. Gordon, Richard Edwards, and Michael Reich, *Segmented Work, Divided Workers: The Historical Transformation of Labor in the United States* (New York, 1982).

[3] See R.H. Tawney, *The Agrarian Problem in the Sixteenth Century* (London, 1912), 266–80; Christopher Hill, *Puritanism and the Revolution: Studies in Interpretation of the English Revolution of the Seventeenth Century* (New York, 1958), 215–38; Maurice Dobb, *Studies in the Development of Capitalism* (New York, 1947); Karl Marx, *Capital*, trans. Ben Fowkes (3 vols., New York, 1977; orig. pub. 1867), 1: 877–901; David J. Rothman, *The Discovery of the Asylum: Social Order and Disorder in the New Republic* (Boston, 1971), 20–29.

persons to eke out a livelihood outside the bonds of contract. Coercive labor codes did not vanish with the triumph of the market, reappearing only at the extraordinary moment of slave emancipation to guide the transition to freedom. On the contrary, in northern states where industrial capitalism and wage labor held full sway – but where sturdy beggars still hovered outside the bounds of commodity exchange – criminal law delivered an unequivocal answer to the almsgiver's dilemma.[4]

The beggar's legal status exposed the ambiguities of contract freedom. For generations reformers and moralists had warned that almsgiving menaced the discipline of the free market, an argument echoed by philanthropists and legislators in the postbellum era. But the new statutes against beggars posed a fundamental ideological problem – that of reconciling legal coercions aimed at free but dependent persons with principles of contract. In a nation just purged of chattel slavery, how could forcible pauper labor be justified?

"A fact it is," declared the New York City philanthropist Henry Pellew in 1879, "pauperism has become incorporated into the social life of this country!" As an officer of the Association for Improving the Condition of the Poor, a group of charitable business and professional men, Pellew claimed to know intimately the changing character of poverty. Speaking at the Conference of Charities, where philanthropists, social scientists, and public officials gathered yearly to devise measures for dealing with the poor, he voiced the fears of a generation of charity reformers. The problem of dependence, Pellew announced, had "assumed alarming proportions."[5]

---

[4] On contract doctrine and the laissez-faire constitutionalism of the courts in the late nineteenth century, see Sidney Fine, *Laissez Faire and the General-Welfare State: A Study of Conflict in American Thought, 1805–1901* (Ann Arbor, 1967), 140–62; Morton Keller, *Affairs of State: Public Life in Late Nineteenth Century America* (Cambridge, Mass., 1977), 343–70; Charles W. McCurdy, "The Roots of 'Liberty of Contract' Reconsidered: Major Premises in the Law of Employment, 1867–1937," *Supreme Court Historical Society Yearbook* (Washington, D.C., 1984), 20–33; William E. Forbath, "The Ambiguities of Free Labor: Labor and the Law in the Gilded Age," *Wisconsin Law Review*, no. 4 (1985), 767–817. For a contrasting analysis of the links between contract doctrine and humanitarian sensibility, see Thomas L. Haskell, "Capitalism and the Origins of the Humanitarian Sensibility, Part 2," *American Historical Review*, 90 (June 1985), 547–66. Eric Foner has maintained that the "compulsory system of free labor" imposed on the freed slaves was an "anomaly" born of the crisis of slave emancipation, and that in the North vagrancy laws did not criminalize the unemployed; see Eric Foner, *Reconstruction: America's Unfinished Revolution 1863–1877* (New York, 1988), 56, 208; Eric Foner, *Nothing But Freedom: Emancipation and Its Legacy* (Baton Rouge, 1983), 51.
[5] Conference of Charities, *Sixth Annual Conference* (Boston, 1879), 217. Of the extensive scholarship on charity and dependency in the late nineteenth-century United

Other observers shared Pellew's bleak views. In newspapers, in annual reports put out by public and private charity agencies, and in investigative studies of city life, accounts proliferated of destitution and swarms of street beggars. "From our great warehouses, plethoric with the accumulated products of every quarter of the globe; from the palatial stores of our opulent merchants . . . and from their princely residences . . . you have but to pass the length of a block and turn a corner to find yourself confronted with dirt, squalor, and wretchedness," one New Yorker wrote in 1869. "The banker is jostled by the beggar." Yet as a member of the New York State Board of Charities ruefully noted, Americans had always assumed that "the terrible enigmas of pauperism" existing in "the old world, would never trouble the new."[6]

Even in America, however, the problem of dependency had deep roots. Since the early years of the nineteenth century, philanthropists had confronted the distress of the laboring poor who earned barely enough wages to support themselves. But it was only in the postbellum era, when the wage system became predominant, that a majority of the gainfully employed suffered its chronic uncertainties. Even during the best of times wage work left both skilled and unskilled vulnerable to casual labor, pay below subsistence levels, and unemployment – each an expression of the fluctuating rhythms of commodity production. Always living precariously, increasing numbers of laboring people were never far from poverty and, in the worst of times, from complete dependence on alms. Soldiers back from the

States, see especially Mary O. Furner, *Advocacy and Objectivity: A Crisis in the Professionalization of American Social Science, 1865–1905* (Lexington, Ky., 1975); Paul Boyer, *Urban Masses and Moral Order in America, 1820–1920* (Cambridge, 1978); Robert H. Bremner, *From the Depths: The Discovery of Poverty in the United States* (New York, 1956); Robert H. Bremner, *The Public Good: Philanthropy and Welfare in the Civil War Era* (New York, 1980); Lori D. Ginzberg, *Women and the Work of Benevolence: Morality, Politics, and Class in the Nineteenth-Century United States* (New Haven, 1990), 133–212; Thomas L. Haskell, *The Emergence of Professional Social Science: The American Social Science Association and the Nineteenth-Century Crisis of Authority* (Urbana, 1977); Marvin E. Gettleman, "Charity and Social Classes in the United States, 1874–1900," *American Journal of Economics and Sociology*, 22, pt. 1 (April 1963), 313–29, pt. 2 (July 1963), 417–26; Robert W. Kelso, *The History of Public Poor Relief in Massachusetts, 1620–1920* (Montclair, N.J., 1969); Daniel Rodgers, *The Work Ethic in Industrial America 1850–1920* (Chicago, 1974), 222–26; David M. Schneider and Albert Deutsch, *The History of Public Welfare in New York State 1867–1940* (Montclair, N.J., 1969); Frank D. Watson, *The Charity Organization Movement in the United States: A Study in American Philanthropy* (New York, 1971); Walter I. Trattner, *From Poor Law to Welfare State: A History of Social Welfare in America* (London, 1974); Michael B. Katz, *Poverty and Policy in American History* (New York, 1983).

[6] William H. Burleigh, "A City Letter," *Independent*, January 14, 1869; Martin B. Anderson, "Out-Door Relief," in New York State Board of Charities, *Eighth Annual Report* (New York, 1875), 128.

South swelled their ranks; as production faltered with the return of peace, unemployed men paced the streets.[7]

Indigence and unemployment soared during the depression of the 1870s, the worst times the nation yet had seen. As in earlier decades the vast majority relying on alms were hirelings, with common laborers and domestic servants outnumbering persons in other trades. By some estimates, the long years of depression left two million without work across the country, roughly one in every six of those gainfully occupied in 1870. The poor lined up at soup kitchens, and growing numbers lodged in police stations and poorhouses. In Brooklyn, for example, nearly a tenth of the population received public outdoor relief during 1877. In crowded poorhouses, in the rising costs of alms, and in the spectacle of thronging beggars, charity agents saw signs that social problems once deemed uniquely European had taken root in America. "No one could have walked the streets during the past winter" without learning a "humiliating" fact, lamented a New York City philanthropist in 1874; "this city is rapidly traveling in the track of the worst capitals of Europe, in the direction of abundant street paupers." Labor advocates said practically the same thing. "Our republic is a sham," declared a writer in the *National Labor Tribune* in 1875. "It generates as many millionaires and beggars as any European monarchy."[8]

---

[7] See Boston Industrial Aid Society for the Prevention of Pauperism, *Thirty-Third Annual Report* (Boston, 1868), 7; "Out-Door Poor," *Monthly Record of the Five Points House of Industry*, 9 (February 1866), 149. On poverty, wage dependency, and charitable reformers in the antebellum era, see Raymond A. Mohl, *Poverty in New York, 1783–1825* (New York, 1971); Carroll Smith-Rosenberg, *Religion and the Rise of the American City: The New York City Mission Movement, 1812–1870* (Ithaca, 1971); Christine Stansell, *City of Women: Sex and Class in New York, 1789–1860* (New York, 1986), 19–37, 44–54, 63–75, 193–214. On the wage economy, unemployment, casual labor, and poverty in the late nineteenth century, see Alexander Keyssar, *Out of Work: The First Century of Unemployment in Massachusetts* (New York, 1986); Katz, *Poverty and Policy*; Eric Monkkonen, ed., *Walking to Work: Tramps in America, 1790–1935* (Lincoln, 1984); Paul T. Ringenbach, *Tramps and Reformers 1873–1916: The Discovery of Unemployment in New York* (Westport, Conn., 1973); Sidney L. Harring, "Class Conflict and the Suppression of Tramps in Buffalo, 1892–1894," *Law and Society Review*, 11 (Summer 1977), 873–911.

[8] Remarks of Rev. Dr. John Hall, in Conference of Charities, *First Annual Conference* (Boston, 1874), 31; J.F. Bray, "Industrial Liberty," *National Labor Tribune*, April 24, 1875; Joseph Cook, *Boston Monday Lectures. Labor, with Preludes on Current Events* (Boston, 1880), 55; "Labor and Wages," *National Labor Tribune*, September 2, 1876; W.B. Rogers et al., "Pauperism in the City of New York. A Report from the Department of Social Economy," *Journal of Social Science Containing the Transactions of the American Association*, 6 (July 1874), 74–83; "Station-House Lodgers," *New York Tribune*, February 28, 1876; *Reports of the Board of Police, to the [Chicago] Common Council* (Chicago, 1874–83); Boston Chief of Police, *Annual Reports* (Boston, 1875–77); Seth Lowe, "The Problem of Pauperism in the Cities of Brooklyn and New York," in Conference of Charities, *Sixth Annual Conference* (1879), 202; Keyssar, *Out of Work*, 1–4, 342–43; Hace S. Tishler, *Self-Reliance and Social Security* (Port Washington, N.Y., 1971), 20–21.

The beggar was the most conspicuous figure of dependency and, in contemporary opinion, the most loathsome – a suspect figure who allegedly thrived on deception rather than on work, someone who got something for nothing. In his 1877 address to the Conference of Charities, Francis Wayland, the dean of the Yale School of Law and an influential proponent of criminal laws against beggars, put in rhyme what other charity reformers phrased more soberly:

> He tells you of his starving wife,
>   His children to be fed,
> Poor little, lovely innocents,
>   All clamorous for bread –
> And so you kindly help to put
>   A bachelor to bed.

Most beggars were said to be "idle from choice," not "necessity," and they were often classed with vagabonds, vagrants, and the legion of unemployed transients whom charity reformers denounced as "tramps" in the 1870s. Supposedly, the beggar only pretended to seek work, "coining his unblushing falsehoods as fast as he can talk" while violating the divine rule of labor that charity agencies took as their watchword: "He that will not work, neither shall he eat." Brazenly advertising their need, adroitly manipulating conscience, beggars extorted their unearned gain by "stratagem rather than by force," claimed Jacob Riis in his famous study of slum life. It was mainly such tricky beggars, attested Boston philanthropists, "who infest the streets, whine at your houses, beset your stores." The verdict of the New York City police chief was that the "tramp-beggar" with a "hoarse voice" and "half-starved countenance" was usually a "fraud."[9]

On alms seekers' occupations, see *Fourteenth Annual Report of the Chicago Relief and Aid Society to the Common Council of the City of Chicago* (Chicago, 1872), 83–84; Massachusetts Bureau of Statistics of Labor, *Eighth Annual Report* (Boston, 1877), 192–93; New York Association for Improving the Condition of the Poor, *Thirty-Fifth Annual Report* (New York, 1878), 24–25; Frederick H. Wines, *Report on Crime, Pauperism, and Benevolence in the United States at the Eleventh Census: 1890* (Washington, D.C., 1895), 844–47.

[9] Francis Wayland, "The Tramp Question," in Conference of Charities, *Fourth Annual Conference* (1877), 119–20; Boston Industrial Aid Society, *Fortieth Annual Report* (1875), 6–7; New York Association for Improving the Condition of the Poor, *Thirtieth Annual Report* (1873), 73; Jacob A. Riis, *How the Other Half Lives: Studies among the Tenements of New York* (New York, 1971; orig. pub. 1890), 192; Associated Charities of Boston, *Third Annual Report* (Boston, 1882), 12; George W. Walling, *Recollections of a New York City Chief of Police* (Montclair, N.J., 1972; orig. pub. 1887), 449. See also Levi Barbour, "Vagrancy," in Conference of Charities, *Eighth Annual Conference* (1881), 132; Samuel Leavitt, "The Tramps and the Law," *Forum*, 2 (October 1886), 190–200; Ringenbach, *Tramps*; Katz, *Poverty and Policy*, 157–237; Monkkonen, *Walking to Work*; Michael Denning, *Mechanic Accents: Dime Novels and Working-Class Culture in America* (London, 1987), 149–66.

Measuring the true extent of beggary was no simple task. Beggars reputedly circled from one charity agency to the next – "busy dependents," the metropolitan reformer Charles Loring Brace termed them, who survived by a "science of alms." In 1892 one journalist counted as many as six thousand street beggars in New York City. But their exact numbers and genuine disposition were difficult to gauge because they revolved nightly through different station houses and ranged between the city and the countryside. No systematic count was made of wandering beggars in the late nineteenth century. Yet diverse observers maintained that most were able-bodied young men and, even though pauperism was commonly ascribed to immigrants, that they were as often native-born as foreign-born.[10]

The problem of begging touched the lives of both rich and poor; it was not hidden away inside poorhouses but rather seemed to spread everywhere, like one of the proverbial plagues, a sign of economic and social chaos as alarming to labor reformers and city missionaries as to charity, police, and prison officials. But it was philanthropic reformers presiding over private agencies and the new state boards of charity who studied the problem most intently and framed the debate. Assailing indiscriminate alms, they enjoined "kind-hearted, gushy people" not to allow beggars to live without selling their labor. They claimed that begging was "contagious." As a Boston philanthropist balefully declared in 1879, "Picture for a moment the return of the professional mendicant, laden with booty, into the same tenement house where other men and women are working hard and earning less. What influence can be worse for all who see that begging pays better than work?" The lesson of charity reform was that traditional benevolent practices invited the laboring poor to live in idleness and to tell fantastic tales, thereby sapping their morals and productive capacity while burdening the public with their support.[11]

[10] Charles Loring Brace, *The Dangerous Classes of New York, and Twenty Years' Work among Them* (Montclair, N.J., 1967, orig. pub. 1872), 384; Thomas Knox cited in Helen Campbell, *Darkness and Daylight; Lights and Shadows of New York Life* (Hartford, 1969; orig. pub. 1895), 584; Boston Industrial Aid Society, *Fortieth Annual Report* (1875), 7. See Conference of Charities, *Fourth Annual Conference* (1877), 106, 104; Massachusetts Board of State Charities, *Fourth Annual Report* (Boston, 1868), 130; "Station-House Lodgers"; Leavitt, "Tramps and the Law," 198; Harring, "Tramps in Buffalo," 875–76; Katz, *Poverty and Policy*, 166; "Report of the Chief of the State Detective Force of the Commonwealth of Massachusetts for the Year Ending December 31, 1877," in *Massachusetts Public Documents 1877* (Boston, 1878), no. 37, 18–23; Louisa Lee Schuyler and Edith Grace Putnam, "Out-Door Relief in New York County," in New York State Board of Charities, *Ninth Annual Report* (1876), 134.

[11] Conference of Charities, *Eighth Annual Conference* (1881), 132; William R. Stewart, *The Philanthropic Work of Josephine Shaw Lowell* (New York, 1911), 133; "Address of Robert Treat Paine, Jr." (1879), in *Associated Charities of Boston. Publications* (n.p.,

In the eyes of charity reformers there was a clearly etched "line of distinction" between laboring for wages and begging. The hireling was an independent person, self-supporting and able to maintain a household, one who participated in the vast social exchange of the marketplace and obeyed its rules – the polar opposite of the slave. The beggar was a dependent person, who had no permanent home and who neither bought nor sold but preyed on others. The hireling abided by the obligations of contract; the beggar eluded them. Charity reformers derived their view of beggary from the "best thought of the day" – the teachings of classical political economists and other "men of science." Comprising a constituency of state officials, prominent industrialists and businessmen, scholars, and moral reformers, most of whom had been abolitionists, they were heir to an intellectual tradition that dissociated relations of personal dependence from transactions based on free contract. That indeed had been the ideological lesson of slave emancipation, the basis for vindicating the free wage system.[12]

But in the eyes of laboring men no such distinct line existed between wage work and begging, either in fact or theory. They hardly found the beggar an admirable figure, and they deplored both the spread of pauperism and the cost of supporting dependent persons in poorhouses and by outdoor alms. Yet they claimed that most beggars became so, not by choice, but rather, as Samuel Gompers said, due to "circumstances over which they had no control." Many workingmen doubted that hireling labor represented independence. Furthermore, they pointed out that laborers repeatedly crossed back and forth from depending on wages to depending on alms – from inside to outside the wage contract. For them the beggar was neither

n.d.), 8. See also David Thelen, *Paths of Resistance: Tradition and Dignity in Industrializing Missouri* (New York, 1986), 103–8; on early modern injunctions against indiscriminate alms, see Hill, *Puritanism and Revolution*, 215–38.

[12] New York Association for Improving the Condition of the Poor, *Thirtieth Annual Report* (1873), 77; New York State Charities Aid Association, *Fifth Annual Report* (New York, 1877), x. Enlightenment political thought had coupled hirelings with beggars as dependent persons; see C.B. Macpherson, *The Political Theory of Possessive Individualism: Hobbes to Locke* (New York, 1962), 107, 144–48. On the ideological distinction drawn in the nineteenth century between independent hirelings working under wage contracts and dependent paupers, see Gertrude Himmelfarb, *The Idea of Poverty: England in the Industrial Age* (New York, 1984), 159–63; Robert Steinfeld, "Property and Suffrage in the Early Republic," *Stanford Law Review*, 41 (January 1988), 335–76. On longstanding fears that wandering beggars evaded the "moral police of family life," see Cook, *Monday Lectures*, 85–88; Douglas L. Jones, "The Strolling Poor: Transiency in Eighteenth Century Massachusetts," in Monkkonen, ed., *Walking to Work*, 24–30; Rothman, *Discovery of the Asylum*, 156; Edmund Morgan, *The Puritan Family: Religion and Domestic Relations in Seventeenth Century New England* (New York, 1944), 144–47; John Demos, "The American Family in Past Time," *American Scholar*, 43 (Summer 1974), 438.

a deviant nor a disingenuous figure, but one who personified, in an
extreme way, the dependence and compulsions implicit in the wage
contract itself. Workingmen denied that they were "voluntary beggars." The beggar, explained the labor reformer Ira Steward, reflected the condition of a "large class": those without means to employ themselves, who "must either sell days works, or live upon
charity, or starve to death."[13]

According to laboring men, their only choice was often begging
or starving, if they would not steal. They described men who were
willing to work but were found "walking about in enforced idleness"
for lack of purchasers of their labor:

> For hours along the crowded streets,
>   With aimless steps I've trod,
> Without a home or hope in life,
>
> . . . .
>
> My useless arms have failed to win
>   A crust, a place to stay.
> Earth has no work; no room for me!

During the depression of the 1870s labor journals figured that there
were as many as four million men out of work and printed reports
of their wanderings. "I am a vagrant and vagabond," stated one
wanderer. "I was working at my trade. Business became dull, and
hands were dropped from time to time. My turn came. . . . I wandered to the next town for some kind of employment, and so from
place to place, everywhere hearing how I might possibly get work in
the next village. . . . Distance made me a stranger and necessity a
beggar." This was the condition of "100,000 men as decent." Another "Wanderer" described traversing seventeen states in a single
year but finding only six weeks of work. In his daybook, where he
recorded his disbursements, one overseer of the poor confided that
he could not help believing these stories, though "Most Everyone
says '*Let them freeze.*'"[14]

---

[13] U.S. Congress, Senate, *Report of the Committee of the Senate upon the Relations between
Labor and Capital* (5 vols., Washington, D.C., 1885), 1: 371; "A Tale of a Tramp,"
National Labor Tribune, November 10, 1877; Ira Steward, "Causes of Increased
Wages" [1870s], Ira Steward Papers, State Historical Society of Wisconsin, Madison;
"Resolutions of the Boston Eight Hour League, May 31, 1876," *Workingmen's Advo-
cate*, June 10, 1876. See also "Tramps," *National Labor Tribune*, September 4, 1875,
July 8, 1876, August 14, 1875; "The Tramp," *Journal of United Labor*, December
1883; "Tramps," *Carpenter*, January 1882; "Tramp! Tramp!," *John Swinton's Paper*,
May 24, 1885; J.F. Bray, "Reform Our Social System," *National Labor Tribune*, Sep-
tember 4, 1875; "Report of the Special Committee on Labor," Illinois House of
Representatives (Springfield, 1879), 11.

[14] "Letter to the Workingmen," issued by J.C.C. Whaley, William Sylvis, and William
Jessup of the National Labor Union, in "Capital and Labor," *Revolution*, June 4,
1868; "J.M.," "Out of Work," *Journal of United Labor*, April 10, 1886; "Crime,

Even in prosperous years hireling men might intermittently rely on begging. By their own calculations, even the most skilled workmen were usually without work three to four months a year. Then, as the carpenter P.J. McGuire explained, they were likely to "ramble through the streets, sit in the parks, look around, and wait until there is word." They managed to "live only by ways . . . best known to the poor," turning to the soup-houses and station houses. Allegedly, it was these virtuous men, husbands and fathers, who joined the ranks of street beggars expert in soliciting alms.[15]

Such an interpretation was unacceptable to charity reformers. Though not unaware of the material causes of poverty, they found it inconceivable that wage contracts could generate the need to beg. Rather, they attributed the dependence of an able-bodied man on alms to his depravity, disinclination, and skill in avoiding the "discipline of hunger and cold." Regarding wage labor as the obverse of dependency, they postulated that beggars simply lacked compulsion to work.[16]

Poverty – Their Causes," *Workingman's Advocate,* December 21, 1867; "Correspondence from New York," *Workingmen's Advocate,* January 11, 1868; "Tramps," *National Labor Tribune,* September 24, 1875; "The Army of Tramps," *National Labor Tribune,* May 27, 1876; "The Coming Time," *National Labor Tribune,* January 16, 1875; "Tale of a Tramp," *National Labor Tribune,* November 10, 1877; "Tramps," *National Labor Tribune,* September 4, 1875; "Records of the Poor," Daybook of William O'Gorman, Overseer of the Poor, Newtown, New York, entries for December 21, 1874, December 25, 1873, March 15, 1874, New York Historical Society, New York, New York. See also Terence Powderly, "My Painful Experience as a Tramp," *American Federationist,* 3 (September 1901), 332; Ira Steward, "Unemployment," in Steward Papers; George McNeill, ed., *The Labor Movement: The Problem of To-Day* (Boston, 1887), 576–82; P.J. McGuire, "The Working Class – Its History and Struggles," *Carpenter,* April 1884; Michael Davis, "Forced to Tramp: The Perspectives of the Labor Press, 1870–1890," in Monkkonen, ed., *Walking to Work,* 141–65.

15 U.S. Congress, Senate, *Relations between Labor and Capital* 1: 319, and see pp. 757, 747, 215. On labor advocates' indictment of the economic conditions that led to enforced idleness and begging, see also "Social and Political Liberty," *Workingmen's Advocate,* April 21, 1877; "Workingmen's Wages," *National Labor Tribune,* April 6, 1878; "Idleness in New York," *John Swinton's Paper,* January 20,1884; "The Tremendous Work of Idleness," *John Swinton's Paper,* December 28, 1884; Ira Steward, "Less Hours," Steward Papers; Edward H. Rogers, *Eight Hours a Day's Work. A Lecture* (Boston, 1872), 5–18. On the insecurity of working-class life in the late nineteenth century, see Katz, *Poverty and Policy,* esp. pp. 9–13, 183; Keyssar, *Out of Work,* 50–53, 147.

16 Anderson, "Out-Door Relief," 100, 102, 118. On charity reformers' tendency to note structural causes while imputing begging largely to volition, see, for example, Boston Industrial Aid Society, *Thirty Second Annual Report* (1867), 9–10; Massachusetts Board of State Charities, *Eleventh Annual Report* (1875), xcii; Illinois Board of State Commissioners of Public Charities, *Fourth Biennial Report* (Springfield, 1877), 98, 204–8; Rogers, "Pauperism in the City of New York," 74; Conference of Charities, *Eighth Annual Conference* (1881), 15. By the 1890s, more charity reformers had articulated the links between the wage system and dependency, yet earlier even those who acknowledged unemployment advocated forced pauper labor. See, for

To the kind-hearted almsgiver, charity reformers issued grave warnings; but to the beggar, they did more than preach. Their organizations were dedicated to suppressing mendicancy and "voluntary idleness." And they collaborated with lawmakers in securing the enactment of new criminal legislation. At the yearly Conference of Charities, which met under the auspices of the American Social Science Association, philanthropists gathered to elaborate measures for confining beggars to jails and compelling them to work in return for alms. To extract labor from unworthy paupers – as Franklin B. Sanborn, a charity reformer who had been a radical abolitionist, bluntly affirmed in 1878 – "work-houses are very convenient."[17]

Massachusetts was the first of the northern states to enact new laws against beggars. In 1866 the legislature, which was dominated by Republicans, passed an "Act Concerning Vagrants and Vagabonds." The 1860 criminal code had punished beggars along with a motley band of streetfolk – jugglers, tricksters, common pipers and fiddlers, pilferers, brawlers, and lewd persons. But the new statute dwelled on the crime of begging. It was promoted by the Board of State Charities, which explicitly called for "additional legislation" sentencing "sturdy beggars" to "enforced labor." Directed against idle persons without "visible means of support," the act punished at forced labor for not longer than six months in a house of correction or workhouse:

all persons wandering abroad and begging, or who go about from door to door, or place themselves in the streets, highways, passages or other public places to beg or receive alms.[18]

Notably, just a month before the new law took effect Congress had enacted the Civil Rights Act, thereby voiding the southern Black Codes, which, among other things, had punished freed slaves for vagrancy and idleness. At the very moment when Republicans in Congress were enshrining the legal supremacy of free labor as a

example, Conference of Charities, *Fourth Annual Conference* (1877), 102–10. On the opposition between individualist and environmental theories of pauperism, see Haskell, *Professional Social Science*; Katz, *Poverty and Policy*; Boyer, *Urban Masses*; Ringenbach, *Tramps and Reformers*.

[17] Franklin B. Sanborn to William P. Letchworth, in New York Board of State Charities, *Twelfth Annual Report* (New York, 1879), 230. See also "Unemployed Labor" (lecture of Joseph Cook), *Boston Daily Globe*, January 22, 1878; Associated Charities of Boston, *Third Annual Report* (1882), 11.

[18] "An Act Concerning Vagrants and Vagabonds," *Massachusetts Statutes* (Boston, 1866), ch. 235; *Massachusetts General Statutes* (Boston, 1860), ch. 165, sec. 28, p. 820; Massachusetts Board of State Charities, *Second Annual Report* (Boston, 1866), xcviii–ix; see also Massachusetts Board of State Charities, *Third Annual Report* (1867), 251.

cornerstone of Reconstruction, their brethren in Massachusetts were engaged in constructing an apparatus of labor compulsions.

Within two decades states throughout the North had enacted similar laws against nomadic beggars. Charity reformers and state officials joined in promoting involuntary pauper labor laws, enactments that coincided with scientific philanthropy's assault on "indiscriminate" private almsgiving and public outdoor relief. Labor advocates bitterly opposed the legislation on the grounds that it violated the personal liberty of poor men who were honestly looking for work. Yet vagrancy or "tramp" acts, as they were sometimes called, were passed in state after state: in Pennsylvania in 1871, 1876, and 1879; in Illinois in 1874 and 1877; and in New York in 1880 and 1885. The New England states adopted a series of harsh measures during the late 1870s, and Massachusetts passed several additional statutes. Municipal ordinances were also enacted. Although the wording of the laws varied, all made begging a crime punishable by arrest, imprisonment, and compulsory labor. The Illinois vagabond law of 1874, for example, required that beggars be held in jails or workhouses for up to six months, whereas the 1845 criminal code had provided that they be hired out at public auctions for no longer than four months' service. A further revision in 1877 revoked their right to a jury trial. Under the 1880 New York act, roving beggars were punished at hard labor in penitentiaries, whereas the earlier rule had sent all but the "notorious offender" to local poorhouses. In some states, sentences extended as long as two years. The intent of the new laws, as Franklin Sanborn and Francis Wayland explained in 1880, was to "convert" the vagrant beggar into a "fast prisoner."[19]

Many of the statutes were the direct accomplishment of charity reformers. Among the main tasks the Conference of Charities assigned itself was showing how "legislation ought to travel." As one member declared, "suppression of vagrancy and begging" was

---

[19] Conference of Charities, *Seventh Annual Conference* (1880), 278, 23. On the vagrancy laws, see Leavitt, "The Tramps and the Law," 190–200; Conference of Charities, *Sixth Annual Conference* (1879), 24–26; *Ill. Rev. Stat.* (1845), 175–76; *Ill. Rev. Stat.* (1874), 392–93; *1877 Ill. Laws*, 87–89; *N.Y. Rev. Stat.* (1859), 2: 879; *1880 Laws N.Y.*, ch. 176; Kenneth Kann, "Working Class Culture and the Labor Movement in Nineteenth-Century Chicago" (Ph.D. dissertation, University of Chicago, 1977), 146; see also Harring, "Tramps in Buffalo"; Ringenbach, *Tramps and Reformers*, 11–29; Keyssar, *Out of Work*, 135–38, 253–54; Rodgers, *Work Ethic*, 226–28; Davis, "Forced to Tramp"; David Montgomery, *Citizen Worker: The Experience of Workers in the United States with Democracy and the Free Market during the Nineteenth Century* (New York, 1993), 83–89. Some vagabond laws exempted "resident" alms seekers and as an alternative to jail provided for fines, with a usual maximum of $20 (the 1877 Illinois law raised the maximum fine from $20 to $100). Paupers generally lacked such sums, so if convicted, they usually were incarcerated, and it was difficult for beggars to prove residence.

"probably the most important work" of charity reform. In the words of Theodore Roosevelt, Sr., a delegate at the 1877 conference, paupers "must be made to work." Even before the charities conference organized the effort both public and private philanthropic agencies vigorously promoted laws against begging, all of which entailed forced labor. By 1866, New York City charity officials had resolved that the only way to prevent sloth was through "compulsory labor." A few years later a commissioner of the New York State Board of Charities advised that the laws must be made "more stringent" regarding "vagabonds and professional beggars." In Illinois charity, police, and prison officials all pressed in the 1870s for what one police chief termed a "good vagrant law." And both the Boston Industrial Aid Society and the New York Association for Improving the Condition of the Poor, agencies closely tied to the Republican Party, advocated penal laws and forced labor as a cure for begging. The New York State Charities Aid Association was especially tenacious, pledging to "abolish beggary" and to compel "lazy vagabonds to work" and preparing bills for the legislature. Its members belonged to New York City's elite – merchants, industrialists, ministers, lawyers, physicians, and professors. On its board sat Frederick Law Olmsted and E.L. Godkin as well as eminent charity reformers such as the elder Theodore Roosevelt, Charles Loring Brace, Josephine Shaw Lowell, and Louisa Lee Schuyler. Not only the best men of the day but their wives and daughters too were authors of the vagrancy laws.[20]

In Massachusetts, charity officials, lawmakers, and the police joined in extending the reach of the new legislation. In 1867, as a

[20] Conference of Charities, *Seventh Annual Conference* (1880), 23; Conference of Charities *Eighth Annual Conference* (1881), 131; Conference of Charities, *Fourth Annual Conference* (1877), xxii; New York City Commissioners of Public Charities and Correction, *Seventh Annual Report* (New York, 1867), xxix; Anderson, "Out-Door Relief," 102; Chicago Board of Police, *Report* (Chicago, 1876), 12; New York State Charities Aid Association, *First Annual Report* (New York, 1873), 7; New York State Charities Aid Association, *Third Annual Report* (New York, 1875), 24; New York State Charities Aid Association, *Sixth Annual Report* (1878), 20–22, 128–33; New York State Charities Aid Association, *Eighth Annual Report* (1880), 5, 83–85. See also New York Association for Improving the Condition of the Poor, *Thirtieth Annual Report* (1873), 74, 83; Chicago House of Correction, *Fifth Annual Report of the Board of Inspectors* (Chicago, 1876), 13–14; Illinois Board of Public Charities, *Fourth Biennial Report* (1877), 98; Boston Chief of Police, *Annual Report* (1876), 34; Boston Industrial Aid Society, *Fortieth Annual Report* (1875), 7; Boston Industrial Aid Society, *Forty-First Annual Report* (1876), 4, 10; Kann, "Working Class Culture," 146–47, 167–73; Iver Bernstein, *The New York City Draft Riots: Their Significance for American Society and Politics in the Age of the Civil War* (New York, 1990), 162–68, 172–84, 190–91. On labor reformers' opposition to vagrancy statutes, see "The Albany Quacks," *John Swinton's Paper,* April 12, 1885; "The Tramp Bill," *John Swinton's Paper,* April 26, 1885.

member of the Massachusetts Board of State Charities, Franklin Sanborn pointed out that a "class of wretches" was still roaming about,
despite the statute enacted the year before. In 1872 the secretary of
the charities board, Edward L. Pierce, proposed that overseers of the
poor in each town should have the authority to extract some type of
labor from alms seekers – "chopping wood, picking stones" – in
return for food or a night's lodging. In 1875, as a member of the
legislature, Pierce successfully introduced this measure, which subjected beggars who refused to work to conviction as vagabonds and
forced labor. Three years later the legislature was again involved in
amending the vagrancy law. It held hearings, which disclosed "extraordinary differences of opinion upon nearly every point." Charity
agents endorsed harsher sanctions, and the chief of the state detective force advocated a pass system, summary prosecution of beggars,
and strict work compulsions. But labor reformers led by Ira Steward
testified that vagrant laws were not "politic or humane" and instead
proposed laws reducing the hours of work and banning labor-saving
machines.[21]

Outside the legislative hearing rooms some ten thousand unemployed men agitated for public works and more extensive outdoor
relief. They assembled on Boston Common and marched to City
Hall, where a delegation presented a memorial stating their demands – a demonstration that was similar to those in other cities
during the 1870s and equally unsuccessful. The mayor responded
that he had neither funds nor authority to furnish work and that
doing so would be "very bad policy," since it would encourage dependence on government for support, "aggravating the evils" of
destitution. Nor were legislators in the statehouse persuaded by labor's demands. They did not pass an eight-hour law and concluded
that limiting the use of the machinery would "send us all . . . to the

---

[21] Massachusetts Board of State Charities, *Third Annual Report* (1867), 196; Massachu-
setts Board of State Charities, *Eighth Annual Report* (1872), 29–30, 24; Massachusetts
Board of State Charities, *Twelfth Annual Report* (1876), 93–94; "An Act Concerning
Vagrants," *General Statutes of Massachusetts* (1875), ch. 70; "Tramps," *Boston Daily
Globe,* January 22, 1875; "At the State House," *Boston Daily Globe,* March 6 and
March 13, 1875; "The General Court," *Boston Daily Advertiser,* February 24, 1875;
"Report and Bill Concerning Vagrants," in Massachusetts House of Representatives,
Legislative Documents (Boston, 1878), no. 100, pp. 1–2, 10, 19–20; "The Legisla-
ture," *Boston Daily Globe,* January 18 and January 23, 1878; "Report of the Chief of
the State Detective Force of the Commonwealth of Massachusetts for the Year
1877." On laboring men's demands in Massachusetts and elsewhere, see Rogers,
Eight Hours a Day's Work; "The Tramp Nuisance," *Carpenter,* November 1884; "How
to Give Work to the People," *Carpenter,* November 1885; "The Eight-Hour Law,"
Journal of United Labor, March 10, 1885; "The Millions Who Can't Find Work while
Millions Are Worked to Death," *John Swinton's Paper,* November 2, 1884; Keyssar,
Out of Work, 191–202.

poorhouse." The outcome of their inquiries was a statute giving the chief detective the duty of pursuing vagrant beggars and enforcing the law. Still, in 1880 the legislature again tightened the rules with an act that declared begging "*prima facie* evidence" of being a tramp and imposed a penalty of up to two years' confinement in the state workhouse.[22]

Although charity reformers professed to transform dealings with wandering beggars, they acknowledged the importance of English precedents. They spoke approvingly of Elizabethan codes that relieved the worthy poor while setting vicious beggars to work, and especially of the New Poor Law of 1834 that granted public charity to sturdy paupers only if they agreed to enter a workhouse. Josephine Shaw Lowell lauded the principle of a workhouse test, affirming that charity was ideal when "persons not in danger of starvation will not consent to receive it." Nevertheless, by commanding the summary arrest and forced labor of beggars, the American legislation did not grant dependent persons, even in theory, that formal right of free choice.[23]

Like the New Poor Law, however, the vagrancy statutes belonged to a wider attack on paternalistic customs of charity. Doles of money, food, or kindling; soup kitchens set up on the streets; lodgings at police stations – all these traditional forms of outdoor alms constituted an "unmitigated evil" that not only destroyed the "habit of industry" but also taught the poor to view dependence as "a right" rather than a stigmatized status. Intoning the dominant precepts of laissez-faire, charity reformers especially condemned public outdoor alms and maintained that sturdy beggars had no right to state sup-

---

[22] " 'Give Us Work,' " *Boston Daily Globe*, January 20, 1878; see also "The City," *Boston Daily Globe*, January 6, 1878; "Report and Bill Concerning Vagrants," 1–2, 5, 19–20; "An Act Concerning Vagrants," *General Statutes of Massachusetts* (1878), ch. 160; Massachusetts Board of State Charities, *Fifteenth Annual Report* (1879), 82–83; "An Act for the Protection of the People of the Commonwealth against Tramps," *General Statutes of Massachusetts* (1880), ch. 257; "The Legislature," *Boston Daily Globe*, April 8 and April 16, 1880. See Herbert Gutman, "The Failure of the Movement by the Unemployed for Public Works in 1873," *Political Science Quarterly*, 80 (1965), 254–76; Kann, "Working Class Culture," 80, 220–40.

[23] Stewart, *Lowell*, 160. On reformers' claims of radical change, see, for example, New York State Board of Charities, *Ninth Annual Report* (1876), 29. For a discussion of English legal precedents, see Conference of Charities, *Fourth Annual Conference* (1877), 102–4; New York State Charities Aid Association, *Third Annual Report* (1875), 26; Anderson, "Out-Door Relief," 112–14. On the 1834 New Poor Law, see Himmelfarb, *The Idea of Poverty*, 147–76; Michael E. Rose, *Relief of Poverty, 1834–1914* (London, 1972), 9–14; Karl Polanyi, *The Great Transformation: The Political and Economic Origins of Our Time* (New York, 1944), 101–4, 163–66; Mitchell Dean, *The Constitution of Poverty: Toward a Genealogy of Liberal Governance* (New York, 1991). On the coincidence of the New Poor Law and British slave emancipation, see David Brion Davis, *Slavery and Human Progress* (New York, 1984), 122, 340 n. 26.

port, even through public works. They denounced all such subsidies not only as vestiges of feudalism but as socialistic entitlements, as a shameful form of state guardianship that bred "degradation and dependence" and made the state's relation to the destitute virtually the same as that "between master and slave."[24]

Precisely because the able bodied were not entitled to be dependent, many philanthropists claimed they should be left to starve or to live by selling their labor. Yet even officials such as Lowell, who applauded hunger as a stimulus to industry, also acknowledged the existence of genuine want and valued charity as a "preventive of violence." Moreover, as Lowell further observed, even if the state recognized no right to alms, cunning beggars moaning that "they were starving" would still survive on the benevolence of the conscience stricken.[25]

The vagrancy laws offered a solution to this intricate set of problems by converting the dependency of sturdy beggars into a crime. A commissioner of the New York State Board of Charities announced the rule emphatically: "The policy of the law should be to treat as criminals those who levy upon the public for support while able to earn their own living." Since the state was not bound to give gifts of charity, reformers reasoned, it could justly grant the able bodied public alms only as an act of penal authority. There was no right to relief unless the poor suffered "punitive treatment" and fell under "the category of tramps, vagrants, and so forth." Nor should the state provide work to the poor except in almshouses or "as part of their penal servitude."[26]

This supposedly new system of charity rested squarely on state coercion. Ideally, reformers averred, almsgiving was meant to be a purely private and voluntary moral obligation. But, as Lowell argued,

[24] "Report of the Standing Committee on Out-Door Relief," in New York State Board of Charities, *Seventeenth Annual Report* (1884), 157; Rogers et al., "Pauperism in the City of New York," 78–79; New York Association for Improving the Condition of the Poor, *Thirty-Second Annual Report* (1875), 67. See also New York State Board of Charities, *Ninth Annual Report* (1876), 131–34; Illinois Board of Public Charities, *Fourth Biennial Report* (1877), 97, 203; Associated Charities of Boston, *Fourth Annual Report* (Boston, 1883), 22; Associated Charities of Boston, *Seventh Annual Report* (Boston, 1886), 13; Boston Overseers of the Poor, *Fourteenth Annual Report* (Boston, 1878), 6; Katz, *Poverty and Policy*, 6, 14, 124, 191–92; Fine, *Laissez Faire and the General-Welfare State*.

[25] "Report of the Standing Committee on Out-Door Relief," 143–44. For charity officials' recommendation that in obedience to natural law, able-bodied paupers should be left to starve, see, for example, Illinois Board of Public Charities, *Fourth Biennial Report* (1877), 98, 200; Boston Industrial Aid Society, *Thirty-Fourth Annual Report* (Boston, 1869), 8.

[26] Anderson, "Out-Door Relief," 102; Henry E. Pellew, "Out-Door Relief Administration in New-York City," in Conference of Charities, *Fifth Annual Conference* (1878), 56; New York State Charities Aid Association, *Third Annual Report* (1875), 27.

to prevent the poor from gaining a right to "live upon others," the state should support none "except those whom it can control." Other refomers were just as categorical. Dependency must be "as far as possible punishable," Henry Pellew declared in 1879. "Nothing but coercion will avail."[27]

By punishing dependent persons the vagrancy laws also impinged on private relations of charity. Though no law forbade giving, the beggar committed a crime simply by asking. Nor did guilt vary with the cause of need. "Harsh as it may seem," explained Francis Wayland, even those searching for work must be convicted for begging: "when those who honestly desire employment, but can find nothing to do, are reduced to the necessity of begging from door to door, they must . . . be classed with those unwilling to labor."[28]

It did not matter, then, whether the genesis of dependency lay in the poor refusing offers of work or having none to accept; for beggars to subsist outside the matrix of contract obligations had become a crime. Here, philanthropists argued, was a method of transforming beggars into independent hirelings – to compel them to obey the rules of the market and enter into transactions of voluntary exchange. Like their British predecessors, they presumed that when begging was outlawed and public alms made repulsive, the poor "might be taught to prefer" to sell their labor "for pay." Perhaps some of these reformers might have been pricked by doubt, torn between traditional ideals of benevolence and the harsh precepts of the market. But they made no public avowals of private uncertainty, nor did they appear to lack foresight into the consequences of the laws they proposed. They spoke of uplifting the poor and ultimately eradicating dependency, but in the meantime, of punishing beggars with forcible labor. In the workhouse, they claimed, "if discipline were very strict and hard labor were enforced . . . the inmates might prefer to earn an honest living outside." Exalting volition, they spoke in the same breath of coercion.[29]

---

[27] "Report of the Standing Committee on Out-Door Relief," 160; Henry E. Pellew, "Pauperism in the State of New York. – the Value of Industrial Training and Enforced Labor," Conference of Charities, *Sixth Annual Conference* (1879), 220. On the distinction between voluntary private almsgiving and public relief, see Josephine Shaw Lowell, *Public Relief and Private Charity* (New York, 1884); Richard T. Ely, *Social Aspects of Christianity, and Other Essays* (New York, 1889), esp. pp. 92–93. On the vast expansion of state power implicit in the reformed English poor law system of the nineteenth century, see Himmelfarb, *The Idea of Poverty*, 164–68.

[28] Wayland, "Tramp Question," in Conference of Charities, *Fourth Annual Conference* (1877), 118.

[29] New York State Charities Aid Association, *First Annual Report* (1873), 23; Theodore Roosevelt, Josephine Shaw Lowell, and Edward Donnelly, "Communication to the Mayor of New York in Regard to the Official Charities of the City," in New York State Board of Charities, *Eleventh Annual Report* (New York, 1878), 211. See also

In linking forced labor to wage relations, charity officials laid bare the place of compulsion in a free market economy. Presumably dependent by choice and debased by their own habits, wandering beggars appeared impervious to sanctions that presupposed inner discipline. As Edward Pierce put it, "The low nature of the vagrant lacks any principle or purpose impelling him to labor." And where nature was lacking, the alternative was the "deterrent force of the criminal law."[30] Augmenting the fear of hunger and the moral appeals of reformers, the laws against begging gave free labor a foundation in legal compulsion.

The legal justification for punishing beggars received classic statement in Christopher G. Tiedeman's *Limitations of Police Power,* the most influential treatise on state authority written in the late nineteenth century. The gist of the offense, explained Tiedeman, was not idleness or listless wandering, for a citizen was bound neither to "produce something" nor to have a home. Nevertheless, a man had a duty to "take care of himself." According to Tiedeman, the crime lay in having no means of support – becoming a "public burden." Virtually all the vagrancy statutes contained the phrase, "without visible means of support," identifying the offending deed as dependency.[31]

As proof of lack of support, old and tattered clothes, or even a "dilapidated condition," were not enough to convict. Nor was it always lawful to search a man's pockets to discover that he had no money before arresting him. Simply begging, however, was unimpeachable evidence of guilt. "If a man is found supporting himself in his journeyings by means of begging," Tiedeman declared, "no doubt that would be deemed sufficient evidence of not having proper means of support." Undoubtedly, almsgivers were accomplices to the crime, yet the law dealt differently with those of means and those without. No "rightful law" could prevent almsgivers from

New York State Board of Charities, *Ninth Annual Report* (1876), 30; Boston Industrial Aid Society, *Thirty-Second Annual Report* (1867), 9; New York Association for Improving the Condition of the Poor, *Thirtieth Annual Report* (1873), 78. On connections drawn by authors of the Tudor poor laws between free labor contracts and vagabond laws, see Hill, *Puritanism and Revolution,* 221–22.

[30] Massachusetts Board of State Charities, *Eighth Annual Report* (1872), 20; see also New York Association for Improving the Condition of the Poor, *Thirtieth Annual Report* (1873), 74.

[31] Christopher G. Tiedeman, *A Treatise on State and Federal Control of Persons and Property in the United States* (2 vols., New York, 1975; orig. pub. 1900), 1: 149, 143–44. This is the second edition of the treatise best known by the title cited in the text: Christopher G. Tiedeman, *A Treatise on the Limitations of Police Power in the United States Considered from both a Civil and Criminal Standpoint* (St. Louis, 1886). See also Theodore Dwight Woolsey, "Nature and Sphere of Police Power," *Journal of Social Science Containing the Transactions of the American Association,* 3 (1871), 97–114.

disbursing their property, but the state could "prohibit public and professional begging, and, under the vagrant laws, punish those who practice it." It was "certainly constitutional" to put beggars in the workhouse. Validating the principles of charity reform, jurists affirmed that in a nation where labor was free, dependent persons ought to be viewed as criminals and forced to work. "There is, in just principle," posited a treatise on criminal law, "nothing which a government has more clearly the right to do than to compel the lazy to work."[32]

Under the vagrancy statutes the process of justice was summary. On sight or upon a complaint, officers of the law had a duty to arrest all offenders and carry them to the nearest municipal justice or police court, where, without money for bail, they were locked up until the day of trial. No warrant was required for the arrest, and the suspects were usually tried without a jury. The New York City Board of Police Justices noted that the procedure of conviction "is very simple; indictment and jury trial are unnecessary, the justice must proceed summarily; he can not organize a court of special sessions to try the prisoner." Reversing the ordinary rule, suspects were presumed guilty unless they could rebut police testimony with "a good account of themselves." Convicts were removed to "places of industry," where they were set at tasks such as hauling coal and brick; breaking stone; laying pipes; and making bricks, brushes, and shoes; less often, they were hired out under private prison labor contracts.[33]

Great discretion fell to the police. Officers could make arrests simply on suspicion, without even witnessing the beggar in the act. Often, the police accompanied charity agents on home visits to the poor in order to bring beggars to judgment. "No class of person has better opportunities or facilities for learning the real necessities and true condition of the poor than those who are constantly patrolling the localities in which the poor live, and whose duties bring them continually into contact with this class," police officials boasted, "mendicants are traced to their haunts, their claim to charity investigated, and . . . they are prosecuted." According to a New York City

[32] Tiedeman, *State and Federal Control* 1: 144–45, 149–50; Joel Bishop, *New Commentaries on the Criminal Law* (2 vols., Chicago, 1892), 1: 273–74.

[33] Statement of Board of Police Justices, "The Vagrancy Act and Its Enforcement," in New York Association for Improving the Condition of the Poor, *Thirty-Sixth Annual Report* (1879), 14; Tiedeman, *State and Federal Control* 1: 99–100, 142, 146; Walling, *Recollections,* 388, 449. See also Massachusetts Board of State Charities, *Twelfth Annual Report* (1876), 165–66. On the types of penal labor in houses of correction and workhouses, see Chicago House of Correction, *Sixth Annual Report of the Board of Inspectors* (1877), 28; Board of Directors for Public Institutions of the City of Boston, *Twenty-Second Annual Report* (Boston, 1879), 43; New York City Commissioners of Public Charities and Correction, *Twenty-Second Annual Report* (1882), 155.

detective, a "few simple propositions" governed "this street begging business." No subtlety was necessary in law enforcement: "beggars of every class should be driven from the street, under penalty of imprisonment." In particular, the sturdy beggar with "brawny arms and perfect health" deserved punishment. "A good square look at one of these creatures . . . begets an impulse to kick him into the street."[34]

Quite often the police yielded to such impulses, kicking and beating suspected vagrants. Laboring men in New York City reported that police officers sometimes assaulted and arrested them when they were simply sitting on curbs or lingering on stoops. One man was standing on Tenth Avenue when, he alleged, "without provocation," an officer "came up and said, 'What are you tramps doing here insulting respectable people?'" and struck him "several violent blows on the head with his baton and kicked him." Even men sitting on the streets outside their own homes, showing no signs of being beggars, risked being accosted and arrested – as was Max Moskovits, who was resting on his own stoop on Essex Street, on the Lower East Side. "Get out of here you bastard," one officer reportedly threatened him, "or I will lock you up."[35]

The accused stood trial before a police court justice. Observers noted that in this tribunal cases often took "less than a minute." Police officers read the charges, and the magistrate delivered verdicts instantly as the prisoners came before him. If convicted beggars could post bond of several hundred dollars, they could bring appeals to the lowest state court, where they might obtain a jury trial. Yet very few appear to have exercised that right, and those who did usually were found guilty again. When a man was poor or common looking, a critic of the legal system remarked, he could easily find himself "behind prison walls without his knowing even upon what charge he had been put there and without having made the slightest defence." The commissioners of the workhouse in New York City

[34] Boston Chief of Police, *Annual Report* (1873), 49; Walling, *Recollections*, 194, 387, 449; John Warren, Jr., *Thirty Years' Battle with Crime; or, The Crying Shame of New York as Seen under the Broad Glare of an Old Detective's Lantern* (New York, 1970; orig. pub. 1875), 211, 198. On charity agencies' use of the police to investigate the poor in their homes, see, for example, Schuyler and Putnam, "Out-Door Relief in New York County," 131; Associated Charities of Boston, *Fourth Annual Report* (1883), 16.

[35] Complaints of George Satterwhite (December 24, 1893) and Max Moskovits (November 11, 1892) in New York Senate, Counsel of the Committee of the New York Senate Appointed to Investigate the Police Department, "Examination of Trials by the Police Board from January 1, 1891, to May 1, 1894" (typescript, May 1, 1894), New York Historical Society, New York, New York, 87, 99. See Matthew H. Smith, *Sunshine and Shadow in New York* (Hartford, 1869), 300–307, 363–64; Lillian W. Betts, *The Leaven in a Great City* (New York, 1902), 13; Eric Monkkonen, *Police in Urban America, 1860–1920* (New York, 1981).

described the process of punishment as an ordeal of "humiliation
and self-abasement" from the moment offenders were "huddled
into the gloomy prison van at the Tombs, till they are . . . marshalled
into gangs . . . marched off to the place where they are to do pen-
ance . . . and after being scrubbed and ventilated, assigned to hard
work."[36]

Despite the reports of swift retribution, charity reformers complained that too often the vagrancy codes remained a dead letter.
They claimed that the police were not zealous enough in making
arrests and that judges acquitted the poor. As the chairman of the
Boston Overseers of the Poor argued, "Our judges, we fear, acting
under a tender regard for the personal liberty of those brought before them, hesitate to sentence to the workhouse worthless persons."
Some judges did display notable regard for the liberty of the poor.
In a series of rulings in 1877 and 1878, a judge in the criminal court
of Cook County, Illinois, declared that the state vagabond act of
1877 was unconstitutional in denying the right of trial by jury, and
he discharged all the prisoners appealing their convictions under
that act. Supervisors of the Chicago House of Correction assailed the
rulings for nullifying the "grand results" of increased convictions
under the new statute.[37]

Equally noteworthy was an 1876 Maine case that involved a law
authorizing overseers of the poor to commit to the workhouse propertyless persons who did not labor: " 'all persons able of body to
work, and not having estate or other means to maintain themselves,
who refuse or neglect to do so.' " The state supreme court held that
the law was an "arbitrary exercise of power" that violated the Fourteenth Amendment. Pointedly, the court drew a parallel between
North and South – between impoverished Yankees and freed slaves.
"If white men and women may be thus summarily disposed of at the
north, of course black ones may be disposed of in the same way at

---

[36] Smith, *Sunshine and Shadow in New York*, 167; "A Day in Court," *Arena*, 2 (August
1890), 330–31; New York City Commissioners of Public Charities and Corrections,
Eighteenth Annual Report (1878), ix. On the appeals process in Massachusetts, see,
for example, Suffolk Superior Court, Criminal Case Files, Box 76B (1874–75), cases
2190, 1090, 3060; Box 78B (1877–81), cases 2045, 2030, Massachusetts State Archives, Boston. On the infrequency of appeals in vagrancy cases, see Tiedeman, *State
and Federal Control*, 146. On the criminal justice system, see Allen Steinberg, *The
Transformation of Criminal Justice: Philadelphia, 1800–1880* (Chapel Hill, 1989).

[37] Massachusetts Board of State Charities, *Twelfth Annual Report* (1876), 178; "The
People, ex. rel., Hattie Brown," *Chicago Legal News*, December 8, 1877, 96; In re
Scully and O'Leary, *Chicago Legal News*, November 12, 1878, 27–28; Chicago House
of Correction, *Eleventh Annual Report of the Board of Inspectors* (1882), 20; Chicago
House of Correction, *Sixth Annual Report of the Board of Inspectors* (1877), 12; Chicago
House of Correction, *Seventh Annual Report of the Board of Inspectors* (1878), 14. On
charity reformers' allegations of lax enforcement of the vagrancy laws, see Confer-
ence of Charities, *Thirteenth Annual Conference* (1886), 193–94; "Report and Bill
Concerning Vagrants," 2, 9; Chicago Board of Police, *Report* (1878), 18.

the south; and thus the very evil which it was particularly the object of the fourteenth amendment to eradicate will still exist." Yet the court overturned the vagrancy conviction not because the law in dispute compelled work, but because it did not require a judicial trial, thereby violating the constitutional guarantee of due process. The objection lay not "in the fact that ... persons ... may be restrained of their liberty," declared the court. "Not in committing them to the workhouse, but in doing it without first giving them an opportunity to be heard." Though underscoring the links between the rights of dependent citizens in the North and of ex-slaves in the South, the holding expressly vindicated forced pauper labor when rooted in proper legal process.[38]

Courts throughout the country upheld the vagrancy legislation, ruling that it was indeed a crime for people "not having estate" to subsist without labor – either for wages or in exchange for alms.[39] Though charity reformers were unsatisfied with the amount, thousands were arrested and confined each year for begging and vagrancy. The crime statistics were notoriously imprecise; nonetheless, they amply indicated how widely the force of law was brought to bear on the poor. During the 1870s and 1880s, both in New York City and in Chicago, the police arrested thousands of persons annually on vagrancy charges. Reportedly, in one winter month in 1876 – at the height of hard times – the number of vagrancy arrests in New York City rose to twenty a day. Not all who were arraigned were convicted, but vagrancy was the most common minor offense after drunkenness, assault, and disorderly conduct, and it was well known that the police easily secured vagrancy commitments when lacking evidence of more serious crimes. Prison officials reported that the new laws "largely increased the numbers held as vagrants." Just after the Illinois enactment of 1877, for example, annual vagabond convictions in Chicago alone rose to nearly twelve hundred, more than twice the number a year before. From time to time, philanthropists noted approvingly, the police swept the poor off the streets, "arresting in one day, through a sudden and simultaneous movement, some 500 street-beggars, and subjecting them, through the courts, to the legally appointed penalties." According to Jacob Riis, in the late 1880s over half the arrests for begging in New York City were likely to end in convictions.[40]

[38] *Portland v. Bangor*, 65 Maine 120, at 120, 121 (1876).
[39] See Tiedeman, *State and Federal Control*, 147; "The People, ex. rel., Cain v. Hitchcock," *Chicago Legal News*, June 29, 1878, 329–30; "The Vagrant Act," *Chicago Legal News*, February 1, 1879, 162.
[40] Massachusetts Commissioners of Prisons, *Seventh Annual Report* (1878), 14; New York Association for Improving the Condition of the Poor, *Thirtieth Annual Report* (1873), 74; Riis, *How the Other Half Lives*, 194. On the imprecision of the criminal

To punish anyone simply for lacking means of support was, for many workingmen, evidence enough that the vagrancy acts were unjust. Just as they disagreed with charity reformers about the causes of begging, so labor spokesmen also saw the rules of law differently than treatise writers, the courts, and the police. Holding the poor in "penal servitude" violated the principle of voluntary labor and turned free citizens into slaves, they protested. "What will they not do with the poor workman who happens to be thrown out of work?" demanded a writer in the *National Labor Tribune*. "Why arrest him and place him in the lock-up. Do you call this a free country?" Others argued that every man had an irrevocable right to go "traveling around in search of a day's work" and should not be "enslaved in the penitentiaries" because he asked for alms along the way. A man was "not a law-breaker" because he begged from "necessity."[41]

Knowing firsthand the stimulus of hunger, laboring men testified

statistics, see New York State Charities Aid Association, *Fifth Annual Report* (1877), 11. On the tendency of the police to secure vagrancy convictions when lacking evidence of other offenses, see "Report and Bill Concerning Vagrants," 7. On the incidence of vagrancy convictions relative to other offenses, see Frederick H. Wines, *Report on the Defective, Dependent, and Delinquent Classes of the Population of the United States, as Returned at the Tenth Census (June 1, 1880)* (Washington, D. C., 1888), 506; Wines, *Report on Crime, Pauperism, and Benevolence*, 355; New York Senate, "Report of the Secretary of State on the Statistics of Crime in the State, for the Year Ending October 31, 1886," (Albany, 1887), 202–7; Massachusetts Bureau of Statistics of Labor, *Eleventh Annual Report* (1880), 170–71, 182–85; testimony of John R. Commons, in *Report of the Industrial Commission on the Relations and Conditions of Capital and Labor Employed in Manufactures and General Business* (19 vols., Washington, 1901), 14: 38. On vagrancy arrests and convictions, see Chicago Board of Police, *Annual Reports* (1872–85); Chicago House of Correction, *Annual Reports of the Board of Inspectors* (1872–1885), esp. *Fifth Annual Report* (1876), 20, and *Sixth Annual Report* (1877), 21; Office of the Superintendent of Police of the City of New York, "General Order No. 209" (1876), in New York State Charities Aid Association, *Fifth Annual Report* (1877), 76; Police Department of the City of New York, *Annual Reports* (New York, 1866–86); Children's Aid Society, *Thirty-Sixth Annual Report* (New York, 1888), 12; N.Y. Senate, "Report of the Secretary of State on the Statistics of Crime for 1886," 223; Pellew, "Out-Door Relief Administration in New-York City," 59; Boston Chief of Police, *Annual Reports* (1870–87); Massachusetts Bureau of Statistics of Labor, *Eleventh Annual Report* (1880), 142–69; Massachusetts Commissioners of Prisons, *Annual Reports* (Boston, 1875–80); Board of Directors for Public Institutions of the City of Boston, *Annual Reports* (Boston, 1867–84); Ringenbach, *Tramps and Reformers*, 11. For charity officials' approving accounts of the strict enforcement of the vagrancy laws, see Conference of Charities, *Fourth Annual Conference* (1877), xxiv; Massachusetts Board of State Charities, *Twelfth Annual Report* (1876), 167–81. On high rates of vagrancy and disorderly conduct convictions in antebellum Philadelphia and the discretion of magistrates, see Steinberg, *Transformation of Criminal Justice*, 123–28, 178.

41 "Tramps," *National Labor Tribune*, September 4, 1875; "Who Is a Tramp?" *National Labor Tribune*, January 12, 1878; "The Tramp Bill," *John Swinton's Paper*, April 26, 1885; "A Tale of a Tramp," *National Labor Tribune*, November 10, 1877. See also "Tramps," *Workingman's Advocate*, March 6, 1875; George McNeill, *The Eight Hour Primer. The Fact, Theory and the Argument* (New York, 1889), 2; testimony of Samuel Gompers and Adoph Strasser, in U.S. Congress, Senate, *Relations between Labor and Capital* 1: 371–72, 463.

to the opposition between the ideal of free contract and the coercive provisions of the vagrancy laws. They claimed that necessity itself was a dreadful compulsion, which compromised the legal right to choose when, for how long, and for whom to labor. All too often poor men made "contracts only against their will . . . compelled by the force of circumstance." The vagrancy laws revoked even this formal right of free choice by enlisting punitive state power as an instrument of labor compulsion. In the judgment of labor advocates, the rule of consent enshrined by slave emancipation and set forth in treatises on contract law stood in conflict to statutes ordering beggars to be jailed and "compelled to work, whether they want to or not." They objected that as in "the time of Henry the VIII" the state had decreed that "it is a crime to be out of employment and money." Such legislation, they argued, had no place in a nation committed to freedom and instead represented a throwback to bondage – a system "worthy the days of fugitive slave laws," which reduced to "white slavery an army of men who do not belong to a servile race."[42]

As charity reformers saw the question, however, there was nothing inconsistent about endorsing both the principle of state coercion and the rules of the free market. It was rare when their publications did not offer tribute to the "natural laws" of political economy and the superiority of free labor. Nor did they doubt that the genius of American institutions was to entitle "every man to act with perfect freedom," bargain for the "best price," and "refuse to sell his labor"; and they maintained that "no law ought to be made in a free country to prevent his doing so."[43]

The key point was that even free persons could not choose to beg instead of agreeing to sell their labor for a wage, no matter how low. However much charity reformers espoused full liberty in bargain making, they deplored the existence of a "large class who make begging a trade . . . who will only do such work and at such wages as suit them." Not forced pauper labor, they insisted, but begging and alms transgressed the laws of the market, disturbing the "voluntary play" of commodity exchange and the operation of supply and demand.[44] Thus the vagrancy laws were represented as the guarantee – not the nullification – of voluntary transactions.

[42] Testimony of John Jarrett in U.S. Congress, Senate, *Relations between Labor and Capital* 1: 1155; see also p. 86; D.H. Johnson, "Tramps," *National Labor Tribune,* April 13, 1878; J.E. Emerson, "Tramps," *National Labor Tribune,* December 1, 1877; "Tramps," *Workingman's Advocate,* January 15, 1876; "Tramps," *National Labor Tribune,* August 17, 1875.

[43] New York Association for Improving the Condition of the Poor, *Thirty-Second Annual Report* (1875), 68; Anderson, "Out-Door Relief," 126; Boston Industrial Aid Society, *Thirty-Eighth Annual Report* (1873), 10.

[44] Boston Industrial Aid Society, *Thirty-Ninth Annual Report* (1874), 6; New York Association for Improving the Condition of the Poor, *Twenty-Seventh Annual Report*

That reasoning gained credence in leading texts of political economy. Liberal economists of the postbellum era set forth both the
doctrine of voluntary labor and the necessity of legal compulsion.
"Nobody can compel you," stated Edward Atkinson, explaining the
ideal of wage work defined by the abolition of slavery. "You sell your
time to another man, and he pays you what your work is worth to
him; and if you think it is worth more you can say 'Good-by' . . . and
you can do something else." Yet, like legal theorists, economists justified the coercive aspects of the vagrancy laws while also preaching
the gospel of free labor. All hirelings were entitled to seek the best
market unhindered by "social and legal restraints," affirmed Francis
Amasa Walker. Yet it was of the "highest economical consequence"
that "something of a penalty" be put on the "pauper condition." In
his landmark reformulation of classical economics, *The Philosophy of
Wealth,* John Bates Clark expressly approved "work-houses for
tramps." While celebrating America as a free society, which had
been purged of all bondage "since slavery was abolished in the
Southern land," both economists and lawyers joined philanthropists
in defending the legitimacy of involuntary pauper labor.[45]

Although Yankees professed to the contrary, nowhere did the contradictory aspects of contract freedom emerge more plainly than in the
South in the aftermath of slave emancipation. There, northern liberators imposed free labor policies that brought to light the coercive un-
derside of market relations. They abjured slavery's paternal bonds
and extolled the ideal of voluntary labor. Yet simultaneously they punished as vagrants freed slaves who refused to enter into wage contracts
and set them to work. It was not only across the Atlantic in the English
poor law that charity reformers found an example; paradoxically,
slave emancipation furnished a native model of forced labor. The abolition of slavery distilled fundamental problems of dependency and
discipline that were endemic in pauperism, bequeathing a distinctive
ideology and set of precepts to charity reformers in the North.

(1870), 45. And see New York State Charities Aid Association, *Fourth Annual Report*
(1876), 48; New York State Board of Charities, *Ninth Annual Report* (1876), 132.

[45] Edward Atkinson, *The Margin of Profits: How It Is Divided, What Part of the Present Hours
of Labor Can Now Be Spared* (New York, 1887), 10, 17; Francis Amasa Walker, *The
Wages Question: A Treatise on Wages and the Wages Class* (New York, 1876), 183; Francis Amasa Walker, *Political Economy* (New York, 1883), 423, and see pp. 269, 418;
John Bates Clark, *The Philosophy of Wealth: Economic Principles Newly Formulated* (Boston, 1886), 196; Atkinson, *Margin of Profits,* 103. Richard Ely differed in noting that
the vagrancy laws oppressed the innocent poor, yet he thought workingmen were
"undoubtedly going too far" by demanding their complete abolition. See Richard
T. Ely, *An Introduction to Political Economy* (New York, 1889), 75–76; Ely, *Social Aspects
of Christianity,* 83–112.

Throughout the proclamations of the Freedmen's Bureau ran a double message: an affirmation of former slaves' right to liberty and a warning that freedom barred dependence. The bureau sought to dispel the notion that its mission was charitable, aiming its words both at former slaves and at northerners who shunned the prospect of permanently supporting a free black population. "Freedom does not mean the right to live without work at other people's expense," the bureau declared in 1865. "A man who can work has no right to a support by government or by charity." Though entitled to choose the buyers of their labor, former slaves were not free to refuse all wage work. The bureau made explicit the double meaning of emancipation: "While the freedmen must and will be protected in their rights, they must be required to meet these first and most essential conditions of a state of freedom, *a visible means of support, and a fidelity to contracts.*"[46]

According to the bureau's chief, Oliver Otis Howard, the duty of government was not to " 'feed the niggers in idleness,' " as enemies of Reconstruction charged. Rather, the bureau aimed to induce former slaves to work and scrupulously subjected all applicants for aid to a "rigid examination," turning away all who were fit to labor. If the freedmen "failed to contract," Howard explained, "they incurred the odium of being a 'lazy, idle, and worthless race,' besides running the risk of starving." Though pledging to prevent a recurrence of bondage, Howard was not fully consistent in either his convictions or his policies. "I repeatedly cautioned my officers against any substitute whatsoever for slavery," he avowed. Nonetheless, he affirmed that "a little wholesome constraint" could not be avoided, and even led to "larger independence."[47]

Agents of the bureau had great latitude in exercising "wholesome constraint." They did not hesitate to compel former slaves to enter into yearlong contracts binding them to fieldwork. Their strictures constantly juxtaposed the contrary principles of consent and coercion. In July 1865 an assistant commissioner for Louisiana issued an edict epitomizing the contradiction in bureau policy: "That freedmen everywhere be *enjoined to work,* and in doing so, they will, in all cases, enter into *free and voluntary contracts* with employers of their

---

[46] *Orders Issued by the Commissioner and Assistant Commissioners of the Freedmen's Bureau,* 39th Cong., 1st sess., House Exec. Doc. 70 (1865), 155, 139. See Foner, *Reconstruction,* 152–53.

[47] Oliver Otis Howard, *Autobiography of Oliver Otis Howard* (2 vols., New York, 1907), 2: 214; *Report of the Commissioner of the Freedmen's Bureau,* 39th Cong., 2nd sess., House Exec. Doc. 1 (1866), 772; Howard, *Autobiography* 2: 246, 247, 221. See also *Orders Issued by the Commissioner and Assistant Commissioners of the Freedmen's Bureau,* 39th Cong., 1st sess., House Exec. Doc. 70 (1865), 58.

own choice." Similar rules were promulgated throughout the southern states. In Georgia, for example, the bureau forced freedpeople to accept work on plantations, and the duty of local agents was to "make contracts for them" – agreements that were to be treated as "binding . . . as though made with the full consent of the freed people."[48] Stationed in the South to guarantee free labor practices, agents of the national government created a scheme of compulsory contract.

Such measures culminated in penal laws against vagrancy. In response to freedpeople's efforts not only to negate the dominion of former masters, but also to resist the impersonal discipline of wage contracts, the bureau imposed a system of legal coercions to prompt the sale of their labor.[49] As Howard saw it, "idleness" was an intractable problem, and he reported that neither persuasion nor threats overcame the freedmen's reluctance to make contracts. Therefore, he turned to legal sanctions against those who preferred to survive outside the contract system: "At last I urged for such freedmen the use of the vagrant laws," though "leaving out the whipping post." Instead, the penalty was a prison term or bound labor on plantations and public works.[50]

The many complexities of contract freedom, dependence, and legal compulsion had been signaled by the 1864 report of the American Freedmen's Inquiry Commission, which led to the bureau's formation. Written by the antislavery reformers Samuel Gridley Howe, Robert Dale Owen, and James McKaye, the report warned against governmental paternalism that would inadvertently restore bondage "under the guise of guardianship." It advised that former slaves must be "self-supporting," not protected or burdened by special laws for "colored people" but treated "as any other freeman." And though holding that only the market's "natural laws" should govern wage labor and that ex-slaves "should be subjected to no compulsory contracts as to labor," it recommended vagrancy laws "as apply equally to whites."[51]

---

[48] *Orders Issued by the Commissioner and Assistant Commissioners of the Freedmen's Bureau,* 39th Cong., 1st sess., House Exec. Doc. 70 (1865), 10 (emphasis added), 65, and see pp. 58–59, 149. See Foner, *Reconstruction,* 161.

[49] On the dual aspects of former slaves' aspirations to freedom, see Julie Saville, *The Work of Reconstruction: From Slave to Wage Laborer in South Carolina, 1860–1870* (New York, 1994).

[50] Howard, *Autobiography* 2: 247.

[51] *Communicating the Final Report of the American Freedmen's Inquiry Commission to the Secretary of War,* in, *Report of the Secretary of War,* 38th Cong., 1st sess., Sen. Exec. Doc. 53 (1864), 109–110. See Thomas C. Holt, " 'An Empire over the Mind': Emancipation, Race, and Ideology in the British West Indies and the American South," in *Region, Race, and Reconstruction: Essays in Honor of C. Vann Woodward,* ed. J. Morgan Kousser and James M. McPherson (New York, 1982), 283–313.

The commission's report endorsed principles and procedures already established by the Union army. By 1862, army officials had ordered that fugitive slaves must be saved from "idle and vicious habits . . . that they should work; and as they are yet too ignorant, thoughtless and improvident to think and act judiciously for themselves, they must be subjected to wholesome rules and restraints." Later military ordinances required former slaves to toil on plantations and commanded that transgressors must be arrested as vagrants and forced to work, sometimes specifying that all persons loitering around the camps, "either white or black," should be set at penal labor rather than be allowed to "roam in idleness." The Freedmen's Bureau elaborated these precepts. As the assistant commissioner for Mississippi, Col. Samuel Thomas, explained the punishment for refusing to contract to former slaves:

If you do not contract with the men who wish to employ you, what do you propose to do? You cannot live without work of some kind. Your houses and lands belong to the white people, and you cannot expect that they will allow you to live on them in idleness. . . . The government hopes you will do your duty, and in return will secure you all the rights of freemen. . . . [I]f then you are found idle you may be taken up and set to work where you will not like it. The State cannot and ought not to let any man lie about idle, without property, doing mischief.

It was "nonsense" to think that by entering "a contract you will somehow be made slaves," Thomas insisted. Rather, he warned, "Your danger lies exactly in the other direction. If you do not have some occupation you will be treated as vagrants, and made to labor on public works."[52]

While northern emissaries of freedom were suppressing "idleness" through compulsory labor, southern legislatures were pursuing a similar agenda through the infamous Black Codes enacted immediately after the war. Among their other provisions, the codes

[52] Ira Berlin, Thavolia Glymph, Steven F. Miller, Joseph P. Reidy, Leslie S. Rowland, and Julie Saville, eds., *Freedom: A Documentary History of Emancipation, 1861–1867*, ser. 1, vol. 3, *The Wartime Genesis of Free Labor: The Lower South* (New York, 1990), 380–82, 419, 316–18; "The Freedmen in Virginia," *Liberator*, July 7, 1865; *Message from the President Communicating Reports of Assistant Commissioners of the Freedmen's Bureau*, 39th Cong., 1st sess., Sen. Exec. Doc. 27 (1865), 36–37. See also *Orders Issued by the Commissioner and Assistant Commissioners of the Freedmen's Bureau*, 39th Cong., 1st sess., House Exec. Doc. 70 (1865), 155, 174, 139, 28–29, 52; "Fullerton's Address to the Freedmen of Louisiana," *National Anti-Slavery Standard*, November 11, 1865; Leon Litwack, *Been in the Storm So Long: The Aftermath of Slavery* (New York, 1979), 319–21, 366–71; Foner, *Reconstruction*, 153–70; Barbara J. Fields and Leslie S. Rowland, "Free Labor Ideology and Its Exponents in the South during the Civil War and Reconstruction" (paper delivered at Organization of American Historians Annual Meeting, 1984).

required black persons to enter into wage contracts and prohibited vagrancy. For example, the antebellum Mississippi vagrant law, which had punished with fines and imprisonment an Elizabethan array of deviants – "rogues and vagabonds, idle and dissipated persons, beggars, jugglers, or persons practicing unlawful games or plays, runaways, common drunkards, common night-walkers, pilferers, lewd, wanton, or lascivious persons" – was rewritten to govern "freedmen, free negroes and mulattoes . . . without lawful employment or business." The Alabama Black Codes defined a vagrant as a "stubborn or refractory servant; a laborer or servant who loiters away his time, or refuses to comply with any contract for any term of service without just cause." The penalty for black vagrants was hard labor in jails and on chain gangs, or they could be hired out to individual employers for a term of involuntary service. Though by the postbellum era white persons were no longer subject to penal sanctions for breaking labor contracts and were not forced specifically to perform them, under many of the Black Codes freed slaves were arrested for quitting work and were either returned to their employers or imprisoned as vagrants.[53]

Northerners responded selectively to the coercions aimed at the freedpeople, crying out that the Black Codes, but not Yankee free labor policy, resurrected slavery. Writing to Senator Lyman Trumbull about the mind-set of the "great mass of the southern people," a Union soldier stationed in Meridian, Mississippi, observed, "It is their hope, and intention, under the guise of vagrant laws, &c, to restore all of slavery but its name." Under the southern legislation, declared General Benjamin F. Butler, "vagrancy or indisposition of a negro to work is a crime for which the negro shall be sold in servitude." Abolitionists also condemned the Black Codes as a return to "practical slavery." Yet, though the Freedmen's Bureau drew criticism from northerners, most did not equate its forcible labor laws with bondage. Rather, leading exponents of Yankee habits of industry – "a hundred merchants" in the citadel of the Boston Board of Trade, as Wendell Phillips indignantly remarked – backed coercion in the conquered states: "a stringent vagrant law that shall whip men to work."[54]

[53] *Laws in Relation to Freedmen*, 39th Cong., 2nd. sess., Sen. Exec. Doc. 6 (1866), esp. pp. 192, 170. See also Robert J. Steinfeld, *The Invention of Free Labor: The Employment Relation in English and American Law and Culture, 1350–1870* (Chapel Hill, 1991).
[54] Letter of C.E. Lippincott to Lyman Trumbull, August 29, 1865, Lyman Trumbull Papers, Library of Congress, Washington, D.C.; Letter of Benjamin F. Butler to Thaddeus Stevens, November 20, 1865, Thaddeus Stevens Papers, Library of Congress; "The Report of Gen. Schurz," *National Anti-Slavery Standard*, December 30, 1865; "South Carolina Re-Establishing Slavery," *Liberator*, November 24, 1865; "Speech of Wendell Phillips, Esq., at the Brooklyn Academy of Music, Tuesday Evening, February 18, 1866," *National Anti-Slavery Standard*, February 24, 1866. On

It is hard to suppose that Yankees wholly overlooked the parallels between the Black Codes and their own rules for converting slaves into wage laborers. At least some bureau officials were troubled about imposing vagrancy sanctions on freedpeople who were "idle from necessity" rather than from choice, and they cautioned against punishments that replicated slavery. But for most northerners the crucial difference between the two sets of ordinances lay in their racial character; bureau law did not discriminate by race. At Howard's orders, the bureau extended existing vagrant rules "made for free people" to former slaves, a policy formally blind to color. By contrast, northerners denounced the Black Codes for imposing extraordinary punishments on "account of color" and operating "most iniquitously upon the freedmen." South Carolina policy was a case in point. In January 1866 the bureau nullified the Black Codes in the name of equal rights, declaring that "all laws shall be applicable alike to all the inhabitants." The bureau's own rules, which withheld charity from the able bodied and authorized hiring out convicted vagrants to planters, provided that rules "applicable to free white persons, will be recognized as the only vagrant laws applicable to the freedmen." In the Yankee worldview, it was not legal coercion that contravened free labor, but its unequal application based on race.[55]

In supervising the transition to freedom, northern officials openly defended the propriety of forcing former slaves to work. "A vagrant law is right in principle," the head of the bureau in Mississippi affirmed.

I cannot ask the civil officers to leave you idle, to beg or steal. If they find any of you without business and means of living, they will do right if they treat you as bad persons and take away your misused liberty.

Among the rights guaranteed to former slaves, none gave them liberty to "saunter about neglecting their business," to be without a

---

abolitionists' criticism of bureau officials, see "Fullerton's Folly," and "Freedmen in Louisiana," both in *National Anti-Slavery Standard*, November 18, 1865. But this indictment was singular, prompted by singularly outspoken disregard for freedpeople's liberty and dignity. Though enforcing identical policies, bureau officials in other states met with no such criticism. In defending the Black Codes, however, southern whites did not fail to underscore their similarity to bureau regulations. See Foner, *Reconstruction*, 208. On abolitionists' support for the bureau, see James M. McPherson, *The Struggle for Equality: Abolitionists and the Negro in the Civil War and Reconstruction* (Princeton, 1964), 178–91, 341, 349–50.

[55] *Orders Issued by the Commissioners and Assistant Commissioners of the Freedmen's Bureau*, 39th Cong., 1st sess., House Exec. Doc. 70 (1865), 95, 52; *Report of the Commissioner of the Freedmen's Bureau*, 39th Cong., 2nd sess., House Exec. Doc. 1 (1866), 741; Montgomery, *Citizen Worker*, 85–86. See also Howard, *Autobiography* 2: 278; Harold M. Hyman, ed., *The Radical Republicans and Reconstruction, 1861–1870* (New York, 1967), 218–19, 281; Foner, *Reconstruction*, 149–51, 153–55.

livelihood and take up begging. As a Tennessee bureau official told his staff, this constraint was intrinsic to freedom: "the peace and good order of the community, and the success of free labor, depend largely upon the vigor and thoroughness of your action in relation to vagrants." Rather than being anomalous to the New South, institutions of emancipation erected on forced labor and vagrancy decrees had counterparts throughout the world in nations implementing the abolition of slavery. Invalidating ex-slaves' aspirations to subsist through self employment and independent property ownership, American architects of freedom – like those elsewhere – defined the alternatives as either wage labor or unlawful dependence.[56]

The lessons of emancipation quickly traveled north, where they guided the cures devised for begging. For like the former slave, the Yankee poor had neither masters nor property, and both subsisted by selling their labor or by depending on alms.[57] And many who became apostles of charity reform after the Civil War, and who had long opposed slavery, studied the progress of free labor in southern society. Not only did they survey the situation from afar; many journeyed and lived in the South, where they inspected up close and helped to install the wage system, compiled reports on relations between former masters and slaves, supervised plantations, and worked as missionaries among the freedpeople. On returning north, where their own city streets were filled with beggars, they brought back more than recollections of burning sunlight and of gangs of freed slaves picking endless rows of cotton.

The career of Edward Pierce suggests the itinerary of many philanthropists. A Boston lawyer with impeccable antislavery credentials, Pierce held positions in both the South and the North that clothed his views on dependency with state power. Appointed in 1862 by Secretary of the Treasury Salmon P. Chase to oversee the famous wartime experiment with free-labor cotton cultivation in the Sea Islands of South Carolina, Pierce then served as secretary of the Massachusetts Board of State Charities, and soon after guided a vagrancy law through the Massachusetts legislature. As he traveled the length

---

[56] *Message from the President Communicating Reports of Assistant Commissioners of the Freedmen's Bureau*, 39th Cong., 1st sess., Sen. Exec. Doc. 27 (1865), 36; *Orders Issued by the Commissioner and Assistant Commissioners of the Freedmen's Bureau*, 39th Cong., 1st sess., House Exec. Doc. 70 (1865), 53. See Wilhelmina Kloorsterboer, *Involuntary Labour since the Abolition of Slavery: A Survey of Compulsory Labour throughout the World* (Leiden, Holland, 1960); Thomas C. Holt, *The Problem of Freedom: Race, Labor, and Politics in Jamaica and Britain, 1832–1938* (Baltimore, 1992), 179–87.

[57] On definitions in early English law of vagabonds as masters, bound neither to the land nor to a lord, see Sir Frederick Pollack and Frederic William Maitland, *The History of English Law Before the Time of Edward I* (2 vols., Cambridge, 1923; orig. pub. 1898), 1: 30.

of the country his thoughts on freedom consistently allowed for compulsion. At Port Royal, Pierce warned the former slaves that "if they were to be free, they would have to work, and would be shut up or deprived of privileges if they did not," and he envisioned "the workhouse or even the prison" as punishment. Yet he opposed the Black Codes, not only for discriminating against freedpeople, but also for classifying the breach of labor contracts as a crime. Back in Boston a decade later, echoing ideas he had uttered at Port Royal, Pierce affirmed that criminal law must compel begging vagabonds to work – a punishment not "interfering with personal liberty." On both sides of the Mason–Dixon line he justified penal coercion in transforming dependent persons into free laborers.[58]

In the famous venture in the Sea Islands Pierce worked closely with the Educational Commission of Boston, a group of reformers and professional men dedicated to elevating the condition of the freed slaves. The commission's first chairman was the Reverend Edward Everett Hale, an abolitionist who, like Pierce, went on to advocate vagrancy laws and forced pauper labor. Hale became an officer of the Boston Industrial Aid Society, which drew its members from the same circle as the Educational Commission and was devoted to suppressing street beggary.[59]

Still other prominent charity reformers had studied the transition from slave to free labor. Josephine Shaw Lowell traveled in the South with the Freedmen's Association after the war and became a principal exponent of workhouses. Even more striking was the route of the Yankee reformer Samuel Gridley Howe. In 1863, shortly before being appointed chairman of the Massachusetts Board of Charities, Howe had toured the South as a member of the Freedmen's Inquiry Commission, which had defended the merits of vagrancy laws for blacks and whites alike. While the Freedmen's Bureau disseminated these precepts across the South, Howe reiterated them in dealing with beggars on his own home ground. Under his direction the Massachusetts Board of State Charities named "Punishment for Vagrancy" the first rule of scientific alms and sponsored the vagrant

---

[58] A.W. Stevens, ed., *Addresses and Papers of Edward L. Pierce* (Boston, 1896), 72, 85, 152–54; Massachusetts Board of State Charities, *Eighth Annual Report* (1872), 20, 30. See James Ford Rhodes, "Memoir of Edward L. Pierce," *Proceedings of the Massachusetts Historical Society*, 18 (1903–1904), 363–69; George F. Hoar, "Edward Lillie Pierce," *Proceedings of the American Antiquarian Society*, 12 (October 1897), 197–210. On the contradictory strains of Pierce's policies in the Sea Islands, see Willie Lee Rose, *Rehearsal for Reconstruction: The Port Royal Experiment* (New York, 1981), esp. pp. 21–62.

[59] See Rose, *Rehearsal for Reconstruction*, 21–62; Boston Industrial Aid Society, *Fiftieth Annual Report* (1885), 5–12; Conference of Charities, *Fourth Annual Conference* (1877), 108–10.

law of 1866, claiming it had "introduced a new feature" to charity by imposing "enforced labor for the paupers who can work, but will not."[60]

Shaped by their southern experience, charity reformers both renounced paternal obligations to the poor and interpreted the compulsory aspects of contract freedom to require punishing beggars. They did not expressly equate their undertaking with that of instilling in former slaves a desire to labor as hirelings. Yet other Yankees, even without the benefit of personal experience, frankly observed how apt a model slave emancipation provided for curing dependency. In 1878 the *Boston Daily Globe* urged that plans devised for the "lately emancipated negroes" should be used to solve "the great questions . . . of suppressing the vagrant practices of the idle." This editorial appeared amid the agitation over the vagabond bill enacted that year. According to the *Globe*, "What was in 1865 considered as eminently practical, is equally so now." The experience of war and emancipation not only honed efficient techniques of philanthropy but also schooled Yankees in ways of forcing the poor to work. The endeavor of replacing the slave system by wage contracts recast conceptions of dependence, obligation, and labor compulsion. Just as the ideal of free labor was transported south, so its coercive elements – articulated in rules governing freedpeople – were carried back north.[61]

What could not be so easily echoed in the North was the logic that justified compelling freed slaves to put their labor up for sale. Slave emancipation represented an apocalyptic moment, but problems of

[60] Massachusetts Board of State Charities, *Twelfth Annual Report* (1876), lxxiv; Massachusetts Board of State Charities, *Fifth Annual Report* (1869), xvii. See also Stewart, *Lowell*, 48–49; Haskell, *Emergence of Professional Social Science*, 92–97.

[61] "Providing for the Unemployed," *Boston Daily Globe,* January 19, 1878. My interpretation departs from that of most other historians who, in analyzing the ideology and policies of the charity organization movement, have focused on the expert techniques of public administration that charity reformers honed from the experience of the Civil War and Reconstruction. See, for example, George Frederickson, *The Inner Civil War: Northern Intellectuals and the Crisis of the Union* (New York, 1965), esp. pp. 98–112, 211–15; Bremner, *From the Depths*, 51–57. My interpretation instead stresses the central importance of emancipation, the problems entailed in constructing a free labor system, and the schemes for enforcing a system of voluntary wage labor that charity reformers inherited from the national government's policies toward freed people. Though closer in emphasis, it also differs somewhat from the interpretation offered by Eric Foner, who maintains that the bureau's views on charity and dependency reflected dominant Northern views. See Foner, *Reconstruction*, esp. pp. 152–53. While this was certainly the case, the influence also flowed in the other direction. The bureau's confrontation with the unprecedented task of remodelling the southern labor system and installing contract practices was an important crucible for shaping emerging Yankee conceptions of poverty, dependency, almsgiving, and labor compulsion.

dependency appeared endemic in the North. Nor could Yankee reformers simply restate arguments that Englishmen had used centuries earlier to defend coercive poor laws, for they confronted ideological consequences of emancipation unknown to their forebears. Roughly a quarter of a century earlier, in the British Empire, there had also been striking simultaneity between colonial slave emancipation and the metropolitan enactment of the 1834 New Poor Law. Yet the sanctions against dependency and the labor compulsions that accompanied the American triumph of freedom were more extreme. Whereas the British law granted beggars the choice of entering a workhouse or forgoing alms, the American reform summarily punished them with penal labor. "We come back to the old rule," declared Josephine Shaw Lowell in 1876, "that the man who won't work, shall be made to work." But the task was not simply to make beggars work; it was also to explain how a society rhetorically committed to contract freedom could embrace a rule so at odds with the principle of consent.[62]

Before the emergence of the antislavery movement in the late eighteenth century, the system of forced pauper labor had required no special justification. It had coexisted in the Atlantic economy with other forms of bound labor that ranged along a continuum from indentured servitude to chattel slavery, and in both England and America spokesmen of the propertied classes used identical arguments on behalf of slavery and compulsory pauper labor. Members of Parliament and American slaveholders shared a common conception of labor discipline, and philosophers as different as Thomas Hobbes and the antislavery advocate Francis Hutcheson expressly recommended enslavement as a punishment for vagabonds and idlers.[63]

Yet as antislavery beliefs came to prevail on both sides of the Atlantic, reformers and statesmen pulled apart the strands of arguments that once had been intertwined. Abolitionists were hardly uninterested in questions of labor discipline or even opposed to compulsory pauper labor or workhouses, but in advocating such measures, they no longer conflated them with slavery. Instead they distinguished between systems of bound labor. The theory that beg-

[62] New York State Charities Aid Association, *Fourth Annual Report* (1876), 102. See also the report of Edward Everett Hale in Conference of Charities, *Fourth Annual Conference* (1877), 102–4; Himmelfarb, *Idea of Poverty*, 160; Davis, *Slavery and Human Progress*, 122, 340 n. 26.

[63] See Edmund S. Morgan, *American Slavery/American Freedom: The Ordeal of Colonial Virginia* (New York, 1975), 319–27, 338–39; David B. Davis, *The Problem of Slavery in the Age of Revolution 1770–1823* (Ithaca, 1975), 263–64; Furniss, *Position of the Laborer in a System of Nationalism*, 42, 67, 80–116.

gars must be set to work endured. What shifted were the justifications, the styles of argument, that exponents of free labor throughout the Anglo-American world used to defend traditional modes of
coercion that fell short of outright slavery.[64]

In the aftermath of emancipation northerners turned to two lines
of argument to explain the paradox that in guarding ex-slaves' freedom, they impressed them into involuntary labor. On the one hand,
they claimed that devices such as vagrancy laws and compulsory contracts were merely temporary expedients needed to mediate the transition from slavery to freedom. As O.O. Howard maintained, these
were extraordinary measures, required to educate persons accustomed to bondage in the ways of the market and the wage system: "I
would have been glad to have adopted precisely the same methods
of regulating labor as obtained in the northern States, but neither
the planters nor the freedmen were yet prepared for this." On the
other hand, northerners implied that former slaves would never be
ready for complete freedom, citing racial inferiority as grounds for
coercion. Although the rules of the Freedmen's Bureau did not discriminate by race, many who endorsed them fell back on longstanding apologies for involuntary servitude. According to Wendell Phillips, even Yankees could still be found arguing "there is a race
among us that obliges us to go back to compulsion."[65]

Neither of these arguments spoke exactly to the predicament of
charity reformers who rewrote the poor law in the North, for they
faced a situation almost as different from circumstances in the
South as from those in England in centuries past. The northern vagrancy codes were not intended as temporary expedients. Nor were
they devised (as both the Tudor statutes and the Reconstruction
measures had been) to promote the transition to commodity relations and the creation of a wage-laboring class. Rather, they were
designed for a society long accustomed both to free labor and to
market transactions, where hirelings were not in scarce supply but
often too abundant, especially during the depression of the 1870s.
Nor did beggars comprise a separate race, as the freedpeople did;
though philanthropists often equated paupers with immigrants and

---

[64] On the ambiguities of abolitionists' views on labor compulsion, see Davis, *Slavery in
the Age of Revolution*, 241–54, 260–66, 357–59, 453–67.

[65] *Report of the Commissioner of the Freedmen's Bureau*, 39th Cong., 2nd sess., House Exec.
Doc. 1 (1866), 772; "Speech of Wendell Phillips, Esq.," *National Anti-Slavery Stan-
dard*, February 24, 1866. See Foner, *Reconstruction*, 208; Barbara J. Fields, "Ideology
and Race in American History," in Kousser and McPherson, eds., *Region, Race, and
Reconstruction*, 165; Holt, " 'An Empire over the Mind,' " 284–88, 303; Morgan,
American Slavery/American Freedom, 316–37; Davis, *Age of Revolution*, 299–306; C.
Vann Woodward, "Unfinished Business," *New York Review of Books*, 35 (May 12,
1988), 22–27.

blamed their individual traits on "poor stock," they did not classify them as a different species of being or presume that their stock made them unsuited to free labor. The enactment of the northern vagrancy laws, therefore, represented a paradox similar, but not identical, to that posed by emancipation, and it had to be justified in different terms.[66]

Not even the most steadfast proponents of the laws could escape the problem: a society priding itself on having abolished slavery was forcibly extracting labor from dependent persons. Edward Everett Hale admitted the profound questions at stake – the "difficulty under our system of personal liberty" of granting overseers of the poor "penal powers." The philanthropist Henry Pellew conceded that the "embryo" of such "difficulties" lay in the "supposed antagonism between free and enforced labor." Yet he claimed this was a specious objection, a "prejudice and misunderstanding" that would disappear with a "full discussion" of the advantages of coercion.[67]

It was the rule of commodity exchange that charity reformers invoked to sweep away the "misunderstanding" regarding enforced labor. In defending the vagrancy acts they spoke most commonly in the idiom of the marketplace. As in any bargain, they claimed, so in almsgiving, the beggar owed something in return: a share of labor – surrendered willingly or not – for a portion of food or a night's lodging. The New York State Board of Charities stated the rule emphatically: "In the case of the able-bodied, no aid should be extended to them except upon their rendering an equivalent therefor, by their labor."[68] Philanthropists intoned this injunction again and again. Images of commerce, the language of buying and selling, of equivalence and payment, pervaded their discussions. The poor must be "made to work in payment for what they have received," declared the New York State Charities Aid Association. As a student at Harvard, Edward Pierce had been struck by the primacy of exchange; it was the theme of a prize-winning essay that he wrote on contract law. As a charity official, he returned to it, announcing that forced labor obliged the beggar "to pay his way." Both public and private phil-

---

[66] Massachusetts Board of State Charities, *Second Annual Report* (1866), xxii. See also Dobb, *Studies in the Development of Capitalism,* 23–25, 231; Katz, *Poverty and Policy,* 94, 103, 134–35, 177. It was not until the 1890s that nativism developed into racial determinism. See John Higham, *Strangers in the Land: Patterns of American Nativism 1860–1925* (New York, 1970), 131–57.

[67] Conference of Charities, *Fourth Annual Conference* (1877), 107; Conference of Charities, *Fifth Annual Conference* (1878), 57. See also Massachusetts Board of State Charities, *Eighth Annual Report* (1872), 30.

[68] New York State Board of Charities, *Ninth Annual Report* (1876), 29; quoted by Josephine Shaw Lowell, in New York Charities Aid Association, *Fourth Annual Report* (1876), 40.

anthropic agencies affirmed the justice of requiring paupers to "render an equivalent." More important than the liberty of the poor, as Hale argued in 1877, was the principle inscribed in the vagrancy laws: "That in all cases, a return in work be extracted in proportion to the relief thus given."[69]

In compelling beggars to work in exchange for alms, charity reformers professed simply to uphold the rules of the market. Every sale, as William Blackstone had written, required a "*quid pro quo,*" and it was a settled rule of contracts that the law would enforce only agreements entailing reciprocity – that a valid contract required "consideration." Indeed, the rule of reciprocity marked the dividing line between economic and moral transactions. The notion of "proper exchange" was foreign to the "field of morals," the economist Arthur Latham Perry explained in 1868, but there was "nothing else but proper exchange within the field of economy." In the "language of political economy," he went on, to produce meant nothing other than to "render a service for an equivalent." Through a deft translation, philanthropists applied these precepts to their project of reform, showing the worth of compulsory labor. As Pellew declared in 1878, "Even in giving out-door relief the principle of obtaining some return, some *quid pro quo* . . . should be insisted upon."[70]

The sturdy beggar who refused to pay a share of labor was a "swindler," said charity reformers. Like a thief, he looked on the public as a "vast, intangible body" to "plunder without remorse." Citing the labor theory of property, charity reformers averred that every cent of unrequited alms amounted to robbery, just as if the beggar had gone pilfering from door to door. What made the pauper and the criminal alike was that both took something for nothing, receiving "benefits, without rendering an equivalent in return." As an antidote to such swindling practices the vagrancy laws held beggars

[69] New York State Board of Charities, *Ninth Annual Report* (1876), 29; New York State Charities Aid Association, *Fourth Annual Report* (1876), 40; New York State Charities Aid Association, *Thirteenth Annual Report* (1885), 17; Edward L. Pierce, "The Consideration of a Contract, Part I," *American Law Register,* 2 (March 1854), 257–79; Edward L. Pierce, "The Consideration of a Contract, Part II," *American Law Register,* 2 (May 1854), 385–400; Edward L. Pierce, "The Consideration of a Contract, Part III," *American Law Register,* 2 (June 1854), 449–59; Massachusetts Board of State Charities, *Eighth Annual Report* (1872), 30; Conference of Charities, *Seventh Annual Conference* (1880), 245; Conference of Charities, *Fourth Annual Conference* (1877), 110. See also Ginzberg, *Women and the Work of Benevolence,* 197–98.

[70] William Blackstone, *Commentaries on the Laws of England* (4 vols., Chicago, 1979; orig. pub. 1765–69), 2: 442–46; Arthur L. Perry, *Elements of Political Economy* (New York, 1868), 44, 91; Conference of Charities, *Fifth Annual Conference* (1878), 57. See also Edward Atkinson, "What Makes the Rate of Wages," *Journal of Social Science Containing the Transactions of the American Association,* 19 (December 1884), 56–57.

strictly to the rule of exchange, transforming charity into a punitive bargain.[71]

In insisting on the paramount importance of exchange relations, charity reformers translated the principles of contract into a justification for involuntary labor. A contract ordinarily signified both consent and reciprocity. By splitting apart these interlocking principles, charity reformers demonstrated how easily the ideal of contract – when transposed onto poor relief – could be made to stand for compulsion. It required no more than a rhetorical inversion, a substitution of words. Instead of naming slavery as a referent, the authors of the vagrancy laws spoke in terms of "earning," thereby likening forced pauper labor not to bondage, but to wage work. It was wrong to give the "slightest aid," Francis Wayland postulated in 1877, "which is not earned by an equivalent amount of labor." According to such arguments, compulsory labor gave almsgiving the form of a wage contract. As one charity official explained, if beggars chose not to work, the "public has the same right to exact from them labor as it has to exact labor from those to whom it pays wages." Throughout the commercial world agreement usually took priority over the notion of fair exchange; but in the economy of charity, exchange annulled volition. Philanthropists used the language of contract – the rule of "rendering an equivalent" – to legitimate an exchange relation that plainly violated the principle of consent.[72]

Like any other market transaction, then, the duty to the poor was reduced to an exchange of commodities. The accomplishment of scientific philanthropy was not only to rediscover the virtues of vagrancy statutes and workhouses, but also to give a new ideological configuration to charity: to impose a commodity form on the obligation between almsgiver and beggar, to convert a dependency relation into a relation of contract. Charity, by tradition, was the very essence of a paternal relationship, one remote from the world of sharp bargaining, and the beggar the exemplar of dependency. "Nobody but a beggar chuses to depend chiefly upon the benevolence

[71] New York State Board of Charities, *Twelfth Annual Report* (1879), 260; Conference of Charities, *Fourth Annual Conference* (1877), 48; Illinois Board of Public Charities, *First Biennial Report* (1871), 17, 18. See also New York Association for Improving the Condition of the Poor, *Twenty-Seventh Annual Report* (1870), 61; Wayland, *Elements of Political Economy*, 119, 153; Bishop, *Commentaries on the Criminal Law* 1: 274.

[72] Conference of Charities, *Fourth Annual Conference* (1877), 119; Anderson, "Out-Door Relief," 100. See also Boston Industrial Aid Society, *Forty-Seventh Annual Report* (1882), 6. On the preeminence of principles of consent over notions of fair exchange in nineteenth-century contract doctrine, see Morton J. Horwitz, *The Transformation of American Law 1780–1860* (Cambridge, 1977), 160–210. On English poor law reformers' conception of the wage contract, see Himmelfarb, *The Idea of Poverty*, 162–63.

of his fellow-citizens," Adam Smith had written. But using Smith's own vocabulary, American philanthropists remodeled charitable benevolence in the image of a contract. The only choice they left beggars was to enter the matrix of exchange relations, to yield up their labor under a compulsory charitable contract. None was so unflinching in stating this hard fact or renouncing the ethos of paternalism as Josephine Shaw Lowell. Even in dealing with the poor widow, the most pathetic figure of dependence, Lowell declared, it was always "a good thing to drive a hard bargain" rather than give "a dollar without . . . equivalent" and leave the widow to spend "her days in idleness and her nights in debauchery."[73] The rules of the market were no more a mystery to benevolent women than to benevolent men, both of whom claimed that forcing beggars to work freed them from a kind of bondage.

Sentiment held little place in the new code of almsgiving. Philanthropists continued to speak of uplifting and redeeming the poor, fusing an older rhetoric of Christian charity with the usages of political economy. But, for all their moral concerns, they disowned a paternal obligation to the sturdy poor, insisting that the strict law of *quid pro quo* must govern both public and private alms, that the issue was not "tenderness" but "material return." They claimed that the best charity was the personal sort that created a bond between giver and receiver, but they conceived of that bond in terms of contract more than sympathy. The "exercise of feelings of humanity" belonged to the household realm, they argued. This was precisely the model of obligation prescribed by theorists of liberalism, the creed of scientific thinkers who deciphered all social exchange, other than that inside the home, according to the calculus of contract. As the sociologist William Graham Sumner explained the virtue in the harsh rule of equivalence, to be dependent – to make no return – was to renege on the rights of freedom itself. "A free man," wrote Sumner in 1883, "derogates from his rank if he takes a favor for which he does not render an equivalent."[74]

Out on the streets, philanthropists distributed cards bearing the legend, "What to Do with Beggars," and warning, "Do Not Give." In

[73] Adam Smith, *An Inquiry into the Nature and Causes of the Wealth of Nations* (New York, 1937; orig. pub. 1776), 14; Lowell, *Public Relief and Private Charity*, 93.
[74] New York State Board of Charities, *Fifth Annual Report* (1872), 37; Boston Industrial Aid Society, *Thirty-Fourth Annual Report* (1869), 7; Associated Charities of Boston, *Third Annual Report* (1882), 11; William Graham Sumner, *What Social Classes Owe to Each Other* (New York, 1972; orig. pub. 1883), 39. See also Stewart, *Lowell*, 156; Massachusetts Board of State Charities, *Eighth Annual Report* (1872), 24; Conference of Charities, *Fourth Annual Conference* (1877), 46–51; Conference of Charities, *Fifth Annual Conference* (1878), 53–72; Katz, *Poverty and Policy*, 200–201.

the words of Edward Everett Hale, charity reformers gave benevolence a new meaning: "they so worked on the public, that men began to believe that it is wicked to give money to a beggar."[75] Among rich and poor, reformers inculcated this creed, remodeling charity as a market relation, recasting the ideal of reciprocity into a justification for coercion. Here was the source of the almsgiver's dilemma, the sin of giving to a street beggar who gave nothing in return, which proved so troubling to good Samaritans such as William Dean Howells.

The vagrancy laws purportedly rescued beggars – against their will – from the abject status of taking favors without rendering an equivalent. For, according to the new political economy of charity, it was not forced labor but rather alms without work that threatened to reduce the poor to slavery. The object of the legislation, its authors claimed, was not to set paupers in bondage, but to hold them fast within the world of exchange. The laws secured the supremacy of contract relations by bringing even dependent persons under their terms. They were "equitable enactments," affirmed the New York Association for Improving the Condition of the Poor, "based on contract and individual rights."[76]

In so arguing, charity reformers gave new moral legitimacy to labor compulsions that came perilously close to slavery. Under the vagrancy laws the state enforced the sale of labor – through an involuntary exchange – wherever beggars contrived to avoid the natural sanctions of hunger and cold. In an age of supposedly untrammeled freedom in the marketplace, legal coercions were resurrected to assure the supremacy of wage labor. The system of unfree pauper labor dated back to premodern times. But in reconciling that tradition with the rules of the market, Americans in the late nineteenth century spoke in a distinctly modern language of contract.

[75] Associated Charities of Boston, *Third Annual Report* (1882), 21; Boston Industrial Aid Society, *Fiftieth Annual Report* (1885), 11.
[76] New York Association for Improving the Condition of the Poor, *Twenty-Eighth Annual Report* (1871), 59. For the argument that pauper's degradation was worse than that of the slave, see Walker, *The Wages Question*, 88.

4

The Testing Ground of Home Life

Implicit in the ethos of contract that denied a man food unless he worked was the assumption that his wages ought to be at least enough to keep him from starving. But this primal reciprocity was hardly thought to constitute free labor's hallmark; for even slavery, as abolitionists admitted, involved the exchange of labor for sustenance. Despite classical political economy's grim lessons of supply and demand, which taught that the free market inevitably put hirelings at risk of starving, the moral legitimacy of wage labor in the era of slave emancipation rested on the promise that free commodity relations would afford more than slavery's equities – more than brute survival. But how much more? By what measure did the wage contract distinguish free men from chattel property?

That question was intently debated by a multitude of economists, moralists, and reformers from the early nineteenth century onward. In America as in the Old World, they offered an array of technical definitions and arithmetical formulas as they pondered the equities of the wage contract. Yet nearly all Americans came to agree on one measure of exchange value – that home life differentiated the wages of freedom and bondage. Speaking on behalf of the former slaves to a New York audience in November 1865, the Reverend Henry Ward Beecher gave voice to this free labor gospel. "The slave is a man and he will respond to human influence. Although a black man may never be a Yankee, he will follow hard after. Why should he, an ill-compensated and bewhipt drudge work willingly?" Beecher asked. "Give him the prospect of a home, a family that is not marketable, and he will work."[1] In postbellum America the promise of a home unscathed by the market distinguished the rewards of free contract and chattel slavery.

The creed announced by Beecher presupposed that the wage contract would sustain the marriage contract. Indeed, no axiom had been more important to abolitionism, which had constantly contrasted the morality of free market relations to the evils of the slave

[1] *National Freedman*, November 1865, 332.

system on the grounds that all free, laboring men had a right to an inviolate household.[2] Even the most ill-paid hireling, as Beecher claimed, could be assured of a family "not marketable." But in the years directly after slave emancipation, the nation's first social-scientific investigations of the free labor system in the North found to the contrary. A principal object of these studies was to discover if wage labor supported home life. Public questions of political economy were thus intimately linked to private household circumstances. Yet the empirical data did not corroborate the vaunted ideological distinction between the traffic in slaves and the traffic in free labor based on contract – for it showed that poor men's families were likely to be marketable.

As a symbol of slavery's downfall, the image of the orderly home was as powerful as the ideal of cotton cultivation by free labor. Nowhere was this expressed more clearly than in the ideas of freedom put forward by antislavery advocates who aided in reconstructing southern society. As the famous fugitive slave Harriet Jacobs wrote in 1864 from a Virginia freedpeople's settlement where she taught school: "When we went round visiting the homes of these people, we found much to commend them for. Many of them showed marks of industry, neatness, and natural refinement. In others, chaos reigned supreme. There was nothing about them to indicate the presence of a wifely wife, or a motherly mother. They bore abundant marks of the half-barbarous, miserable condition of slavery, from which the inmates had lately come."[3] The home therefore stood as a touchstone of emancipation's progress; its neatness symbolized the rights and duties of freedom, its chaos the legacy of slavery – a difference defined by women's place within.

At the very outset of emancipation Yankees in the South had emphasized the connection between free labor and home life. Concern with freedpeople's housekeeping was widespread, as was the notion that their newfound domestic rights offered the key incentive to wage labor. These issues were made central in discussions of freedom by both men and women, white and black reformers, state officials and missionaries from private benevolent societies. One of the first to enunciate them was Edward Pierce. While overseeing cotton plantations in the Sea Islands in 1862, he lamented to the Lincoln administration that freedpeople did not eat meals together as a family

[2] See Amy Dru Stanley, "Home Life and the Morality of the Market," in *The Market Revolution in America: Social, Political, and Religious Expressions,* ed. Melvyn Stokes and Stephen Conway (Charlottesville, 1996), 74–96.
[3] "Letters from Teachers of the Freedmen," *National Anti-Slavery Standard,* April 16, 1864.

and that their houses and bodies were as dirty as they had been under slavery. "Whosoever under our new system is charged with their superintendence," he declared, "should see that they attend more to the cleanliness of their persons and houses, and that, as in families of white people, they take their meals together at table." Worrying fastidiously about housework – as well as about growing cotton – he defined his mission as instilling "the love of wages, of offspring, and family" to spur free labor. "Where I came from all were free," he told the ex-slaves, "we did not sell children or separate man and wife; but all had to work." The promise was that black households would resemble white ones, that freedmen's wives and children would not be commodities, that freedom protected the home from the market's incursions.[4]

Northerners pledged that in exchange for hard work freedpeople would earn the right to maintain the traditional dependency relations of the household. They affirmed that wage labor would support wives' unpaid domestic work – unlike in slave families, but like in idealized white families. Just days after Appomattox, Republican legislators brought this message to the South. As Senator Henry Wilson declared to a gathering of black people in Charleston, South Carolina: "Freedom does not mean that you are not to work. It means that when you do work you shall have pay for it, to carry home to your wives and the children of your love." To the freedwomen in the same audience, Congressman William D. Kelley stated: "Remember, my friends, that you are to be mothers and wives in the homes of free men. You must try to make those homes respectable and happy." This was the exchange at the nub of the Victorian domestic ideology that portrayed the household as a sphere separate from the cash nexus. As Yankees habituated former slaves to market incentives, they claimed that the *quid pro quo* for a free man's labor was a wife at home.[5]

Yet freedwomen's fieldwork was as integral to the Yankee emancipation program as tributes to home life, even though abolitionists had highlighted the conflict between domestic ideals and slave

[4] Ira Berlin et al., eds., *Freedom: A Documentary History of Emancipation, 1861–1867*, ser. 1, vol. 3, *The Wartime Genesis of Free Labor: The Lower South* (New York, 1990), 128, 143, 131–32. See also Thomas C. Holt, "Gender in the Service of Bourgeois Ideology," *International Labor and Working-Class History*, 41 (Spring 1992), 29–36.

[5] Both addresses were quoted transcribed in Lydia Maria Child, *The Freedmen's Book* (New York, 1968; orig. pub. 1865), 260, 262. See Nancy F. Cott, *The Bonds of Womanhood: 'Woman's Sphere' in New England, 1780–1835* (New Haven, 1977); Mary P. Ryan, *Cradle of the Middle Class: The Family in Oneida County, New York, 1790–1865* (New York, 1981); Linda Kerber, " 'Separate Spheres, Female Worlds, Woman's Place': The Rhetoric of Women's History," *Journal of American History*, 75 (1988), 9–39; Stanley, "Home Life."

women's plantation labor. Almost from the war's start the Union
army had to deal with great masses of destitute freedwomen and
children who lived in, or had fled to, occupied territory or who
trailed the troops to be with their enlisted male kin. The prevailing
response was to return them to field labor, a policy that held sway
throughout Reconstruction. As the American Freedmen's Inquiry
Commission recommended in 1863, farming abandoned plantations
was "expedient and profitable . . . even though chiefly by women
and children." The Freedmen's Bureau refused to discriminate by
sex or age in obliging ex-slaves to work. "I have assembled as many
freedmen as possible . . . and address them upon their duties as well
as their rights," one Virginia bureau agent reported in 1866, "and
endeavor to instill into them . . . how absolutely necessary it is that
every member of each family who was able to do so should work."[6]
Here the agenda of emancipators converged with the efforts of former masters to reclaim the labor of entire black households.

But the work rules that healed sectional differences clashed with
the aspirations of former slaves to construct an autonomous family
economy. Emancipation brought not only freedwomen's withdrawal
from the fields, but freedmen's assertion of the right to provide for
their families. "What induces a colored man to take a wife?" asked
the Freedmen's Inquiry Commission. In response, one South Carolina freedman testified, "there are more married than ever I knew
before, because they have a little more chance to mind their families
and make money to support their families." This ideal did not bar a
wife's productive labor at home, but it did run counter to her hiring
by white employers and was inseparable from the desire to own land.
As the South Carolina freedman further attested, "The people here
would rather have the land than work for wages. I think it would be
better to sort out the men and give land to those who have the
faculty of supporting their families."[7] In the eyes of many former
slaves, independent land ownership rather than wage labor salvaged
the home from the market.

Yankees who worked and traveled in the South after the war, however, saw no conflict between celebrating domesticity and indiscrim-
inately enjoining wage labor, even as they fussed about the sloppy
housekeeping of freedpeople. Rather, leading accounts of postbel-

[6] *Preliminary Report Touching the Condition and Management of Emancipated Refugees, Made
to the Secretary of War by the American Freedmen's Inquiry Commission, June 30, 1863*, in
Report of the Secretary of War, 38th Cong., 1st sess., Sen. Exec. Doc. 53, (1864), 14; G.
Buffum to O. Brown, December 28, 1866, quoted in Elizabeth Regosin, " 'God
Almighty's Law' or State Law?: The Freedmen's Bureau and the Legalization of Slave
Marriages" (unpublished seminar paper, March 1991).
[7] Berlin et al., eds., *Freedom*, 252, 253.

lum southern life grew lyrical at the sight of freedwomen and children performing gang labor in the cotton fields. As Whitelaw Reid
described a Mississippi plantation in 1866, "A quarter of a mile
ahead of the plows a picturesque sight presented itself. Fifty women
and children . . . were scattered along the old cotton rows, chopping
up weeds, gathering together the trash that covered the land, firing
little heaps of it, singing an occasional snatch of some camp-meeting
hymn, and keeping up incessant chatter. . . . Most of them were
dressed in a stout blue cottonade . . . heavy brogans of incredible
sizes on their feet, and gay-checkered handkerchiefs wound about
their heads. . . . The moment the sun disappeared every hoe was
shouldered. . . . In a moment the whole noisy row was filing across
the field toward the quarters . . . looking as much like a caravan
crossing the desert as a party of weary farm-laborers."[8] No abolitionist portrayal of a southern plantation had been so benign.

By no means did northerners explain how freedwomen could at
once work in the fields and do the cleaning and cooking at home
that were as much tokens of freedom as wage labor. Instead they
simply avowed that abolition had ended the traffic in human chattels
that destroyed home life – that contract relations entailed reciprocity
between free labor and the right to a family. As General Rufus Saxton asked of freedmen in August 1865, "Could you rise . . . against a
government which has given you a right to yourselves, your wives,
and children, and taken from you the overseer, the slave trader, the
auction block?" Meanwhile, Saxton admonished, "Your first duty is
to go to work . . . and provide food, clothing, and shelter for your
families. Bear in mind that a man who will not work should not be
allowed to eat."[9]

The symbolic polarity of home life and bondage invoked to defend wage labor after emancipation stood at the center of antislavery
conceptions of freedom. Abolitionists readily granted that the free
market ethos of competitive individualism was not synonymous with
the ideal of domestic affection, an argument famously advanced by
the proslavery thinker George Fitzhugh. Nevertheless, they held that
only a free market in labor, as in other commodities, ensured that
the household would remain inviolate – a sphere insulated from
commerce. It was a staple of abolitionism to counterpose free society,
where home and marketplace were allegedly separate realms, to

[8] Whitelaw Reid, *After the War: A Tour of the Southern States 1865–1866*, ed. C. Vann
Woodward (New York, 1965; orig. pub. 1866), 486–87.
[9] "Circular No. 2, To the Freedmen of South Carolina, Georgia, and Florida, Issued
by Brigadier General R. Saxton, August 16, 1865," in *Report of the Joint Committee on
Reconstruction, at the First Session, Thirty-Ninth Congress* (New York, 1969; orig. pub.
1866), 231, 230.

what the former slave William Wells Brown called the "southern market," where human beings were "struck off to the highest bidder." It was also common for abolitionists to counter arguments about wage slavery by contrasting hirelings' domestic situation to that of bondsmen. As William Lloyd Garrison asked with regard to the condition of "the most degraded and dependant free laborer, ... Can any power take from him his wife and his children?"[10] To abolitionists, home life gave proof of the wage contract's moral and economic legitimacy, marking a crucial difference between the commodity relations of freedom and slavery.

By definition, therefore, the wages of the most degraded free man imaginable had to be enough to sustain his rights at home. That was an antislavery article of faith. Abolitionists were far more preoccupied with depicting the squalor of slave cabins and the brutality of involuntary servitude than with charting the wages of free labor. Yet they not only admitted that poverty existed and that wages fluctuated with supply and demand, they also agreed that paying a "small pittance" for a man's labor was not "just or equal." As Garrison wrote, "The absence of the necessaries of life is indeed a sore calamity." Still, he claimed that the poorest hireling was better off than the slave. "Wretched, however, as is his lot . . . he is still a man – still a freeman . . . still the owner of his own body . . . still a husband." Abolitionists argued that while slaves were stripped of both the fruits of their labor and household rights, it was as much the birthright of all free men to claim property in their wives and children as in themselves and their wages. Regarding the freedman, they prophesied, "his earnings would be his . . . his comforts would be his – his wife, his children would be his; the apprehension of forcible separation would depart."[11] Unlike the bondsman, the hireling could count himself free because the sale of his labor entitled him to be master at home.

That theory had been handed down from none other than Adam Smith, who was preoccupied not simply with the question of wages

[10] "Chattel Slavery and Wages Slavery," *Liberator*, October 1, 1847; C. Peter Ripley, ed., *The Black Abolitionist Papers. Volume 4; The United States, 1847–1848* (Chapel Hill, 1991), 247. See also George Fitzhugh, *Sociology for the South, or the Failure of Free Society* (New York, 1965; orig. pub. 1854); David R. Roediger, *The Wages of Whiteness: Race and the Making of the American Working Class* (London, 1991), 83.

[11] "Slavery Better than Poverty?" *Liberator*, December 24, 1841; "Birney's Responses," *Emancipator*, August 1835. Though not addressing the issue of home life, the following are informative: Jonathan A. Glickstein, " 'Poverty Is Not Slavery': American Abolitionists and the Competitive Labor Market," *Antislavery Reconsidered: New Perspectives on the Abolitionists*, ed. Lewis Perry and Michael Fellman (Baton Rouge, 1979), 195–218; Eric Foner, *Politics and Ideology in the Age of the Civil War* (New York, 1980), 34–53.

but with the economic and moral differences between free labor and
slavery. In propounding free market doctrine, Smith postulated that
commodity relations and family bonds were wholly congruent – that
the traffic in free labor must inevitably support the customary dependencies of the household; otherwise, hirelings would not differ
from slaves. He emphasized that free men toiling at the most brutish
drudgery were elevated far above the slave's "miserable life," for
they were "paid for the work they do" and had "also the liberty of
marriage." Indeed, Smith theorized that the wage bought men their
liberty as husbands: like other forms of property ownership, it constituted the economic basis of a man's rights at home. "Especially in
the lower ranks," he wrote, the wife owed her "maintenance . . .
intirely to her husband, and from this dependence it is that she is
thought to be bound to be faithfull and constant to him." Conversely, a male slave could cohabit with a female slave but never
assert claim to her person or service because she was "not maintained by his labour . . . nor any way supported." For Smith a principal reward of the free labor contract was a husband's right to maintain a dependent wife.[12]

Yet Smith's wage doctrine was not without ambiguities. *The
Wealth of Nations* offered three disparate conceptions of the wage.
First, Smith defined it as equivalent, in some measure, to the wealth
produced by labor, an idea indebted to the labor theory of property. In the "original state," he explained, the whole product was
labor's "natural recompense," but with the onset of land and capital accumulation, the whole was divided up into rent, profit, and
wages, and labor's recompense decreased. Analytically, however, the
wage still signified a property right in the fruits of toil and suggested rough equity in the shares of landlord, capitalist, and labor.
Second, Smith defined the wage simply as labor's price as a commodity, a cost determined by supply and demand. Following Daniel
Defoe, who observed in 1704 that wages "rise and fall as . . . the
employers and the workmen, balance one another," Smith wrote
that the "market price" of labor, like other goods, was set by competitive bargaining regulated by "the proportion between the quantity which is actually brought to the market, and the demand."
Third, Smith defined the wage in terms of family survival – the
amount necessary to "continue the race of journeymen and servants."[13]

[12] Adam Smith, *Lectures on Jurisprudence,* ed. R.L. Meek, D.D. Raphael, and P.G. Stein
(Oxford, 1978; orig. pub. 1763), 178, 191, 178.
[13] Adam Smith, *An Inquiry in the Nature and Causes of the Wealth of Nations,* ed. Edwin
Cannan (New York, 1937; orig. pub. 1776), 64–66, 56, 57, 80. Defoe quoted in
Michael Wermel, *The Evolution of Classical Wage Theory* (New York, 1938), 24.

In Smith's political economy, perpetuating the stock of labor out-ranked the primacy of supply and demand as a law of wages. Differing with earlier economic thinkers, he eschewed poverty as a spur to labor and held that wages could not fall below the cost of family subsistence, that they depended on both the cost of necessaries and the state of the labor market. "A man must always live by his work," he declared, "and his wages must at least be sufficient to maintain him. They must even upon most occasions be somewhat more; otherwise it would be impossible for him to bring up a family, and the race of such workmen could not last beyond the first generation." Smith presumed a sexual division of labor entailing the wife's "attendance on the children," and he advocated "liberal" wages to foster "the marriage and multiplication of labourers." And he insisted that free men must be compensated differently than slaves – on the basis of family subsistence, not individual "wear and tear" – yet he also argued that hirelings were more frugal than slave masters and that free labor was "cheaper in the end" than slavery. He found it too "tedious" to compute the cash needed for family support; but he moralized that this was the least sum "consistent with common humanity." Considerations of wealth, freedom, and ethics thus fused in Smith's teaching on the rewards of wage labor and home life.[14]

Well before Smith's time, theorists of the wage had assumed that a man must earn enough to maintain a family, incorporating gender relations into their analysis of economic law. Writing in the seventeenth century, Sir William Petty claimed that wages were determined by what men needed "to live, labour, and generate." Locke reasoned that a man's wages must at least "make him live" and "maintain himself and family by his labor." In the nineteenth century Smith's followers on both sides of the Atlantic continued to reason in this way. For all of these economists, the wage retained multiple meanings. It was a token of exchange, the *quid pro quo* for free labor. It signified labor's price, its money value in a market economy. It also stood for labor's share of the wealth created under capitalist forms of industry. Adherents of strict Manchester doctrine claimed that labor was paid from a "wage fund," a sum of wealth saved by employers; innovators argued that wages came from ongoing industry, varying not with the fund of accumulated capital but with the extent of present production. But none disputed the tenet that a man's wages, as John Stuart Mill wrote, must support "himself, a wife, and a number of children."[15]

[14] Smith, *Wealth of Nations*, 67–68, 80, 81, 74.
[15] Petty quoted in Karl Marx, *Capital*, trans. Ben Fowkes (3 vols., New York, 1977; orig. pub. 1867), 1: 430; Locke quoted in Wermel, *Classical Wage Theory*, 26, and see pp.

Even the most dismal of the classical writers on free market society presupposed that the wage must maintain family life. Thomas Malthus disagreed with Smith that common humanity precluded labor's price from falling below this level, bleakly observing that it had not yet stopped "premature mortality" due to starvation. In Malthus's view, it was simply supply and demand that fixed wages high enough to maintain a stationary population. David Ricardo was just as matter-of-fact. Affirming that wages must be left to market competition like other commercial contracts, he granted that they would drop as population increased. Yet he held that labor's "natural price" must allow hirelings to "perpetuate their race" and that it reflected the price of "necessaries and conveniences required for the support of the labourer and his family." Though the classical "iron law" of wages dictated that the market's free play would push wages down to the barest subsistence level, it also presumed the necessity of home life to produce and reproduce free labor as a commodity.[16]

American economists echoed this doctrine. One of the earliest and most influential restatements was Francis Wayland's *The Elements of Political Economy,* a treatise first published in 1837, which went through many editions. Wayland stressed that wages did not vary with family size and that members of very large laboring households risked starving. Nonetheless, he declared that "physiological laws" defined the "natural minimum" of wages as a sum adequate to keep "the species" from extinction – adequate at least for a "virtuous and frugal" laborer to "support himself and wife, and two children."[17] In both emergent and advanced industrial economies, the principle of natural wages was rooted in the conception of natural household dependencies.

From liberal political economy, therefore, Yankee apostles of free labor drew the lesson that men's wages reconciled the worlds of market and home. Classical wage doctrine underpinned the antislavery image of the hireling as master of a household who sold his labor to pay for maintaining his wife and children. Smith was not fully

14–31, 48–64, 126, 132, 140–41; John Stuart Mill, *Principles of Political Economy with Some of Their Applications to Social Philosophy* (New York, 1965; orig. pub. 1848), 450, 401. For a contrasting analysis, which underscores not an intellectual tradition, dating from the Enlightenment, that linked wages to the needs of hireling men and their families but rather the newness of such wage doctrine in the late nineteenth century, see Lawrence B. Glickman, *A Living Wage: American Workers and the Making of Consumer Society* (Ithaca, 1997), 51–53, 57–77.

16 Thomas R. Malthus, *Principles of Political Economy Considered with a View to Their Practical Application* (2nd ed., New York, 1968; orig. pub. 1836), 222, 223; David Ricardo, *The Principles of Political Economy and Taxation* (London, 1965; orig. pub. 1817), 52. See also Wermel, *Classical Wage Theory.*

17 Francis Wayland, *The Elements of Political Economy* (Boston, 1852), 292, 294, 193.

consistent in his views on domestic economy and female labor, for he affirmed the tenet of male support but also stated that the "labour of the husband and wife together" must earn enough for the family, leaving unclear whether both unpaid housework and wage work counted as earning value for the household. Yet his successors unequivocally equated the natural wage solely with the sale of male labor. Though aware that theory and fact – natural and market prices – did not always correspond, they considered such cases aberrations rather than chronic features of the market. According to Francis Amasa Walker, an American authority on the wage economy in the late nineteenth century, there was an inexorable rule "in all states of human society" enjoining men to the "support of one adult female." And the theory was that above all in the United States, "where political freedom and social ambition exist," the hireling would "gladly deny himself the wages his wife might earn, in order that she may 'keep the house' " – that his own labor would sell for enough to establish a boundary between his home and the market.[18]

This economic theory did not simply shape antislavery defenses of the wage contract before and after slave emancipation; it underlay both the bourgeois ideal of separate spheres and labor agitation for a family wage dating from the early nineteenth century. By the Gilded Age, a remarkably wide range of commentators who addressed the issue of growing class inequality agreed that a free man's wages should at least maintain his family intact and his wife at home. As the minister Joseph Cook warned in one of his famous Boston Monday Lectures in 1878, "if our institutions are to endure," labor's price must equal the "cost of producing labor," a price that "ought to include the expense of keeping wives at home to take care of little children." Legal doctrine was exceptional in giving no recognition to this ideal of exchange, for at law the wage meant neither a normative natural price nor a property right, but merely a sale price ruled by contract. Yet social theorists who excluded moral precepts from their understanding of free market relations nonetheless presumed a male breadwinner who sustained the private domain. "In a free state," wrote Smith's disciple William Graham Sumner, "every man is held and expected to take care of himself and his family." Implicit in this domestic duty was the premise that men could fulfill it by dint of their wages as well as by other forms of wealth.[19]

---

[18] Smith, *Wealth of Nations*, 68; Francis Amasa Walker, *First Lessons in Political Economy* (New York, 1889), 257; Francis Amasa Walker, *Political Economy* (New York, 1883), 296; Francis Amasa Walker, *The Wages Question: A Treatise on Wages and the Wages Class* (New York, 1876), 126.

[19] Joseph Cook, *Boston Monday Lectures. Labor, with Preludes on Current Events* (Boston, 1880), 226, 228; William Graham Sumner, *What Social Classes Owe to Each Other*

Even the charity reformers who viewed dependence on alms as a
crime believed that the price of men's labor must support dependency within the home, that the natural wage was a rule as fixed as
supply and demand. "It may . . . be assumed," announced the New
York Association for Improving the Condition of the Poor in 1870,
"that every able-bodied man in this country may support himself and
family comfortably." Those most opposed to giving alms to starving
men, who insisted on the exchange of forced labor for charity, insisted that the wage bargain must enable the hireling to maintain his
household. As Josephine Shaw Lowell argued, "if he cannot do this,
there is something radically wrong with us."[20]

Following slave emancipation, therefore, in both the North and
the South, home life came to represent the proving ground of free
contract relations. But differences of region and race affected how
Yankees promulgated this worldview. The promise of inviolable family bonds issued to former slaves did not carry with it the corollary
that men alone should sell their labor for a wage. In the blunt words
of one freedpeople's schoolbook, "All the members of your family
have heretofore been accustomed to work in the field. . . . The father, mother, and children together have toiled the livelong day. At
present this cannot be changed." This was hardly the image of separate spheres ascendant in the North – an image in which every man,
no matter the "scanty remuneration for his daily labors," was re-
warded by the "bliss of home" unqualified by commodity relations,
by his status as "lord of such a paradise" where his wife presided
with "soothing kindness" to "sweeten his labors," by his absolute
right to her housework. Since the rise of abolitionism, white citizens
had been taught that a fundamental difference between freedom
and slavery lay not simply in home life but in women's place at
home.[21]

In August 1883, when far-reaching congressional hearings on the
wage system were convened in New York City, the inquiry began with

(New York, 1972; orig. pub. 1883), 39. See also Christopher G. Tiedeman, *A Treatise
on the Limitations of Police Power in the United States Considered from Both a Civil and
Criminal Standpoint* (St. Louis, 1886), 571; Martha May, "Bread before Roses: Workingmen, Labor Unions and the Family Wage," in *Women, Work and Protest: A Century
of U.S. Women's Labor History*, ed. Ruth Milkman (Boston, 1985), 1–21; Alice Kessler-
Harris, *A Woman's Wage: Historical Meanings and Social Consequences* (Lexington, Ky.,
1990), 6–32.

[20] *Twenty-Seventh Annual Report of the New York Association for Improving the Condition of
the Poor* (New York, 1870), 69; *Seventeenth Annual Report of the New York State Board of
Charities* (New York, 1884), 160–61.

[21] Rev. I.W. Brinkerhoff, *Advice to Freedmen* in *Freedmen's Schools and Textbooks,* ed. Robert C. Morris (6 vols., New York, 1980; orig. pub. 1864–65), 4: 29–30; *Universalist
and Ladies' Repository,* April 19, 1834, quoted in Cott, *Bonds of Womanhood,* 69–70.

a journey into the homes of the laboring classes. For two days the investigating committee explored the tenement districts, walking through streets where factories abutted living quarters, stopping to question storekeepers about the price of groceries. But the principal concern, as the legislators told their guide, was that "you get us into the houses." Inside the many tenement dwellings they visited, they took stock of the rooms, furniture, utensils, and food, and they asked about wages and household expenses – with the object of discovering the condition of "the people who really live by their labor." The burgeoning of state investigation into the labor question in the late nineteenth century led directly to the study of proletarian home life.[22]

The groundwork for the congressional expedition had been laid a decade earlier in the surveys into working-class existence conducted by the Massachusetts Bureau of Labor Statistics. By this time, tenement life was a well-established field of inquiry. Since the early nineteenth century, reformers and government officials had explored the world of the laboring poor for purposes varying from religious salvation to public health to scientific charity. Simultaneously, the tenement sketch became a popular literary genre. So commonplace had tours of the tenements grown that some inhabitants, noted the Massachusetts bureau in 1875, "betrayed an indisposition to have their private life inquired into." Like other investigators, the bureau depicted a world of astonishing wretchedness. "You that are incredulous of the narrative," it challenged, "go, look, be nauseated, be convinced." But the bureau studies differed from others in focusing on labor. "To some extent there is now a distribution of wealth, through the wage system," declared the bureau in 1871; "how meager the share of some, can be seen by visiting the tenement houses."[23] In the tenements the bureau examined neither the moral character of the poor nor the environmental determinants of morality, but rather the wage system's effects on laboring households.

Just as Massachusetts was first to apply the lessons of slave eman-

---

[22] U.S. Congress, Senate, *Report of the Committee of the Senate upon the Relations between Capital and Labor* (5 vols., Washington, D.C., 1885), 1: 94. See also William R. Brock, *Investigation and Responsibility: Public Responsibility in the United States, 1865–1900* (New York, 1984), esp. pp. 88–115, 148–84. On the development of professional social science in the United States, see Thomas L. Haskell, *The Emergence of Professional Social Science* (Urbana, 1977); Mary O. Furner, *Advocacy and Objectivity: A Crisis in the Professionalization of American Social Science, 1865–1905* (Lexington, Ky., 1975). See also Joan Wallach Scott, *Gender and the Politics of History* (New York, 1988), 112–38.

[23] Massachusetts Bureau of Statistics of Labor, *Sixth Annual Report* (1875), 202; Massachusetts Bureau of Statistics of Labor, *Second Annual Report,* (1871), 528, 551. On antebellum tenement investigation, see Christine Stansell, *City of Women: Sex and Class in New York, 1789–1860* (New York, 1986), 193–203.

cipation regarding dependency and forced labor in the North, so it
was also first to duplicate the scrutiny of ex-slave homes in Yankee
dwellings in order to test the promise of free labor against the realities of laboring life. But different groups of reformers pursued these
northern variants of emancipation policy. While abolitionists-turned-
charity officials rewrote the poor law, labor reformers acting as statisticians inaugurated the Commonwealth's inquiry into the relation
between home life and wage labor. The first deputy chief of the
Massachusetts Bureau of Labor Statistics was the radical labor advocate George McNeill; its titular head was the elderly Boston Brahmin
Henry K. Oliver, a onetime factory superintendent who sympathized
with labor reform. In its first report of 1870 the bureau stated its
objective of exploring "The Wage System and Its Results," starting
with the "Homes of Low-Paid Laborers in the City of Boston."[24]
While for Yankee missionaries in the South the cabins of freedpeople
measured their progress out of slavery, for the bureau the home was
the testing ground for the wage system in the North.

During three days in December 1869 the bureau's staff explored
the Boston tenement district, inspecting premises inhabited by immigrants and nativeborn, and by whites and blacks. The intent was
not to search into *"private affairs, from motives of mere curiosity,"* but
instead to gather empirical data "upon the great question of Labor."
The investigators compiled inventories of destitute rooms with only
a few sticks of furniture, which were sometimes "a marvel of neatness" but usually were only as clean as "could be expected." In an
English couple's single room, typical of many others, there was "one
bed, two old tables, four old chairs out of repair, a stove, a few
cooking utensils, and tubs." The tenement inspection yielded
"dreadful pictures . . . of want and degradation" – of households
like those of "fellow-laborers in London."

Here, as well as there, will be found, in the labyrinthal slums of cities, in
narrow courts, dark lanes, and nasty alleys, wretched tenements . . . packed
full of men, women, and children, as thick as smoked herrings in a grocer's
box. Here they breed, here they live (!), and here they die.

Boston's many "low-paid laborers" were too poor, the bureau concluded, to have "a home of decency and comfort."[25]
The evidence gathered in the tenement home visits was of free

[24] Massachusetts Bureau of Statistics of Labor, *First Annual Report* (1870), 158, 164.
See also Dumas Malone, ed., *Dictionary of American Biography* (20 vols., New York,
1936), 14: 18–19, 12: 150; James Leiby, *Carroll Wright and Labor Reform: The Origin
of Labor Statistics* (Cambridge, Mass., 1960).
[25] Massachusetts Bureau of Statistics of Labor, *First Annual Report*, 25, 168, 173, 170,
35, 88, 182.

labor in crisis. More often than not, the bureau found that the husband's pay was so low that the wife also worked for wages, a revelation in conflict with prevailing notions of the link between contract freedom and northern home life. Thus in the household with the four broken chairs, the husband earned only $1.25 a day as a common laborer and the wife took in washing. According to the bureau, this domestic economy was as standard within the tenement houses as poor food and furniture: while the men, when they could find employment, worked in jobs ranging from common labor to furniture making, their wives mostly went out scrubbing or took in laundry, which hung all over the rooms drying. In such families, reported the bureau, "No cheerful smile greets a returning father whose six days' earnings pay for but five days' meat." Rather, poverty destroyed domesticity. It "kills love and all affection, all pride of home . . . nay, emasculates home of all its quickening powers." On returning home, the "hapless father, seeking rest and comfort after toil, and finding neither, takes to the loafing spots of the streets . . . and the high road of ruin is opened before him." The bureau's most striking tenement images were of wives "toiling at wash-tub and iron board" for other families and of men whose wages left them destitute of home life.[26]

Not only did this study of the wage system differ from other tenement surveys, it belied assumptions about the natural reciprocities of the free market. Unlike many metropolitan investigators, the bureau ascribed family disorder to poverty, not the reverse. And it openly condemned the fact that the sale price of all men's labor did not enable wives to attend to the "duties of the household . . . indicated by the whole family relation." Unlike Yankee witnesses to free labor in the postbellum South, the bureau adhered strictly to the classical wage doctrine that defined men as family breadwinners and women as dependents, using this as a standard for assessing social conditions in Boston. It averred that "under a proper organization of society," the workingman "would accrue such recompense of his daily toil, as would secure the family comfort from his earnings alone." It pointed to the homes of the low-paid laborers, stating that something was "radically wrong" with the exchange relations generated by the wage system. "The people in all the places we visited," the bureau observed, "barely live."[27]

Subsequent bureau studies threw into further question the harmony between wage labor and home life and the free man's untrammeled rights in a dependent wife and children. Repeatedly, the bureau affirmed that a man's wages should support his "whole family"

[26] Ibid., 170, 161, 163, 178.   [27] Ibid., 179, 158, 178.

and that his wife's "appropriate place and duties are at home." But its empirical research disclosed the opposite – that the market in free labor often absorbed entire households, changing "homes into houses." The bureau's statistical data showed that in the early 1870s a Massachusetts family of four to five persons could survive on about $700 a year, but that men's average yearly wages amounted to less than $600, while those of unskilled men had dropped to $433.90. "Not in Boston alone are . . . miserable homes to be found," reported the bureau in 1873. Especially among the "great army" of unskilled, "But for the aid of wife and children at the wash-tub or in the mill, absolute want would stare them in the face."[28]

The 1871 report featured a telling colloquy between bureau investigators and a mule spinner about the conditions of domestic economy – "an inside view of operative life at home." The mule spinner could be said to stand for all hireling men who had lost property in their wives' labor. He testified that his wife also worked in the mill, and therefore he did much of the cooking and cleaning.

For breakfast we manage thus: I get up at 5 o'clock and . . . get the meal ready. . . . I get home at 7 o'clock, and help along supper until she gets home. . . . I generally lay in bed until about 7 o'clock Sundays. . . . [T]hen it takes wife and me about all the time to wash, clean and scrub up the house.

Incredulous that a man would have to do housework, the bureau asked, "Is this the common way in which operatives in your town live?" The mule spinner replied, "Yes . . . those that have wives that go to the mill." With respect to the hireling man such as this, the bureau concluded, "really he has no home. He goes to a dreary house . . . where neither brilliant light, nor glowing warmth, nor well-dressed wife, nor carpet . . . allure."[29]

Though the bureau's staff was changed in 1873 amid mounting controversy over its ties to labor radicalism, its surveys of home life continued to challenge free labor assumptions. The new bureau chief was Carroll Wright, a statistician who had practiced law and served as a state senator and whose sympathies lay more with elite social science than with labor reform. Yet Wright's bureau reiterated

---

[28] Massachusetts Bureau of Statistics of Labor, *Second Annual Report* (1871), 533; Massachusetts Bureau of Statistics of Labor, *Third Annual Report* (1872), 340; Massachusetts Bureau of Statistics of Labor, *Second Annual Report*, 533; Massachusetts Bureau of Statistics of Labor, *Fourth Annual Report* (1873), 107, 108. On the wage and family budget statistics, see Massachusetts Bureau of Statistics of Labor, *Second Annual Report*, 445, 417; Massachusetts Bureau of Statistics of Labor, *Fourth Annual Report*, 116, 85, 93; Massachusetts Bureau of Statistics of Labor, *Third Annual Report*, 341.

[29] Ibid., *Second Annual Report*, 476, 477, 540.

that a man's labor should sell for enough to maintain his family and that wives' wage labor was "the most harmful wrong." In 1874 it conducted a thoroughgoing inquiry into the "Condition of Workingmen's Families," visiting 397 homes across the state, examining wages, living quarters, diet, and the cost of food, clothing, rent, and other necessities – a study designed to "satisfy the most exacting students of social economy." Reflecting the fall in prices caused by the onset of economic depression in 1873, this study showed that a family of five could now live on about $600 a year, but that the average yearly wages of all men were only $574.89 and that unskilled men made as little as $221 a year. "If it were not for the labor of women and children, the wives and offspring of laboring men," the bureau found, "the average laborer could not make the ends of the year meet." The most exacting methods of social-scientific inquiry indicated that men's labor did not sell for a natural price.[30]

But the bureau hardly adopted the stance of scientific objectivity; rather, its perspective was explicitly moral, reflecting the antislavery ideal that all men were entitled to be masters of a family of dependent persons. For the bureau, the wage contract's virtue turned on whether the market price of men's labor ensured this household right. "It seems natural and just that a man's labor should be worth, and that his wages should be, as much as, with economy and prudence, will comfortably maintain himself and family," the bureau declared. "The broad and pertinent inquiry is, Does the wage system, as now existing in the world, do what is acknowledged is 'natural and just' and right?" In this inquiry slavery served as a negative standard of measure. Precisely because bondage provided for the slave's "bodily wants," free labor must assure a greater award. A man's pay should not force "him to overwork his wife with home and outside duties" or to still by his children's wages "their cries for bread," the bureau claimed. "It is plain that there is an error in that price and form of labor that will not permit a man to support his family without drawing on the vital powers of those to whom we must look to make his place good." This landmark government study did not go so far as to question the wage system's perpetuity. But it did find that existing commodity relations thwarted home life – that wage labor "unsexed men and women" and threatened "coming generations" by drawing whole families into the labor market – and

[30] Ibid., *Sixth Annual Report* (1875), 193, 183, 192, 380, 359, 338, 108. See also Daniel Horowitz, *The Morality of Spending: Attitudes toward the Consumer Society in America, 1875–1940* (Baltimore, 1985), ch. 2; David Montgomery, *The Fall of the House of Labor: The Workplace, the State, and American Labor Activism, 1865–1925* (New York, 1987), 136.

it looked to enlightened public opinion and, more heretically, even to legislation to enforce a natural wage.[31]

Other state labor bureaus followed in the path of Massachusetts, entering inside homes to assess the wage system. In 1882 the Illinois bureau surveyed Chicago families and reported that the difference between men's wages and the minimum cost of subsistence was "painfully apparent from the tenements they occupy, the clothes they wear, and the food and fuel they consume." A year later it examined over two thousand households in Illinois in order to reveal "in statistical form, the effect of the wage system." Not only did it show that a family of four to five persons needed $550 a year to live, but that men's wages averaged only $525.27 and wives and children, who were naturally "dependents," had to be "contributors" to family income. Its investigators also peered into pots and larders, inspected furnishings, measured the size and cleanliness of rooms, and witnessed everyday existence, which they often described as a "miserable affair altogether" as they recorded what they had seen, heard, and smelled. "This minute catalogue," explained the bureau, "portrays more vividly than any mere array of figures can the common current of daily life among the people." During the 1880s the New York bureau collected similar data. It focused on Manhattan tenement apartments that were also sweatshops, where husbands, wives, and children did wage work in the same rooms in which they lived. These homes, noted one bureau member, were "horrible rookeries."[32]

The 1883 congressional investigation into the wage system took statesmen on the same tenement tour as the bureau statisticians; and inside the government chambers where they conducted hearings their questions also turned from the equity of wages – "Do workingmen of the country . . . think that they get a fair share of the wealth they produce?" – to circumstances at home. They asked how laborers lived, what they ate, the kind of beds they slept in, the state of their dwellings. They pressed for the intimate details of domestic life, not from prurient curiosity but as a way to gauge what a man's labor was actually worth. "We desire to know the condition of the laboring men," the congressional examiners declared, "the adequacy of the compensation . . . for the support of their families, the

[31] Massachusetts Bureau of Statistics of Labor, *Sixth Annual Report*, 193, 194, 108, 109, 108.
[32] Illinois Bureau of Labor Statistics, *Second Biennial Report* (1883), 288, 289; Illinois Bureau of Labor Statistics, *Third Biennial Report* (1884), 137, 331–33, 255, 269, 370, 357; New York Bureau of Labor Statistics, *Third Annual Report* (1886), 175. See also New York Bureau of Labor Statistics, *Second Annual Report* (1885), 146–81.

manner in which they live, the houses they occupy, and all the facts."
Listing their expenses – meat at 20 cents a pound, a few "squalid
tenement" rooms at 15 dollars a month – laboring men answered
that wages were "[n]ot at all sufficient for a man of family."[33]

Testimony that hireling men could not afford to marry had far
more impact than claims that they did not earn the real value of
their labor. The committee's encounter with one telegraph operator,
himself a single man, exemplified how the hearings unfolded:

Q. . . . Do you consider the rates of compensation received by operators adequate for their reasonable and comfortable support? – A. No, sir; not taking
into account the value of their services and the length of hours that they are
required to work.

Q. Well, is the amount of money which they receive sufficient to furnish a
man a comfortable house, good lodging, food, and clothing, and the other
ordinary comforts of civilized life? – A. Yes, if he denies himself the privileges
of nature and remains in single blessedness all his days. . . .

Q. You think it is entirely inadequate to support a family?

A. Entirely so. . . . [A]s to the support of a family, families can *exist*, of course,
on a very small amount of money. . . . Telegraph operators as a rule are
single men. . . .

Q. You speak of the operators as a rule being unmarried. . . . Do you attribute that fact, to any great extent, to the inadequacy of their pay? – A. Yes, sir;
I should think that that had great influence on their condition in that respect.

As workingmen spoke of the dissonance between the wage system
and marriage, the committee grew attentive. "What I want to know
is the actual fact; are there few or many married men among the
operators?" asked one examiner. Was it due to "an indisposition"
or "economical reasons why they should be reluctant to assume that
relation?" Always the reply was poor wages, and the reluctance was
allegedly widespread. For example, bakers, a very low-paid group,
were often "unmarried, for the reason that their limited incomes do
not permit them to marry." Reputedly, even skilled craftsmen did
not marry due to "prudential motives." As one Boston printer
stated, "I find in a great many instances that they do not take unto
themselves helpmeets, being afraid to incur the responsibilities of
married life." Though, in fact, the likelihood of men raising families
did not vary strictly with their wages, the marriage rate did fall
sharply during the depression of the 1870s. Ample evidence con-

---

[33] U.S. Congress, Senate, *Relations between Capital and Labor* 1: 683, 315, 570, 569, 144.

fronted the committee of family life undercut by free market relations.[34]

The investigation elicited many tales of husbands whose wage dependence rendered their rights at home uncertain. These men
hardly seemed like lords of a domestic paradise. "What is the social
air about the ordinary machinist's house?" the committee asked.
"Are there evidences of happiness and joy and hilarity?" The witness
responded that most machinists, after working with files and chisels
for ten hours a day, "were pretty well played out when they come
home, and the first thing they think of is having something to eat
and sitting down, and resting, and then of striking a bed." But he
continued, "instead of a pleasant house it is every day expecting to
lose his job . . . his wages being pulled down . . . and staring starvation in the face makes him feel sad, and the head of the house being
sad, of course the whole family are the same, so the house looks like
a dull prison instead of a home." Again and again, often citing labor
bureau statistics as authority, workingmen testified that most men of
their class could not support a family on their own, and that even
the price of the whole family's labor was barely enough. With regard
to Massachusetts textile operatives, one witness explained that "even
when their wives have gone to work in a mill . . . they have seemed
to go down-hill entirely, wear poor clothes, and have to stint themselves in many things." Others explained that only the best-paid
craftsmen, such as puddlers, who earned $3.50 a day, had "home
comforts" – good food, clothes, furniture, more rooms, carpets, and
wives who kept house.[35]

As noteworthy as labor's testimony were the committee's questions. Two decades earlier the Freedmen's Inquiry Commission had
interrogated freedmen about home life under slavery, while Yankee
liberators had inspected their cabins for signs of moral and material
improvement. So, too, did the congressional inquiry into the wage
system concentrate on the home. Yet it produced evidence at odds

---

[34] Ibid., 143–44, 150, 194–95, 118, 437, 42, and see pp. 41–49. See also Massachusetts
Bureau of Statistics of Labor, *Sixth Annual Report,* 359; Illinois Bureau of Labor
Statistics, *Second Biennial Report,* 292–93; Carroll Wright, *A Report on Marriage and
Divorce in the United States, 1867 to 1886; Including an Appendix Relating to Marriage
and Divorce in Certain Countries in Europe* (Washington, D.C., 1889), 135–36.

[35] U.S. Congress, Senate, *Relations between Labor and Capital* 1: 758–59, 20–21, and see
pp. 59, 488–89, 570; U.S. Congress, Senate, *Relations between Labor and Capital* 3:
488. See also Lizabeth A. Cohen, "Embellishing a Life of Labor: An Interpretation
of the Material Culture of American Working-Class Homes, 1885–1915," in *Labor
Migration in the Atlantic Economy: The European and American Working Classes during the
Period of Industrialization,* ed. Dirk Hoerder (Westport, Conn., 1985), 321–52; Dor-
ethee Schneider, " 'For Whom Are All the Good Things in Life?': German-
American Housewives Discuss Their Budgets," in *German Workers in Industrial Chicago,* ed. Hartmut Keil and John B. Jentz (Dekalb, 1983), 145–60.

with the assurances confidently put forward in the era of slave emancipation that free market relations safeguarded family life. Like the
state labor bureau studies, the congressional inquiry came to document how free labor was destroying the household's natural dependencies.

In the tenements, government investigators discovered that the
freedom of northern hirelings was far from secure – that is, if, as in
antislavery thought, the home was viewed as a crucial measure of
freedom for men who owned nothing but their own labor. The
home was the place, the laboratory, where the contract rights of
work and marriage could be tested simultaneously. Well before the
turn of the century, when women reformers in settlement houses
shocked the public by mapping the suffering of families not fully
supported by the sale of men's labor, this ground was surveyed by
government social science that had been shaped at its formative moment by labor reform.[36] Homes of only one room with a few pieces
of broken furniture, which were gloomy as a prison, did not much
resemble the antislavery vision of family life. Nor for men like the
mule spinner, who did housework before dawn because his wife also
worked in the mill, did the wages of free labor afford a family "not
marketable."

The plantations of the Old South were worlds away from the Yankee
tenement houses of the Gilded Age, but the horror that filled abolitionist writing on home life under slavery echoed powerfully in
northern labor reform after the war. As well as putting their interior
lives on display, hireling men carried out their own inquiries into
the relationship between wage labor and family existence; they supplied the grist for public investigation and directly influenced its
categories of analysis. Yet their interpretation was distinctive in point-
ing to inevitable conflict between the wage contract and family
bonds. In their view, the fusion of household and market that increasingly characterized hireling home life in the North was indistin-
guishable from slavery.

This was the viewpoint set forth by Samuel Gompers in his 1881
indictment of cigar making in tenement dwellings in New York City.
Like clothing sweatshops, the tenement cigar shops infamously fused
home and work. But the cigar shops were of very recent vintage,
emerging not at the rise of industrial transformation early in the

---

[36] See Kathryn Kish Sklar, *Florence Kelley and the Nation's Work: The Rise of Women's
Political Culture, 1830–1900* (New Haven, 1995); Sonya Michel and Seth Koven,
"Womanly Duties: Maternalist Politics and the Origins of Welfare States in France,
Germany, Great Britain, and the United States, 1880–1920," *American Historical
Review,* 95 (October 1990), 1076–1108.

century, but in the 1870s, when a new device, the cigar mold, allowed employers to split up the craft into unskilled tasks and enlist
whole families, most of them Bohemian immigrants, to prepare the
tobacco and make cigars at home. In a series of essays titled "The
Curse of Tenement-House Cigar Manufacture," printed in labor
newspapers in both German and English, Gompers documented the
misery of these families in order to promote state abolition of this
labor system. He presented scenes reminiscent of antislavery tracts –
scenes of filthy, crude living quarters, and of households menaced
by commodity production. But in Gompers's portrait the family was
not sacrificed on the altar of chattel slavery, but "to the Moloch of
wage slavery."[37]

Gompers was nothing but forthright about the object of his tenement survey, which predated the formation of the New York labor
statistics bureau. He toured Manhattan's Lower East Side, where he
had grown up. He explained that the idea was to "see with our own
eyes . . . the rooms in which people live and work, are born and die."
Each cigar-making family, he reported, occupied two or three small
rooms, furnished with a table, a stove, a few wooden chairs, a bed,
and some cheap pictures; the hours of labor began before sunrise
and lasted far into the night; none but infants were exempt from
work; and the piece-rate wages for the entire family's labor hovered
at a meager subsistence level. But he also saw it as "his duty to drag
out of its dark hiding place . . . what a devouring, poisonous cancer
the pursuit of the almighty dollar, through exploitation, oppression,
and sacrifice of our fellow men, has created in our midst." For Gompers the tenement cigar shop epitomized the evils of free market
relations.[38]

To reveal how wage relations wholly contaminated the home,
Gompers focused on the dirtiness of the rooms and the work of
women. "The filth, stench of tobacco, etc. are nauseating," he wrote.
The tobacco lay everywhere, drying on the floor, spread over the
stove, stored in cans in the bedrooms, piled next to the beds: "always, in every room, tobacco, filth, and human beings, thrown together." These rooms did not represent refuges from the market in
labor; rather, inside them "husbands, wives, and children sit unceas-

[37] "A Translation of a Series of Articles by Samuel Gompers on Tenement-House
Cigar Manufacture in New York City" in *The Samuel Gompers Papers. Volume 1: The
Making of a Union Leader, 1850–86*, ed. Stuart B. Kaufman (Urbana, 1986), 172–
210, quotes at pp. 173, 185. See "Pestilence in the Cigar," *Workingman's Advocate*,
October 3, 1874 and October 10, 1874; Eileen Boris, " 'A Man's Dwelling House Is
His Castle': Tenement House Cigarmaking and the Judicial Imperative," in *Work
Engendered: Toward a New History of American Labor*, ed. Ava Baron (Ithaca, 1991),
114–41.
[38] "Gompers on Tenement-House Cigar Manufacture," 174, 181.

ingly at their work" and family bonds were eroded. "The 'shop' has completely taken over the living quarters. . . . [I]t is probably impossible to dream of anything but tobacco in this atmosphere." Gompers pictured the husband at night, still making cigars, "dressed in an undershirt, drawers, and apron." But the dominant images were of women and children. "In one room we saw a mother who had just begun to nurse her child but had not interrupted her work of making wrappers. That is how people work in these factories; not a moment must be lost – the mother with the babe at her breast." In another shop, on East Second Street, "a young woman was sitting at the worktable, rolling cigars with her hands, her feet rocking a cradle in which lay a baby: the poor child was sick, terribly emaciated, and its shrunken features seemed to say: 'How can I stay alive in such a place?' "[39]

These images were surely calculated to recall the appeals of antislavery. Indeed, Gompers presented the scene of the woman rolling cigars while rocking a cradle in a part of his survey titled "Slaves of the Tobacco Industry." Here he also despaired about family meals, illustrating how the food itself embodied the terms of bondage in the tenements. "The 'dinner' consisted . . . mainly of cooked or smoked sausage or something similar which does not need to be prepared first," he noted. "The housewife would lose too much valuable time cooking a meal; she has other work to do: making wrappers and rolling cigars." Elsewhere in the survey, sounding like Yankees outraged by chattel slaves' lack of a family table, he grieved that "time and again . . . meals were often taken at the worktable and during work," a situation reflecting "an existence beneath human dignity." The dirty rooms, the sick children, the uncooked food, the absence of family meals – all these figured as signs of the intrusion of commodity relations into northern homes, homes in which wage work defied free labor doctrine by allowing wives no time for housework.[40]

Images remindful of antislavery were central, too, in labor reform portrayals of workplaces separated from living quarters, where wives nonetheless toiled beside husbands whose labor sold for a price less than the cost of family subsistence. The condition of Hungarian immigrants in the Pennsylvania coke works violated the traditions of a "race of freemen," argued Terrence Powderly, the leader of the Knights of Labor. He explained that the women were not hired directly, yet they accompanied their menfolk to the coke ovens early each morning. Like an abolitionist, he was horrified by a labor system that extracted cash value from women who worked while partly

[39] Ibid., 180, 176, 182, 183, 185. [40] Ibid., 184, 187, 197.

naked and burdened with babies. "At one of the ovens, I saw a woman drawing the hot coke from the chamber. She had no covering on her head, and very little on her person. Her only attire consisted of a short, coarse chemise and a pair of cowhide boots. In a freight-car close by stood another woman forking the coke as it came to the car. . . . Her person from the waist up was exposed. When she stooped over to handle the coke, she caught her hair between her teeth to keep it out of her way. Her feet were incased in a pair of heavy shoes; her legs were exposed from the knees down. Her babe, which she had brought to the works with her, lay in front of the car." For all the differences between free labor in the coke works and slave labor in the cotton fields, Powderly's outcry paralleled abolitionist images of dehumanized slaves. But unlike radical abolitionism, it asserted race privilege in addition to free men's rights.[41]

Despite shared symbolism, then, there were fundamental differences between labor reform and antislavery understandings of the link between the wage contract and home life. These differences were longstanding, and expressed not simply diverging racial ideals but more polar views of the market in free labor. Since the rise of the labor movement its spokesmen had condemned market relations that slashed men's wages below the price of family subsistence and converted the labor of wives and children into commodities. Simultaneously they contended that poverty was a form of bondage – a claim that locked them in ideological battle with abolitionists. As a New York City tailor declared in 1860, wages were "so low that it requires a man and his wife and children should work very long hours . . . to enable them to drag out a miserable existence." Weaving together the themes of race, family, and commodity relations, arguing that the "condition of free white men" was a "state of slavery more infinitely galling and insupportable than that of the African negro," the tailor contrasted southern planters who maintained slave families to "Shylocks in the Free States" who "care not how many families they may ruin, so long as they can realize fortunes out of their blood and bones." Whereas abolitionists defended free labor as the bedrock of domesticity, hirelings argued that market relations made poor men's home life just as precarious as the slave's.[42]

Nor did labor reformers' protest against the abolitionist worldview abate with the downfall of slavery. To the contrary, as their denunci-

[41] George E. McNeil, ed., *The Labor Movement: The Problem of To-Day* (Boston, 1887), 421, 420.
[42] Henry Mullins, *A Voice from the Workshop* (New York, 1860), 8, 9, 10. Though the evidence cited in the text counters his claim that labor's critique of wage slavery crystallized only after slave emancipation, see, in regard to antebellum labor assertions of white supremacy, Roediger, *Wages of Whiteness*, 65–87.

ations of wage slavery intensified after the war, so too did their arguments that free labor was antagonistic to marriage and family life.
This was one of the main ideas taught by the Boston labor advocate
Ira Steward, who collaborated with George McNeill and whose outlook therefore stamped the early investigations of the Massachusetts
Bureau of Labor Statistics. In an 1865 pamphlet Steward enunciated
the hireling interpretation of the law of wages: "Because, fathers are
paid low wages they send their children . . . into factories and shops.
. . . Because, husbands are underpaid they consent that their wives
may crowd the labor market. . . . And because, single men are not
paid enough for their daily labor, they do not marry." Steward issued
a scathing critique of antislavery doctrine and the inequities of the
wage contract in an essay on "Poverty" that was published in the
1873 bureau report, along with statistical tables on wages and living
costs. "There is a closer relation between poverty and slavery," he
wrote, "than the average abolitionist ever recognized." He argued
that "wealth is the master and poverty is the slave of 'the great law
of supply and demand,' " and he emphasized the outcome on family
life. It was not necessary to have "studied Malthus and his theories"
to see that "little mouths are not properly fed," to understand that
poverty "decides marriages." Making palpable the "terrible equivalents" produced by labor's sale price, Steward offered a class analysis
of the dirty home that traced its unwholesome effluences far beyond
the tenement neighborhoods: "The dirt of the poor man's hovel is
the miasma of the rich man's parlor."[43]

What was new in this agitation about home life was the stress that
labor reformers in the postbellum era laid on dirt and housework in
conveying the plight of poor men and their families.[44] Perhaps this
reflected heightened public awareness of pestilence and sanitary
measures. But for laboring men the dirty home offered a particularly
vivid way of symbolizing their loss of both a domestic domain and
property in their wives's dependent labor, the very contract entitlements that, together with self ownership, defined men as free. And
it was a symbol that at once reflected and challenged the ascendant
reform view that the tidy home was a sign of the moral worth of both
the southern freedpeople and the northern poor. This symbol was

[43] Ira Steward, "A Reduction of Hours and Increase of Wages" (Boston, 1865), in *A Documentary History of American Industrial Society*, ed. John R. Commons (11 vols., Cleveland, 1910), 9: 300; Ira Steward, "Poverty," in Massachusetts Bureau of Statistics of Labor, *Fourth Annual Report* (1873), 411–39, quotes at pp. 411, 419, 415, 416, 411, 414. See also Glickstein, " 'Poverty Is Not Slavery' "; Foner, *Politics and Ideology*, 34–53.

[44] Antebellum labor advocates focused on family life and a male family wage, but not on housework. See Elizabeth Blackmar, *Manhattan for Rent, 1785–1850* (New York, 1989), 123–24.

the counterpart of images of mothers forking coke into freight cars and of tenement apartments where women rolled cigars and men worked in their underwear; it denoted the condition of families in which wives did no housework and husbands were not masters.

Labor advocates debated at length, "What Is Labor Worth?" and among themselves did not always agree about the answer. They studied the census and the data on wages and expenses collected by labor bureaus and trade union statisticians. Like other reformers, they affirmed the link between eating and working; as the preamble to the Knights of Labor constitution declared, "In the sweat of thy brow shalt thou eat bread." Yet laboring men quoted this biblical injunction to discredit not beggars' unearned alms but what they saw as capital's unearned profits, the taking of "Something for Nothing" that left labor "to starve in sight of the wealth it creates." Wages, they insisted, equaled no more than between a sixth and a tenth of the proceeds of industry, not nine-tenths, as liberal economists such as Edward Atkinson had calculated.[45] Invoking a labor theory of wealth, they demanded the "fruits of their labor," the "first reward," a "full share," and the "just and full value of labor." All of these formulas disputed the rule of supply and demand, but they also expressed varying ideals of a just alternative.[46]

A wealth of ambiguity lay in the claim that hirelings were entitled

---

[45] Knights of Labor, *Proceedings of the [Third] General Assembly* (Minneapolis, 1879), 150; "Something for Nothing," *Journal of United Labor,* July 1883; Ira Steward, "Wages and Wealth," Ira Steward Papers, Wisconsin State Historical Society; U.S. Congress, Senate, *Relations between Labor and Capital* 1: 760; "Labor and Law," *Locomotive Firemen's Magazine,* November 1884. See also "One-Sixth!" *National Labor Tribune,* February 1, 1877; "Our Neglected Interests," *National Labor Tribune,* October 17, 1874; "Whither Do We Travel?" *National Labor Tribune,* Dec 18, 1875; "The Crusade against Trade Unions," *Workingman's Advocate,* June 16, 1877; Edward Atkinson, "What Makes the Rate of Wages?" *Journal of Social Science Containing the Transactions of the American Association,* 19 (December 1884), 47–116, quotes at pp. 60, 96, 108; Edward Atkinson, *The Margin of Profits: How It Is Now Divided, What Part of the Present Hours of Labor Can Now Be Spared* (New York, 1887), 92–93; David A. Wells, *Recent Economic Changes* (New York, 1889), 406–22.

[46] "Danger Ahead," *National Labor Tribune,* October 30, 1875; G.K.H, "Trades' Unions. – II," *Workingman's Advocate,* May 26, 1866; "Declaration of Principles" of the Central Labor Union, *John Swinton's Paper,* October 14, 1883; "Tramps," *National Labor Tribune,* July 15, 1876. For recent assessments of wages, profits, and prices in this era, see James Livingston, "The Social Analysis of Economic History and Theory: Conjectures on Late Nineteenth-Century American Development," *American Historical Review,* 92 (February 1987), 93–137; Montgomery, *Fall of the House of Labor,* 47, 171–72; David M. Gordon, Richard Edwards, and Michael Reich, *Segmented Work, Divided Workers: The Historical Transformation of Labor in the United States* (New York, 1982), 95–96, 147; Howell J. Harris et al., "Symposium on the Fall of the House of Labor by David Montgomery," *Labor History,* 30 (Winter 1989), 93–137. My analysis is not intended to challenge the finding that aggregate real wages were rising during this era, but rather to highlight contemporaries' conflicting perspectives.

to the fruits of their labor. The most radical interpretation was that labor should earn all the value it created and that capital, as the socialist Albert Parsons argued, simply constituted "unpaid for labor." Yet the dominant idea among labor spokesmen was that wages represented a share, and wealth the "joint product" of labor and capital. Though some excluded rent and interest from the equation, most accepted employers' profits as legitimate in principle. From the National Labor Union in the 1860s to the National Industrial Congress in the 1870s to the Knights of Labor in the 1880s, labor associations variously called for a "fair share," a "larger proportion," an "equal share," a "proper share." And just as the fruits of labor had more than one meaning, there were differing approaches for obtaining them, from reforming to abolishing the wage system. The eight-hour day, the cooperative commonwealth, trade unions, money reform, socialism, the single tax all had a mass following and promised to end the injustice of low wages.[47]

But these many formulations derived from a common core of belief about the relation between freedom and equivalence in exchange. The aim of labor spokesmen was to expose what both classical economics and antislavery thought obscured – the irony that voluntary wage contracts obeying the laws of the market revolved around the same quid pro quo as slavery. Laboring men decried the "Market Value of Free-Born Slaves" and claimed that it was "unjust and immoral" to "put human labor on the market to be knocked down to any bidder," to set its "value according to demand and supply." They drew on antislavery language in attacking the traffic in labor and in arguing that unrequited work amounted to bondage. Yet at the same time they disclaimed the antislavery valorization of wages as a token of freedom, on the grounds that the existing nature of this exchange merely replicated the reciprocity between master and slave. They insisted that hirelings were like slaves in being powerless to "compel an exact equivalent." As George McNeill wrote, it was a travesty of the "theory of freedom of contract" to suppose that

[47] Speech of A.R. Parsons, in *Journal of United Labor*, July 1883; Thomas Phillips, untitled manuscript fragment, circa 1870s, Thomas Phillips Papers, Wisconsin State Historical Society, Madison; "Platform of the National Labor Union, adopted 1867," in Commons, ed., *A Documentary History of American Industrial Society* 9: 177; "Platform of the National Industrial Congress," *Workingman's Advocate*, January 2, 1875; Knights of Labor, "Declaration of Principles," *John Swinton's Paper*, October 14, 1883; "Capital and Labor," *Locomotive Firemen's Magazine*, February 1885; G.K.H., "Trades' Unions. – II." See also David Montgomery, "Labor and the Republic in Industrial America: 1860–1920," *Mouvement Social*, 111 (April-June 1980), 201–15; Leon Fink, *Workingmen's Democracy: The Knights of Labor and American Politics* (Urbana, 1983), 6, 9–10; Daniel T. Rodgers, *The Work Ethic in Industrial America, 1850–1920* (Chicago, 1974), 215–16; Glickman, *A Living Wage*, 61–77.

any man would willingly "sell his labor for a mere loaf of bread for himself and family."[48]

It was in the sense, therefore, of being dispossessed of both their own labor's proceeds and the service of their wives – of being disentitled both at work and at home – that hireling men spoke of themselves as wage slaves. In doing so they laid bare not only the surplus value derived from wage work that led to capital accumulation, but also the economic value of unpaid housework. Elite reformers and moralists romanticized housework as part of woman's separate sphere, but its economic significance was hidden in a capitalist culture that took money as the sole index of value.[49] As laboring men described dirty rooms and uncooked food they were not simply reckoning their own slavish wages; they were also bringing to light the worth of housework lost when their wives' labor became a market commodity.

To men who were unsure of being able to feed their families, the value of housework in balancing wages with subsistence needs was anything but invisible. "It is the wife," explained the *Workingman's Advocate*, "who has to study how long she must make the bag or barrel of flour last." As one shoemaker confessed, "it is only through my wife's frugality that we are able to trail along." But housework's value appeared most dramatically in testaments to the cost of its absence, such as Gompers's account of how a man lived on wages of 17 cents an hour:

In some instances his wife takes in sewing and does chores for other people, while in other instances that I know of they work in a few of the remaining laundries where women are still engaged. . . . By this means the home, of course, is broken up; indeed there is hardly the semblance of a home, and in these instances where the wife goes out to work no meal is cooked. . . . Of course, when the wife is at home although the living is very poor, it is cooked; she cooks what can be purchased with the portion of the 17 cents per hour remaining after the payment of rent, and the cost of light, fuel, &c.

[48] J. Normandy, "Market Value of Free-Born Slaves," *John Swinton's Paper*, May 18, 1884; P.J. McGuire, "The Working Class. – Its History and Struggles," *Carpenter*, April 1884; "Wage Slaves," *Journal of United Labor*, August 1883; "Wages Slavery and Chattel Slavery," *Journal of United Labor*, May 25, 1884; "Slavery," *Workingman's Advocate*, August 25, 1866; McNeill, ed., *Labor Movement*, 479, 481. See also David Brion Davis, "The Perils of Doing History by Ahistorical Abstraction: A Reply to Thomas L. Haskell's *AHR Forum* Reply," in *The Antislavery Debate: Capitalism and Abolitionism as a Problem in Historical Interpretation*, ed. Thomas Bender (Berkeley, 1992), 304; Sean Wilentz, "Against Exceptionalism: Class Consciousness and the American Labor Movement," *International Labor and Working-Class History* (Fall 1984), 1–24.

[49] See Jeanne Boydston, *Home and Work: Housework, Wages, and the Ideology of Labor in the Early Republic* (New York, 1990), 36–37.

Defending higher wages, laboring men argued that the "wife can
have more time for household duties. . . . The man can then come to
his cleaner and clearer home." Meanwhile, they figured free labor's
current price again and again in terms of children who were "dirty
and ragged," food like "smoked or salted meat that required no cooking," and homes that were in a "deplorably filthy condition."[50]

Against these everyday household scenes that evoked slavery, laboring men set up images of plebeian life divided into separate sexual spheres. They idealized the division between the worlds of the
market and the household no less than did genteel exponents of
free labor and Victorian domesticity; their model of Yankee home
life could have been drawn from *Uncle Tom's Cabin*. Their version of
this ideology was distilled in a "Labor Poem" printed in the *National
Labor Tribune* in 1874 that depicted a husband leaving work and a
wife and children at home:

> Though coarse his fare, and scant his means of life,
> Thought of his children and loving wife
> Makes rich amend for all his toil and strife.
> As fades the last ray of setting sun,
> His home is reached, his daily task is done;
> His young ones watching at the open door
> He sees with joy, and hastens on the more.
> Within the housewife, partner of his weal,
> Prepares with busy hand the evening meal. . . .
> Arrived within, she greets him with a smile
> And sweet caress – the welcome home. . . .

Here, too, home life was the reward for drudgery, even though the
means of living were scant. And, as in other visions of separate
spheres, the husband was master at home, a "very king," the sovereign of a "domestic castle." Such images went hand in hand with
refrains linking men's wages to the dependent relations of the
household, which claimed that it was "God's purpose" for man to
"maintain his wife and his children by his labor." For hireling men,
the ideal of separate spheres had enormous potency because it sym-
bolically negated not only the vanquished world of slavery but life in
the tenements.[51]

[50] "Let the Wife Be Heard," *Workingman's Advocate,* November 22, 1873; Knights of
Labor, *Proceedings of the [Eighth] General Assembly* (Minneapolis, 1884), 595; U.S.
Congress, Senate, *Relations between Labor and Capital* 1: 278; George E. McNeill, *An
Argument in Favor of a Legislative Enactment to Abolish the Tenement-House Cigar Factories,
in New York and Brooklyn* (New York, 1882), 15; New York Bureau of Labor Statistics,
Second Annual Report (1885), 181, 154, 156.
[51] "Home, Wife and Children," *National Labor Tribune,* December 12, 1874; W. Whit-
worth, "Saturday Night," *Journal of United Labor,* March 5, 1887; "The Children of

The heart of labor's outcry was that the wage contract did not keep separate the realms of market and home, but rather collapsed them into one by pricing free men's labor no higher than the rewards of slavery. What government investigators left unstated, workingmen made explicit. Only in name were their homes inviolate, their rights absolute as masters of a household, their dependents secure from the marketplace. It was in the free market, not the slave auction, they argued, that their wives and children were sold, to earn wages by serving other men. "As a rule," wrote Ira Steward, "everything a poor man has is for sale." In McNeill's words, the free laborer was "a man without the rights of manhood . . . homeless, in the deep significance of the term." Other hirelings argued that wage labor consumed not only men within the "machinery of commerce," but whole families on the "altar of greed." Using antislavery guidelines, these men declared themselves unfree.[52]

Over a century earlier Enlightenment theorists of contract freedom had equated wage labor and marriage as relations of household dependency, drawing an analogy between hired men and wives. Antislavery theory disrupted this analogy, legitimating wage labor by counterposing the formal freedom and equality of contracting parties in the marketplace to the benevolent dependencies of the home – the antithesis symbolized by separate spheres. But the argument of labor reform in the Gilded Age was that the market was boundless, that commodity relations now suffused the household, even permeating, within tenement shops, the inner recesses of the home: the food, the rooms, the bonds between husbands and wives, and mothers and children. Which was to argue that the wages of contract reproduced slavery.

By the end of the century, the labor protest surrounding home life and the social-scientific surveys of laboring households registered in the rise of a new school of political economy that sought to reconceptualize the ethics of market exchange. Its leaders were professors who had inherited antislavery beliefs and were struck by the distress of the laboring poor. They made their professional mark by forming the American Economic Association in 1885, declaring at its found-

Mechanics," *Workingman's Advocate,* August 4, 1866; John Mason, "From a Laborer," *National Labor Tribune,* January 2, 1875. See Glickman, *A Living Wage,* 46–47.

[52] Ira Steward, "The Power of Wealth," Ira Steward Papers, Wisconsin State Historical Society; McNeill, ed., *Labor Movement,* 455; "Resolution of the Massachusetts Federation of Trades," in U.S. Congress, Senate, *Relations between Labor and Capital* 1: 70. For a differing interpretation, emphasizing postbellum labor leaders' accommodation to and legitimation of the regime of market relations and wage labor, see Glickman, *A Living Wage.*

ing the urgency of solving social problems created by labor relations. They dissented from classical economics in the name of evangelical Christianity, and they were profoundly concerned with wages, as John Bates Clark explained in his germinal ethical treatise, *The Philosophy of Wealth*: "The problem thrust upon society is not merely how to divide a sum, but how to adjust rights and obligations. . . . If it is humanly possible to thus settle the questions at the basis of the law of wages, no scientific work can be more immediately and widely beneficent."[53] The scientific ideal of the ethical apostates was to settle questions of labor's price by discovering a new moral paradigm of free market relations, a paradigm that would truly reconcile the wage contract with home life.

The scholarship written by the principal spokesmen for the ethical school – Clark at Smith College, Richard T. Ely at Johns Hopkins University, Henry Carter Adams at the University of Michigan – did not offer tenement descriptions; instead, like the classical literature, it explicated concepts such as wealth, value, capital, money, labor, and wages. But unlike the classical texts, its subject matter was not limited to traditional economic themes and its standpoint was avowedly sociological and openly critical of existing class relations. "I took upon myself a vow to write in behalf of the laboring classes," was Ely's response to the poverty he saw as a young man in New York City in the early 1880s. Thus his 1889 *Social Aspects of Christianity*, typifying ethical methods of inquiry, advocated a "juster distribution of wealth" and termed the belief that wages exceeded profits "quackary and jugglery which must delight Satan." Nor was wealth the only scale of equity. Though the ethical economists did not directly contribute to the study of laboring homes, it was nonetheless in light of the "claims of family life" that they examined work and wages and attacked the classical view that supply and demand was divinely ordained.[54]

Whereas classical political economy assumed as a matter of material necessity that men's wages must perpetuate the stock of laborers, ethical political economy deplored the moral consequences of the

[53] John Bates Clark, *The Philosophy of Wealth. Economic Principles Newly Formulated* (Boston, 1886), 108–9. See also "Constitution of the American Economic Association," *Publications of the American Economic Association*, 1 (1886), 35–42; Dorothy Ross, *The Origins of American Social Science* (New York, 1991), 98–122; Sidney Fine, *Laissez Faire and the General-Welfare State: A Study of Conflict in American Thought* (Ann Arbor, 1956), 169–251; Furner, *Advocacy and Objectivity*.

[54] Ely quoted in Ross, *Origins of American Social Science*, 105; Richard T. Ely, *Social Aspects of Christianity, and Other Essays* (New York, 1889), 77; Henry Carter Adams, "Relation of the State to Industrial Action," *Publications of the American Economic Association*, 1 (January 1887), 471–549, 506. See also Richard T. Ely, *The Social Law of Service* (New York, 1896), 257.

gap between that theory and the reality of laboring life. Outspoken in their indictment of the unregulated marketplace for overturning family dependencies, the ethical economists affirmed that wives and children belonged at home. Ely's *Introduction to Political Economy* assailed the effect of low wages and the displacement of skilled men that forced entire families into the labor market: "The home is thus demoralized, and the rising generation becomes weak in body and mind and depraved in character." In an 1887 essay addressing the depravity of commerce, Henry Carter Adams claimed that the existing wage system would "ultimately result in race-deterioration." It must be possible, he argued, "to produce cottons without destroying family life." Not only did the ethical school credit hirelings' bitterness about wages, it also represented the home as the most glaring symbol of the inhumanity of the traffic in free labor, thereby hewing more closely to the vision of labor reform than that of antislavery.[55]

Notably, too, the new political economy used old proslavery arguments, not to acclaim the merits of bondage but to condemn contemporary free market relations. In an article entitled "How to Deal with Communism," John Bates Clark warned of the danger that lay in deepening divisions between rich and poor, borrowing the language of Fitzhugh's *Cannibals All!* as he likened the wages of free labor to chattel slavery. "We do not enslave men now-adays. The emancipation proclamation ended all that, did it not? We offer a man a pittance, and tell him to take it and work for us from morning till night or starve; but we do not coerce him. . . . We do not eat men – precisely. We consume the product of their labor; and they may have virtually worked body and soul into it; but we do it by such indirect and refined methods that it does not generally occur to us that we are cannibals."[56] An anxious meditation on the themes of working and eating, Clark's linkage of cannibalism with the free market gave new authority to the wage-slavery argument that paying starving men a pittance for their labor placed them in a condition of bondage.

In the eyes of the ethical economists, contract freedom was as illusory as wage slavery was real. Looking for the underlying cause of low pay, they traced it to the regime of contract itself – to the endur-

[55] Richard T. Ely, *An Introduction to Political Economy* (New York, 1889), 173; Adams, "Relation of the State to Industrial Action," 506, 505. On ethical economists' sympathy with wage grievances, see also Henry Carter Adams et al., "The 'Labor Problem,'" *Scientific American Supplement*, 22 (August 21, 1886), 8861–63 and (August 28, 1886), 8877–80; George B. Newcomb, *Political Economy in Its Relation to Ethics* (1885), Pamphlet Collection, Wisconsin State Historical Society.
[56] John Bates Clark, "How to Deal with Communism," *New Englander*, 37 (July 1878), 533–42, 540.

ing, but unacknowledged, economic dependence of hirelings who were formally free. While Clark graphically identified free laborers with slaves, Ely was even more direct in arguing that contract tenets had not produced "beneficent results" but were a fiction that disguised the enslavement of wage earners. "The condition of the ordinary laborer who is free to make his own bargains, or who, as we say, lives under the *regime* of free contract," he wrote in his *Introduction to Political Economy,* generally constitutes "the practical dependence of the laborer on account of the pressure of economic necessity; at times, indeed, a dependence which virtually amounts to slavery." This was the condition of sweated laborers, "kept prisoners in the dens where they work." Henry Carter Adams similarly inveighed against liberty of contract as a shibboleth of classical economics.[57] In spite of their antislavery heritage, the ethical economists maintained that the triumph of free contract had irrevocably altered the form of exchange between property owners and the unpropertied, but not the relationship of authority and submission characteristic of unfree labor.

In so arguing, the ethical school claimed not simply to be engaging in criticism but to be laying the foundation for a new theory of wages and a new science of market relations. The belief was that class strife could be averted through a political economy reformulated in recognition of free labor's inequities. This project began with the denial that human labor was a commodity. As Clark wrote in *The Philosophy of Wealth,* "The statement so frequently met with in works on Political Economy that 'Labor is a commodity and is governed by the same laws as other commodities' is one of the mischievous errors that still cling to the science." Only labor's products should be defined as commodities, and never the human faculties that produced wealth, or else "the whole man will have to be classed as a commodity." This error of classification was "disastrous in its practical results," Clark held, for it gave rise to the notion that supply and demand acted "promiscuously on everything bought and sold." All of the leading ethical economists objected that labor differed fundamentally from other market goods because it was attached to a human personality, just as abolitionists had abjured treating slaves as commodities.[58]

But the trademark of the ethical project was disavowing the moral dualism of separate spheres; and here the home took on utmost importance in the new political economy. Among the core proposi-

---

[57] Ely, *Political Economy,* 77, 35, 36; Adams, "Relation of the State to Industrial Action."
[58] Clark, *Philosophy of Wealth,* 21, 7, 110. See also, for example, Ely, *Political Economy,* 161.

tions of bourgeois social thought was that the ethos of the market
and that of the household were opposed to one another, but that
these realms were mutually reinforcing precisely in their antinomies
– that family altruism counterbalanced ruthless buying and selling
while free market relations nourished home life. This proposition
gave meaning to the divide between public and private, as well as to
the idea of separate sexual spheres. It was essential to both classical
economics and the antislavery faith that yoked wage labor and home
life. But the ethical economists cried out that the moral schism between home and market was corrosive of life in both realms. By their
lights, these realms had to remain spatially separate but become eth-
ically one, with the ethos of the home transposed into the market.

Again Clark's *Philosophy of Wealth* led the way in setting out the
ethical position. He mapped the spiritual cleavage between the public world of the market and the private world of the household,
showing its historical origins and its modern perversities. He retold
the story of market society's development, how in antiquity competitive commodity exchange arose between strangers at the border, or
"mark," of village life, in liminal places removed from communal
experience, and how in the present day this moral distance still divided home and market, rupturing both social life and individual
consciousness. A "tribal conscience" governed in the village, but on
the mark "there was 'higgling,' the contention between buyers and
sellers. . . . Modern society consists of the fusion of the two," Clark
wrote. "We are appalled by the moral dualism in which we live . . .
the necessity of a twofold life." There was "one code for the family
. . . a different one for mercantile life" – a "good bargain" was
"morally, a bad bargain," necessarily unequal. In a culture that di-
vorced household ethics and market relations, "a sensitive conscience must be left at home when its possessor goes to the office or
the shop." This was why men's labor sold for less than the price of
family survival.[59]

The ethical ideal was to fuse these separate spheres, not by placing
market relations inside the home or wives and children outside it to
sell their labor, but rather by remodeling the wage contract in the
image of the household's benevolence. Sympathy would mediate the
cash nexus. Hard bargaining would be transmuted into organic
bonds between buyers and sellers of free labor. Adam Smith had
described self interest as the only ground on which to meet one's

---

[59] Clark, *Philosophy of Wealth*, 155–56, 162, 157. Both Ely and Henry Carter Adams
followed Clark in deploring these dualisms. See Ely, *Political Economy*, 65–68; Adams,
"Relation of the State to Industrial Action," 504–6. See also Jean-Christophe Agnew, *Worlds Apart: The Market and the Theater in Anglo-American Thought, 1550–1750*
(New York, 1986), 17–56.

adversary in commodity exchange, "We address ourselves, not to their humanity but to their self-love, and never talk to them of our own necessities but of their advantages." But the ethical economists placed humanity at the center of a redeemed wage system, exalting mutual obligations that transcended market dealings. The keywords in their vocabulary were morality and personal responsibility, the exemplar of which was the home. "Competition without moral restraints is a monster . . . completely antiquated," wrote Clark, acerbically adding that even "the troglodyte had a family, and, within the precinct of his home, was ruled by higher motives." The new political economy proposed to widen the precinct of the home among men who were no longer cave dwellers, to impose its higher values on the marketplace. The rule would be a "just price," as buyers of human labor responded compassionately to the necessities of the sellers.[60]

Paradoxically, only where the home and market were morally one would these spheres stay physically separate, and the household remote from the traffic in labor; this was the bedrock of the ethical argument. If the ethos of the family entered into commodity relations between men, the labor of wives and children would be protected from sale. It was to the fact of "dual existence" – the counting of "harshness and inhumanity" as vices at home but market virtues – that Henry Carter Adams attributed free labor's propensities to destroy family life and cause "race-deterioration." Conversely, joining a man's paternalistic impulses with the wage relationship would produce a new calculus of exchange. "It is taken for granted with us that a man's self-interest includes wife and children," explained Ely. "If self-interest becomes so broad in its scope as to identify self with humanity as now with one's family, we have Christian altruism. What is wanted is to extend the circle of self-interest." Economic man would become a man of sentiment, master of a household whose benevolent practices would encompass the marketplace.[61]

In ethical economics, therefore, home life did not represent the moral counterweight to the free market but instead a new paradigm for commodity relations. This idea converged with labor reform's invocations of Christian brotherhood and the Golden Rule as alternatives to acquisitive individualism. But the images of contract that labor reformers counterposed to the market belonged to the world of dem-

[60] Smith, *Wealth of Nations*, 14; Clark, *Philosophy of Wealth*, 151, 163, 168–69. See Adams, "Relation of the State to Industrial Action," 548; Washington Gladden, *Working People and Their Employers* (Boston, 1876), 169, 172–73, 181; Ely, *Social Aspects of Christianity*, 85, 93–95, 101.

[61] Adams, "Relation of the State to Industrial Action," 504–6; Ely, *Political Economy*, 151–52.

ocratic politics, not to the household – they spoke of the cooperative commonwealth, of a republic of labor, of industrial democracy. By contrast, in taking home life rather than political democracy as a model of exchange, the ethical economists envisioned equity in wage relations that would remain fundamentally hierarchical. "It lies in the nature of things," wrote Ely of hirelings' subordination at work; "the demand of ethics is not equality." And in remodeling the sale of labor in the form of reciprocity at home, the ethical economists inverted the traditional narrative that celebrated labor's liberation from the dependencies of the household. Not only did they argue that wage dependency at its worst resembled slavery; they saw much to value in the "feudal feeling." For them, free labor's ideal endpoint was something very close to the old-fashioned paternalism of Christian charity, extended from the home to the marketplace.[62]

It is unlikely that the ethical rewriting of political economy directly affected labor's price or altered individual conscience on a mass scale. However, through the idea of morally fusing the home and the market it did help lay the intellectual groundwork for the American welfare state that was emerging at the turn of the century. Proclaiming government a "moral agency" – an expression of collective will legitimately be endowed with the power to regulate the free market and thereby raise the ethical plane of commodity relations – the new political economy attacked both laissez-faire and the moral dualism of modern life. Although the ethical school did not propose state fixing of wages, on the theory that this was coercive, it did advocate enacting protective labor laws that would bar wives and children from wage work in order to lessen "the evils of the present system." The state would bear the duty of imposing the household's moral codes on the market in free labor, abridging contract freedom in the interest of traditional family dependencies.[63]

In an 1883 address to a freedmen's aid society the black minister Alexander Crummell sorrowfully considered the progress of his race

---

[62] Ely, *Social Aspects of Christianity*, 97, 125; Ely, *Political Economy*, 67. See also Christopher Tomlins, "Subordination, Authority, Law: Subjects in Labor History," *International Labor and Working-Class History*, 47 (Spring 1995), 56–90. On labor's Christian doctrine, see, for example, McNeill, ed., *Labor Movement*, 468–69; Herbert Gutman, "Protestantism and the American Labor Movement: The Christian Spirit in the Gilded Age," in Gutman, *Work, Culture, and Society in Industrializing America: Essays in American Working-Class and Social History* (New York, 1976), 79–117.

[63] Adams, "Relation of the State to Industrial Action," 510, 507–8. See also Alice Kessler-Harris, *A Woman's Wage*. See Michel and Koven, "Womanly Duties"; Sklar, *Florence Kelley*; Linda Gordon, "Putting Children First: Women, Maternalism, and Welfare in the Early Twentieth Century," in *U.S. History as Women's History: New Feminist Essays*, ed. Linda K. Kerber, Alice Kessler-Harris, and Kathryn Kish Sklar (Chapel Hill, 1995), 63–86; Susan Lehrer, *Origins of Protective Legislation for Women, 1905–1925* (Albany, 1987).

since the abolition of slavery. His measure of freedom was the home and women's place within it. The "old plantation hut" was still the dwelling place of former slaves, he mourned. Emancipation Day had brought the freedwoman "no invisible but gracious Genii who, on the instant, could transmute the rudeness of her hut into instant elegance, and change the crude surroundings of her home into neatness, taste, and beauty." Both home life and housework remained wishes unfulfilled. "With her rude husband she still shares the hard service of a field-hand. . . . Her furniture is of the rudest kind. The clothing of the household is scant. . . . She has rarely been taught to sew . . . [or] the habitudes of neatness, and the requirements of order." What Crummell still dreamed of was a world where women would be "helpers of *poor* men" – "thrifty wives of the honest peasantry of the South" – creating "homes of Christian refinement" even in "the cabins of the humblest freedmen."[64] Yet obstacles to this vision had been planted at the outset of emancipation by the decree of northern liberators that the economic need for wives' wage work outweighed the moral value of separate spheres and freedmen's rights to dependent labor at home. Freedom did not earn former slaves a home life untouched by the market.

By 1883, few in the North were concerned with freedpeople's households; this issue faded from view with the end of Reconstruction. Instead it was Yankee tenement homes that drew the attention of labor reformers and social scientists with an antislavery pedigree. A decade before Crummell's address, government statisticians in Massachusetts tested the equities of the wage contract in the tenements, finding that most men's labor cost less than family subsistence – that wages did not afford decent food and furniture, tidy rooms, or the rights of husbands to their wives' housework. Just two years before Crummell spoke of freedom and home life, Samuel Gompers went to the tenements to show that hirelings lived like slaves, in a world where the traffic in free labor engulfed the household rather than sustaining it as a precinct separate from the market. Turning these revelations on their head, ethical political economy held that the spirit of the home must pervade the market to assure that free labor's rewards did not recreate the reciprocities of bondage. Charity that began at home would be the model for the wage contract rather than market relations being the model for charity. The fruits of both empiricism and theory, all these studies of home

[64] Alexander Crummell, *Africa and America: Addresses and Discourses* (Springfield, Mass., 1891), 67, 68, 81, 82. Crummell's thought influenced a generation of black intellectuals; the 1883 address was cited by both W.E.B. Du Bois and Anna Julia Cooper. See W.E.B. Du Bois, *Darkwater: Voices from within the Veil* (New York, 1969; orig. pub. 1920), 171; Anna Julia Cooper, *A Voice from the South* (New York, 1969; orig. pub. 1892), 24.

life confounded the antislavery promise that hireling men's families would not be for sale.

Following slave emancipation the legitimacy of contract freedom thus turned on the question of home life. In both the North and the South the wage contract was at once defended as freedom and condemned as slavery through images of the household. For both exponents and critics of wage labor, the physical separation of home and market embodied the difference between free men entitled to be masters of a family and slaves without domestic rights. By the Progressive Era, it had become common for reformers to justify the regulatory state and above all labor laws for women by arguing that these spheres were fusing in a way that endangered the future of the white race, an argument carrying the ideological force of debates over slavery and freedom that transcended regional boundaries.[65] But these representations of home life rested on an ideal of marriage that was itself the subject of political criticism and legal reform in the postbellum era.

[65] See Florence Kelley, *Some Ethical Gains through Legislation* (New York, 1969; orig. pub. 1905); Kathryn Kish Sklar, "Two Political Cultures in the Progressive Era: The National Consumers' League and the American Association for Labor Legislation," in Kerber, Kessler-Harris, and Sklar, eds., *U.S. History as Women's History*, 36–62; Kessler-Harris, *A Woman's Wage*, 33–56.

5

Wage Labor and Marriage Bonds

When Congress debated the meaning of slave emancipation the galleries overhead were filled with women. There they would have heard statesmen equate freedom with contract but also affirm that abolition did not transform the bonds of marriage – that "A husband has a right of property in the service of his wife." One of those listening in the congressional gallery was Frances Gage. Reflecting on the debate, she observed: "I would not say one word against marriage. . . . But let it be a marriage of equality. Let the man and woman stand as equals before the law."[1] That aspiration was central to antislavery feminism in the nineteenth century.

In the wake of emancipation it fell not to Congress but to state lawmakers to reconcile the traditional rules of marriage with the new circumstances of wage work, which increasingly rendered wives' labor a commodity for sale on the market. The core of the problem was a wife's right to her own labor, wages, and person – a property right that the wage contract presumed but the marriage contract denied. Legislatures throughout the country responded by enacting "earnings laws" that entitled wives to the fruits of their waged labor, thereby seeming to address feminist claims about the anomalies of marriage in free society. Here was a set of rights that appeared to replicate the contract rights afforded to former slaves. Yet the analogy was not so clear-cut, for the reforms did not nullify a husband's legal title to his wife's service at home.[2]

As a child, Frances Gage had spent hours in her father's library. Along with Shakespeare, Milton, Butler, and Johnson, she read *Black-*

[1] Eric Foner, "The Meaning of Freedom in the Age of Emancipation," *Journal of American History*, 81 (September 1994), 435–60, quote at p. 456; Elizabeth Cady Stanton, Susan B. Anthony, and Matilda Joslyn Gage, eds., *History of Woman Suffrage* (3 vols., Rochester, N.Y., 1887), 2: 112–17, quote at p. 115.

[2] See Amy Dru Stanley, "Conjugal Bonds and Wage Labor: Rights of Contract in the Age of Emancipation," *Journal of American History*, 75 (September 1988), 471–500; Reva B. Siegel, "Home as Work: The First Woman's Rights Claims Concerning Wives' Household Labor, 1850–1880," *Yale Law Journal*, 103 (March 1994), 1073–1217.

stone's Commentaries, which she remembered was "rather dry . . . for a little girl." Yet from Blackstone she learned a "startling intelligence," that wives could not buy and sell, make contracts, or own property, even in themselves – that under the " 'Common Law, husband and wife are one.' " She was troubled by the law, even as a child. For other feminists the encounter with legal doctrine came later. They studied common law treatises, statutes, and court rulings; they researched marriage rules in primitive societies as well as biblical injunctions, tracing both the secular and sacred genesis of the marriage contract. They quoted Shakespeare, finding in *The Taming of the Shrew* a husband's vivid representation of his wife as chattel property:

> I will be master of what is mine own.
> She is my goods, my chattel; she is my house,
> My household stuff, my field, my barn,
> My horse, my ox, my ass, my anything.

Elizabeth Cady Stanton summed up the feminist view of the marriage contract as a slave code. "If the contract be equal, whence come the terms 'marital power,' 'marital rights,' 'obedience and restraint,' 'dominion and control'?" she asked in 1868, quoting the language of the law. "According to man's idea, as set forth in his creeds and codes, marriage is a condition of slavery."[3]

Since its inception the woman movement had underscored the legal symmetry between slavery and marriage, deploring the wife's lack of personal and property rights and calling for statutory reform of the common law rules of coverture. The husband was "to all intents and purposes her master," stated the Seneca Falls Declaration of Sentiments. Among the demands of the First National Woman's Rights Convention held in 1850 was amending the prop-

[3] Frances Dana Gage, "Looking Back," *Woman's Advocate,* 1 (January 1869), 1–2; "Woman's Position in the Nineteenth Century," *Revolution,* September 8, 1870; Paulina W. Davis, *A History of the National Woman's Rights Movement for Twenty Years* (New York, 1871), 31; *Report of the International Council of Women, March 25 to April 1, 1888* (Washington, D.C., 1888), 226; Elizabeth Cady Stanton, "Marriages and Mistresses," *Revolution,* October 15, 1868; Elizabeth Cady Stanton, "Miss Becker on the Difference in Sex," *Revolution,* September 24, 1868. See also Samuel E. Sewall to Caroline Dall, June 9, 1854, Caroline Dall Papers, Massachusetts Historical Society, Boston; Caroline H. Dall, *The College, the Market, and the Court; or, Woman's Relation to Education, Labor, and Law* (Boston, 1867), 271–306; Letter of Elizabeth Cady Stanton to Senator F.P. Blair, October 1, 1868, Elizabeth Cady Stanton Papers, Library of Congress, Washington, D.C.; Lucy Stone, "Fourth of July," *Woman's Journal,* July 9, 1870; Lucy Stone, "Marriage a Penal Institution to Woman," *Woman's Journal,* September 16, 1871; "The History of Morals," *Revolution,* July 1, 1869; "Women in All Ages," *Revolution,* September 15, 1870; "St. Paul Once More," *Woman's Journal,* March 26, 1870; Matilda Joslyn Gage, "Woman, Church, and State," in Stanton et al., eds., *History of Woman Suffrage* 1: 753–99.

erty laws affecting husband and wife. Stanton relentlessly called for more than property reforms, claiming that the question of marriage itself lay at the heart of woman's enfranchisement; but others feared that such arguments might appear to promote "free love." At an 1858 woman's rights meeting controversy erupted over an indictment that read: "*Resolved,* That the slavery and degradation of woman proceed from the institution of marriage; that by the marriage contract she loses control of her name, her person, her property, her labor, her affections, her children, and her freedom." The problem identified by the resolution was not simply title to real property but the wife's utter loss of sovereignty of self.[4]

At first the most frank discussion of the link between the marriage contract and woman's emancipation occurred in private correspondence. In a letter probably written in 1851 Stanton confided her thoughts to her cousin Gerrit Smith, an abolitionist leader. Using the slavery analogy, she emphasized the connection between sexual relations and property rights, and the conflict between marriage and self ownership.

Our laws, our customs, our fashions, are founded in some philosophy . . . – all those relating to woman in the false one that God made woman for man – to grace his home, to minister to his necessities, to gratify his lust, hence our laws make her a mere dependent, she has no rights to houses or lands, to silver or gold, not even to the wages she earns. She is given in marriage like an article of merchandize. . . . [A]nd she that is given never dreams that she herself has the most sacred right to her own person. . . . The rights of humanity are more grossly betrayed at the altar than at the auction block of the slave-holder.

Writing to Susan Anthony in 1853, Stanton named marriage the key question but also conceded the difficulty of raising it. "I do not know that the world is quite willing or ready to discuss the question of marriage. . . . It is in vain to look for the elevation of woman so long as she is degraded in marriage. . . . The right idea of marriage is at the foundation of all reforms. . . . I feel this whole question of woman's rights turns on the point of the marriage relation, and sooner or later it will be the question for discussion." Others agreed privately but avoided public debate. "It seems to me that all that pertains *intrinsically,* to marriage is an entirely *distinct* question, from ours," Lucy Stone wrote

[4] Stanton et al., eds., *History of Woman Suffrage* 1: 70; Siegel, "Home as Work," 1113, 1104 n. 108. See also Elizabeth B. Clark, "Matrimonial Bonds: Slavery and Divorce in Nineteenth-Century America," *Law and History Review* 8 (Spring 1990), 25–54; Norma Basch, *In the Eyes of the Law: Women, Marriage and Property in Nineteenth-Century New York* (Ithaca, 1982); Blance Hersh, *The Slavery of Sex: Feminist-Abolitionists in America* (Urbana, 1978); John C. Spurlock, *Free Love: Marriage and Middle-Class Radicalism in America, 1825–1860* (New York, 1988).

to Stanton in 1856, troubled by Stanton's view that "the *marriage* question must come up" at women's rights meetings. "Its magnitude too, is immeasurable, and there ought to be a convention, especially to consider that subjection – but it ought not be mixed with ours, it seems to me. Not that it is not just as imperative, and sacred, but because they do not belong together." Speaking for many advocates of women's rights, Elizabeth Peabody wrote to Caroline Dall in 1859, "The truth is that marriage and its troubles are rather too delicate a subject to admit of a great deal of talk."[5]

But the marriage question came into the open at the 1860 National Woman's Rights Convention. A furor arose when Stanton demanded not only legal equality under the marriage contract but greater freedom of divorce to remedy the wife's subjection. Though motions to strike her resolutions from the record were voted down in the interest of uncensored debate, there was an outcry against "begging onto our platform" the sanctity of the bond between husband and wife. "That noisy alien 'Marriage & Divorce,' " Wendell Phillips letter reproached Stanton by letter, "hath no right in our house." Other feminists spoke of her "distressing speech." One woman wrote to Dall that Stanton's resolutions had damaged the repute of women's rights advocates by giving "the public the impression that they advocated the abolishment of the marriage relation."

Some of the Woman's Rights people . . . are dissatisfied at what they deem the unwise courage of the last Convention in prematurely discussing the marriage question. . . . I believe that the marriage question is of primary importance, lying as it does at the root of all society, yet I cannot help seeing that the discussion of this question in the spirit in which it seems to have been discussed – not having been present, I know it only from hearsay – has damaged the cause greatly in public estimation.

For most feminists the equality of husband and wife was the limit of marriage law reform and divorce a taboo subject. "Were this discussion admitted, Conventions would be a mob, and it would be years before the riot would cease sufficiently for those who demand nothing but equality, to be heard," wrote another of Dall's correspondents. "God forgive us if we destroy the *family!*"[6]

---

[5] Stanton to Smith, January 5, 185[1?], Stanton to Anthony, 1853, Stone to Stanton, September 17, 1856; all in Stanton Papers, Library of Congress, Washington, D.C., Box 1; Peabody to Dall, February 21, 1859, Caroline H. Dall Papers, Massachusetts Historical Society, Box 2. See also Elizabeth Griffith, *In Her Own Right: The Life of Elizabeth Cady Stanton* (New York, 1984).

[6] Stanton et al., eds., *History of Woman Suffrage* 1: 716–42; Phillips to Stanton, August 21, 1860; Letters of E.G. to Dall, June 1, 1860, Mary L. Booth to Dall, June 5, 1860, E.A. Lukens to Dall, November 23, 1860; all in Dall Papers, Box 3. See Stanton et al., eds., *History of Woman Suffrage* 2: 388–89; *Woman's Journal,* June 4, 1870; *Woman's Journal,* July 2, 1870; *Woman's Journal,* October 22, 1870; *Woman's Journal,* November

Nevertheless, the question of marriage became entrenched on feminist platforms. There was unanimity regarding the ideal of an equal marriage contract – of emancipating wives to own their persons, labor, and wages. Virtually all feminists could agree that freedom entailed transforming the marriage bond, however much they disputed the legitimacy of divorce. Many joined in likening the wife and the slave, while contrasting coverture's disabilities to the rights of property and contract afforded by emancipation. Postbellum feminist agitation gave pride of place not only to suffrage but also to law reform that would grant wives contract freedom, making them masters of themselves. The common watchword was "equality in and out of marriage," despite the disagreement over whether marriage should be dissolvable at will, like other contracts. "The contract of marriage is by no means equal," argued Stanton repeatedly, insisting that the slave codes and the laws governing wives were "nearly parallel." This was also the view of those who shunned talk of divorce. Feminists aimed "simply to equalize" – "to protest against anything which involves inequality, whether in the control of persons, property or children," maintained Thomas Wentworth Higginson. "Of course they talk about oppression and emancipation. . . . Whoever is pledged to obey is technically and literally a slave, no matter how many roses surround the chains." No advocate of women's rights quarreled with Frances Gage's protest that all the states in the Union "deny the wife of a man almost everything that we to-day call our Civil Rights."[7]

Thus feminists claimed that marriage belonged at the very center of public debate over the outcome of slave emancipation. To their way of thinking, this was the question of contract that logically fol-

5, 1870; *Woman's Journal,* December 3, 1870; *Woman's Journal,* December 9, 1871; *Revolution,* December 1, 1870; *Revolution,* June 1, 1870; *Revolution,* May 18, 1871; *Golden Age,* October 7, 1871; *Golden Age,* September 9, 1871; Ellen Carol DuBois, *Feminism and Suffrage: The Emergence of an Independent Women's Movement in America 1848–1869* (Ithaca, 1978), 184, 192; William Leach, *True Love and Perfect Union: The Feminist Reform of Sex and Society* (New York, 1980), 144–52; William O'Neill, *Everyone Was Brave: A History of Feminism in America* (Chicago, 1969), 14–36; Hendrik Hartog, "Lawyering, Husbands' Rights, and the 'Unwritten Law' in Nineteenth-Century America," *Journal of American History,* 84 (June 1997), 67–96; Richard W. Fox, "Intimacy on Trial: Cultural Meanings of the Beecher-Tilton Affair," in *The Power of Culture: Critical Essays in American History,* eds. Richard Wightman Fox and T. J. Jackson Lears (Chicago, 1993), 103–32.

7 Statement of Julia Ward Howe at the 1871 Convention of the American Woman Suffrage Association, in *Woman's Journal,* December 9, 1871; Stanton, "Marriages and Mistresses"; Elizabeth Cady Stanton, "The Woman and the State," *Revolution,* August 19, 1869; Thomas Wentworth Higginson, "Simply to Equalize," *Woman's Journal,* June 24, 1871; Thomas Wentworth Higginson, "Obey," *Woman's Journal,* June 25, 1870; *Proceedings of the Eleventh National Woman's Rights Convention, Held at the Church of the Puritans, New York, May 10, 1866* (New York, 1866), 44.

lowed abolition, for it distilled the inequality of the sexes and the continuing ownership of persons. Attacking all forms of "domestic slavery," they pointed out that "equal rights" was nothing other than the core of the Yankee program of freedom in the South. Indeed, some of their arguments – for example, Gage's words about a "marriage of equality" – found their way into Congress during polemics about the meaning of emancipation for women. As the *Woman's Journal* explained in 1870, "that there should be absolute equality of rights in marriage . . . we have always advocated." Yet this advocacy grew more intense after emancipation, as feminists argued for extending the principles of contract freedom to marriage while insisting that equality would reinforce the sanctity and permanence of home life. They advanced this position in speeches, essays, and legislative campaigns, calling for reform of the legal rights and duties of husband and wife. The typical woman's rights agitator, according to the *Nation's* portrayal, "attends four conventions a month, travels ten thousand miles, and 'corners' eight members of Congress, and reduces three twaddling ministers, and an old fogy of a judge, and a flippant male editor, to appalled silence during the winter campaign." The congressional gallery was simply one of many feminist venues.[8]

In conceiving of marriage as an equal contract, feminists were up against not only common law tradition but new doctrine formulated by legal and political thinkers of their own day. The new doctrine held that marriage was peculiar among free contracts, that it alone – unlike either contracts of sale or contemporary wage contracts – created a relation of status. "In law writings generally, marriage is denominated a contract; yet it is said to be more than a contract, and to differ from all other contracts," explained Joel Bishop in his 1873 treatise, *Commentaries on the Law of Marriage and Divorce.* "All is submerged in the status."[9] Postbellum jurisprudence thereby af-

---

[8] "The English Common Law In Utah," *Woman's Journal,* January 24, 1874; Sen. Edgar Cowan, citing Gage in the 1866 congressional debates, in Stanton et al., eds., *History of Woman Suffrage* 2: 115; "Marriage and Divorce," *Woman's Journal,* November 5, 1870; "The Two 'Movements' among Women," *Nation,* January 19, 1871. See also Ellen Carol DuBois, "Outgrowing the Compact of the Fathers: Equal Rights, Woman Suffrage, and the United States Constitution, 1820–1878," *Journal of American History,* 74 (December 1987), 836–62; Leach, *True Love and Perfect Union,* 190–212; Sarah Barringer Gordon, " 'The Liberty of Self-Degradation': Polygamy, Woman Suffrage, and Consent in Nineteenth-Century America," *Journal of American History,* 83 (December 1996), 815–47; Eric Foner, *Reconstruction: America's Unfinished Revolution 1863–1877* (New York, 1988), ch. 6.
[9] Joel Bishop, *Commentaries on the Law of Marriage and Divorce and Evidence in Matrimonial Suits* (2 vols., Boston, 1873), 1: 3, 13. See also Michael Grossberg, *Governing the Hearth: Law and Family in Nineteenth-Century America* (Chapel Hill, 1985), 21–24, 291–92; Nancy F. Cott, "Giving Character to Our Whole Civil Polity: Marriage and the

firmed the difference articulated in antislavery theory between the
dependencies of marriage and the formal equality and freedom that
wage labor ostensibly shared with all other contracts.

Law writers carefully distinguished between marriage and other
contract relations. Bishop's treatises were among the leading expositions of the new jurisprudence on marriage. A Boston lawyer who
left his practice, Bishop also wrote on contracts and criminal law but
was most acclaimed for his study of marriage. His *Commentaries* pro-
pounded the ruling theory that the relation between husband and
wife was the basis of both the family and civil society, and that public
interest in procreation and the orderly exercise of sexual passion
gave the state exclusive sovereignty over marriage, which was why it
differed from contracts that were simply private transactions. "The
institution of marriage . . . has ever been considered the particular
glory of the social system" and was "the first among the institutions
of human society," wrote Bishop. "Everywhere the doctrine is received, that men and women should not follow their mere animal
instincts in their social relations to one another, but that they should
'pair off.'" Although marriage originated in consent – on the
"threshold of a contract" – it was exceptional in that the terms were
not fixed by a meeting of minds and the contract could not be ended
at will. It was:

the civil status of one man and one woman united in law for life, under the
obligations to discharge to each other and the community, those duties
which the community by its laws holds incumbent on persons whose association is founded on the distinction of sex.

At law, marriage alone represented a hybrid of contract and status:
"its nature as a contract is merged in the higher nature of the status.
And though the new relation – that is, the status – retains some
similarities reminding us of its origin, the contract does in truth no
longer exist, but the parties are governed by the law of husband and
wife."[10]

Postbellum jurisprudence echoed older treatises in conceptualiz-
ing marriage as fundamentally a legal relation of personal dominion
and dependence. Law enforced "Scripture Injunction" by recogniz-

Public Order in the Late Nineteenth Century," in *U.S. History as Women's History:
New Feminist Essays,* ed. Linda K. Kerber, Alice Kessler-Harris, and Kathryn Kish Sklar
(Chapel Hill, 1995), 107–21; Gordon, " 'Liberty of Self-Degradation.' "

[10] Bishop, *Commentaries on the Law of Marriage and Divorce,* 1: 9, 1, 10, 2. See also James
Schouler, *Law of the Domestic Relations* (Boston, 1905; orig. pub. 1870), 12–17; P.
Lucie, "American Marriage Law – The Scottish Interests of Joel P. Bishop," *Juridical
Review* (June 1985), 119–32.

ing in "husbands the right to command, and in wives the duty of obedience," commented Bishop. The exchange of service for support remained the essential legal rule, in spite of the circumstances of wage work that compelled both wife and husband to sell their labor. "If he is poor," Bishop wrote, "still the duty is on him to maintain her." His duty constituted "her own labor and skill" his property "in the most absolute sense." Due to his dominion, she could "have no will of her own." Other treatise writers also elucidated the wife's unfreedom, stressing her condition of servitude and the husband's rights as a master under the common law. Marriage law bore the imprint of the "feudal system," stated Parson's *Law of Contracts*. "In general, whatever she earns she earns as his servant, and for him; for in law, her time and her labor, as well as her money, are his property. . . . He is her husband; he is the stronger, she is the weaker; all that she has is his." Where later treatises differed from earlier ones was in speaking of status to distinguish marriage from other contracts. By contrast, though wage work was also a property relation involving legal subordination, postbellum labor jurisprudence used the language of contract freedom and did not describe a hireling as having no will of his own. Underscoring these distinctions, Bishop explained that the proper usage was "status of marriage" rather than the older term, "contract of marriage."[11]

The new vocabulary was rooted in the theory of marriage as wholly different from a commercial contract – which was precisely the contrast denied by postbellum law in regard to the wage contract, despite the claims of hirelings that human labor should not be defined as a commodity. While extolling the sale of labor as a free contract relation, the law refused to recognize marriage as ordinary commerce or husband and wife as "bargainers with each other . . . as seller and buyer." Bishop found "the idea, that any government could, consistently with the general well-being, permit this institution to become merely a thing of bargain between men and women . . . too absurd to require a word of refutation." He quoted a recent ruling by a Rhode Island court that bluntly construed marriage as an unfree, paternal relation of the household rather than equating it

---

[11] Joel Bishop, *Commentaries on the Law of Married Women under the Statutes of the Several States, and at the Common Law and in Equity* (2 vols., Boston, 1873–75), 1: 26, 32–33, 140, 22; Theophilus Parsons, *The Law of Contracts* (3 vols., Boston, 1873), 1: 373, 379, 384; Bishop, *Commentaries on the Law of Marriage and Divorce* 1: 14. See also Thomas M. Cooley, *A Treatise on the Constitutional Limitations Which Rest upon the Legislative Powers of the States of the American Union* (Boston, 1868), 339; Schouler, *Law of the Domestic Relations*, 54–57, 71; Karen Orren, *Belated Feudalism: Labor, the Law, and Liberal Development in the United States* (New York, 1991); William E. Forbath, "The Ambiguities of Free Labor: Labor and the Law in the Gilded Age," *Wisconsin Law Review*, no. 4 (1985), 767–817.

with market exchange: " 'It is no more a contract than serfdom, slavery, and apprenticeship are contracts; the latter of which it resembles in this, that it is formed by contract.' " At law, marriage represented no pure and simple commodity relation.[12]

The political theory of the day viewed marriage in the same light. According to Theodore Dwight Woolsey of Yale University, terming marriage a contract reflected a failure of language rather than the true nature of the relation. Marriage was both worldly and divine, a "special definite mode of moral and social life" for which contract was a misnomer, he argued in an 1869 study of divorce. His treatise, *Political Science,* taught that though contract often served as the symbol of "great transactions of a moral or religious kind," it did not express their essence. Marriage, he wrote, was not truly of the "contract species." And the husband, he remarked, was the "housemaster."[13]

The dissociation of marriage and contract was also resonant in contemporary theology. Especially influential was an 1870 book *The Nation* written by the Episcopal theorist Elisha Mulford. Seeking to reveal the divinity of family and state, he argued that both embodied transcendent principles and neither derived from contract. He objected not only to liberal social contract theory but also to the "representation of the origin of the family in a contract." For him, contract was both tenuous, because formed by those who "remain separate parties," and profane, because contaminated by the tenets of possessive individualism and commerce. Contract represented the "agreement of parties in the exchange of equivalents, and each remains a possessor. . . . The principle is not the foundation, but the dissolution of the organization of society." Social exchange conceived of as contract, Woolsey warned, was measured solely by "commercial profit and loss" and "defined by regulations in bargain and sale," replicating the ethos of the marketplace.[14]

Yet the marriage doctrines of postbellum law and theology were

---

[12] Parsons, *Law of Contracts* 1: 374; Bishop, *Commentaries on the Law of Marriage and Divorce* 1: 9, 8.

[13] Theodore Dwight Woolsey, *Essay on Divorce and Divorce Legislation, with Special Reference to the United States* (Littleton, Colo., 1982; orig. pub. 1869), 235–36; Theodore Dwight Woolsey, *Political Science or the State Theoretically and Practically Considered* (2 vols., New York, 1878), 1: 79, 99. See Woolsey letters to the Rev. Samuel Warren Dike, December 3, 1878; April 24, 1879; May 21, 1879; August 22, 1881; Samuel Warren Dike Papers, Library of Congress, Washington, D.C. Though not addressing Woolsey's views on marriage, see Louise L. Stevenson, *Scholarly Means to Evangelical Ends: The New Haven Scholars and the Transformation of Higher Learning in America, 1830–1890* (Baltimore, 1986), 1–16, 21, 67, 82–83, 102–17.

[14] Elisha Mulford, *The Nation: The Foundations of Civil Order and Political Life in the United States* (New York, 1870), 54–55, 279, 219, 5, 277, 48, 34, 280–81. See William Gladstone, "Present-Day Papers: Problems of the Family," *Century Magazine,* 39 (1889–90), 385–95.

hardly identical, for jurists never denied the moral validity of contract. Nor did Woolsey's political theory question contract's cultural ascendancy. Rather, the endeavor of secular thinkers was to draw a line indicating the spheres where contract belonged as an instrument of exchange and image of social relations and where it did not. That line cordoned off marriage and the household. Because contract had become so closely linked to commodity relations, so thoroughly soaked with a market meaning, it could not convey the organicism, benevolence, and permanence ideally associated with marriage. As a symbol of liberal individualism, it could not also represent paternalistic bonds. In law, contract simultaneously came to be enshrined as a constitutional right and discredited as a paradigm for marriage. For Woolsey it embodied "natural reason" and the "advance of human society," even though marriage was not of the "contract species."[15] Distinguishing the ambiguities of marriage as status sharpened the legal difference between slavery and contract freedom.

Conversely, that was why feminists invoked contract as a model for equality in marriage, counterposing it to bondage. They argued that marriage should resemble other contracts at law – a claim differing from hirelings' contention that wage labor was unlike other contracts. Nevertheless, both reform aspirations centered on self entitlement, on property in one's own labor and person. Whereas labor advocates held that formal equality under the wage contract disguised the self dispossession entailed in the sale of free labor, feminists condemned the legal inequalities of marriage that deprived wives of the right to self ownership essential to contract freedom. At a meeting of the American Woman Suffrage Association in 1870, Julia Ward Howe set forth the key feminist propositions: "Now, however the matter may stand between man and woman, the State's need of marriage is imperative. And as the State commands marriage . . . the State is bound by every sacred obligation of justice to render the contract an equal one." She assailed the "barbaric element" of the law that denied the wife's right to "her money, and her children, and her body, and her soul."[16] Feminism pronounced equal contract rights the negation of chattel status.

The ideal that marriage should resemble other contracts had expansive implications. It belonged unmistakably to the age of antislavery and emancipation. Taken farthest, it could indeed seem to justify free love principles – that the state should not dictate the rights and duties of husband and wife or the permanence of their bond, that marriage should be absolutely consensual. Thus the distress over

---

[15] Woolsey, *Political Science* 1: 73–74, 79.
[16] Stanton et al., eds., *History of Woman Suffrage* 2: 793–94.

Stanton's proclamations that woman wants "freedom to marry, and to be mistress of herself after marriage; freedom to sunder a yoke she has freely bound." Yet Stanton explained that she opposed only the force of law, not marriage: "My idea is that human law has nothing to do with this relation except as a civil partnership." Attacking status classifications based on unequal property rights, she contended that "marriage should have no more effect on individual property relations than any other partnership" and that the wife should be entitled to the same contract freedoms as other persons – to buy and sell, to own property, "to claim her right to herself, soul and body." Over and over she claimed that marriage should be legally equivalent to other free contracts. "Let the State be logical: if marriage is a civil contract, it should be subject to the laws of all other contracts." That would grant wives a "deed to themselves."[17]

For most feminists, however, the freedom sought in obliterating legal differences between marriage and other contracts stopped at equal rights within the relation while forbidding unlimited liberty of escape through divorce. Still, this was a profound challenge, for it entailed abolishing husbands' dominion over their wives and gave rise to the claims about self entitlement. "Love" and "Ownership" were as opposite as freedom and slavery, argued a writer in the *Woman's Journal* in 1871. "The idea of ownership has been hitherto inseparable from the idea of love.... [T]o the universal mind of man ownership, bondage, slavery, is implied in the word love, and the property right ... is vested in the man.... Ownership in love! Could there be a greater contradiction in terms?"[18] Reformers who dissociated woman's enfranchisement and free love nonetheless saw self ownership as the root question of marriage.

Yet to propose contract as the solvent of a wife's slavery did not imply that marriage should be considered identical to a contract of sale. Though feminists idealized the equal rights of contract that were culturally linked to commerce, they did not view the marketplace as a model for marriage. Rather, they distinguished possessive individual-

[17] Thomas Wentworth Higginson, "The Cleveland Convention," *Woman's Journal*, December 3, 1870; "The New York Revolution," *Woman's Journal*, October 22, 1870; "Marriage and Divorce," *Woman's Journal*, November 5, 1870; Letter of Stanton to Isabella Beecher Hooker, April 27, 1869, Isabella Beecher Hooker Papers, Library of Congress; "The Slave-Women of America," *Revolution*, October 6, 1870; Davis, *History of the National Woman's Rights Movement for Twenty Years*, 65–66; Stanton, "Marriage and Divorce," *Revolution*, October 29, 1868. See also Leach, *True Love and Perfect Union*, 179.

[18] Lydia Fuller, "Love versus Ownership," *Woman's Journal*, April 15, 1871. See also "Marriage and Divorce," *Woman's Journal*, November 5, 1870; Thomas Wentworth Higginson, "Simply to Equalize," *Woman's Journal*, June 24, 1871; Linda Gordon, *Woman's Body, Woman's Right: A Social History of Birth Control in America* (New York, 1976), 95–115.

ism from commodity relations. While arguing that the wife should be
entitled to buy and sell, make contracts, and own property, including
herself, they denounced marriage as a market relation based on the
buying and owning of women – "though the transaction," as Lydia
Maria Child wrote, "is gracefully covered with veils and flowers." One
sense in which feminism did see eye-to-eye with the law was in rejecting the notion of husband and wife as buyer and seller. "Love is the vital essence," affirmed Stanton. Others spoke of "equal companion-
ship" and "partnership," seeking language denoting neither market
reciprocity nor dominion and dependence. The relation was supposed to be sentimental but not paternalistic; the image was of contract but not a contract evocative of the marketplace.[19]

This was the concept of freedom underlying the ideal of marriage
as an equal contract. In feminism, just as in abolitionism, contract
freedom represented the opposite of slavery, and self entitlement
the foundation of all rights. Yet feminism, unlike abolitionism, represented existing marriage as an emblem of slavery rather than freedom – as a descent through contract into bondage. Though speaking
in different terms, the law described a similar passage into unfreedom. It defined marriage not as slavery but as status, starkly distinguishing the relation of husband and wife from other free contracts
premised on formal equality. Thus, explained Lydia Maria Child,
"the radical difficulty at the basis of this whole subject is that women
are considered as *belonging* to men."[20] Such reasoning both drew on
and countered the tenets of law and abolitionism. For feminism envisioned equal contract rights crossing over the threshold of marriage and affording wives the freedom of ex-slaves.

It was hardly coincidental that the debate over marriage proceeded
alongside the empirical inquiry into home life. Both reflected the

[19] Lydia Maria Child, "Concerning Women," *Woman's Journal*, October 21, 1869;
Stanton, "Marriage and Divorce," *Revolution*, October 22, 1868; Letter of Lydia
Maria Child in *Woman's Journal*, November 11, 1870; Sarah F. Norton, "Marriage
versus Freedom," *Woodhull & Claflin's Weekly*, October 22, 1870; "Happy Marriages," *Woman's Journal*, February 18, 1871; Amelia Bloomer, "A Proposed Remedy
for Wife Beating," *Woman's Journal*, September 14, 1872; H.W.M., "Property Rights
of Women under the Roman Law," *Woman's Journal*, January 8, 1876; "Address of
Jane G. Swisshelm at the Illinois Woman Suffrage Association," *Revolution*, February
23, 1871; "Apollo Hall Resolutions," *Revolution*, June 15, 1871; Jane Croly, *For Better
or Worse* (Boston, 1875), 104. In suggesting that feminists neither wholly endorsed
nor wholly repudiated market tenets, nor divided neatly into those who invoked
and those who rejected these tenets, my interpretation differs both from accounts
that stress feminists' market paradigm of marriage and those that stress their criticism of possessive individualism. See Clark, "Matrimonial Bonds"; Leach, *True Love
and Perfect Union*, 7–12.
[20] Lydia Maria Child, "Concerning Women," *Woman's Journal*, October 21, 1869.

ascendance of contract freedom, though one concerned the wife's legal emancipation, and the other the husband's loss of masterhood due to the traffic in free labor. They intersected in revealing the ideological stakes of opposing claims to the wife's labor – the household property that the Thirteenth Amendment's authors assured would not be denied to free men after the abolition of slavery. Interest in this issue reached wide due not only to arguments over equal rights but to the circumstances of wage work that led wives to sell their labor as a commodity.

By no means was government social science alone in documenting the hireling condition of wives in the postbellum North. Though the census did not report the number of wives who earned wages until 1890, impressionistic evidence – found in the penny press, vaudeville scripts, advice manuals, and sentimental novels – corroborated the surveys of the state bureaus of labor statistics. Here is how a rhyme featured in the 1879 collection *Dick's Irish Dialect Recitations* depicted the political economy of marriage among the working classes:

> "Where's Pat?" Shure, now, ye are taysin;
> Who knows, when a man is away?
>
> . . . .
>
> "Out of work?" Shure ye are right, miss,
> Not a ha'porth he's done for a year.
> Git along, is it? Why 'tis the washin'
> And scrubbin' that kapes us all here.
>
> . . . .
>
> I'm airning our pennies for bread. . . .

And in describing the wife's wage work as unnatural, all sorts of reformers and moralists joined government investigators and labor advocates. As Josephine Shaw Lowell maintained in her discussion of home visits to the poor, when a husband was able bodied it was "injurious" and "a disgrace that his overburdened wife should be called upon to earn even fifty cents a week toward the support of the family."[21]

Concern over the transformation of Yankee wives' labor into a market commodity stood in stark contrast to northern attitudes toward the wage labor of freedwomen in the South. Indeed, the equanimity of northerners in insisting that the wives of freedmen toil as

---

[21] William B. Dick, *Dick's Irish Dialect Recitations. A Collection of Rare Irish Stories, Poetical and Prose Recitations, Humorous Letters, Irish Witticisms, and Funny Recitals in the Irish Dialect* (New York, 1879), 97; William R. Stewart, *The Philanthropic Work of Josephine Shaw Lowell* (New York, 1911), 147. See also Joseph A. Hill, *Women in Gainful Occupations, 1870–1920* (Washington, D.C., 1929).

field hands made all the more notable their troubled response to the wives who worked as cigar makers, scrub women, and sweated seamstresses on their own home ground.

Even while assuring former slaves that their marriages would never again be torn apart by sale, northerners who assisted in the transition to freedom took for granted that both husbands and wives would sell their labor to former masters. Speaking to South Carolina freedmen, Edward Pierce promised that they would "not have their wives . . . sold off"; yet he saw nothing objectionable in including pregnant women in the category of "half hand." Similarly, northern schoolteachers, who gauged ex-slaves' fitness for freedom by the cleanliness of their cabins, approvingly portrayed the employment of mothers in the fields. "It was not an unusual thing," wrote Elizabeth Botume, "to meet a woman coming from the field, where she had been hoeing cotton, with a small bucket or cup on her head, and a hoe over her shoulder, contentedly smoking a pipe and briskly knitting as she strode along. I have seen, added to all these, a baby strapped to her back." This placid scene, where wage work and domesticity benignly fused, resembled neither the antislavery images that had counterposed southern cotton fields to northern hearths nor the gloomy depictions of postbellum Yankee tenements.[22]

The Freedmen's Bureau hardly defined the sale of labor by freedmen's wives as inconsistent with northern free labor principles. On the contrary, the bureau deprecated as idle the freedwoman who only did unpaid household work – who refused to turn her labor into a commodity. "Do the women work in the field? Do they work indoors, and in what way?" inquired an 1866 bureau circular that was distributed to local agents supervising government plantations in Virginia. The responses exemplified the bureau's program across the South. "It is impossible for the freedman to support himself and his family by working five days a week and keeping a wife and daughter in idleness," one agent declared. "Unless something is done by the Bureau in this county to induce the freedman to make the female members of their families work in the crops next year there will be destitution amongst them."[23] Refusing to discriminate by sex in en-

[22] Ira Berlin, Thavolia Glymph, Steven F. Miller, Joseph P. Reidy, Leslie S. Rowland, and Julie Saville, eds., *Freedom: A Documentary History of Emancipation, 1861–1867*, ser. 1, vol. 3, *The Wartime Genesis of Free Labor: The Lower South* (New York, 1990), 192, 144, 131–32; Elizabeth Hyde Botume, *First Days amongst the Contrabands* (Boston, 1893), 53.

[23] *U.S. Bureau of Refugees, Freedmen, and Abandoned Lands. Records of the Assistant Commissioner for the State of Virginia* (Washington, D.C.), Record Group 105, reel 44, p. 674; Mecklenburg County to O. Brown, August 31, 1866, Record Group 105, reel 45, p.

forcing the duty of work, discounting all but wage labor as idleness, the bureau denied the virtues of housework also instilled by apostles of free labor.

The bureau's views on freedwomen's industry were not all that different from the interests of ex-masters, though not overlaid with the same feelings of personal outrage. Planters, too, dismissed housework as idleness while asserting claims to female labor that conflicted with the entitlements of freedmen as husbands. They appealed to the bureau to require wives to enter into labor contracts and return to the fields because men's work alone was not sufficient to raise the crop or worth enough for family subsistence. "Allow me to call your attention to the fact that most of the Freedwomen who have husbands are not at work – never having made any contract at all – Their husbands are at work, while they are as nearly idle as it is possible for them to be, pretending to spin – knit or something that really amounts to nothing," one planter complained to the bureau chief in Georgia. "I think it would be a good thing to put the women to work. . . . Are they not in some sort vagrants as they are living without employment?" The planter both reaffirmed his ownership as a master and conceded the new terms of the labor contract by stating that he was "willing to carry my idle women to the Bureau & give them such wages as the Agent may think fair." Used to having chattel labor fully at his own disposal, he devalued the spinning and knitting of former slaves at home as doing nothing. This view was widely shared across the South. Against the loss of their entitlements of race and property, former masters protested that freedwomen aimed "to play the lady and be supported by their husbands like white folks." For them, the exchange of a husband's support for a wife's service at home symbolized white supremacy, but when mirrored in black marriages was a sign of profligacy.[24]

Yankee liberators were not so blunt in denigrating the domestic aims of freedpeople; their approach was more contradictory. They affirmed that ex-slaves would not be sold away from each other as commodities but also held that the wife's labor must be equally as

36. See also Elizabeth Rogosin, " 'God Almighty's Law' or State Law?: The Freedmen's Bureau and the Legalization of Ex-Slave Marriages" (unpublished paper, March 1991).

[24] M.C. Fulton to Brig. Gen. Davis Tilson, April 17, 1866, quoted in Ira Berlin, Stephen F. Miller, and Leslie S. Rowland, "Afro-American Families in the Transition from Slavery to Freedom," *Radical History Review*, 42 (1988), 89–121, quote at pp. 112–13; Dorothy Sterling, ed., *We Are Your Sisters: Black Women in the Nineteenth Century* (New York, 1984), 321. See also Foner, *Reconstruction,* 85–86; Jacqueline Jones, *Labor of Love, Labor of Sorrow: Black Women, Work, and the Family, from Slavery to the Present* (New York, 1985), 59–60; Laura F. Edwards, *Gendered Strife and Confusion: The Political Culture of Reconstruction* (Urbana, 1997), 147–52, 166–67.

available as the husband's for purchase in the free market. In shaping the outcome of abolition, they placed a higher premium on wage work than on housework, despite paeans to the tidy home as an emblem of freedom. This policy had been set at emancipation's advent. Without apology, the Freedmen's Inquiry Commission had ranked the value of labor above the stature of women as a gauge of cultural supremacy. "It has been sometimes said . . . that the grade of civilization in a nation may be measured by the position which it accords to woman. A stricter test is the degree of estimation in which labor is held there," the commission moralized.[25] Yet, though speaking in universal terms, the commission offered no guidance as to whether the precepts governing the extraordinary circumstances of emancipation should also apply above the Mason–Dixon line to persons who had never been chattel and who had been reared in the faith that woman's place at home marked a fundamental difference between freedom and slavery.

In the North, meanwhile, the buying and selling of the wife's labor represented a problem of a seemingly different nature. Employer interests aside, there the question was not how to induce wives to work for wages but why they were becoming hirelings and what this portended – the economic, moral, and legal implications of converting wifely labor into a market commodity. The difference in perspective turned not on spoken ideas about regional distinctiveness, but on unspoken ideas about race – on the sense that marriage bonds differed for white laborers in the North and black laborers in the South. This was a legacy of slavery that abolition did not fully overcome. In regard to neither region of the country did Yankee reformers, officials, and social scientists offer an explicitly racial construction of home life, for their outlook was more ambiguous. They affirmed equal rights, whereas former masters boasted of race privilege. Yet assumptions about race, whether unconscious or simply unacknowledged, colored Yankee views of the wife as hireling, the extent of a husband's property rights in her service, and the value of housework in both the North and South. It was these beliefs that could make the interplay of the wage contract and marriage contract appear as a social problem in northern tenements but not on southern plantations.[26]

In his 1876 study, *The Wages Question*, Francis Amasa Walker

---

[25] *Final Report of the American Freedmen's Inquiry Commission to the Secretary of War* in *Report of the Secretary of War*, 38th Cong., 1st sess., Sen. Exec. Doc. 53 (1864), 25.

[26] On the power and complexity of racial ideology, see Barbara J. Fields, "Ideology and Race in American History," in *Region, Race, and Reconstruction: Essays in Honor of C. Vann Woodward*, ed. J. Morgan Kousser and James M. McPherson (New York, 1982), 143–77.

dwelled on neither free labor in the South nor the fieldwork of freedmen's wives. But in examining industrial capitalism in the North, he emphasized that as market dependency made households increasingly reliant on cash and as unskilled wage work grew common, wives' labor was scarcely exempt from sale. Ironically, he argued, industrial transformation lent housework new significance. He began with the "great industrial change" – the "necessity" that drew wives into the "market of wage labor" and altered traditional family economy. "All which now enters into domestic consumption must come in from without," leading both the husband and wife to "go out and bring in a part of it. At the same time the extension of water and steam power has made the labor of women useful in a thousand operations for which their strength was formerly inadequate." He went on to stress the losses at home: "In the eagerness to increase the family income it is not sufficiently considered that, in the absence of the wife and mother, great loss must necessarily be sustained in the expenditure of that income; and . . . the ill-effects on the health of the family." It was implicit that the white working classes, rather than freedpeople, were under discussion.[27]

Yet enunciated for the first time in a treatise on capitalist industry was the idea that housework had economic value. Though obscured by the rise of the wage economy and the cultural dominion of money, that value was now brought to light as more and more wives became hirelings – through recognizing benefits lost at home. The claim that unpaid wifely labor created family wealth was a longstanding one of feminism. But for political economy this was a revelation, just as it was a new finding for postbellum labor reform. The theory was that a wife's labor was more valuable as housework than as wage work: if it was owned by her husband rather than bought by other men. If put up for sale, its value was no longer hidden, but obvious. "In families where bread comes hardly, the services of the house are foregone," for the "wife . . . no longer working as of old for the head of the house, go[es] out to seek strange employers and be jostled in public places," wrote Walker. "It would often be truer economy to forego wages to be earned at the expense of leaving the home uncared for." He pointed to "Waste in food, clothing, utensils." Here, the dependent wifely labor belonging to a husband was not discredited as producing no wealth.[28]

[27] Francis A. Walker, *The Wages Question: A Treatise on Wages and the Wages Class* (New York, 1876), 380, 381.
[28] Ibid., 380, 381. See Chapter 4 of this volume. On the invisibility of the economic value of housework in the antebellum era, see Jeanne Boydston, *Home and Work: Housework, Wages, and the Ideology of Labor in the Early Republic* (New York, 1990); Alice Kessler-Harris, *Out to Work: A History of Wage-Earning Women in the United States*

In charting the spread of wives' wage labor, other experts on northern industry also weighed the value of housework against the costs of wage work. The 1875 report on the "Condition of Working-men's Families" by the Massachusetts Bureau of Labor Statistics deemed the sale of the wife's labor "a false economy." As Carroll Wright wrote, its effects were "baneful," especially contrasted to a wife's economizing at home: "In personal care of her children, as compared with hired service; in the making and repairing of their clothing as against an outlay for those purposes, or the purchase of ready-made articles; in the instruction of her daughters in domestic matters to render them helpmeets in the future to their husbands; in the preparation of good food and such utilization of that purchased as 'to waste not and want not.' " Matter of factly, the report concluded that reasons of economy as well as of morality militated against wives selling their labor: "they would save more by staying at home than they gain by outside labor." By the turn of the century, housework no longer appeared removed from the market but instead wedded to the cash economy. As a settlement house worker in New York City admiringly observed of housewives who earned wealth by saving at home: "many working-men's wives could give post-graduate courses in the use of money."[29]

In these studies, unlike in Yankee assessments of former slaves' condition, there was no discounting of unsold wifely labor as idleness – no indictment of wives who remained outside wage contracts. Rather, stress was laid on conflicting claims to the wife's labor under the marriage contract and the wage contract, on the complexities arising from its status as both a husband's entitlement and a commodity. From this vantage, housework now seemed to possess economic value. Yet the larger point was that hireling wives in the North were serving two masters. Only "before coming and after returning from work," lamented the Massachusetts Bureau of Labor Statistics, could a wife cook, clean, and sew.[30] That was not the complaint of the Freedmen's Bureau.

(New York, 1982), 71. These accounts do not note that housework's value became newly visible in postbellum economic theory and labor protest with the spread of wives' wage employment. Studies stressing the exceptional nature of feminist arguments that housework created wealth also ignore this trend. See Leach, *True Love and Perfect Union*, 193–94; Siegel, "Home as Work." See also Nancy Folbre, "The Unproductive Housewife: Her Evolution in Nineteenth-Century Economic Thought," *Signs*, 16 (1991), 463–84; Wally Secombe, "The Housewife and Her Labour under Capitalism," *New Left Review*, 83 (January–February 1974), 3–24; Jean Gardiner, "Women's Domestic Labour," *New Left Review*, 84 (January–February 1975), 47–58.

[29] Massachusetts Bureau of Statistics of Labor, *Sixth Annual Report* (Boston, 1875), 360–61, 442; Lillian W. Betts, *The Leaven in a Great City* (New York, 1902), 260–61.

[30] Massachusetts Bureau of Statistics of Labor, *Third Annual Report* (1872), 79; see also p. 340.

According to the 1875 survey of "Workingmen's Families" in Massachusetts, wives were wage laborers in only 12 of the 397 cases examined. This amounted to three percent of the sample households of skilled and unskilled, and immigrant and nativeborn workingmen throughout the state. But a wider investigation the following year put the number at ten percent. The difference may have arisen from the deepening economic depression, yet it also suggested the difficulty of statistical measurements. For the 1870 study of Boston tenement life, which concentrated on "Low-Paid Laborers," had shown that wives intermittently earned wages in almost half of the households inspected. An 1884 Illinois survey of some two thousand families put the total at five percent, though it found twice that figure among the wives of unskilled laborers. Particularly hard to quantify was "transient labor," a wife's "casual labor by chance at scrubbing or washing," which, as the New York State Bureau of Labor Statistics explained in 1886, prevailed in the tenements – "the hiving ground of wash and scrub-women." Despite the statistical discrepancies, however, the general perception was of an increase in wives' wage labor. It was "notorious that many families" were becoming dependent on the "scant earnings" of a wife's "chance work," observed the Massachusetts Bureau of Labor Statistics.[31]

Social-scientific and charitable investigations indicated that wives were likely to work not only as scrubwomen but also in manufactories, mills, and tenement shops. They pervaded the sweated needle trades. As one charity journal explained, women brought their babies to work, keeping them asleep with doses of paregoric while they operated sewing machines. But more often wives did wage labor at home, taking in both sewing and washing. Or they worked beside their husbands and children, producing clothing and cigars in the tenements. Very common was the case of a Massachusetts wife who worked as a "custom Comfortable-maker" at home, earning five dollars a week but able to find work for only twenty weeks a year. By the 1880s more married than single women (mainly "Bohemian" but

[31] Massachusetts Bureau of Statistics of Labor, *Sixth Annual Report* (1873), 368; Massachusetts Bureau of Statistics of Labor, *Seventh Annual Report* (1876), 48–49; Massachusetts Bureau of Statistics of Labor, *First Annual Report* (1870), 164–85; Illinois Bureau of Labor Statistics, *Third Biennial Report* (Springfield, 1884), 274, 272; New York Bureau of Labor Statistics, *Third Annual Report* (New York, 1886), 165, 166; Massachusetts Bureau of Statistics of Labor, *Second Annual Report* (1871), 200. Because much of the wives' wage labor was not only casual but done at home, it defied the original census categories. In 1890, when the census began to report this data, it most likely understated the totals in listing wives as comprising twelve percent of all working women, and not quite five percent of all wives as being engaged in gainful occupations. See Hill, *Women in Gainful Occupations*, 76–77. On the limits, ambiguities, and findings of census data, see Massachusetts Bureau of Statistics of Labor, *Fourth Annual Report* (1873), 51–57; Hill, *Women in Gainful Occupations*; Kessler-Harris, *Out to Work*, 109–41.

also "American") worked as cigar makers in New York City. Some
wives moved back and forth between factory and home labor, but as
one clothing worker said, "I might as well work at home and have
the comfort of seeing that the children were all right. . . . It's wages
that's the trouble," she sighed, "do you know how they cut them?"
They were also found, sometimes with their husbands, in type foun-
dries, printing shops, hardware establishments, laundries, and sewing machine works as well as in shoe, box, and textile factories.[32]

Wives became hirelings in a range of ways. One was to accept
offers issued by clothing manufacturing firms that both sold sewing
machines and gave out piecework to be finished at home, thereby
engaging wives as both consumers and wage laborers, bringing the
market into the household. Advertisements in newspapers beckoned,
"Work! Work! Work! Given out which may be done at home to pay
for any First-Class Sewing Machine," and promised sewing on "all
kinds of Ladies' Undergarments, Suits, Wrappers and Aprons, Gents'
Coats, Pants, Vests and Shirts." In the sweated trades, subcontractors
also went "around among the people" in neighborhoods filled with
recent immigrants, soliciting the labor of housewives. Another way
wives found work was by registering with charities or women's protective unions. Just as there were woodyards where male beggars
could work for alms, so there were similar arrangements that
prompted wives to sell their labor. Benevolent agencies provided
that poor women could do ten hours of domestic service for as little
as 75 cents; sewing too was common "charity work." As philanthropists in New York City noted, "employment given to married women"
was a "popular form of charity." Yet to some charity reformers, the
worst kind of alms made wives into "the breadwinner of the family"
rather than their husbands.[33]

---

[32] *Advocate and Family Guardian*, 42(February 16, 1876), 47; Massachusetts Bureau of
Statistics of Labor, *Third Annual Report* (1872), 73; Helen Campbell, *Prisoners of
Poverty* (Boston, 1970; orig. pub. 1887), 34; New York Bureau of Statistics of Labor,
Third Annual Report (1886), 24, 32–59; "Children's Work," *National Labor Tribune*,
February 3, 1877; U.S. Congress, Senate, *Report of the Committee of the Senate upon the
Relations between Labor and Capital, and the Testimony Taken by the Committee* (4 vols.,
Washington, D.C., 1885), 1: 413–14, 750. See also Massachusetts Bureau of Statis-
tics of Labor, *Second Annual Report* (1871), 521–28; Massachusetts Bureau of Statis-
tics of Labor, *Third Annual Report* (1872), 59–112, 266–68, 278, 288; New York
Bureau of Statistics of Labor, *Second Annual Report* (New York, 1885), 149–78; Lillie
B. Chase Wyman, "Studies of Factory Life: Among the Women," *Atlantic Monthly*,
67 (September 1888), 315–21; *Report of the Tenement House Committee of the Working
Women's Society, of 27 Clinton Place* (New York, 1892), 8.
[33] Advertisements of the Boston firms Engley & Rice and Willard & Cutter, in *Woman's
Journal*, July 9, 1870; John R. Commons, ed., *Trade Unionism and Labor Problems* (New
York, 1967; orig. pub., 1905), 318; Associated Charities of Boston, *Sixth Annual
Report* (Boston, 1885), 36; New York State Charities Aid Association, *Fourth Annual
Report* (New York, 1876), 53; *Monthly Record of the Five Points House of Industry*, 17

Evidence of how hireling wives saw their own situation is as scant as their earnings were. They rarely testified in government hearings on the wage system, and though questioned when social-scientific investigators came to study their homes, their responses went largely unrecorded. They were often described, rarely quoted. Sometimes urban sketches and labor journals featured statements reputed to be theirs, which related the problems of work and poverty that fell on both husband and wife. " 'Tis only a dollar a day he's been earning this many a day. . . . An' how we'll live on that, an' the rint due reg'lar . . . no matter how bare the dish?'' an Irish washerwoman living in a New York City tenement supposedly burst out. " 'Shure an' if I hadn't the washin' we'd be on the street this day.' " In an account of garment workers' home life, a German woman told how she and her husband sewed jackets incessantly, unable to pause for meals:

It is early that we begin, – seven, maybe, – and all day we shall sew and sew. We eat no warm essen. On table dere is bread and beer in pitcher and cheese to-day. . . . Now, we stand eats as we must, and sew more and more. Ten jackets to one day . . . we go not out. It is fourteen hours efery day.

Expressing a keen sense of exchange value in a market economy, an 1875 letter from a "Miner's Wife" to the *National Labor Tribune* explained that the problem was that "every marketable commodity" was not "equally cheap, with labor."[34]

The statements ascribed to wives spoke to the central economic issue: the dominance of commodity production and wage dependence that at once made support by a husband more uncertain and wage labor by a wife more necessary. By law and custom, he was the provider; yet she converted money into family sustenance and often made up the difference when his wages fell short. In myriad ways the market's extension into family economies involved her in commodity relations, belying the idea that the spheres of women and commerce were separate. There was the "zest of bargaining" in the streets, as

(January 1874), 152; Stewart, *Philanthropic Work of Josephine Shaw Lowell*, 147. On wives' application at protective unions and low-paid sewing as charity work, see *Revolution*, January 21, 1869; Massachusetts Bureau of Statistics of Labor, *First Annual Report* (1870), 361; Boston Industrial Aid Society, *Forty-Second Annual Report* (Boston, 1877), 19. On antebellum antecedents, see Christine Stansell, *City of Women: Sex and Class in New York 1789–1860* (New York, 1986), 103–29; Elizabeth Blackmar, *Manhattan for Rent, 1785–1850* (New York, 1989), 124–26.

34 Helen Campbell, *Darkness and Daylight; or Lights and Shadows of New York Life* (Hartford, 1969; orig. pub. 1891), 266; Campbell, *Prisoners of Poverty*, 106; "From a Miner's Wife," *National Labor Tribune*, April 10, 1875. See also George Ellington, *The Women of New York, or the Underworld of the Great City* (New York, 1869), 601; Matthew Hale Smith, *Sunshine and Shadow in New York* (Hartford, 1869), 170. In the 1883 congressional hearings on labor, one wife appeared briefly as a witness. See U.S. Congress, Senate, *Relations between Labor and Capital* 4: 140.

wives bought groceries from pushcarts bearing milk, fruit and vege-
tables, fish, and kindling. Some laboring men claimed to give "every
cent" to their families, while women reported cooking "the soup
bone as long as you can smell beef on the water."[35] Not only did
wives turn parts of their homes into commodities by taking in renters
and boarders, they dealt with pawnbrokers and charity agents.
Dishes, irons, clothing, and pots filled pawnshops lining tenement
districts – as home visitors to the poor observed, wives had to "pawn
most of their things to pay the rent." And a wife's work also was
proving that the need for alms was "bona fide" to these visitors. "*Do
not show suspicion,*" charities advised their agents. "But a wife may be
wisely influenced to keep her rooms and children neat." Through
housework she showed her family worthy of charity. All of these enterprises coexisted with her wage work, and none was new; for wives
had added to household income with both paid and unpaid work
since colonial times. But the wage system's pervasiveness was new to
the postbellum era, as was the transformation of more and more
wives' labor into a market commodity.[36]

[35] Alvan F. Sanborn, *Moody's Lodging House and Other Tenement Sketches* (Boston, 1895),
139–45; Ellington, *Women of New York*, 577–78; U.S. Congress, Senate, *Relations between Labor and Capital* 1: 236, and see p. 369; "A Woman's Opinion," *National
Labor Tribune,* January 16, 1875.
[36] Boston Industrial Aid Society, *Thirty-Second Annual Report* (Boston, 1867), 14–15;
Monthly Record of the Five Points House of Industry, 10 (August 1866), 59; *Advocate and
Family Guardian,* 42 (May 16, 1877), 120; "Records of the Poor," Day Book of William O'Gorman, Overseer of the Poor, vol. 1, October 6, 1873, October 16, 1873, November 20, 1873, New York Historical Society, New York, N.Y.; "Rules and Sugges-
tions for Visitors of the Associated Charities," in Associated Charities of Boston,
Publications (n.d.), 2; Associated Charities of Boston, *Third Annual Report* (Boston,
1882), 13. On pawnshops, see Smith, *Sunshine and Shadow,* 214; Edward Crapsey, *The
Nether Side of New York; or, the Vice, Crime and Poverty of the Great Metropolis* (Montclair,
N. J., 1969; orig. pub. 1872), 134. On charity, see New York State Board of Charities,
Eighth Annual Report (New York, 1875), 14; W.B. Rogers et al., "Pauperism in the City
of New York," *Journal of Social Science,* 6 (July 1874), 76; Massachusetts Board of State
Charities, *Third Annual Report* (Boston, 1867), 193. On wives' unpaid and paid work
and the political economy of marriage in early America, see Laurel Thatcher Ulrich,
Good Wives: Image and Reality in the Lives of Women in Northern New England 1650–1750
(New York, 1980); Boydston, *Home and Work;* Stansell, *City of Women,* 11–18, 43–52,
74–81, 103–29, 193–216; Blackmar, *Manhattan for Rent,* 49, 121–25, 171; Joan Jen-
sen, *Loosening the Bonds: Mid-Atlantic Farm Women, 1750–1850* (New Haven, 1986);
Nancy Grey Osterud, *Bonds of Community: The Lives of Farm Women in Nineteenth-Century
New York* (Ithaca, 1991); Mary Blewitt, *Men, Women, and Work: Class, Gender, and Protest
in the New England Shoe Industry* (Urbana, 1990); Thomas Dublin, "Women and Out-
work in a Nineteenth-Century New England Town: Fitzwilliam, New Hampshire,
1830–1850," in *The Countryside in the Age of Capitalist Transformation: Essays in the Social
History of Rural America,* ed. Steven Hahn and Jonathan Prude (Chapel Hill, 1985),
51–70; Amy Dru Stanley, "Home Life and the Morality of the Market," in *The Market
Revolution in America: Social, Political and Religious Expressions,* ed. Melvyn Stokes and
Stephen Conway (Charlottesville, 1996), 74–96.

The collapse of marriage as a relation of male support and female dependence drew anxious commentary from both inside and outside the world of northern hirelings. Connections were made explicit between husbands who might be led to street begging and wives to wage labor. State officials noted not simply that convicts were increasingly "taken up because they are poor and paupers" and that masses of men roved the country "driven from place to place by want," but also that a significant portion were "breadwinners . . . 'off looking for work.' " Labor newspapers disclosed the crisis of marriage. As a New York City workingman reported in 1876: "The streets are full of half-starved men and women seeking employment. Families are breaking up, selling their furniture and travelling about separated. Station houses are full of tramps." Women sent in notices to labor papers seeking news of missing husbands, explaining that lack of work and unpaid rent caused "absent men." Meanwhile, charity agents wrote of threadbare homes, of wives supporting families with a needle or scrub brush, and of husbands out of work, injured, in jail, or nowhere to be found. "How many, many wives we find deserted," they observed; "husbands are not able to get work, though they are sober, respectable men." And feminists attacked the common law's blindness to the changing economics of marriage that turned "multitudes of wives" into wage laborers with "idle" husbands. The transformation came into focus at the 1883 congressional hearings on labor. When asked how families lived, one carpenter answered, "The Lord only knows. Pawn-brokers thrive pretty well. . . . The women go out and earn part of the living."[37]

Thus labor supposedly belonging to a husband was increasingly sold outside the marriage bond. That hardly endowed him with a property right to his wife's service. Rather, the traffic in free labor, in the North as well as in the South, hastened his wife into a wage contract. His own economic dependence effectively yielded her a

[37] Commissioners of the Illinois State Penitentiary, *Report of the Commissioners of the State Penitentiary* (Springfield, 1867), 41; Illinois Bureau of Labor Statistics, *Second Biennial Report* (Springfield, 1883), vii; Massachusetts House of Representatives, *Report and Bill Concerning Vagrants* (Boston, 1878), 7; "Our New York Letter," *National Labor Tribune*, January 22, 1876; "A Woman's Voice," *National Labor Tribune*, May 6, 1876; "Come Home Benjamin," *National Labor Tribune*, June 6, 1874; "Where Is He?" *National Labor Tribune*, September 25, 1875; *Advocate and Family Guardian*, 41 (July 16, 1875), 168; *Advocate and Family Guardian*, 41 (October 1, 1875), 228; *Advocate and Family Guardian*, 42 (February 16, 1876), 47; *Advocate and Family Guardian*, 43 (September 1, 1877), 205; *Advocate and Family Guardian*, 42 (June 1, 1876), 127; "A Lawyer's Objections," *Revolution*, June 25, 1868; U.S. Congress, Senate, *Relations between Labor and Capital* 1: 319. See also "Charity's Good Deeds," *New York Times*, January 17, 1876; Jonathan B. Harrison, *Certain Dangerous Tendencies in American Life, and Other Papers* (Boston, 1880), 106–27.

hireling's freedom – a condition in conflict with her status as a wife. Whether because he had no work, did not earn enough wages, was ill or in prison, or had simply left home, as a husband's half of the marriage contract went unfulfilled, his wife put her labor on sale. Though in tenement sweatshops she was still likely to work with him, neither bargaining nor earning a wage on her own, her labor was no longer exclusively his. But this was most obvious where her labor was a commodity bought and sold independently of him. "In the olden time the weaver sat in his little home with his family around him blithely joining in his labor," the minister R. Heber Newton wrote regretfully in 1886, but now wives "crowd the labor market."[38]

Perhaps it was because northerners had never thought of slave husbands and wives blithely laboring together under a master's whip that they could unambivalently affirm the virtue of freed wives' wage work. Conversely, perhaps it was because, whether consciously or not, they distinguished by race in understanding both the property rights of men at home and the value of housework that they dwelled on opposing claims to Yankee wives' labor. What riveted the attention of northern hirelings and their investigators alike was the discordance between the marriage contract and the wage contract – the very contract relations that represented slavery's opposite. In spite of common law rules, it had become clear that a poor man could not maintain a wife and therefore lost absolute rights to her labor as she acquired an independent economic identity by selling her service as a market commodity. "In our large cities thousands of women toil to support families," the sociologist Lester Ward expostulated in 1883, "how false is the assertion that men perform the labor of support, while women confine themselves to maternal and domestic duties."[39] The underlying question reflected the essential ambiguities of contract freedom: how could hireling wives be said to belong body and soul to their husbands?

On this question the congressional authors of slave emancipation had offered no guidance. Even as an abstract proposition, they had not contemplated the meaning of a wife selling her labor. For their vision of former slaves entitled to contract freedom rested on the belief that wage work and marriage were complementary, not contracts involving opposing claims to female labor. Indeed, they had foreclosed debate on whether liberties granted to former slaves

---

[38] "Heber Newton on Labor," *New York World*, May 17, 1886. See Blackmar, *Manhattan for Rent*, 124–25.
[39] Lester Ward, *Dynamic Sociology, or Applied Social Science, as Based upon Statistical Sociology and the Less Complex Sciences* (2 vols., New York, 1883), 1: 644.

would also afford wives individual rights and thereby transform marriage into an equal contract at law. Their response to this prospect was an unequivocal, "Oh, no."[40] Nonetheless, the postbellum era saw the rewriting of state law to clarify the wife's position as a hireling. Enacted amid empirical investigations into laboring home life as well as feminist agitation equating marriage law with slavery, "earnings" statutes gave wives title to their own labor and wages – a right known in the law as *emancipation*.[41]

More than semantics linked a wife's emancipation under the earnings laws to the conversion of chattel slaves into free persons. The transformation in both instances revolved around contract and personal dominion over labor. Onetime masters lost property rights in the service of dependents as wives and ex-slaves were entitled to sell their labor and own their wages. And these acts of emancipation occurred almost simultaneously. By 1887, some two-thirds of the states had enacted earnings laws; though a few dated from before the Civil War, the great tide of reform came afterward. Many of the earnings laws expressly entitled the wife to make contracts. In some ways they resembled married women's property acts passed earlier in the century; yet the enactments governed very different forms of wealth acquired by women of different classes.[42] The property laws applied to real and personal property, including land, chattels, and even business enterprises, which were traditionally conveyed along kin lines by gift or inheritance. The earnings laws applied to wages paid for work, validating the status of a wife's labor as a commodity. In principle, they placed her contract rights on a new foundation – on her title to her own labor, rather than to property owned sepa-

---

[40] *Congressional Globe,* 39th Cong., 1 sess., 1782. See Chapter 1 of this volume. In 1867 Congress passed a law for the District of Columbia that permitted the wife to own property but did not grant her either contract rights or a property right in her labor and wages. See *Congressional Globe,* 39th Cong., 2nd sess., 302, 1114–15, 1239, 1765.

[41] Joseph Warren, "Husband's Right to Wife's Services," *Harvard Law Review,* 38 (February 1925), 421–46; *Harvard Law Review* (March 1925), 622–50.

[42] See Elizabeth Warbasse, "The Changing Legal Rights of Married Women, 1800–1861" (unpublished doctoral dissertation, Harvard University, 1960); Richard H. Chused, "Married Women's Property Law, 1800–1850," *Georgetown Law Journal,* 71 (June 1983), 1359–1425; Basch, *In the Eyes of the Law;* Suzanne D. Lebsock, "Radical Reconstruction and the Property Rights of Southern Women," *Journal of Southern History,* 63 (May 1977), 195–216; Richard H. Chused, "Late Nineteenth Century Married Women's Property Law: Reception of the Early Married Women's Property Acts by the Courts and Legislatures," *American Journal of Legal History,* 29 (1985), 3–35; Siegel, "Home as Work"; Carl N. Degler, *At Odds: Women and the Family from the Revolution to the Present* (New York, 1980), 332; Sara Zeigler, "Wifely Duties: Marriage, Labor, and the Common Law in Nineteenth-Century America," *Social Science History,* 20 (Spring 1996), 63–96. Early earnings laws included: an 1852 Kentucky law, an 1855 Massachusetts law, an 1860 New York law.

rately from her husband. The earnings reform registered the wage
system's ascendance by altering the rights of husbands and wives who
owned little besides labor. As the *American Law Review* explained in
1880, wives had become members of "economic classes new to the
public thought."[43] Like the freedom granted to former slaves, the
wife's "emancipation" fostered the indiscriminate sale of labor in
the marketplace.

Unlike slave emancipation, however, the earnings acts did not
represent an entire redrafting of the law of the household. The legislation was passed in "piecemeal" fashion and abounded in "unset-
tled and discordant" principles, remarked legal writers. Rather than
annulling the marriage bond, it both preserved "marital rights" and
entitled the wife to enter into commodity relations unmediated by
her husband. It established both her rights and her duties of contract, protecting her wages against the claims not only of her husband but also of his creditors. At the same time it allowed creditors
direct access to her pay for debts she incurred. At least with respect
to market dealings – her sale of labor and purchase of goods – the
earnings acts diluted the legal presumption of a wife's dependence
and a husband's dominion. But her newfound "right to her labor"
did not abolish his claims to her service at home. The language of
the acts was contradictory. On the one hand, they "presumed" that
a wife performed "all work and labor" on her "separate account"
and allowed her to "receive, use and possess her earnings." But on
the other, they denied her right to be paid for "any labor" done for
husband and children, preserving her husband's right to unwaged
housework. Not fully, then, did the earnings acts redefine marriage
in terms of contract freedom.[44]

Nor did state legislatures record for posterity the meaning they
attached to the wife's emancipation. In contrast to verbatim reports
of congressional debate on abolition, silence shrouds lawmakers' intent in passing the earnings acts. Virtually no evidence remains of
argument in statehouses. For example, there was reportedly a long
debate over an 1874 Massachusetts act, but only fragments were transcribed, such as that one legislator spoke of "more even justice,"
while another attacked the reform as "too radical a change to be

---

[43] "General Notes," *American Law Review*, 14 (November 1880), 788.
[44] Warren, "Husband's Rights to Wife's Services," 622; Schouler, *Law of the Domestic
Relations*, 5; George E. Harris, *A Treatise on the Law of Contracts by Married Women,
Their Capacity to Contract in Relation to Their Separate Statutory Legal Estates, under
American Statutes* (Albany, 1887), i, ii, 45, 114; J.C. Wells, *A Treatise on the Separate
Property of Married Women Under the Recent Enabling Statutes* (Cincinnati, 1878), iii, iv,
73, 77. See, for example, *Statutes of Massachusetts* (Boston, 1874), ch. 184; *Public
Laws of the State of Illinois* (Springfield, 1869), 255.

worthy of consideration." These legislators seem not to have explicitly invoked the abolition of slavery as a model or to have assigned a sweeping emancipatory meaning to the hireling wife's contract rights. Rather, they appear to have responded to issues closer at hand – to signs of crisis in proletarian marriage and reasons advanced by feminists for the plight of laboring wives. No more than their counterparts in Congress did they interpret equal rights to require woman's enfranchisement. According to a lawyer who wrote often for the *Woman's Journal*, earnings reform was only a "patching of the Common law . . . to meet emergency." The wife won rights to her labor and wages simply from "expediency or necessity, and not from a sound philosophical view of the case."[45]

Yet if "expediency" carried the earnings laws to enactment, sometimes "philosophical views" intruded into the political process, though they were never admitted into the final language of the statutes. Enough evidence exists to piece together some of the public discussion surrounding two important statutes: an 1869 Illinois law and the Massachusetts law of 1874.[46] In these cases feminists confronted legislatures with calls for woman's emancipation as well as with more pragmatic arguments that the circumstances of laboring homes falsified the premises of common law rules of marriage.

While Illinois lawmakers deliberated on an earnings statute in February 1869, Stanton described the feminist presence at the state capitol. "On arriving at Springfield, we found the Chicago delegation all ready to besiege the Legislature. . . . We have met with members of the bar and judges of the Supreme Court" and the "Ex-Secretary of State, escorted us to the House and Senate and introduced us to the heads of the departments. We had two pleasant interviews with Gov. Palmer." This would turn out to be one of the last common endeavors of the women's rights movement before it split into rival suffrage associations later that year. The strategy had been planned at a Chicago convention, where antislavery leaders such as William Wells Brown appeared alongside Stanton, Anna Dickinson, and other feminists. In Springfield the agitation aimed broadly at the "enfranchisement of women." But the specific cause was earnings reform. Myra Bradwell, the editor of the *Chicago Legal News*, drafted the statute, and the committee testifying on its behalf included Bradwell and her husband, who was a state judge, as well

---

[45] *Boston Daily Globe*, March 27, 1874, p. 2; David Plumb, "Woman in the Law," *Woman's Journal*, July 16, 1870. On postbellum legislative disinterest in woman's enfranchisement, see DuBois, *Feminism and Suffrage*, 79–202; Leach, *True Love and Perfect Union*, 174–77; O'Neill, *Everyone Was Brave*, 16–17; Degler, *At Odds*, 331–33.

[46] See *Statutes of Massachusetts* (1874), ch. 184; *Public Laws of the State of Illinois* (Springfield, 1869), 255.

as Stanton and Mary Livermore. Stanton did not recount the appeals
made to the legislature. Yet in her legal journal Bradwell wrote of
the suffering of hireling wives whose husbands failed to support
them, announcing a rationale for the legislation:

shoddy creditors of the husband have ... been taking to pay his debts the
money earned by the honest toil of the wife, for the purpose of supporting
her ragged, starving children, which a drunken or unfortunate husband
failed to provide for.

Livermore, too, was interested in the condition of women who
earned a "small amount by scrubbing the Bridewell in Chicago" and
whose husbands seized their wages. Probably, such tales of necessity
punctuated more philosophical calls for the wife's emancipation,
shaping a swift patching of the common law. "In ten days," exulted
Livermore, "the older law was stricken from the statute books, and,
today, the married women of Illinois can control every penny of their
property."[47]

But the earnings law drew no endorsement from Chicago laboring men, who noted its passage only perfunctorily. It was not among
their legislative demands in 1869, which instead concerned convict
labor, apprenticeship regulations, and lien laws. Though they may
have agreed with feminists about the distress of laboring families,
their remedies differed. Seeking to protect the prerogatives of skilled
craftsmen, they apparently saw little merit in law that simply entitled
wives to their wages. Rather, they espoused traditional marriage doctrine. The wife of a laboring man should be "the brightener of his
house, and the wise and careful manager of his family," reasoned
the Chicago *Workingman's Advocate*, while the husband's duty was
"support of his family."[48] Yet it was the breakdown of this traditional

---

[47] Stanton et al., eds., *History of Woman Suffrage* 2: 371; and see pp. 368–69; "Law
Relating to Women," *Chicago Legal News*, October 31, 1868; "The Milwaukee Con-
vention," *Revolution*, March 11, 1869; Livermore quoted in Leach, *True Love and
Perfect Union*, 180. On the feminist legislative campaign, see also "The Chicago
Convention," *Revolution*, February 25, 1869; "Western Operations," *Revolution*,
March 4, 1869; "Editorial Correspondence," *Revolution*, March 11, 1869;
"Woman's Property Rights in Illinois," *Revolution*, March 25, 1869; *Illinois State
Journal*, March 3, 1869, p. 2; March 4, 1869, pp. 1–2; March 5, 1869, p. 2; March
10, 1869, p. 2; March 13, 1869, p. 1; and "The Laws of Illinois," *Chicago Legal News*,
April 4, 1869.

[48] For laboring men's legislative activity and conventional views on marriage, see *Chicago Tribune*, January 13, 1869, 4; "City Matters," *Workingman's Advocate*, January
30, 1869; "Correspondence," *Workingman's Advocate*, February 13, 1869; "The Apprenticeship Law," *Workingman's Advocate*, February 20, 1869; "City Matters," *Workingman's Advocate*, March 20, 1869, March 27, 1869, and April 17, 1869; "Female
Labor and Its Reward," *Workingman's Advocate*, September 21, 1867; "What's a
Wife?" *Workingman's Advocate*, August 8, 1868; "Ladies' Department," *Workingman's
Advocate*, May 7, 1870. See also Kessler-Harris, *Out to Work*, 68–70, 84–86; Martha May, "Bread before Roses: American Workingmen, Labor Unions, and the

relation between husband and wife in laboring homes that the earnings law ratified.

The Illinois enactment thus illustrated the ambiguous politics of earnings reform, an ambiguity deriving not only from unstated legislative motives but also from explicit feminist arguments. For lawmakers the parallel between slave emancipation and wives' contract freedom appeared not to be worth writing into legislation or even debating. Conversely, for feminists this emancipatory parallel was central – but so, too, was their retributory linking of a wife's right to her wages with wrongs committed by her husband. Though incommensurable, both arguments framed their defense of earnings reform.

Through the earnings laws feminists sought guarantees that hireling wives would be slaves no more. They envisioned the laws as not only reconstructing marriage in the image of an equal contract but granting the wife property in herself by allowing her to own her labor and wages. Exactly how they testified within legislative chambers is unclear, but since the antebellum era their calls for earnings reform had focused on self ownership and been cast in terms of slavery and emancipation. As Frances Gage argued in 1855, "the woman and the slave" were reduced to the same condition by the "law which gives the husband and the master entire control of the person and earnings of each."

We must own ourselves under the law first. . . . Let us assert our right to be free. Let us get out of our prison-house of law. Let us own ourselves, our earnings, our genius; let us have power to control as well as to earn and to own.

By the postbellum era, only suffrage assumed higher priority for feminists than earnings legislation; this was a reform of marriage law on which they could agree. Drawing on ascendant contract principles, they argued that the wife was robbed of the "results of her labor" and she must be emancipated to sell her labor and keep her wages – that marriage law and free labor were in conflict. "Repeal the slave code for wives," demanded an 1869 article in the *Revolution*, "the law which says, 'All that she can acquire by her labor, service or act, during coverture, belongs to her husband.' . . . Emancipate wives."[49]

Family Wage," in *Women, Work and Protest: A Century of U.S. Women's Labor History,* ed. Ruth Milkman (Boston, 1985), 1–21; see also Chapter 4 of this volume.
[49] Stanton et al., eds., *History of Woman Suffrage* 1: 843, and see pp. 28, 577; *Woman's Journal,* May 9, 1874; "Woman's Wages," *Revolution,* January 21, 1869. At an 1867 meeting of the American Equal Rights Association, Gage reiterated these words. See Stanton et al., eds., *History of Woman Suffrage* 2: 211–12. See also *Revolution* May 16, 1868; *Proceedings of the Tenth National Woman's Rights Convention Held at the Cooper Institute, New York City, May 10th and 11th, 1860* (Boston, 1860), 89; Siegel, "Home as Work."

For the wife, therefore, feminists claimed the freedom belonging
to other hirelings. Notably, this claim – unlike the wider debate over
wifely wage work – recognized no distinction between the households of northern laborers and those of southern freedpeople. Contending that the husband unjustly owned the wife's labor and appropriated the value of both her paid and unpaid work in exchange for
subsistence, feminists heralded the transformation of all wives from
bound laborers into free laborers. "She is a beggar of all beggars, a
slave of all slaves," they wrote of a wife without contract rights. They
pointed to the freedwife in the South, not to assess the virtues of
housework and fieldwork, but to show that her emancipation was
incomplete because she was not entitled to her wages. Frances Ellen
Watkins Harper reported in outrage that freedmen "hired out their
wives and drew their pay." Frances Gage stressed that freedwomen
in the Sea Islands hesitated to marry and lose the right to their
wages. According to feminists, rights of independent wage labor
were fundamental to the emancipation of wives, irrespective of race.
What had led her to demand "rights, in common with other
women," explained Harper in 1866, was finding that, as a wife, she
could not even own the implements of her wage work: "the very
milk-crocks and wash tubs." Sojourner Truth spoke of freedom as
entitling woman to keep her own money in her pocket as well as to
work. Addressing Yankee working women, Susan Anthony proclaimed the wife's sovereignty over "her own person, and her own
earnings." For feminists, the "inalienable right" of a wife to own
and sell her labor and to possess its fruits transcended differences of
race.[50]

Yet if feminists defended earnings reform in the name of wives'
inalienable rights, they also argued that worthless men had alienated
their rights as husbands. The image of the emancipated wife almost
always accompanied that of the unfit husband. Although both images were meant to legitimate her rights as a hireling, one suggested
that she was inherently entitled to contract freedom, and the other

[50] "The Pecuniary Independence of Wives," *Revolution*, June 10, 1869; William Still,
The Underground Railroad. A Record of Facts, Authentic Narratives, Letters, &c. (Philadel-
phia, 1872), 773; Stanton et al., eds., *History of Woman Suffrage* 2: 197, 115; see also
p. 391; "Proceedings of the Eleventh Woman's Rights Convention, May 1866," in
Frances Smith Foster, ed., *A Brighter Coming Day: A Frances Ellen Watkins Harper Reader*
(New York, 1990), 217; Stanton et al., eds., *History of Woman Suffrage* 2: 194; "The
Working Women's Association," *Revolution*, June 3, 1869; "Pecuniary Independence of Wives." See also "The Woman Question among the Freedmen," *Woman's
Journal*, May 9, 1874; "Man's Chivalry to Woman," *Revolution*, September 16, 1869;
Henry B. Blackwell, "Side Issues," *Woman's Journal*, August 19, 1871; "Marriage a
Penal Institution to Woman," *Woman's Journal*, September 16, 1871; "Constitu-
tional Equality," *Woodhull & Claflin's Weekly*, December 8, 1870; Dall, *The College,
the Market, and the Court*, 361–62; Mari Jo Buhle, *Women and American Socialism,
1870–1920* (Urbana, 1981), 49–60; Leach, *True Love and Perfect Union*, 158–212.

that he had broken his half of the marriage contract. One reflected abstract ideals of personal sovereignty and self proprietorship, the other a moralistic reading of laboring home life. "No matter how . . . abusive, drunken, or wasteful," wrote Stanton, still, the husband was "master of his wife and all her earnings." Sojourner Truth stated the case in much the same way. The "colored women," she reputedly said, "go out washing . . . and their men go about idle . . . and when the women come home, they ask for their money and take it all, and then scold because there is no food." Through accounts of husbands who did not fulfill their duty as breadwinners, feminists aimed to prove that wives were not dependent and had literally earned rights in their own labor.[51]

This justification comported with empirical inquiries in linking the collapse of male support to the sale of wives' labor, but it differed in stressing depravity rather than the toll of wage dependence on marriage. In feminist eyes, a hireling husband's economic impotence was largely his own fault. Though the dissolute husband was also a stock character of temperance reform, the setting was distinctly proletarian in earnings reform, with feminists portraying the "suffering" of wives of the "lower class." As Anthony declared, she became a "woman's rights woman" on discovering, while doing temperance work, that "no married woman had any legal right, even to the fifty cents she earned over the wash-tub." Livermore explained that her interest in the Illinois earnings law had been aroused by the story of a drunken butcher, recently released from jail, who seized his wife's wages to buy liquor. Myra Bradwell, who gained her view of laboring life as an officer of a Sewing Women's Protective Union in Chicago, wrote of "drunken" and "unfortunate" husbands whose wives worked. The "Prospectus" of the *Revolution* summed up the argument: "A woman toils from Monday morning till Saturday night, earning a scanty living for a besotted husband and hungry children, and at the end of every week her wages become [his] property . . . this legalized serfdom we aim to revolutionize." Such claims may well have drawn lawmakers' sympathy while keeping laboring men aloof from earnings reform.[52]

[51] Elizabeth Cady Stanton to Isaac Fuller, March 21, 1860, Stanton Papers, Library of Congress; Stanton et al., eds., *History of Woman Suffrage* 2: 193. Recent scholarship suggests that the 1860 New York earnings law was principally a concession to feminist demands for suffrage and that wage-earning wives were too few and too powerless to exert political pressure. See Basch, *In the Eyes of the Law,* 164–65, 195–99. At issue, however, was not simply women's ability to shape the law, but also legislators' response to the uncertainty of male support and to wives' independent economic dealings.
[52] Dall, *The College, The Market, and the Court,* 308; Anthony quoted in a report on a women's rights meeting at Mount Vernon, New York, in "Women in Council," *Revolution,* September 24, 1868. See also Stanton et al., eds., *History of Woman Suffrage,*

The morality tales feminists spun about plebeian marriage were not phrased in the idiom of law; still, they had everything to do with contract. The point was that husbands had broken their half of the marriage bargain and ought to lose any claim to their wives' earnings – a point that was both legal and sociological. The problem, as a writer in the *Revolution* spelled out, was that there was no "protection for the wife when, from unwillingness or inability, the husband's part of the contract is not fulfilled." Relying on images of a broken contract, feminists translated their idiosyncratic perceptions of laboring domestic economy into a politics of wives' rights. They indicted not only malingering husbands but also the legal rules that obscured both the fact and the value of the wife's labor. In all ages and all households wifely toil was essential to family survival, feminists argued, but the "legal fiction of dependency" was most apparent when the wife was a hireling. Faulting men as husbands and as lawmakers, they attacked the specious rules of the marriage contract by speaking of the distress of laboring homes. "The wife earns her living," they insisted. "Multitudes of men do not support their wives and families." In the economics of working-class marriages that drew the wife into wage earning, feminists found stark evidence of the uncertainty of her husband's support and the value of her labor.[53]

Perhaps inside state legislatures feminists did not argue in just the same way as on their own platforms, yet it is likely that in appealing to lawmakers they defended the wife's emancipation on the grounds of both right and retribution. In Springfield in 1869, Stanton may have echoed her earlier statements to the New York legislature (which she reiterated in many speeches and essays), claiming that the wife "holds

1: 493–97, 525; L. Noble, "Notes on the Woman's Rights Agitation," *Nation,* January 20, 1870; "Law Relating to Women"; "Married Women's Earnings," *Chicago Legal News,* November 21, 1868; "Prospectus," *Revolution,* October 20, 1870. Bradwell highlighted the significance of the earnings reform to wives of the working class, "Social Science Association," *Chicago Legal News,* October 31, 1868. See also "Married Women's Right of Property," *Revolution,* May 14, 1868. On Bradwell's work among wage-earning women, see "The Sewing Women's Union," *Workingman's Advocate,* May 5, 1866. On feminists' troubled efforts to establish a coalition with wage-earning women, see "The Women in Council," *Workingman's Advocate,* October 10, 1868; DuBois, *Feminism and Suffrage,* 126–61. On the gender imagery of female moral reformers, see Carroll Smith-Rosenberg, *Disorderly Conduct: Visions of Gender in Victorian America* (New York, 1985), 20–22, 46, 243–44. Images of brutal, dissolute, working-class husbands appeared throughout feminist discussion of marriage and law reform. For a rare discussion in a labor newspaper linking the wife's wage earning to the husband's failure to perform his part of the marriage contract, see Ida H. Harper, "Woman's Work," *Locomotive Firemen's Magazine,* September 1885.

53 Mary Gooding, "Criminals, Idiots, Women and Minors," *Revolution,* January 21, 1869; Henry Blackwell, "Are Wives Supported?" *Woman's Journal,* April 30, 1870; Kate Gannett Wells, "The Nation on Replies to Dr. Clarke," *Woman's Journal,* July 11, 1874; "A Lawyer's Objections," *Revolution,* June 25, 1868.

about the same legal position that does the slave of the Southern plantation. She can own nothing, sell nothing. She has no right even to the wages she earns; her person, her time, her services are the property of another." Livermore may also have testified then, as she would later argue in other settings, that marriage law was "an outrage upon womanhood. . . . The wife is lost sight of entirely – literally swallowed up as Jonah was swallowed by the whale" and that earnings reform was intended "for the poor and down-trodden women, the wives of drunkards and wife-beaters." Since in 1867 Illinois legislators had already confronted the problem of women unsupported by men by passing a law enabling a deserted wife to sue her husband for maintenance, they might have been receptive to the idea that worthless husbands should not be entitled to their wives' wages.[54]

In the case of the 1874 Massachusetts earnings law, it is uncertain whether feminists gained a hearing from the legislature, though they claimed credit for the enactment. The earnings law formed part of a comprehensive married women's property statute, which amended an earlier act allowing wives only a conditional right to their wages. At a meeting of the Massachusetts Woman Suffrage Association in January 1874, an influential Boston lawyer, Samuel Sewall, presented a statement on the injustice of marriage law, whereupon the gathering resolved to demand that the state legislature "secure an equality of rights for husband and wife." Sewall's preoccupation with earnings reform was evident in his 1868 treatise entitled *The Legal Condition of Women in Massachusetts.* For years Boston feminists had protested the wife's legal status, but, as Lucy Stone later observed, some were more effective advocates than others: "That married women in this State . . . are entitled to what they can earn outside the family . . . is due in great measure to Mr. Sewall."[55]

---

[54] Stanton et al., eds., *History of Woman Suffrage* 1: 599; "American Woman Suffrage Association, Mass Convention," *Woman's Journal,* May 21, 1870; "Annual Meeting of American Woman Suffrage Association," *Woman's Journal,* October 24, 1874; see also "Act in Relation to Married Women," *Public Laws of Illinois* (1867), 132–33.

[55] Report of the Annual Meeting of the Massachusetts Woman Suffrage Association, in *Woman's Journal,* January 31, 1874; unpublished, handwritten summary of Sewall's career (December 29, 1888), National American Woman Suffrage Association Papers, Library of Congress, Washington, D.C.; see also Samuel E. Sewall, *Legal Condition of Women in Massachusetts* (Boston, 1886; orig. pub. 1868; rev. 1870, 1875, 1886). The married women's property bill was first introduced from the House Judiciary Committee in 1873 and referred to in the next legislative session. See *Journal of the House of Representatives of the Commonwealth of Massachusetts* (Boston, 1873), 414, 434. An 1855 Massachusetts statute had provided that the wife "may" labor on her own account, *Acts and Resolves of Massachusetts* (Boston, 1855), ch. 304, sect. 7, but the 1874 law declared that all work performed for other than husband and children "shall, unless there is an express agreement on her part to the contrary, be presumed to be on her separate account," *Statutes of Massachusetts* (1874), ch. 184. See "New England Woman's Rights Convention," *Revolution,* November 26, 1868.

This may have been claiming too much credit. Feminists were not alone in stressing the adversity of laboring wives, and by the time the Massachusetts legislature debated the earnings act, conflicts between wage labor and the marriage relation had been amply documented in the Commonwealth. Moreover, along with amending the property rights of husband and wife, the legislature enacted two other laws in 1874 addressing strains in the marriage contract, legislation that feminists had not initiated. One authorized the state supreme court to compel husbands to maintain their abandoned wives, which opponents claimed tacitly condoned separation, especially among the "lower classes of the people." The other statute altered the poor law to provide wives access to local public charity independent of their husbands' domicile. As the Committee on Public Charitable Institutions explained, it was "proper and desirable that deserted wives, and those having unsteady and improvident husbands" gain the security of alms. In answer, then, to the uncertainty of male support, lawmakers fashioned three different legal remedies. The poor law yielded a wife public support, and the maintenance law obliged her husband to support her privately. But the earnings rule entitled her to support herself by selling her labor and keeping her wages. While granting the wife contract rights, the legislature also reaffirmed her dependence.[56]

Feminists recognized both the achievements and the limits of the earnings measure. "The law no longer declares the husband to be a master and the wife a slave," rejoiced Sewall in the *Woman's Journal.* "The wife's wages are no longer her husband's but her own, unless she chooses to make them his." Others hailed the wife's entitlements as a hireling while attacking the clauses of the law that denied her right to be paid for services done for her own husband. "It is a great gain, when a wife is legally entitled to what she earns outside of her family," wrote Lucy Stone, "when a wife can make a contract as though she were unmarried." Yet she pointed out, "All that a wife earns in her family still counts for nothing." Wendell Phillips saw multiple motives in legislation entitling the wife to enter into commodity relations. Years earlier he had observed that she would surely not be the only one to gain from law acknowledging the sale of her labor and clarifying her status in the marketplace. The earnings laws,

---

[56] *Boston Daily Globe,* March 23, 1874, p. 2; "Report of the Special Agent for the Sick State Poor," Massachusetts Board of State Charities, *Eleventh Annual Report* (1875), cvi; see also *Annual Report of the Secretary of the Board of State Charities* (Boston, 1874), 83–93; "Act Relating to the Rights of Husbands and Wives and for the Protection of Minor Children," *Statutes of Massachusetts* (1874), ch. 205; "Act for the More Efficient Relief of the Poor," *Statutes of Massachusetts* (1874), ch. 274.

he dryly stated, suited the "bank interest" as much as the cause of the wife's emancipation.[57]

Thus the ambiguities of earnings reform were as apparent in Boston as in Chicago. Whereas congressional Republicans presumed that free wage labor would shore up the marriage bond, state lawmakers conceded hireling husbands and wives distinct legal identities. Yet the earnings laws gave formal sanction to the erosion of the economic underpinnings of marriage without fully annulling the rules of coverture. The legislation simultaneously denied and sustained the theory of marriage as a relation of dominion and dependence – by recognizing the wife's labor as a market commodity while leaving intact the husband's claim to her unpaid housework. Treatise writers hastened to explain that the laws were meant "to do something . . . toward severing the unity between husband and wife, in pecuniary things," but not to transform the wife's "*personal* status" or "accomplish the aims of disorganizing revolutionists." The few clues left by judges about legislative intent suggest that the wife's rights were less a token of immutable freedom than a practical response to rifts and reversals within marriage, which often turned her into a public charge. The earnings laws, commented a justice of the Massachusetts Supreme Court, were designed for "women of the poorer, laboring classes," those

left to struggle against the hardships of life – sometimes with a family of children, abandoned by their husbands, or, still worse, with a drunken, thriftless, idle vagabond of a man, claiming all the rights of a husband, and fulfilling none of the duties of that relation.

What accounted for the reform, found a judge in the District of Columbia, was not merely the new significance of money income – "the great accretions of personal over real property, in modern times" – but the "unhappy recurrence of drunken or profligate husbands with patient and industrious wives." In other words, for lawmakers, the husband's dishonor was the root of the matter rather than the wife's sovereignty.[58]

---

[57] Samuel E. Sewall, "Property Rights of Massachusetts Wives," *Woman's Journal,* May 23, 1874; Lucy Stone, "The Real Estate of Wives," *Woman's Journal,* June 20, 1874; *Proceedings of the Eleventh National Woman's Rights Convention,* 42. On Phillips's support for earnings reform, see his letter to Lucy Stone, August 20, 1852, Blackwell Family Papers, Library of Congress, Washington, D.C. On banks' specific efforts to attract wives as penny depositors with accounts in their own name, see the advertisement, "Rules of the M. F. & M. Savings Bank," *Workingman's Advocate,* January 11, 1873.

[58] Bishop, *Commentaries on the Law of Married Women* 2: 6; Wells, *Treatise on the Separate Property of Married Women,* iv; David Stewart, "Married Women Traders," *American Law Register,* 24 (June 1885), 360; "Married Women's Property Bill," *Chicago Legal*

But intent was one thing and effect another. At least some courts, whose task was to give meaning to statutory language, did contemplate the far-reaching emancipatory implications of the earnings reform – however unintended these were by legislatures. In an 1872 ruling that had an elegiac air, the Illinois Supreme Court stated that the wife's newfound contract rights made her master of herself, and the merchant of her own time. Her right to sell her labor and own her wages, the court declared,

presupposes the right to appropriate her own time. The right to take and possess the wages of labor must be accompanied with the right to labor. If the husband can control, then the statute has conferred a barren right. . . . The ancient landmarks are gone. The maxims and authorities and adjudications of the past have faded away.[59]

The author of the ruling was Judge Anthony Thornton, who in 1866 had been a member of Congress and debated the enactments of slave emancipation. Then he had argued that contract rights fractured the slave relation, an understanding echoed in his later reading of the earnings law. His ruling spoke of a lost world, of a hireling wife freed from paternal bonds:

The foundations hitherto deemed so essential for the preservation of the nuptial contract, and the maintenance of the marriage relation, are crumbling. The unity of husband and wife has been severed. They are now distinct persons.

In this case, the lessons of slave emancipation implicitly informed the understanding of the wife's contract freedom. But the ruling did not deal with the question of housework.[60]

The earnings laws came before the courts in as many ways as wives earned wages. Disputes arose over everything from factory labor to farmwork, nursing, taking in boarders, shoebinding, and toiling in tenement sweatshops. The litigation concerned debt, broken contracts, inheritance, and injury to person and property. Two principal issues were at stake: Who had the right to bring suit to recover for

---

News, January 16, 1869; "Woman Forbidden to Practice Law," *Woman's Journal,* May 23, 1874 (citing the District of Columbia Court of Claims). The observations of the Massachusetts justice were quoted during parliamentary debates over married women's property law in England, which was a roundabout reference but one of the few explicit legal statements of the intent behind the earnings law. See Hartog, "Lawyering, Husbands' Rights, and the 'Unwritten Law.' "

59 *Martin v. Robson,* 65 Ill. 129, at 132, 137 (1872).

60 *Martin v. Robson,* 137. See *Congressional Globe,* 39th Cong., 1st sess., 1156. Thornton favored a narrow construction of the Thirteenth Amendment, which would have confined congressional guarantees of freedom to protection of ex-slaves' contract rights.

the wife's labor, the husband or the wife? And who had the paramount claim to her wages, the wife or the husband's creditors? Underlying both issues was a more fundamental problem: Who owned her labor, the wife or her husband? The earnings reform left unclear the legal boundary between the waged labor the wife owned and the unpaid labor she owed her husband. Yet for hireling husbands and wives, that was the critical question: exactly what sort of labor did the earnings laws protect? As the courts threaded their way through the intricacies of wage earners' economic dealings they directly confronted the contradicition between the wife's contract rights under the earnings laws and her dependent status under the common law. This meant deciding in which cases her labor counted as a commodity and in which cases as housework.

To draw the line between the wife's freedom as a hireling and her dependence at home was no simple task. Marriage law had always been "a labyrinth," explained Joel Bishop's 1875 treatise, *Commentaries on the Law of Married Women*. However, "instead of reducing the labyrinth to smaller proportion" the earnings statutes "added to it" by grafting the wife's contract rights onto the husband's rights of ownership. "Nowhere," wrote Bishop, "have the courts gone so far as to suffer these statutes to undo all the obligations which depend on the marriage status."[61]

There were few legal precedents to guide the courts in construing the wife's right to her wages. Under the earlier property acts, that right had been strictly limited, so long as the marriage remained intact. The restriction stemmed from solicitude for the unity of husband and wife and was also intended to prevent husbands from defrauding creditors by transferring assets to their wives in the form of wages.[62] Though the property acts entitled the wife to apply "time and attention" to her property and to claim income from her separate estate, the "products of her labor or skill" remained her hus-

[61] Bishop, *Commentaries on the Law of Married Women* 2: 198, 22.
[62] See Wells, *Treatise on the Separate Property of Married Women*, 287; Bishop, *Commentaries on the Law of Married Women* 2: 370; C.I.H. Nichols, "Property Rights of Wives," *Revolution*, September 2, 1869; *Gerry v. Gerry*, 77 Mass. 381 (1858). The "custom of London," which permitted wives to act as sole traders and keep the profits of trade, did not apply to the wages of manual labor. Though in equity jurisdictions a husband could grant his wife her wages as a gift, that transaction was not valid against his creditors. Law writers noted that the inapplicability of the property acts to earnings discriminated against the working classes. See Warren, "Husband's Right to Wife's Services," 423; Helen Z.M. Rodgers, "Married Women's Earnings," *Albany Law Journal*, 64 (November 1902), 384–86. See also *Seitz v. Mitchell*, 94 U.S. 580 (1876); *Schwartz v. Saunders*, 46 Ill. 18 (1867). On the "custom of London," see Bishop, *Commentaries on the Law of Marriage and Divorce* 1: 495; William W. Story, *A Treatise on the Law of Contracts Not under Seal* (New York, 1972; orig. pub. 1844), 44. On the voluntary gift of her earnings, see Warren, "Husband's Right to Wife's Services," 421–25.

212 From Bondage to Contract

band's. Only in exceptional situations – when a husband was missing, imprisoned, incapacitated, or had deserted his wife – was she entitled to "earn money by her labor, and take the pay." Whether he was dissolute or simply unlucky, if the husband breached his duty to support his wife, the unity of the marriage bond and the exchange of service for protection collapsed. When, in the language of law, husbands were "banished or had abjured the realm," the rights that women lost in marriage reverted back to them. By endowing the wife with economic rights and obligations, the law protected her own interests as well as those of creditors who relied on her word. In such exceptional circumstances, "no right of the husband could be infringed." Under the earnings statutes the exceptional circumstance became the rule. The statutes undercut the "indissoluble connexion" of marriage, assuming the economic estrangement, if not the actual physical separation, of husband and wife, an estrangement that breached his claim to her labor and created her title to her wages.[63]

According to the courts, it was clear that if the wife "mends a garment for her husband," the work belonged to him. In such instances she could claim no wages for "personal services." It was equally plain that if her husband abandoned her and she lived alone, subsisting by, for example, making suspender straps or doing housework for another man, her earnings were her own. In these cases the sale of her labor had nothing to do with her husband's claims. The New York Court of Appeals articulated the rule:

So where the wife is living apart from her husband, or is compelled to labor for her own support, or the conduct or habits of the husband are such as to make it necessary for her protection that she should control the proceeds of her labor, the jury might well infer that her labor was performed on her separate account.[64]

---

[63] Harris, *Treatise on the Law of Contracts by Married Women*, 131; Wells, *Treatise on the Separate Property of Married Women*, 175; Bishop, *Commentaries on the Law of Marriage and Divorce* 1: 514, 496; Tapping Reeve, *Law of Baron and Femme, of Parent and Child, Guardian and Ward, Master and Servant, and of the Powers of the Courts of Chancery* (Albany, 1863); James Kent, *Commentaries on American Law* (4 vols., New York, 1832), 2: 150. On the legal capacities of deserted wives as a source of "protection," see Harris, *Treatise on the Law of Contracts by Married Women*, 6, 135–36. On the confluence of the interests of wives and creditors, see Kent, *Commentaries on American Law* 2: 154, 157; Story, *A Treatise on the Law of Contracts*, 43.

[64] Bishop, *Commentaries on the Law of Married Women*, 344; *Birbeck v. Ackroyd*, 74 N.Y. 356, 358–59 (1878). See also *Burke v. Cole*, 97 Mass. 113 (1867). In *Brooks v. Schwerin*, 54 N.Y. 343 (1873), the wages of a wife who "worked out by day" for $1.25 a week were declared her own. In *Hazelbaker v. Goodfellow*, 64 Ill. 238, 241 (1872), the court reasoned, "we can entertain no doubt that where the husband deserts his wife and children. . . . he at the same time abandons all claim to their labor and their earnings."

Between the two extremes, however, the distinction between house-work and the wife's wage work on her "separate account" grew more difficult to decipher. The ambiguities turned on the nature and lo-cation of her labor – whether it fell within the category of "house work" and was done inside or outside the home – as well as on the use to which the earnings were put. The issue was clear in cases of "hardship," in which the husband was "unable or unwilling . . . idle or dissolute." But the problem, as the New York court confessed, was that "where the husband and wife are living together, and mutually engaged in providing for the support of themselves and their family, – each contributing by his or her labor to the promotion of the common purpose," there was no evidence indicating the wife's in-tention to "separate her earnings from those of her husband."[65] In such perplexing cases – where labor did not neatly divide into par-cels of property labeled mine and thine – the courts held that the wife's wages still belonged to her husband, an interpretation that returned to the common law rule.

That narrow construction extended the legal definition of house-work to cover virtually all of the wife's wage work, thereby reaffirm-ing the property rights of husbands. Whereas the earnings statutes presumed that the wife labored on her "own account" except for work performed for her family, the courts reversed the presumption. Taking in boarders, nursing the sick, canning fruit, working as a seamstress for five dollars a week, running a hotel – such industry was deemed part of the service the wife owed as the "helpmate of her husband." Accordingly, she had no lawful claim to its proceeds, judges reasoned. As the discharge of her wifely duty, her labor had no economic value aside from her husband's interest in it, and her earnings were liable for his debts. Payment for housework could pro-mote "frauds upon creditors," declared the New York Court of Ap-peals, for the wife could absorb her husband's earnings under "se-cret, unknown contracts."[66]

Despite the earnings acts, it remained the wife's burden to rebut

[65] *Birbeck v. Ackroyd,* 74 N.Y. at 359. See also *Beau v. Kiah,* 4 Hun. N.Y. 171 (1875); *Coleman v. Burr,* 93 N.Y. 17 (1883). In *Birbeck,* the court held that the husband had the right to sue to recover the wages his wife earned while working in a woolen mill, since she did not explicitly declare her intent to make them her own.

[66] *Cunningham v. Hanney,* 12 Ill. App. 437, 438 (1883); *Coleman v. Burr,* 93 N.Y. at 26. See also *Beau v. Kiah,* 4 Hun. N.Y. 171; *Dawes v. Rodier,* 125 Mass. 421 (1878); *Stout v. Ellison,* 15 Ill. App. 223 (1884); *Switzer v. Kee,* 146 Ill. Reports 578 (1893); *Reynolds v. Robinson,* 64 N.Y. 589 (1876); *Carpenter v. Weller,* 22 N.Y. 135 (1878); *Uransky v. Dry Dock East Broadway and Battery Railroad Company,* 117–18 N.Y. 304 (1890); *Blaes-chinka v. Howard Mission and Home for Little Wanderers,* 130 N.Y. 497 (1892); Wells, *Treatise on the Separate Property of Married Women,* 287. For an unusually broad inter-pretation of the earnings laws, see *Adams v. Curtis,* 4 Sup. Ct. N.Y. (Lansing) 164 (1870). See also Siegel, "Home as Work."

the legal presumption that her husband still owned her services. That burden extended even to labor that she sold outside her home. Furthermore, if her wages mingled indistinguishably with her husband's, either in savings banks or common family possessions, she lost title to her earnings as well as to the furniture, clothing, and utensils purchased by the joint fund. The courts frowned on the "confusion of goods" that made ownership difficult to determine. If the wife owned separate property, her husband might even farm her land without subjecting it to his debts. Yet if she saved her money together with her husband's in one bank account, he became the exclusive owner: "To mix it with his money . . . would be, in effect, returning it to him." For when the earnings of husband and wife mixed, neither juries nor creditors had a way to distinguish what belonged to each.[67]

A Massachusetts case illustrated the labyrinthine course of the law that returned a wife's wages to her husband. In 1875 Bridget Hawkins sued a railroad company for losing her clothes, which she had bought with her own wages. She asserted her claim under the earnings law passed the year before. Hawkins was a factory laborer, whose work in a textile mill fell outside the domain of housework. So the jury found in delivering a verdict entitling her to recover the value of her labor, as embodied in her clothes purchased with her own wages. But the Massachusetts Supreme Judicial Court reversed the judgment on appeal, ruling that her wages were not "literally her own" – not hers "separately and exclusively" because she shared them with her husband in a "joint fund." The practice in the Hawkins family, as in many laboring homes, was for the husband to give his wages to his wife, who mixed them with her own to pay for household goods from a common fund of money. It was precisely this

---

[67] Bishop, *Commentaries on the Law of Married Women* 2: 359; *McCluskey v. Provident Institution for Savings,* 103 Mass. 300, 306 (1869). According to the courts, title to the wife's earnings followed from the prior and preeminent right of property. As long as the wife had clear legal title to separate property, her husband could even expend his labor on it without converting it to his own possession or making it liable for his debts. See *Buckley v. Wells,* 33 N.Y. 517 (1865); *Gage v. Dauchey,* 34 N.Y. 293 (1866); *Blood v. Barnes,* 79 Ill. 437 (1875). For the opposite holding, where the husband's management of his wife's property converted it to his possession, see *Wilson v. Loomis,* 55 Ill. 352 (1870); Zeigler, "Wifely Duties." Such actions were mainly suits against law officers, often sheriffs, for seizure of goods in execution for debt. The contrast between the courts' holding in these cases, usually known as "agency" cases, and the earnings cases demonstrates that property ownership remained the essential basis of the wife's legal capacity and ability to shield her assets from her husband's creditors. Her capacity thus remained a highly unusual one. On the hardship this rule imposed on working-class wives, see Rodgers, "Married Women's Earnings," 384–86; *Kelley v. Drew,* 94 Mass. 107 (1866); Wells, *Treatise on the Separate Property of Married Women,* 182.

mingling of earnings, the court held, that made the wife simply "the custodian" rather than "exclusively the owner" of her wages and whatever she bought with them.[68]

Such judgments made a dead letter of the earnings laws, claimed feminists. According to Samuel Sewall, everyone was shocked by the "hard case of Bridget Hawkins." Even before the ruling, essays in the *Woman's Journal* accused judges of "legal pettifogging" and denounced the courts for clinging to precedent and upholding abuses. But the Hawkins case, argued Sewall, represented the "grossest injustice," one that encouraged husbands in debt to "sell and pawn their wives' clothing." The case made a "cruel mockery" of the wife's contract rights and exposed the "great defect" of the law.[69]

The courts thus resolved the ambiguities of the wife's emancipation by holding that in most cases her labor belonged to her husband. Even as judges weighed the opposing claims to her wages – probing her home life while also sifting through her commerce with employers, storekeepers, and moneylenders – they continued to assign her a legal status more akin to that of a bound servant than a hireling. A New York justice put it plainly: "I suppose the husband is still entitled to the services of the wife."[70] As a consequence, the wife's legal rights came to hinge not on ownership of herself and her labor but entirely on her ability to keep her work and wages from her husband's reach, to segregate them as forms of separate property.

This legal rule not only contravened the tenets of the wage contract; it was also contrary to the domestic economy of the laboring poor, in which the wife's wage work and unpaid housework were intertwined. In these households the wife did not simply sell her labor to pay for family necessities, her home was most often the place of her wage work. These were the families in which she could be found sewing at piecework or doing washing in rooms used for "living, eating, work and sleeping," and where the smell of tobacco

[68] *Hawkins v. Providence & Worcester Railroad Company*, 119 Mass. 596, 598–99 (1876).
[69] Samuel E. Sewall, "Husbands and Wives," published essay, source unknown (circa 1878), National American Woman Suffrage Association Papers; Henry Blackwell, "Do Not Appeal to the Courts," *Woman's Journal*, February 7, 1874; Sewall, "Husbands and Wives." In response to the Hawkins cases, Sewall and other Massachusetts feminists promoted a law allowing contracts between husbands and wives, an effort that failed in the legislature in 1878. See Sewall, "Husbands and Wives"; Leach, *True Love and Perfect Union*, 176. On the judicial rulings in married women's cases in the early twentieth century, see Nancy F. Cott, *The Grounding of Modern Feminism* (New Haven, 1987), 186–87; Siegel, "Home as Work."
[70] *Beau v. Kiah*, 4 Hun. N.Y. at 173.

waiting to be made into cigars hovered "over everything, the infant's cradle, the marriage bed."[71] The separate property rule – discriminating not simply between men and women but between women of the propertied and laboring classes – gutted the value of the earnings laws to the hireling wife, for among husbands and wives who owned little other than labor, no clear line separated their work, their wages, or their belongings. As her husband's property, the wife's earnings could be claimed for his debts.

Objects in pawnshops reflected the material significance that the wife's emancipation might have had in laboring homes. Accounts of city life described how the poor lined up every Saturday under the three golden balls that marked the pawnshop, carrying "some little article of little worth" and "receiving a mere pittance in exchange." In one shop on the Bowery clothing and furniture filled entire rooms and the shelves and pigeonholes

overflowed with mechanics' tools, musical instruments, clocks, guns, pistols, swords, drums, boots, shoes, work-boxes, – a complete museum. . . . relics of better days; odd mementoes . . . articles of domestic use of all sort – sometimes unmentionable.[72]

Not even the broadest judicial interpretation of the earnings laws could have remedied the poverty of laboring families. Still, had the courts construed them differently, granting the wife – rather than her husband – first title to her own person, labor, and wages, she might have been better able to guard her household belongings from the claims of debt. Perhaps, as Samuel Sewall argued, she could more often have eluded the pawnbroker's reach. Yet her right to the fruits of her labor was of little value when premised on physical or economic separation from her husband.

Under the earnings laws, marriage became more like any other contract – one of less stark formal inequality between husband and wife. Registering the effects of wage work on home life, the laws struck at coverture's essence: the exchange of service for support that gave the husband dominion over his wife. The law set its imprimatur on the sale of wifely labor as a commodity. Yet the wife remained partly free and partly bound. For her emancipation granted her wages, but left her without clear title to herself and her labor. Only in part did

[71] Massachusetts Bureau of Statistics of Labor, *First Annual Report* (1870), 166–72; Samuel Gompers, "The Curse of Tenement-House Cigar Manufacture," in *The Samuel Gompers Papers*, ed. Stuart B. Kaufman (6 vols., Urbana, 1986), 1: 175. See also Betts, *Leaven in a Great City*, 24, 255, 257–58.
[72] Smith, *Sunshine and Shadow in New York*, 214; Thomas Knox in Campbell, *Darkness and Daylight*, 607.

her contract rights release her from belonging, body and soul, to her husband. As antislavery statesmen had pledged during debates over abolition, the hireling husband retained a property right in his wife's service that was the entitlement of all free men. The wife, remarked Thomas Wentworth Higginson, was only "half way out" of the "feudal shell."[73]

The contract freedom afforded wives, therefore, was not that of either former slaves or other hirelings. Rather, it was hedged by the bonds of marriage. Because the wife lacked unqualified rights of self ownership, the law narrowly founded her claims to her wages on her title to separate property or her estrangement from her husband. Reconciling wage labor with marriage, the earnings reform brought to light a new set of contradictions. Prevailing beliefs defined freedom in terms of the contract right both to sell one's labor for wages and to maintain a household. Yet the legal rules entitling the wife to her wages implicitly denied her status as proletarian while also presupposing her distance from her husband. That was as paradoxical as the persistence of marriage bonds in a land of free men.

[73] Thomas Wentworth Higginson, "Half Way Out," *Woman's Journal,* July 18, 1874.

6

The Purchase of Women

The triumph of contract freedom rested as much on discrediting proslavery visions of free market society as it did on destroying the slave system. As northerners dismantled southern society and addressed the momentous problems of Reconstruction, they simultaneously had to confront crises within their own world that had been forecast by slavery's defenders. In the slaveholders' view, freedom would ultimately bring the end of all domestic order: organic relations of dependency – between master and slave, husband and wife, the propertied and unpropertied – would give way to the cruel hierarchies of free market relations. That was the lesson of history, one southerner had warned the United States Congress in 1857. "When the working classes stepped out of the condition of bondage, by the process of emancipation, they branched into four recurring subordinations – the hireling, the beggar, the thief, and the prostitute."[1]

More than any of the other figures, the prostitute evoked the nightmare of freedom envisioned in the Old South. She stood outside the matrix of the legitimate contracts of labor and of marriage. Yet by exchanging sex as a commodity for money she perversely fused aspects of both, in a way contemporaries found loathsome. Above all, they were haunted by the figure of the streetwalker. In both law and popular thought, she was equated with the beggar, classified as a dependent vagabond who did nothing valuable and bothered passersby. Yet her defining trait was not asking for alms but offering to sell her body. Unlike the beggar, she complied with the spirit of the market. But she negated the law of marriage, which restricted exchanging sex for subsistence to husband and wife and entitled men to women's bodies. Like the wife who earned wages, the streetwalker exposed the conflict between contract freedom and relations of dominion and dependence at home.

By no means did concern over prostitution arise from the abolition of slavery. Streetwalking had been punished since colonial

---

[1] Quoted in Eugene D. Genovese, *Roll, Jordan, Roll: The World the Slaves Made* (New York, 1972), 460.

times, and by the eve of the Civil War, both moral reformers and public officials had mounted crusades against prostitution across the country. Before the war, as after, city inhabitants deplored not only the supply of women on the streets but the demands of their male buyers.[2]

But slavery's downfall gave new meaning to prostitution as a social problem. Partly, the heightened anxiety owed to the growing street trade in female bodies and to unprecedented state efforts to license prostitution as lawful commerce in the postbellum era. Yet the problem went deeper. Prostitution appeared to embody all the forces threatening the legitimacy of contract as a model of freedom. It suggested that the triumph of free labor did not safeguard even the most intimate sexual bonds from the marketplace. And it revealed not simply the corrosive aspects of free market relations but also the fragility of home life as their institutional and emotional counterweight. Reflecting the intersecting crises of wage labor and marriage, prostitution became a dominant symbol in the ideological conflict over both of these contract relations.

As a symbol, prostitution was inseparable from ideas of slavery and freedom. While for slaveowners it had signified Yankee free market relations, for abolitionists it had represented the traffic in slaves. After emancipation, therefore, the streetwalker was so disturbing a presence precisely in her ambiguity – a figure who conspicuously blurred the difference between free and unfree commodity relations, who could be seen as both the essence of contract freedom and a vestige of slavery.

In the eyes of the law, the streetwalker was the beggar's double; their common crime was roving about and soliciting in public. As Edward Pierce explained in an 1870 report to the Massachusetts Charities Board on reforming "habitual offenders," both were species of vagrants who "should be deprived of their liberty." Yet prostitution itself was not illegal. Rather, the wrongdoing was what statutes termed *nightwalking* or *streetwalking* – being "a female who by night

---

[2] See Christine Stansell, *City of Women: Sex and Class in New York, 1789–1860* (New York, 1982); Carroll Smith-Rosenberg, *Religion and the Rise of the American City: The New York City Mission Movement* (Ithaca, 1971); David J. Pivar, *Purity Crusade: Sexual Morality and Social Control, 1868–1900* (Westport, Conn., 1973); Mary P. Ryan, *Women in Public: Between Banners and Ballots, 1825–1880* (Baltimore, 1990), 95–109; John D'Emilio and Estelle B. Freedman, *Intimate Matters: A History of Sexuality in America* (New York, 1988), 49–51, 130–33, 140–45; Timothy J. Gilfoyle, *City of Eros: New York City, Prostitution, and the Commercialization of Sex, 1790–1920* (New York, 1992); Marilyn Wood Hill, *Their Sisters' Keepers: Prostitution in New York City, 1830–1880* (Berkeley, 1993); Barbara Hobson, *Uneasy Virtue: The Politics of Prostitution and the American Reform Tradition* (New York, 1987).

frequents the streets, highways or public places, or goes about or abroad with intent to offer herself for prostitution." Neither state criminal codes nor the police and courts drew a distinction between asking as a beggar and offering as a prostitute; rather, they lumped them together as conditions of criminal dependence. Both paupers and prostitutes were "leeches . . . drawing blood," declared the Charities Board, "helpless, dependent, idle."[3]

During the years immediately following the Civil War state officials charged that prostitutes were multiplying as fast as beggars. According to an 1870 study by the Massachusetts Bureau of Labor Statistics, "Vagrancy, beggary and prostitution in all their phases abound, and are increasing in our midst." That same year the Boston police chief reported increasing complaints about "lewd women . . . perambulating our streets," and his force became famous for making mass arrests of streetwalkers. Preoccupation with the issue was not confined to Massachusetts. In 1875 a New York City detective asserted that prostitution had increased so much throughout the country that America now rivaled France in immorality. The "infamous business," concluded an 1876 government report on crime in New York State, existed "not in quiet and obscurity, but flauntingly, openly, indecently." Seemingly, the traffic in women had grown as common as pleas for alms.[4]

Literary studies of city life lent color to the findings of the state. Observers of the metropolitan underworld portrayed the streetwalker's menacing publicity – her gait, gestures, cries, face, body, and clothes all were catalogued as signs of plebeian vice. By comparison, elite brothels appeared almost respectable. "In all the great cities of the United States . . . and I have been in all of them – the walking of the streets after nightfall by prostitutes has become an alarming evil," claimed one writer, as a man of the world. "The

---

[3] Massachusetts Board of State Charities, *Seventh Annual Report* (Boston, 1871), 11, 12, 37, 38; Massachusetts Board of State Charities, *Second Annual Report* (Boston, 1866), xx. See also Howard Woolston, *Prostitution in the United States prior to the Entrance of the United States into the World War* (New York, 1921), 25–26; Ernst Freund, *The Police Power: Public Policy and Constitutional Rights* (Chicago, 1904), 228–30; Thomas C. Mackey, *Red Lights Out: A Legal History of Prostitution, Disorderly Houses, and Vice Districts, 1870–1917* (New York, 1987), 28–92; Hill, *Their Sisters' Keepers*, 112–27.

[4] Massachusetts Bureau of Statistics of Labor, *First Annual Report* (Boston, 1870), 363; Boston Chief of Police, *Annual Report* (Boston, 1870), 57; John Warren, Jr., *Thirty Years' Battle with Crime; or, The Crying Shame of New York as Seen under the Broad Glare of an Old Detective's Lantern* (New York, 1970; orig. pub. 1875), 76, 37, 14, 32; New York State Assembly, *Report of the Select Committee of 1875 to Investigate the Causes of the Increase of Crime in the City of New York*, Doc. No. 106 (1876), 30. See also Hill, *Their Sisters' Keepers*, 176–79. On mass arrests, see Edward H. Savage, *Police Records and Recollections or Boston by Daylight and Gaslight for Two Hundred and Forty Years* (Montclair, N.J., 1971; orig. pub. 1873), xiii.

stranger need only turn three hundred feet out of Broadway . . . to encounter the most startling evidence of the possibility of total depravity."

To see the worst, stand for the hour before midnight on the corner of Houston and Greene streets. . . . A hundred women apparently will pass. . . . They are poorly dressed, have nothing of beauty in form or face, and are always uncouth or brazenly vulgar in manner.

The accounts described the streetwalker's search for buyers, her "offers to sell her body to a man she never saw before, for fifty cents . . . at least a dozen times within the hour." Reportedly, some women merely asked, "How are you, my dear?" Others dared to "openly solicit you" while "walking past . . . dressed gaudily, though they are ugly in the face." Each evening, a New York man wrote in 1869, "they come out of their dens to the broad pavement, – up and down, down and up, leering at men, and asking for company or for help. . . . [A] woman flitting out from a side street, where she has been watching for her victim, will seize a man by the arm, and cry out, 'Charlie, how are you?' . . . 'Where are you going?' . . . If the party looks after the woman . . . she turns and follows the looker-on."[5]

The scenes mirrored the portraits of begging, though the prostitute was inevitably a woman and the beggar almost always a man. There were the same images of clamoring poverty, of clever streetfolk and gullible victims. There was the same vocabulary objecting to "tramps on the sidewalk, who annoy the passerby." There was the same anxiety about mistaken identity, about confusing prostitutes and virtuous women, as with the unworthy and worthy poor. There was the same mistrust of bodily appearances, the sense that prostitutes hid their physical deformities while beggars falsely advertised theirs. "By day, they look pale and sickly," one city explorer wrote of streetwalkers. "By night they appear to be beautiful, with smiling faces, light and buoyant step. . . . The gas-light is a good friend of theirs, it hides so many defects." Coupling beggars and nightwalkers as the most debased members of the underworld, the street scenes depicted both as carriers of disease. Yet they represented the beggar's contagion as purely moral, the streetwalker's as both physical and moral, emanating from a body corrupted by degenerate sexuality. While beggars spread idleness, streetwalkers spread "loathsome

[5] Edward Crapsey, *The Nether Side of New York, or, the Vice, Crime and Poverty of the Great Metropolis* (Montclair, N.J., 1969; orig. pub. 1872), 142, 138; George Ellington, *The Women of New York or the Underworld of the Great City* (New York, 1869), 302; Matthew Hale Smith, *Sunshine and Shadow in New York* (Hartford, 1869), 427–28. See also Gilfoyle, *City of Eros*, esp. pp. 197–223; John F. Kasson, *Rudeness and Civility: Manners in Nineteenth-Century Urban America* (New York, 1990), 70–111.

diseases." Even to sympathetic onlookers, the streetwalker was "the extremity of abomination – the last gleam of womanhood dead beyond resurrection." By dint of sex, female depravity was considered the worst.[6]

Despite the furor over streetwalkers' growing prevalence, such claims were as familiar as the vignettes documenting them. Since the 1830s, moral reformers had published eye-witness accounts to prove that prostitution was on the rise. A half century later the descriptions of nightwalking predators had acquired a lurid monotony. As Edward Pierce admitted, "these unhappy women . . . the castaways of society, are the theme of a periodical sensation." Literary men meditated on the problem's apparent timelessness. "In walk, manners, dress," one despaired, Broadway streetwalkers "resemble the women of their class, who, three thousand years ago, plied their wretched trade under the eye of Solomon."[7]

But if the streetwalker illustrated the age-old fall of woman, she conversely appeared distinctly modern – she was the quintessential commodity, and she was thoroughly metropolitan. Circulating on sale through the streets, she embodied the vast social and economic changes brought on by the burgeoning of capitalism and city life. As Walter Benjamin would later write in an essay titled "Central Park," the prostitute's allegorical significance in the nineteenth century related directly to the ascendance of the commodity form. "Ever more callously the object world of man assumes the expression of the commodity. . . . The commodity attempts to look itself in the face. It celebrates its becoming human in the whore." So, too, Benjamin wrote that city growth darkly recast prostitution's meaning. "With the rise of the great cities prostitution came into possession of new secrets": one of which was the "labyrinthine character of the city," a labyrinth signifying "death-dealing forces" and "colourfully framed by prosti-

[6] Smith, *Sunshine and Shadow in New York*, 424; Ellington, *Women of New York*, 299; Crapsey, *Nether Side of New York*, 142; Helen Campbell, *The Problem of the Poor: A Record of Quiet Work in Unquiet Places* (New York, 1882), 10–11. See also Ryan, *Women in Public*, 69–73, 111. On representations of beggars and prostitutes, see Catherine Gallagher, "The Body Versus the Social Body in the Works of Thomas Malthus and Henry Mayhew," in *The Making of the Modern Body: Sexuality and Society in the Nineteenth Century*, ed. Catherine Gallagher and Thomas Laqueur (Berkeley, 1987), 83–106; Sander L. Gilman, "Black Bodies, White Bodies: Toward an Iconography of Female Sexuality in Late Nineteenth-Century Art, Medicine, and Literature," in *"Race," Writing, and Difference*, ed. Henry Louis Gates, Jr. (Chicago, 1986), 223–61.

[7] Massachusetts Board of State Charities, *Seventh Annual Report* (1871), 206; Smith, *Sunshine and Shadow in New York*, 427. See also John R. McDowall, *Magdalen Facts* (New York, 1832); William W. Sanger, *History of Prostitution, Its Extent, Causes and Effects Throughout the World; Being an Official Report to the Board of Alms-House Governors of the City of New York* (New York, 1858), 17–19, 29–30; Ryan, *Women in Public*, 69–73; and the commentary quoted in Gilfoyle, *City of Eros*, 30, 51, 55–56; Hill, *Their Sisters' Keepers*, 11, 219 n. 366.

tution." Less eloquently American writers in the late nineteenth century explored these allegorical motifs. Seeking to decipher changes in the culture they inhabited, they saw in the streetwalker an emblem of the estrangement, the spectacular illusion, the lure of the commodity that characterized the city as marketplace – where the street "is a perpetual panorama" and everything "can be purchased."[8]

In an age preoccupied with measuring the quantity of commodity production as an index of wealth, counting the number of prostitutes as an index of sin became something of an obsession as well. Yet statistical surveys were just as impressionistic as literary ones. No standard classification system existed, which created ambiguity about what constituted a prostitute and whether prostitutes with other means of livelihood were included with so-called professionals. Moreover, as the *New York Sun* pointed out in an 1868 article on "Social Evil Statistics," verifying prostitutes' identity could prove hard not simply because they were "migratory" but because their "real character" was often unknown, if they lived in tenements not brothels. Their numbers were as elusive as those of beggars. Probably, the police understated the figures to indicate their triumph over vice, while reformers and writers tended to exaggerate; but where, between the two, the truth lay is unclear. For example, during the late 1860s the police consistently numbered New York City prostitutes at two thousand to three thousand, or about two percent of the city's young female population. Yet others set the number as high as twenty-five thousand. By 1872, the police declared it had dropped to twelve hundred. According to the author of one urban sketch, however, there were almost twice that many streetwalkers alone. The backgrounds of these women were murky too. The vast majority were young and white, and most had apparently been raised in laboring families. It seems that somewhat more were immigrants, particularly Irish, than were nativeborn, though this would be reversed by the century's end. And a substantial minority were married, though, rhetorically, domesticity and prostitution were usually dissociated.[9]

[8] Walter Benjamin, "Central Park," *New German Critique*, 34 (Winter 1985), 32–59; quotes at pp. 42, 53; Smith, *Sunshine and Shadow in New York*, 27–28. See also Susan Buck-Morss, "The Flaneur, the Sandwichman, and the Whore: The Politics of Loitering," *New German Critique*, 39 (1986), 99–140; Christine Buci-Glucksman, "Catastrophic Utopia: The Feminine as Allegory of the Modern," *Representations*, 14 (1986), 220–29; Elizabeth Wilson, *The Sphinx in the City: Urban Life, the Control of Disorder, and Women* (Berkeley, 1991).

[9] *New York Sun*, quoted in "Infanticide and Prostitution," *Revolution*, February 5, 1868. See also Smith, *Sunshine and Shadow in New York*, 371–72, 374; Gilfoyle, *City of Eros*, 58; Crapsey, *Nether Side of New York*, 142; Warren, *Thirty Years*, 30–31; Hill, *Their Sisters' Keepers*, 29–31, 58–62; Hobson, *Uneasy Virtue*, 88–94; Ruth Rosen, *The Lost Sisterhood: Prostitution in America, 1900–1918* (Baltimore, 1982), 44, 138–42; George Kneeland, *Commercialized Prostitution in New York City* (New York, 1913), 101, 164.

Crime statistics spoke to the problem's magnitude but were not considered reliable, either. Nor did the extent of convictions necessarily correspond to the sheer number of prostitutes, for the police had diverse reasons for making arrests, as did judges for handing down verdicts. "No comparison of convictions at different periods for the offence of nightwalking would be of the slightest value," the Boston police commissioner J.M. Bugbee asserted in 1880.[10]

In spite of such disclaimers, the statistics did suggest a cause for prostitution's ebb and flow. In Boston, where the records in fact were comparatively precise, yearly nightwalking arrests and convictions reached new heights during the Civil War, roughly doubling the totals for 1860. Arrests peaked at 473 in 1863, while convictions increased to nearly half that figure. Perhaps the law was more vigilant during wartime. Yet it is at least as likely that the absence of men from home drove more women into the streets to sustain themselves. Indeed, it was common knowledge that despite the temporary opening of some jobs to women, the Civil War brought a "fearful increase" in prostitution. Even the circumspect Mr. Bugbee concluded that "nightwalking . . . would be specially promoted by the war."[11]

As a commodity incarnate, therefore, the prostitute assumed her condition by reason of circumstances more historically specific than – yet inseparable from – the epic growth of capitalism and cities. That the Civil War seems specially to have promoted nightwalking points to the importance of changing relations of female dependency. It sets in relief the link between prostitution and the uncertainties of male support within the household, reflecting how at particular moments sex took on added currency as an object of market exchange as opposed to one of marital reciprocity.

Judging from the fragmentary evidence, the hard times of the

[10] Letter of J.M. Bugbee to Samuel Warren Dike, December 10, 1880, in Samuel Warren Dike Papers, Manuscripts Division, Library of Congress, Washington, D.C.

[11] Warren, *Thirty Years' Battle*, vi; Letter of J.M. Bugbee to Samuel Warren Dike, December 10, 1880. See Arthur Calhoun, *A Social History of the American Family* (3 vols., New York, 1919), 2: 357–63; D'Emilio and Freedman, *Intimate Matters*, 134–35; Ryan, *Women in Public*, 103, 110–11. On Boston nightwalking statistics, see Boston Chief of Police, *Annual Report* (1870), 37; *Annual Report of Police Commissioners* (Boston, 1881), 19; Massachusetts Bureau of Statistics of Labor, *Eleventh Annual Report* (Boston, 1880), 130–69. Note that Boston convictions during the Civil War were roughly half to two-thirds of all arrests.

Many pages could be written about the vagaries of the criminal statistics. Massachusetts was exceptional in having a specific category for nightwalking; other states lumped this offense together with vagrancy and disorderly conduct. But even in Massachusetts nightwalkers were also likely to be arrested and sentenced as vagrants or disorderly persons. Thus nightwalking statistics underrepresent the numbers arrested and punished as nightwalkers. But they do suggest the impact of the wartime experience. For example nightwalking arrests from 1861 to 1865 averaged 401 per year, whereas from 1854 to 1858 they averaged 301 per year.

1870s represented another of those moments. Along with unemployment and poverty, prostitution seems to have increased during the depression year.. From 1875 to 1878 the number of nightwalking arrests and convictions rose sharply again in Boston, not to the peaks of the war era, but still to more than double the figures for the early 1870s. Chicago followed a similar pattern. There, streetwalking fell under the rubric of vagrancy, and in the late 1870s vagrancy arrests more than tripled and convictions more than doubled compared to the numbers recorded early in the decade: in 1872 there were 881 arrests and 673 convictions; in 1876 there were 3,192 arrests and 1,553 convictions. Though it is unclear how many were charged with streetwalking, the Chicago police listed "prostitute" as the most common occupation of all female offenders. New York City police records indicated that the extent of female vagrancy, which was taken to be synonymous with prostitution, swelled by about one-fifth in 1875. The numbers suggest a response to the query posed by city missionaries at the New York Five Points House of Industry in November 1874: "Business men are complaining that trade is almost dead, manufacturing establishments are cutting down their force of laborers. . . . What then the hundreds who will be out of work this winter shall do, becomes a question of interest. . . . [T]here are those who will not steal, and who are ashamed to beg."[12]

In all probability, the very circumstances of postbellum capitalist crisis that both bred more begging and heightened the importance of wives' wage labor to family economy also led more women to sell sex as a commodity. Not only does this correspondence attest to the very old link between prostitution and women's dependency on men. It suggests a newer connection between prostitution and wage dependency in a full-scale market economy, where all forms of personal survival and social exchange, including sexual ones, were mediated by the cash nexus.[13]

As both wage earners and unwaged family members, women confronted the laws of supply and demand. Like all hirelings, they endured unemployment and low pay, which were worsened by gender

[12] *Monthly Record of the Five Points House of Industry* (November 1874), 100. See Boston Chief of Police, *Annual Report* (1870), 37; *Annual Report of Police Commissioners* (1881), 19; Massachusetts Bureau of Statistics of Labor, *Eleventh Annual Report* (1880), 130–69; Chicago Board of Police, *Reports of the Board of Police to the Common Council* (Chicago, 1873–1879); *Reports of the General Superintendent of Police to the City of Chicago* (Chicago, 1880–1883); House of Correction of the City of Chicago, *Annual Reports* (Chicago, 1872–1876); New York City female vagrancy was reflected in police statistics on nightly lodgers, see "Station-House Lodgers," *New York Tribune*, February 28, 1876.
[13] See C.B. Macpherson, *The Political Theory of Possessive Individualism: Hobbes to Locke* (New York, 1962).

conventions that restricted them to a few female trades and presumed their dependence on men, affording them wages often insufficient even for personal subsistence. In the early 1870s Massachusetts statisticians reported that the weekly earnings of many sewing women did not equal the price of board. Stressing the link between casual labor and casual prostitution, experts on urban poverty in New York City wondered, "counting unemployed time which is considerable during the year. . . . how are the poor creatures to command a decent home and clothe themselves?"[14]

At the same time, women confronted men's inability or reluctance to marry and support them, especially at times of prolonged economic depression, as in the 1870s. "There come in so many pecuniary considerations, which form barriers to marriage," the sociologist Lester Ward observed in 1883, "men and women . . . have no legal access to one another." Not only lack of money but also lack of men diminished the supply of male providers. The 1870 census showed that in eastern cities, from Boston to Charleston, women of marrying age outnumbered men. Wartime fatalities combined with the promise of economic opportunity on the frontier to increase what contemporaries recognized as a surplus of women.[15]

Adding to these dilemmas was the difficulty of obtaining alms. If women were young and single, and especially if their virtue was unclear, they had little chance of receiving outdoor charity. As one New York overseer of the poor wrote in his log for October 1873: "Was visited by Mrs. Keinbaugh, wife of Henry Keinbaugh who it seems has deserted his wife, a very young woman but I suspect of doubtful character. . . . Refused application." And as scientific charity attacked indiscriminate alms and outdoor public charity, such refusals became still more common. At the height of the depression of the 1870s, when municipal governments suppressed begging and cut back on public doles of food and money, charity reformers argued that giving wives aid through work disrupted proper domestic econ-

---

[14] "A Working Woman's Statement," Nation, February 21, 1867; Massachusetts Bureau of Statistics of Labor, Third Annual Report (Boston, 1872), 72–92; Monthly Record of the Five Points House of Industry (June 1866), 18. See also "The Working Woman," Boston Daily Globe, May 23, 1874, 5.

[15] Lester Ward, Dynamic Sociology (2 vols., New York, 1883), 1: 625; Ninth Census of the United States (Washington, D.C., 1872), 1: 641–56. See also New York Association for Improving the Condition of the Poor, Twenty-Ninth Annual Report (New York, 1872), 40; Independent, 21 (April 29, 1869); Virginia Penny, Think and Act (Philadelphia, 1869), 109–33; New York Association for Improving the Condition of the Poor, Twenty-Fifth Annual Report (New York, 1868), 45. See also "Do Women Earn Their Own Support?" Revolution, September 1, 1870, 138; "A Part of the Social Problem," Woodhull & Claflin's Weekly, May 24, 1873. By contrast, the 1870 census showed that men outnumbered women in cities further west, such as Chicago, Kansas City, St. Louis, and San Francisco.

omy. "Such a popular form of charity," the New York State Charities Aid Association declared in 1875, "fosters a bad state of things. The women support the family, while the men lounge away their time." A decade later the philanthropist Josephine Shaw Lowell insisted that it was "a great wrong, to give help to the family of an . . . immoral man." That left women to depend on husbands for support.[16]

The prostitute thus emerged on the streets against a backdrop of dependency relations even more complicated than those leading men to beg. Directly and indirectly, women were vulnerable both to the impersonal whims of the market economy and to the official whims of the state.[17] And they were vulnerable to the personal whims of their menfolk, as well. By prostituting themselves, women left the matrix of legitimate dependence for the netherworld of the criminally dependent.

The question of exactly which circumstances of dependency caused prostitution became a topic of intensive social inquiry in the years following the Civil War. Understandably, it was of utmost importance in an era that glorified the overthrow of slavery's dependencies. The inquiry ranged from reform tracts to sensationalistic journalism to government social science, uniting the concerns of moralists, charity and prison officials, feminists, and labor advocates but also exposing their differences. Invariably, the inquiry raised wider questions about the outcome of contract freedom – about conditions in the market and at home and how they were morally and materially joined.[18]

The inquiry was framed by the same set of dualisms as the debate over begging, although the polarities were more subtle. Again the question of causality was posed in either/or terms: choice as opposed to circumstance. But the opposite answer prevailed. While the dominant view was that beggars usually chose their fate, prostitutes were

[16] William O'Gorman, Records of the Overseer of the Poor, April 8, 1873–April 5, 1876, *Daybook*, notation for October 3, 1873; New York State Charities Aid Association, *Fourth Annual Report* (New York, 1876), 51, 53; Josephine Shaw Lowell, *Public Relief and Private Charity* (New York, 1884), 105. See also *Woman's Journal*, May 9, 1874, 149; Mimi Abramovitz, *Regulating the Lives of Women: Social Welfare Policy from Colonial Times to the Present* (Boston, 1988), 137–55; Priscilla Ferguson Clement, "Nineteenth-Century Welfare Policy, Programs, and Poor Women: Philadelphia as a Case Study," *Feminist Studies*, 18 (Spring 1992), 35–58.

[17] See Karen Orren, "The Work of Government: Recovering the Discourse of Office in *Marbury v. Madison*," *Studies in American Political Development*, 8 (1994), 60–80; William J. Novak, *The People's Welfare: Law and Regulation in Nineteenth-Century America* (Chapel Hill, 1996).

[18] See Judith G. Coffin, *The Politics of Women's Work: The Paris Garment Trades, 1750–1915* (Princeton, 1996); Joan W. Scott, *Gender and the Politics of History* (New York, 1988), 139–63; Stansell, *City of Women*, 171–92.

by this time seen mostly as victims of necessity, sometimes not wholly
innocent but nonetheless trapped by social forces beyond their control. Yet there were differing understandings of necessity itself – of
whether it reflected women's dependence on men or the dependencies of free wage labor.

The framework of the inquiry had been established by the landmark 1859 study of prostitution by the physician William Sanger.
This was a massive social-scientific investigation of prostitution's history, extent, and causes. Unlike religious literature on the issue, it
dealt with material conditions rather than with personal sin. Sanger
denied that prostitution either was "voluntary" or arose from "innate depravity"; assuming that women were passionless, he instead
traced their fall to economic necessity. Not only did he reveal the
effects of desertion, abuse, and betrayal by men, he documented the
pressures of low wages and lack of work. "Real necessity forces them
on the town," he argued. "No economist, however closely he may
calculate, will pretend that fourteen cents a day will supply any
woman with lodging, food, and clothes." He estimated that New
York City's prostitutes had increased from five thousand to six thousand during the depression of the late 1850s. For Sanger, the line
between choice and necessity was clear-cut – choosing between prostitution and starvation, "between voluntary dishonor and killing indigence," was no choice at all.[19]

As concern over prostitution rose after the Civil War, material
ways of thinking came to outweigh purely moral ones. Questions of
political economy were more decisive than those of sexual propen-
sity, at least until the advent of the national purity movement in the
1880s. Certainly, older modes of reasoning endured; the discussion
still treated "licentiousness, intemperance . . . all forms of bodily in-
dulgence," as an Anglican bishop wrote in 1872. Meanwhile, ancient
ideas of evil instinct were translated into a new Darwinian vocabulary. Prostitution was an "inherited taint," wrote a physician in the
Popular Science Monthly. Stating that it was necessary "to cut off this
baneful entail of degenerate propensities," scientific philanthropists
held that prostitutes should be jailed for "very long periods" because the "strong evil in their nature [was] strengthened by their
surroundings." Yet hereditary theory was not the only way of linking
evil nature to a modern environment. Moralists assailed the burgeoning culture of consumption, stating that bewitching displays of goods
promoted a devil's bargain between female desire for finery and
male lust, which tempted poor women into "the most sure hell of
which we can know anything." But none of these viewpoints was

---

[19] Sanger, *History of Prostitution*, 488, 523, 532, 578, 575–77, 488.

blind to what the bishop termed the "scarcity of honorable and supporting female employment."[20]

It was not the devil in either classic or modern guise that pervaded the postbellum analysis of prostitution, but the starving needlewoman. Sewing in a sweatshop or her own threadbare room, she was the symbol of necessity. She represented "craving want" – as the *Christian Inquirer* put it, the choice between "starvation or hell." The *New York Herald* illustrated the cause of prostitution by picturing "a wan face and weary fingers, stitching by the light of a candle." This image was entered into the official public record by the 1871 report of the Massachusetts Bureau of Labor Statistics: "Alas, many . . . have confessed to us, some with shame and remorse, others with the defiant question, 'What else could I do?' *that they had sold their womanhood for bread to sustain life.* . . . Realize, if you can, what it is to sit for hours into the night, thinly clad, in a fireless room, toiling for food that in proper supply had not passed your lips for days!" This image never effaced that of sexual betrayal and was overshadowed at the century's end by reports of a vast global conspiracy forcing women to be prostitutes. Yet for a time the needlewoman symbolized the social conditions that set a higher price on a woman's body than on her labor.[21]

This symbol downplayed volition, as did other images of the prostitute as victim. Though the views that prostitutes presented of themselves were almost always mediated by those of reformers and state officials, prostitutes said often enough to trouble their questioners

[20] F.D. Huntington, *The Social Evil: Its Causes, Consequences, and Cure. A Report Made to Citizens of Syracuse* (New York, 1872), 7; Ely Van De Warker, "The Relations of Women to Crime," *Popular Science Monthly*, November 1875–April 1876, 334–44, quote at p. 341; Josephine Shaw Lowell, "One Means of Preventing Pauperism," In Conference of Charities, *Sixth Annual Conference* (Boston, 1879), 193, 197, 199; Robert Laird Collier, *The Social Evil, an Address* (Chicago, 1871), 5; Huntington, *Social Evil,* 7. See also Ronald G. Walters, "The Erotic South: Civilization and Sexuality in American Abolitionism," *American Quarterly*, 25 (May 1973), 177–201. Purity reformers also remained concerned with conditions of female labor and low wages. See, for example, *Philanthropist,* June 1886, May 1890, and June 1890.

[21] Massachusetts Bureau of Statistics of Labor, *Second Annual Report* (Boston, 1871), 206–8; Joseph Cook, *Boston Monday Lectures. Labor, with Preludes on Current Events* (Boston, 1880), 158; *Christian Inquirer,* cited in Penny, *Think and Act,* 99; *New York Herald,* January 12, 1869, reprinted in "The Workingmen of New York," *Workingman's Advocate,* February 6, 1869. See also Savage, *Police Records and Recollections,* 173; Annie Nathan Meyer, *Woman's Work in America* (New York, 1891), 287–88; Mari Jo Buhle, "Needlewomen and the Vicissitudes of Modern Life: A Study of Middle-Class Construction in the Antebellum Northeast," in *Visible Women: New Essays on American Activism,* ed. Nancy A. Hewitt and Suzanne Lebsock (Urbana, 1993), 145–65; Stansell, *City of Women,* 191–92; Gilfoyle, *City of Eros,* 270–76; D'Emilio and Freedman, *Intimate Matters,* 209–10; Joanne J. Meyerowitz, *Women Adrift: Independent Wage Earners in Chicago, 1880–1930* (Chicago, 1888); Rosen, *Lost Sisterhood,* 112–35; Marc T. Connelly, *The Response to Prostitution in the Progressive Era* (Chapel Hill, 1980), esp. pp. 114–35.

that they chose their way of life. One rare autobiography spoke explicitly of "free will," as well as of "basting and seaming and buttonholing for a few dollars a week" while being "light in the head from hunger." But the latter image, in obscuring free will, was more common.[22]

The image of the fallen seamstress was notable, however, in illuminating aspects of wage labor unrecognized in tributes to contract freedom. Harsh realities of the free market that were denied in the beggar's case were widely admitted in the prostitute's. As Boston's police chief asked in 1871: "What more could be done were it the policy to drive these women into the streets for a living? Do our merchants, our tradesmen, our manufacturers, ever think of this?" The same philanthropists who denied that begging was involuntary stressed that the "Great Want" of sewing women led to "repeated if not frequent resorts to the street after nightfall." Even reformers and state officials who were most unsympathetic to unlawful dependence linked prostitution to starvation wages.[23]

Thus the flaws of free labor came to the fore in explaining prostitution, whereas defective character remained primary in explaining begging. Whether one was absolved or accused of personal responsibility for illegitimate dependency turned on differences of sex. Economic categories of analysis were applied to women and moral categories to men – a reversal of customary associations that had complex ideological consequences. The image of the starving needlewoman supported the ideal of female virtue underlying Victorian gender codes, but at the same time it highlighted difficulties of laboring life that did not fall on women alone. "The ruined girl," as the Boston minister Joseph Cook stated in 1878, "is a terrific indictment against the modern system of wages."[24]

Despite the anxious consensus that prostitution was tied to wage work, there was no single understanding of either the deeper roots or cultural meaning of this linkage. Answers to why woman's work paid less than the "wages of sin" bespoke diverging ideals and assumptions about the economic and social order. But the argument was most pointedly joined by feminists and labor spokesmen. Neither group was involved in reform efforts to rescue prostitutes from the streets, a mission of practical uplift that both considered ineffectual. Rather, both approached the problem more polemically, taking the

---

[22] Nell Kimball, *Her Life as an American Madam* (New York, 1970), 141, 143, 183. See Kneeland, *Commercialized Prostitution*, 185.

[23] Boston Chief of Police, *Annual Report* (1871), 63; "A Great Want," *Monthly Record of the Five Points House of Industry*, June 1866, 17–18; "Street Charity – Its Uses and Abuses," *Monthly Record of the Five Points House of Industry*, June 1866, 45.

[24] Cook, *Boston Monday Lectures*, 226.

sale of female bodies as a departure point for attacking in distinctive ways relations of dependency and domination in free market society.

The same year that Sanger's study was published, the feminist reformer Caroline Dall wrote to Wendell Phillips that she was anxious about giving a public lecture on Labor. "I shall have to speak of prostitution," she confided, "as the first result of low wages. You can guess how this will be received, and whether I need courage or no." Dall had reason to be uneasy, for not only was she to speak publicly on a delicate topic, she would criticize political economy, employers, and men. "Lust is a better paymaster than the mill-owner or the tailor," she told a Boston audience in November 1859. "Compare the price of labor with the price of dishonor, and you will cease to be surprised that women fall." Dall denied that the market set female wages, arguing that man-made rules, based on the idea of woman as a household dependent, limited the avenues of her work and devalued its worth. "His own lust of gain stands in the way of her daily bread. . . . A forcing-pump and a siphon has man imposed upon the natural currents of labor." Unlike female evangelical reformers, Dall focused on unequal access to the means of subsistence, not on the sexual double standard. And unlike Sanger (whom she cited), she blamed male dominion for driving women "from the seamstress's chair to the curbstone and the gutter." In her view, prostitution arose not from female "self-support" but from the false doctrine of female dependence.[25]

The themes that Dall broached soon became a mainstay of women's rights. Articles on female wages and the extent of prostitution filled the postbellum feminist press. "We need not wonder at the multiplication of these fearful statistics. Let us no longer weep, and whine, and pray over all these abominations," declared Elizabeth Cady Stanton in 1868. "We believe the cause of all these abuses lies in the degradation of woman."[26]

To feminists' way of thinking, the cure for prostitution lay in destroying the constraints of woman's sphere and all inequality based on sex. "So long as Woman is disfranchised," stated a writer in the *Woman's Advocate*, "so long will she be underpaid; and so long is there very little choice left for her between poverty and starvation,

[25] Letter of Caroline Dall to Wendell Phillips, September 4, 1859, in Wendell Phillips Papers, Houghton Library, Harvard University. The lecture was published in Caroline H. Dall, *The College, the Market, and the Court: Woman's Relation to Education, Labor, and Law* (Boston, 1867), see pp. 135, 140, 137, 143, 175. See also Caroll Smith-Rosenberg, "Beauty, the Beast, and the Militant Woman: A Case Study in Sex Roles and Social Stress in Jacksonian America," in *Disorderly Conduct: Visions of Gender in Victorian America* (New York, 1985), 109–28; William Leach, *True Love and Perfect Union: The Feminist Reform of Sex and Society* (New York, 1980), 263–91.

[26] "Infanticide and Prostitution," *Revolution*, February 5, 1868.

and a life of sin." Writing to the *Revolution,* "A Working Woman"
put it bluntly, "The prices of woman's labor are established by men
almost universally. . . . Surely there is something besides supply and
demand that robs woman of half her earnings."[27] The necessity that
made female choice an illusion here derived not from the market's
natural laws but rather from male contrivances.

In rejecting prevailing wage doctrine, feminists did not simply
dispute classical economic principles, they entered a wider dialogue,
carried out across the industrial world, on woman's place in capitalist
production and the level of her earnings. As the economist Francis
Amasa Walker observed, "A great deal of attention has been directed, in these late days, to the wages received by women" – with
"sentimentalists" opposing the payment of market rates, "as if it
were the business of employers to do anything else," and economists
viewing " 'demand and supply,' as setting the whole question of
women's wages, without recognizing . . . man's volition." Equivocal
about his own views, Walker maintained that women's low pay
marked a "failure of competition" arising from cultural as well as
economic causes.[28]

But feminists held men accountable as a sex for making it more
profitable for women to be prostitutes than to perform wage labor.
Although refusing to explain low wages merely by supply and demand, feminists exploited market precepts in showing how women
calculated – in terms of exchange value – what commodities to put
up for sale. "A certain class of men will pay vice largely, while virtue
starves," objected a writer in the *Woman's Journal.* "Think what a
premium they offer upon vice!" Prostitutes reportedly charged buyers from ten cents to ten dollars, a price higher than the usual wages
for piecework sewing and the rates for work given out as alms, which
fell below 25 cents a day. When the alternatives were working, begging, or starving, choosing to "do worse" at least had the virtue of
economy. But it did not embody the prized freedoms of the market.
Feminists held that women compelled by such choices were "as

---

[27] Nettie Bertrand, "A Working Girl's Thought," *Woman's Advocate,* 1 (February
1869), 79; "What Was Said," *Revolution,* February 4, 1869. See also *Revolution,* October 1, 1868, January 20, 1870; *Woman's Journal,* February 2, 1870, February 12,
1870, March 19, 1870; *Woodhull & Claflin's Weekly,* August 13, 1870, May 20, 1871.
[28] Francis Amasa Walker, *First Lessons in Political Economy* (New York, 1889), 258–59;
Francis Amasa Walker, *The Wages Question: A Treatise on Wages and the Wages Class*
(New York, 1876), 372–79. See also Azel Ames, Jr., *Sex in Industry: A Plea for the
Working-Girl* (Boston, 1875). See Kathleen Canning, " 'The Man Transformed into
a Maiden'? Languages of Grievance and the Politics of Class in Germany, 1850–
1914," *International Labor and Working-Class History,* 49 (Spring 1996), 47–72; Coffin, *Politics of Women's Work;* Scott, *Gender and the Politics of History,* 139–63; Joan W.
Scott, "The Woman Worker," in *Histoire des Femmes en Occident,* ed. Georges Duby
and Michelle Perrot (4 vols., Paris, 1991), 4: 399–426.

much objects of enlightened, philanthropic sympathy, as were, a few years ago, the negro slave women."[29]

In feminist hands, then, the starving needlewoman's plight became an image of slavery. "Only think of intelligent white women, in this free and wealthy country, being compelled to live on a cracker a day! Only think of women making shirts at 8 cents each, to support themselves!" The question, declared a correspondent of the *Revolution*, was whether "southern slavery, bad as it was, ever produced as much suffering or evil."[30] Inspired by a sense of racial prerogatives as well as one of equal rights, this rhetoric echoed workingmen's cries of wage slavery. Yet for feminists the issue of wages, however urgent, was not the essence of the prostitute's subjection. Nor were they referring to other common ideas of bondage, such as being enslaved to one's own passions or actually being impressed into sexual servitude.

Instead, by explaining the material roots of prostitution through analogies to slavery, feminists attacked the condition of women's dependence on men. This was the argument of a speech on "Social Purity" that Susan Anthony delivered across the Midwest in 1875. "The tap-root of our social upas lies deep down at the very foundations of society. It is woman's dependence. . . . Hence, the first and only efficient work must be to emancipate woman from her enslavement." Moving beyond the standard portrait of necessity – the "penniless woman" who earned a "scanty larder" and was tempted by the "gilded hand of vice" – Anthony declared that woman must be "equal – a free and independent sovereign." In her eyes, the prostitute exemplified all women's dependence.[31]

Feminism did not simply contribute to inspecting the causes of prostitution by insisting on inequities in work and wages; its insights went deeper. Advocates of women's rights argued that poverty was a proximate reason why fallen sewing women walked the streets but the underlying reason was men's command over the means of subsistence and the resulting asymmetries of power that shaped all moral values and economic exchange. As Anthony said, "Whoever controls

[29] Helen M. Slocum, "The Causes of Prostitution," *Woman's Journal*, January 18, 1879; Parker Pillsbury, "How the Working Women Live," *Revolution*, May 13, 1869. See Warren, *Thirty Years' Battle*, 102; Kneeland, *Commercialized Prostitution*, 107–8; Oliver Dyer, "The Destitute and Outcast Children of N.Y. City," *Packard's Monthly* (February 1870), 78; Associated Charities of Boston, *Sixth Annual Report* (Boston, 1885), 36. For a less subversive feminist analysis of wages, see Thomas W. Higginson, "The Problem of Wages," *Woman's Journal*, March 19, 1870.

[30] "Woman's Rights," *Revolution*, May 13, 1869.

[31] Ida Husted Harper, *Life and Work of Susan B. Anthony* (3 vols., New York, 1969), 1: 408, 2: 1011, 1007, 1010. See also "Female Labor Question," *Revolution*, October 29, 1868.

work and wages, controls morals." For feminists, prostitution did not represent an exceptional case but an awful example of ordinary affairs between the sexes.[32]

Not only did this argument negate idealistic assumptions about the bonds between men and men, it directly connected wrongs in the market with wrongs at home, challenging the division between public and private life. For feminists, the inequalities and coercions of both realms met in the contract of prostitution – a contract joining "woman's want of bread" with "passional demands on the part of men." Yet by contrasting the prostitute as the exemplar of female dependence to the independent sovereign equal in work and wages, feminists reaffirmed the ideal of contract freedom.[33]

Much of this diagnosis could have been advanced from Gilded Age labor platforms; but not all. Labor reformers condemned women's low wages and argued that extremes of poverty and wealth caused prostitution, offering an economic analysis of immorality by linking the corrupt commerce between men and women to wage labor. They agreed with feminists in ascribing prostitution to unfree social relations. Yet they saw virtue in the dependence of women in marriage, while assailing the dependence of men under the wage contract.[34]

Among workers a story circulated about a seamstress who told her employer she could not live on her wages but earned only the reply to supplement them by prostituting herself. As Samuel Gompers retold it to congressional investigators in 1883, " 'But what shall I do,' she said. . . . 'Oh,' was the answer, 'you can do as many others do; some gentleman will . . . pay your board in full or in part, for the privilege of occasionally visiting you in a friendly way.' " The story was meant to expose free labor's depredations through the special misfortunes of women. It taught that prostitution and the underselling of male labor were two sides of the same coin, evils caused alike by the purchase of female work for a price below subsistence. Workingmen knew well that few commodities were cheaper than women's labor.[35]

[32] Harper, *Susan B. Anthony* 2: 1008.   [33] Ibid. 2: 1006, 1010.

[34] See, for example, *Workingman's Advocate,* December 30, 1876; *Journal of United Labor,* December 25, 1886; *Workingman's Advocate,* August 17, 1867, December 21, 1867; *John Swinton's Paper,* May 18, 1884, March 15, 1885, June 27, 1886.

[35] U.S. Congress, Senate, *Report of the Committee of the Senate upon the Relations between Labor and Capital, and Testimony Taken by the Committee* (4 vols., Washington, D.C., 1885), 1: 291; Carroll D. Wright, *The Working Girls of Boston* (Boston, 1884), 118. See Ira Steward, "Poverty," in Massachusetts Bureau of Statistics of Labor, *Fourth Annual Report* (Boston, 1873), 419, 416; "The Wage-Workers. Address of Ira Steward, of Boston, to the Trades-Unions of This City," *Chicago Tribune,* July 10, 1879,

The image of the seamstress who prostituted herself to live domi-nated labor reform protest in the Gilded Age. She represented the "phantom of want," paid wages so low that they were "scarcely suf-ficient to keep body and soul together." Explaining "why so many needle women lead a life of shame," the Chicago *Workingman's Ad-vocate* described a woman who earned four dollars for working for fourteen full days on an infant's cape that cost seventy dollars in a department store. Her life was alleged to typify the results of wage labor, "a fair sample of the system which is daily driving thousands of these unfortunates from destitution to prostitution."[36]

Again the sewing woman personified asymmetries of power and property, but the dominion was of capital, not of men. Though labor reformers often argued that employers sexually exploited female workers, they analyzed prostitution from the vantage point of wage relations rather than of sex relations, terming men "murderers of women's virtue" not as representatives of their sex but as members of the propertied class.[37] For them, the "villain" in the needle-woman's story was the "shrewd business man" who was probably "the trustee of the Erring Woman's Refuge!!!" – while the prostitute resembled a man so poor that he was forced into crime, a "father ... branded as a thief" for stealing "the necessaries of life." In la-bor's view, the ruined seamstress did not portray a uniquely female condition but one different only in degree from the adversity of other hirelings dependent on wages and caught between starvation and debasement.[38]

Thus the sale of the female body symbolized the crisis of free labor. The sewing woman's fall became a way of illustrating that the buying and selling of free labor as a market commodity produced not only stark class inequality but immoral exchange between the sexes. Just as the bondswoman was the eroticized abolitionist symbol of chattel slavery, so the prostitute was for labor reformers a lurid symbol of contract freedom. But behind the icon of the fallen seam-

clipping in Labor Pamphlet Collections, Wisconsin State Historical Society, Madi-son, Wisconsin.

[36] "Wages for Working Girls," *Workingman's Advocate*, August 17, 1867; "The Wrongs of the Seamstress," *Workingman's Advocate*, December 30, 1876; "Legalized Rob-bery," *Workingman's Advocate*, January 18, 1868. For a differing interpretation of labor's discussion of prostitution, which stresses how the theme of prostitution be-came a platform for consumerist valorizations of wage labor by labor leaders, see Lawrence B. Glickman, *A Living Wage: American Workers and the Making of Consumer Society* (Ithaca, 1997), 35–53.

[37] "The Wrongs of the Seamstress." See also "The Present Need of Woman," *Journal of United Labor*, November 25, 1886.

[38] "The Wrongs of the Seamstress"; "Legalized Robbery"; "Women," *John Swinton's Paper*, May 3, 1885.

stress stood the figure of the hireling man too poor to protect his womenfolk from selling their virtue – a man without property in the persons of women. As a Chicago cigar maker described the condition of laboring men, "their poverty often drove their wives, sisters and daughters to lives of shame."[39]

This aspect of labor thought was expressed in many forums – eight-hour leagues, trade union journals, and socialist tracts – but it was most systematically set forth and documented in the reports of the early Massachusetts Bureau of Labor Statistics, when the labor reformer George McNeill was the bureau's deputy. The bureau's path-breaking studies of laboring home life and women's work offered empirical data linking sexual immorality to relations of wage labor, fueling the outcry over prostitution. The bureau exposed the plight of hirelings who *"sold their womanhood."* As the 1871 report declared, "The wonder is not that so many, but that so few fall!"[40]

The bureau's 1870 investigation of a thousand female laborers in Boston revealed that low pay and seasonal work left many of them – such as seamstresses who earned four cents a shirt – without food and clothing. Deriding moral reforms aimed at prostitution as "ephemeral easements," the bureau declared that wages were "the root of the evil." Rhetorically, it asked, "Is it any wonder that vice, holding out promises of better shelter, food and clothing, tempts so many from the path of virtue? . . . Is it not clear that the cry for 'cheap labor' brings dear cost elsewhere?" The bureau's discussion of prostitution as "hideous sin" punctuated its survey of tenement slums, sweated work, and wage labor by wives and children – all of which demonstrated cheap labor's irredeemably dear cost to domestic economy.[41]

A central aspect of the bureau's analysis was its finding that prostitution had come to rival marriage as a supplement to female wages. It argued that both forms of sexual exchange lowered the price of female labor, and therefore all wages, but it counterposed prostitution as sin to the ideal of husbandly support and wifely dependence. Reflecting the inconsistencies of much of the era's labor reform thought, the bureau endorsed women's economic and political

[39] Illinois General Assembly, House of Representatives, *Report of Special Committee on Labor* (Springfield, 1879), 31.
[40] Massachusetts Bureau of Statistics of Labor, *Second Annual Report* (1871), 207. On the bureau's readership, see, for example, Franklin B. Sanborn, "Poverty and Public Charity," *North American Review,* 110 (April 1870), 342; "Labor in Massachusetts," *Woman's Journal,* June 3, 1876; Cook, *Boston Monday Lectures,* 180–81; Helen Campbell, *Women Wage-Earners: Their Past, Their Present, and Their Future* (New York, 1972; orig. pub. 1893), 111–13.
[41] Massachusetts Bureau of Statistics of Labor, *Second Annual Report* (1871), 207, 202, 229, 197; *Third Annual Report* (1872), 115.

equality as a remedy for prostitution but unequivocally affirmed the principle that "man is the supporter of the household." It argued that the problem lay in violations of this "general rule" – all the cases where men could not support their families and prostitution thereby became an illicit surrogate for proper domestic economy. It was these "frequent exceptions" that rendered sex a market commodity along with the labor of wives and children.[42]

The fallen needlewoman was a sensationalized image in the bureau studies as elsewhere, but the bureau used this image to channel the moral panic over prostitution into scrutiny of free labor and to lay bare the effects of male wage dependence. Its root object of concern was "poor workingmen" – who were out of work and underpaid and who had no claim to either the sexuality or labor of women. It was not in starvation female wages but rather in the situation of men that the bureau finally found why so many women were "driven to desperate means for a livelihood." By focusing on prostitution, as by studying tenement life, the bureau undertook to reveal that free labor had left masses of men without the right to be masters at home.[43]

To the bureau, then, the cause of prostitution was not that women were dependent on men, but the inverse – that the wage dependence of men contravened this rule. This reasoning was worlds away from feminist thought, turning women's vicissitudes into an indictment of the lost rights of men. The bureau quoted testimony from laboring men that female hirelings were "unfit for wives, and especially for mothers." It followed that "those who sold their womanhood" were even more unfit and could be counted as ruined property from the view of men's household interests. Echoing antislavery language, the bureau condemned the fact that women were forced to "the necessity of making merchandise of body and soul." Yet it also represented the traffic in women as a sign of the bondage of men.[44]

The bureau, however, recanted this early analysis under the direction of the elite statistician Carroll Wright. Responding to requests

[42] Massachusetts Bureau of Statistics of Labor, *Second Annual Report* (1871), 229, 225. See also Massachusetts Bureau of Statistics of Labor, *Third Annual Report* (1872), 114–15, 340. On labor activists' demand for a male "family wage," see Martha May, "Bread before Roses: American Workingmen, Labor Unions and the Family Wage," in *Women, Work, and Protest,* ed. Ruth Milkman (Boston, 1985), 1–21; Jeanne Boydston, *Home and Work: Housework, Wages, and the Ideology of Labor in the Early Republic* (New York, 1990), 99, 135, 155; Eileen Boris, *Home to Work: Motherhood and the Politics of Industrial Homework in the United States* (New York, 1994).
[43] Massachusetts Bureau of Statistics of Labor, *Third Annual Report* (1872), 115.
[44] Ibid., 117; Massachusetts Bureau of Statistics of Labor, *First Annual Report* (1870), 123; Massachusetts Bureau of Statistics of Labor, *Second Annual Report* (1871), 207.

238 From Bondage to Contract

for data on sexual crime from an influential moral reformer, the Rev. Samuel Warren Dike, Wright's bureau reopened the issue of prostitution in an 1884 report, *The Working Girls of Boston*. Wright promised Dike that "the matters you inquire about will be included" and devoted the investigation to determining if prostitutes were "recruited from the manufactory." Again the bureau found not only that laboring women often earned less than subsistence wages but that men often could not support their families. Now, however, it disclaimed all links between wage work and prostitution. Seeking to refute the story "flippantly bandied about" that employers recommended prostitution to make ends meet, Wright maintained that working girls were "as virtuous as any class of women" and that "no immoral influences" existed at work. Though in an earlier report he had found that wage labor harmed women's reproductive organs, he now saw it as a prophylactic against immorality, stating that "girls cannot work hard all day and be prostitutes too." According to his data, which contradicted Sanger's, "fallen lives" owed less to "poor pay and hard work" than to seduction or choice. He disputed testimony that "the streets were crowded with working girls . . . soliciting men to accompany them home." Instead he concluded that only convicts and professionals were nightwalkers, that "no working woman ever walks the streets as a prostitute."[45]

Not only was this study meant to defend the honor of Boston's working girls, its stated purpose was also to defend the moral integrity of the capitalist manufactory. Later government surveys followed its lead; the New York Bureau of Labor Statistics dissociated wage labor and prostitution, stating in an 1886 report that "the women who take to a life of shame for want of work or low wages as a peculiar cause, are a minority."[46] But these government counterclaims registered the power of the labor reform argument. The debate over prostitution's causes was also a referendum on free contract relations, with the virtues of free wage labor as much at stake as female virtue.

The broader meaning of this inquiry was summed up by William Lloyd Garrison in an address he gave on prostitution in 1878, near the end of his life. In order to discover the "springs of licentious-

---

[45] Letter of Carroll D. Wright to Samuel W. Dike, January 9, 1882, Samuel Warren Dike Papers, Library of Congress; Wright, *Working Girls of Boston*, 5, 112, 118, 120, 121, 124–25, 123, 126; Massachusetts Bureau of Statistics of Labor, *Sixth Annual Report* (Boston, 1875), 67–112. See also James Leiby, *Carroll Wright and Labor Reform: The Origins of Labor Statistics* (Cambridge, Mass., 1960).

[46] New York Bureau of Statistics of Labor, *Third Annual Report* (New York, 1886), 173. See also Campbell, *Women Wage-Earners*, 210–211; International Council of Women, *Report of International Council of Women* (Washington, D.C., 1888), 135.

ness," Garrison argued that the "quest must be for the underlying causes of poverty." This was a transformation in his thought. For he had once seen poverty as insignificant compared to slavery and had never accepted the analogy between wage slavery and chattel slavery, warning instead about the prospect of "a licentious perversion of liberty." But now he singled out the conditions of both poverty and free labor as causing prostitution. Calling tenement neighborhoods "human hives of misery," and poverty the "chief promoter of prostitution," he quoted the words of a prostitute who enlightened a city missionary about wage labor:

I know you mean well by coming here, but I don't know how much good it will do. Instead of coming here you had better go around to some of these factories and shops that grind a poor girl down to $2 a week, and get them to pay better wages. It's no use; a girl can't live on what she gets.[47]

Garrison emphasized "speculation" and "land monopoly" and "private ownership" in analyzing prostitution, reiterating the arguments of labor reformers with whom he had fervently disagreed concerning the legitimacy of wage labor. "Between the wages of sin and the wages of the sweatshop," he said, "the simple wonder is that so many women in need can hold to lives of chastity." Prostitution cast a different light on the market in free labor, which abolitionism had been central in justifying.[48]

Even Garrison, who deemed slavery an unparalleled wrong, conceptualized prostitution in much the same terms as slavery. Using language he would not have applied to wage labor, he protested that women were "forced to make merchandise of themselves" – that the "human soul" was in "the market, and for sale with the body."[49] This was exactly how abolitionists had decried the commodity relations of slave society and contrasted them to the regime of free contract, although chattel slaves were not said to sell themselves. It was

---

[47] Walter M. Merrill and Louis Ruchames, eds., *The Letters of William Lloyd Garrison: To Rouse the Slumbering Land, 1868–1879* (6 vols., Cambridge, Mass., 1981), 6: 388–89; Aaron M. Powell, ed., *National Purity Congress: Its Papers, Addresses, and Portraits* (New York, 1896), 399, 400, 402, 403; Aaron M. Powell, *Personal Reminiscences* (New York, 1899), 60. See the essays by David Brion Davis in *The Antislavery Debate: Capitalism and Abolitionism as a Problem in Historical Interpretation,* ed. Thomas Bender (Berkeley, 1992), 161–79, 290–309; Jonathan A. Glickstein, " 'Poverty Is Not Slavery': American Abolitionists and the Competitive Labor Market," in *Antislavery Reconsidered: New Perspectives on the Abolitionists,* ed. Lewis Perry and Michael Fellman (Baton Rouge, 1979), 195–218.

[48] Powell, ed., *National Purity Congress,* 403, 400, 402, 404. See also David Brion Davis, *The Problem of Slavery in the Age of Revolution, 1770–1823* (Ithaca, 1975); Bender, ed., *The Antislavery Debate,* 161–79, 290–309.

[49] Powell, ed., *National Purity Congress,* 400, 404. See also Chapter 1 of this volume.

hardly remarkable that prostitution proved immensely troubling to
a society claiming to have abolished the sale of human beings.

The ideological conflict over American slavery drew much of its
moral energy from opposing uses of prostitution as a metaphor for
the worlds of bondage and freedom. Both abolitionists and slaveowners tapped this well of symbolism to attack the venality of relations
between men and women on the other side of the Mason–Dixon
line. But the metaphor's meaning transcended sex. In the debate
between slavery and freedom, prostitution stood for a social system
in which all was for sale, in which the market operated as the arbiter
of human relations – this paradoxically was how antislavery represented life in the Old South and how proslavery represented the
Yankee culture of free contract. After emancipation it was both the
ambiguities and polarities of these charged metaphors that framed
the understanding of prostitution as a social problem.

From the 1830s on, abolitionists and slaveowners accused each
other of extolling a social order founded on flesh peddling. In this
war of words the traffic in women symbolized the commodity relations distinctive to slavery and freedom, respectively; prostitution signified both the market in slaves that nullified contract rights and the
market in free labor that entailed contract rights. Both sides argued
in the name of the household, contending that market values were
not commensurate with domestic affection and that social order required a realm of reciprocity not measured by buying and selling.
Southerners insisted on the analogy between slavery and marriage,
whereas abolitionists insisted on the analogy between slavery and
prostitution. Meanwhile, most northerners claimed that the household and market were separate spheres in free society, whereas slaveowners claimed that prostitution embodied their fusion. Two 1837
tracts exemplified this controversy. The abolitionist George Bourne
attacked slavery's effects on "domestic society" by arguing, "The
slave states are one vast brothel," while the southerner William Gilmore Simms defended the "Morals of Slavery" by arguing, "We in-
vite comparison with the free States" – with the "*prostitution of the
North.*" A way of testing the moral character of slavery and freedom,
prostitution symbolized the negation of home life, on which abolitionists and slaveowners rested the defense of their opposing
worlds.[50]

---

[50] George Bourne, *Slavery Illustrated in Its Effects upon Woman and Domestic Society* (New
York, 1972; orig. pub. 1837), 27; W.G. Simms, "The Morals of Slavery," in *The Pro-
Slavery Argument; as Maintained by the Most Distinguished Writers of the Southern States,*

As the slavery debate intensified, abolitionists used prostitution as a shorthand for southern life. This antislavery symbolism was so entrenched that it lived on long after abolition. "I shall forgive the white South much in its final judgment day," wrote W.E.B. Du Bois in 1920, "but one thing I shall never forgive, neither in this world nor the world to come: its wanton . . . insulting of the black womanhood which it sought and seeks to prostitute to its lust." A metaphor for slavery, prostitution remained an emblem of racial subjugation.[51]

A wealth of meaning lay in this metaphor. Indeed, it denoted both economic relations and sexual exchange, expressing antislavery horror not only at the master's licentious power but at the slave's status as a commodity. In ancient times slaves had been sold as prostitutes, but this linkage was for the most part symbolic in nineteenth-century America. Undoubtedly abolitionists knew that prostitutes and chattel were different, for they contrasted free market relations to slave auctions, involuntary servitude, and forcible sex that increased the wealth in slaves. While lauding volition as the basis of Yankee economy, Wendell Phillips stressed that naked force was involved in the value of sex under the slave system – that "half a million of women are flogged to prostitution." Abolitionists realized that prostitutes were seller and commodity in one, while slaves were simply commodities. But in arguing that the essence of unfreedom was treating human beings as "marketable commodities," they came to conflate slavery and prostitution.[52]

Containing the Several Essays, on the Subject, of Chancellor Harper, Governor Hammond, Dr. Simms, and Professor Dew (Charleston, 1852), 211, 229. (Simms's essay originally appeared in 1837 in the Southern Literary Messenger.) See Ronald G. Walters, The Antislavery Appeal: American Abolitionism after 1830 (Baltimore, 1976), 91–110; Eugene D. Genovese, The World the Slaveholders Made: Two Essays in Interpretation (New York, 1971), 195–202; Larry E. Tise, Proslavery: A History of the Defense of Slavery in America, 1701–1840 (Athens, Ga., 1987), 344–46; Stephanie McCurry, Masters of Small Worlds: Yeoman Households, Gender Relations, and the Political Culture of the Antebellum South Carolina Low Country (New York, 1995), 208–38; Amy Dru Stanley, "Home Life and the Morality of the Market," in The Market Revolution in America: Social, Political, and Religious Expressions, 1800–1880, ed. Melvyn Stokes and Stephen Conway (Charlottesville, 1996), 74–96.

[51] Walters, "The Erotic South," 183; W.E.B. Du Bois, Darkwater: Voices from within the Veil (New York, 1969; orig. pub. 1920), 172. See also Neal K. Katyal, "Men Who Own Women: A Thirteenth Amendment Critique of Forced Prostitution," Yale Law Journal, 103 (December 1993), 791–826; quotes at pp. 796–805.

[52] Karen Halttunen, "Humanitarianism and the Pornography of Pain in Anglo-American Culture," American Historical Review, 100 (April 1995), 303–34; quotes at pp. 324–25; William H. Pease and Jane H. Pease, eds., The Antislavery Argument (New York, 1965), 67, 68. See Stanley, "Home Life and the Morality of the Market"; Chapter 1 of this volume; Gerda Lerner, The Creation of Patriarchy (New York, 1986), 86–100, 123–40. For differing interpretations of abolitionism, stressing the primacy of sexuality, see Walters, "Erotic South"; and criticizing the metaphorical use of

Antislavery literature wedded market themes to sexual coercion. Bourne's tract attacked the slave system for gratifying both "lascivious desires and pecuniary demands" by combining "forcible defilement" with trade in "the *girl-market,*" where "warranted virgins" sold at the highest price. It did not acknowledge prostitution in free society, imputing sexual immorality only to the master-slave relation. Instead it used the slave auction – the "trade in '*breeding wenches*' " that fostered "*the propagation of slaves as articles of merchandize*" – to represent the cash value of women as peculiarly southern. In front of buyers seeking a "*female bargain,*" women chattel were hoisted up and advertised as commodities:

The auctioneer recapitulated their history . . . their personal purity, their age, their capacity for usefulness . . . and they were successively transferred to the highest bidder. . . . The bills of sale were made out in the usual horse-jockeying slang, with the additional guarantee of maidenhood.

At one Alabama auction female slaves were weighed, sold, and "the average price was *seven dollars per pound!*"[53]

For abolitionists, the slave auction epitomized the profane nature of unfree market relations – the condition of the slave as prostitute. "Beauty and innocence, are exposed for sale upon the auction block; while villainous monsters stand around, with pockets lined with gold," raged Frederick Douglass in 1850. "More than a million of women, in the Southern States of this Union, are . . . through no fault of their own, consigned to a life of revolting prostitution." Repeatedly, abolitionists recorded how slaveholders entered into "a bargain for a colored girl" to indicate the inhumanity of southern commodity relations. In "thrilling tones" the antislavery lecturer Sarah Parker Remond told of the flesh trade she had escaped as a free black: "In the open market place women are exposed for sale – their persons are not always covered." And as the place where women were sold away from husbands, parents, and children, the auction illustrated the conflict between slavery and home life. It was there, wrote the black poet Frances Ellen Watkins Harper, that

---

prostitution, see bell hooks, *Ain't I a Woman: Black Women and Feminism* (Boston, 1981), 33–34.

[53] Bourne, *Slavery Illustrated,* 13, 40, 24, 48, 62, 23, 27, 37–38, 62–63 (sole reference to prostitution in free society, p. 114). Yet Bourne tacitly referred to the crusades against northern prostitution of the early 1830s, which were led by moral reformers allied with abolitionist leaders, by hypothetically asking in regard to southern immorality, "Now suppose that the same course of life should be commenced in New-England. . . . The *puritan women* would raise a moral hail-storm and whirlwind." On the campaign against prostitution in the antebellum North, see Smith-Rosenberg, "Beauty, the Beast, and the Militant Women," in *Disorderly Conduct;* Walters, "Erotic South."

"woman, with her love and truth . . . Gaz'd on the husband of her youth, With anguish none may paint or tell."[54]

Not all abolitionists used prostitution as a symbol for slavery, yet they constantly used commercial language – buying, selling, bargaining, leasing – to condemn slavery and to contrast human divinity to the spirit of the market. The goal of antislavery, wrote Angelina Grimké in 1836, was "no longer to barter the *image of God* in human shambles for corruptible things such as silver and gold." Remond decried "the traffic in the bodies and souls of men and women who are 'made but a little lower than the angels.' " Antislavery arguments were filled with images of human beings sacrificed in the marketplace. Speaking to the American Anti-Slavery Society in 1857, Harper vividly described slaveholders as knowing of "a fearful alchemy by which . . . blood can be transformed into gold. Instead of listening to the cry of agony, they listen to the ring of dollars and stoop down to pick up the coin." An unmistakable strain of ambivalence, even abhorrence, toward the market ran through antislavery propaganda. And it was most pronounced in abolitionist claims that commodity relations debased women and destroyed family bonds.[55]

The intent of abolitionists was hardly to discredit all forms of market exchange but rather to isolate the trade in slaves as singularly unacceptable. Yet all the discussion about the evils of setting a price on human faculties and body parts – "blood and nerves," "bodies and souls" – had implications beyond the issue of chattel slavery. For at the very moment abolitionists were attacking the South for its commerce in unfree persons, the North was being transformed by the commerce in free labor. Paeans to contract freedom notwithstanding, the antislavery outcry against turning human life into cash value thereby resonated with potential, if unintended, meaning for free persons grappling with the upheaval caused by the rise of wage labor and market society. As one northern critic of wage slavery wrote:

Wherever wages slavery is substituted for chattel slavery, universal prostitution must ultimately take the place of partial concubinage. . . .

> "*Even Love is sold* . . .
> Is turned to deadliest agony . . .

---

[54] Douglass cited in hooks, *Ain't I a Woman*, 33–34; Charles Whipple, *The Family Relation, as Affected by Slavery* (Cincinnati, 1858), 15; Remond cited in Vron Ware, *Beyond the Pale: White Women, Racism and History* (London, 1992), 78; Frances Ellen Watkins [Harper], "The Slave Auction," *Frederick Douglass' Paper*, September 22, 1854.

[55] Angelina E. Grimké, *Appeal to the Christian Women of the South* (New York, 1836), 26; "Letter from Miss Remond," *Liberator*, November 19, 1858; "Speech of Miss Watkins," *National Anti-Slavery Standard*, May 23, 1857. See Karen Sanchez-Eppler, *Touching Liberty: Abolition, Feminism, and the Politics of the Body* (Berkeley, 1993).

A life of horror from the blighting bane
Of commerce. . . ."

Turning antislavery symbolism against itself, some opponents of the
wage system claimed that prostitution was more emblematic of illusory freedom than of actual bondage.[56]

Thus the antislavery argument was complicated by the problem of
containing its own diatribe against commodity relations, especially as
it used the symbolism of prostitution and pitted the market against
home life. One way out of this predicament was to argue that the
condition of the slave as prostitute was immeasurably worse than that
of the free prostitute, an argument that echoed the abolitionist response to protests about wage slavery. Unlike the prostitute in the
North, the slave was "prostituted by law and stripped of all personal
rights," stated Abby Kelly Foster in 1860. Only bondswomen were
"handed over to the lusts of any slave-breeder, slave-trader, and
slave-holder, who shall wish to outrage them" – "compelled by the
law . . . to live in prostitution." By invoking the formal right of personal freedom central to the antislavery defense of wage labor – by
claiming that the law made prostitution worse in slave society than
in free society – abolitionists distinguished between the market in
women in the South and the North.[57]

But most often abolitionists offered more sweeping vindications
of Yankee commodity relations, arguing that the free market in labor
insulated the household from the cash nexus. The symbolism of the
southern brothel as the polar opposite of the northern home was
essential to their denial that free contracts could produce wage slavery. They contrasted slaveholders' practice of "converting woman
into a commodity to be bought and sold" to family relations in free
society where, as Garrison wrote, even the lowliest hireling was "still
a husband, from whose embrace no ruffian can tear his wife – still a
father, whose children no man may seize, and offer in the shambles
to the highest bidder." Insisting that market and household were
one in the South but separate spheres in the North, abolitionists
fleshed out the meaning of freedom through the negative symbolism
of slavery as prostitution. Furthermore, by refusing to accept the
metaphor of wage slavery but instead using prostitution as metaphor

[56] William Wells Brown, "The American Slave-Trade," *Liberty Bell* (Boston, 1848), 231,
235–36. The northern critic was the labor reformer William West, who engaged
Garrison in the well-known dispute over the evils of chattel and wages slavery. See
"Wages Slavery and Chattel Slavery," *Liberator,* April 23, 1847, 67.
[57] "Spiritualism as a Practical Principle . . . Abby K. Foster applying it to the Pollutions
of Slavery," *Liberator,* August 24, 1860.

for slavery, they represented sex – as opposed to labor – as the essence of self turned into a commodity by chattel slavery.[58]

Meanwhile, slaveholders were constructing a moral defense for their way of life that yoked prostitution to free society. Perhaps in moments of private introspection they saw themselves through antislavery eyes, agreeing with Mary Chesnut that "[i]n slavery, we live surrounded by prostitutes. . . . [O]urs is a monstrous system." But the leading proslavery theorists rejected this image of their social system. Although their ways of defending slavery were not uniform, they all attacked northern depravity, contending that prostitution was the outgrowth not simply of innate passion but of free market relations that substituted exchange value for organic social bonds.[59]

The first postulate in the defense of slavery's morality was that " 'those only who are least guilty, may be permitted to cast the stone!' " This proverb informed the great proslavery works, from essays by William Gilmore Simms and William Harper in the 1830s to George Fitzhugh's treatises on social theory in the 1850s. Simms quoted it in his essay on southern morals, denouncing the "fictions of the abolitionists" and admonishing antislavery writers to examine "the brothels, and the stews, and the alleys" of free society. Instead of dwelling on the supposed "grossness" of slavery, abolitionists should examine the "degraded classes in the free States."[60]

Prostitution was a test case for Simms. He capitalized on the notoriety of the 1831 *Magdalen Report,* an exposé of prostitution in New York City, and on the ties between the Magdalen Society and abolitionism as personified by the reformer Arthur Tappan, who was a leader in both causes. Caustically, he wrote that if abolitionists "demanded of Mr. Tappan a copy of the report," they would learn "that, in the city of New-York alone, not including blacks, there are ten thousand professional prostitutes." Denying that the "prostitution of the South" was the "peculiar result of slavery," he admitted that southerners were sometimes guilty of sexual immorality, "but not as slaveholders." Rather, prostitution arose from natural depravity and existed in all societies as "an incident of humanity, in its

[58] Stephen Foster quoted in Walters, *Antislavery Appeal,* 95; "Slavery Better Than Poverty?" *Liberator,* December 24, 1841. See also C. Peter Ripley, *The Black Abolitionist Papers* (5 vols., Chapel Hill, 1992), 4: 323; David R. Roediger, *The Wages of Whiteness: Race and the Making of the American Working Class* (London, 1991), 83; David R. Roediger, "Frederick Douglass Meets the Slavery Metaphor: Race, Labor and Gender in the Languages of Antebellum Social Protest," in *The Terms of Labor,* ed. Stanley Engerman (Stanford University Press, forthcoming).
[59] Chesnut quoted in Shirley Yee, *Black Women Activists: A Study in Activism, 1828–1860* (Knoxville, 1992), 43.
[60] Simms, "Morals of Slavery," 230, 216, 211, 229.

fallen state.'' Further, he argued on the grounds of race that slavery lessened prostitution's evil by limiting it to bondwomen who had no "sensibilities," no "consciousness of degradation," no "social *status.*" Unlike "white prostitution," the southern alternative did not "debase the civilized.'' Simms emphasized that Tappan's magdalens were "factory and serving girls," as he counterposed slavery's benevolent labor system to the "sufferings of the working class" under the wage system. Accusing free society of "overthrowing all . . . hallowing associations," he called abolitionists to the "aegean duty of cleansing . . . stables.''[61]

Other slaveholders also defended southern sexual morality while assailing wage labor and free market relations. In his 1838 *Memoir on Slavery* William Harper argued both that slavery prevented the misery of laboring families and that white women prostituted themselves only in free society. Contrasting female slaves to prostitutes in New York City, he claimed that no slave was "found in the streets a ghastly wretch, expiring under the double tortures of disease and famine.'' But the moral superiority of the slave system was also that bondswomen alone offered "easy gratification" for "hot passions" whereas northern womanhood learned early " 'to go to market . . . it haggles . . . it is knowing, acute, sharpened.' '' In his *Letters on Slavery* the South Carolina statesman James Henry Hammond also moved from condemning free labor to retorting that the "grand charge" of southern licentiousness was antislavery "tea-table gossip, and long-gowned hypocrisy.'' He claimed that abolitionists projected onto the South abuses of "natural instinct" pervasive in the North. In attacking the "whole Slave region as a 'Brothel,' '' he asked, "Do these people thus cast stones being 'without sin'?''[62]

George Fitzhugh's writings grounded the proslavery argument about relations between the sexes most firmly of all in political economy. Their central theme was that in exalting the market as the measure of human relations, free society destroyed the organic unity of the household embodied in slavery. In *Sociology for the South* he wrote scathingly that freedom's defining social exchange was "hard dealing," its virtue "avarice," its only aspiration "to make the best bargains one can," and its watchword "Caveat Emptor.'' Its "moral

[61] Ibid., 229, 230, 220, 264, 211. See also Lewis Tappan, *The Life of Arthur Tappan* (New York, 1870), 110–25, 163–88; Paul Boyer, *Urban Masses and Moral Order in America, 1820–1920* (Cambridge, Mass., 1978), 12–21.

[62] William Harper, "Memoir on Slavery," in *The Pro-Slavery Argument*, 45, 41, 42, 40, 55; James Henry Hammond, *Two Letters on Slavery in the United States, Addressed to Thomas Clarkson, Esq.* (Columbia, S.C., 1845), 11, 14, 17, 15. See Drew Gilpin Faust, *James Henry Hammond and the Old South: A Design for Mastery* (Baton Rouge, 1982). On Hammond's illicit sexual practice, see Carol Bleser, ed., *Secret and Sacred: The Diaries of James Henry Hammond, a Southern Slaveholder* (New York, 1988), 167–76.

code" was expressed in the adage, "every man for himself, and devil take the hindmost." For Fitzhugh, prostitution reflected the diabolical nature of free society. He admitted that the domestic slave trade cruelly split families, but he countered that brutal necessity forced Yankee girls to "quit the domestic hearth . . . to seek a living among strangers," a topic so painful that "delicacy" forbade its further discussion. Of home life in the North he wrote, "We shall not sully our sheet with descriptions of the marriage relation . . . in free America." Averring that "domestic affection cannot be calculated in dollars and cents," he held that free market relations eroded all paternalistic reciprocity between men and women as well as between masters and servants.[63]

As Fitzhugh saw it, marriage and prostitution were alike in free society, both representing commercial contracts that reduced sex to a market commodity. In the North the "holy ordinance" of marriage, he argued, was "a mere civil contract, entered into with no more thought, ceremony or solemnity than the bargain for a horse." Like other slaveholders, he insisted that the analogy in southern society was between marriage and chattel slavery, stressing the "intimate connexion" between these two domestic bonds based on hierarchies of dominion and dependence. Ominously he warned, "Marriage is too much like slavery not to be involved in its fate." He found in prostitution a symbol for all the corrosive forces of freedom that threatened the household and that were distilled in the market relation of contract. To transform the family from a "temple of the Gods" into a "den of prostitutes," he wrote, was the upshot of Yankee liberty and equality.[64]

But that was precisely what abolitionists argued about slavery. However much slaveholders and abolitionists differed over the merits of freedom and bondage as systems of production and reproduction, they agreed that these elements of the social order were inexorably joined – that the buying and selling of human labor could not be separated from family relations. What they could not agree on was which form of commodity relation annulled home life: the market in free labor or the market in slaves. A principal irony of their differences was that both used prostitution as a symbol for the deformities of a world where the market was transcendent. For abolitionists, it symbolized slavery, a traffic in bodies and souls opposed to the contract rights of labor and marriage. For slaveholders, it symbolized

---

[63] George Fitzhugh, *Sociology for the South, or The Failure of Free Society* (New York, 1965; orig. pub. 1854), 39, 38, 133, 200, 51, 250, 195, 106. See also Genovese, *The World the Slaveholders Made.*

[64] Fitzhugh, *Sociology for the South,* 195, 206, 205, 195.

free society, where individuals were bound together merely by contracts no different from bargains for a horse.

When freedpeople in Georgia gathered to celebrate the anniversary
of emancipation on January 1, 1866 they were asked to recall their
condition as slaves. "This is a day of gratitude for the general destruction of slavery," proclaimed the black minister Henry McNeill
Turner. "This trafficking in human blood, buying and selling, sepa-
rating man and wife." That same year officials in Massachusetts
sounded a tocsin for the country, warning how "at night the sad
procession of fallen women walks abroad." As foes of slavery rejoiced
at the downfall of the southern traffic in human beings, Yankees
confronted an openly prospering street trade in women – trade that
belied sweeping claims that the buying and selling of human commodities had been abolished. For all the debate over its causes, prostitution was understood to be a sale of the self. According to the
1872 classic, *The Dangerous Classes of New York,* the prostitute sold
"that which is in its nature beyond all price . . . she perverts a passion
and sells herself." At law, prostitution meant "setting one's self to
sale." In a culture that equated slavery with commodified selves, the
nightwalking procession thus suggested that a form of bondage still
persisted and that slaveholders' talk of abolitionists casting stones
had not been off the mark.[65]

The conflict between northern prostitution and antislavery ideology had been no less apparent before the Civil War, but it was
heightened in the years thereafter. This was due not simply to contemporary reports that the sheer number of prostitutes had risen.
Nor was it due alone to the significance of slave emancipation. What
was also new in the postbellum era were legislative proposals to deal
with the procession of streetwalkers by licensing and regulating this
commerce – by transforming it from criminal dependence to a lawful
market relation. In short, the state would authorize the traffic in
women though it had abolished all traffic in slaves. In an 1869 essay
on the "Social Evil," the abolitionist Parker Pillsbury assailed the
"unhallowed brokerage" that would be established by state licensing
of prostitution. "It is just as was slaveholding and slave-breeding in
this country before the war." In an inversion of antebellum antislavery symbolism that had portrayed the South as a brothel, slavery was

---

[65] Edwin S. Redkey, ed., *Respect Black: The Writings and Speeches of Henry McNeal Turner*
(New York, 1971), 10; Massachusetts Board of State Charities, *Second Annual Report*
(1866), xx; Charles Loring Brace, *The Dangerous Classes of New York and Twenty Years'
Work among Them* (New York, 1872), 116; *Carpenter v. the People,* 8 Barb., 603, 610,
611 (1850).

now the symbol for the sale of women in free society, rather than vice versa.[66]

Ironically, the first American experiment with lawful prostitution occurred during the Civil War as an army measure implemented in the South less than a year after the Emancipation Proclamation. In August 1863 Union officials in Nashville, Tennessee imposed a license system after trying unsuccessfully to transport the city's white prostitutes out of the state to protect northern soldiers from venereal disease. The licensing system involved compulsory medical inspection of prostitutes, hospital treatment, health certificates, weekly fees, and punishment in the workhouse for violators. Initially, the rules only covered white women but were later extended to prostitutes of all races. The following year the United States Sanitary Commission, together with Union army doctors, installed a similar system in Memphis. The measures were enforced until the war's end and were intended not simply to control disease but also to create public order by clearing prostitutes from the streets. The Memphis order barred " 'Street walking,' soliciting, stopping or talking with men on the streets . . . language or conduct in public which attracts attention; visiting the public squares." In other parts of the South, Union officers used vagabond laws for the same purpose, punishing women who lived "by licentiousness" at penal labor, while after the war some agents of the Freedmen's Bureau made marriage virtually compulsory among former slaves. Yet in wartime Tennessee, in the midst of waging a contest for freedom, the Union validated the sale of sex as a commodity in a trade that was strictly regulated rather than organized, like the market in free labor, on the principle of laissez-faire.[67]

---

[66] "The Social Evil," *Revolution*, December 23, 1869. See Pivar, *Purity Crusade*. It is important to note that the postbellum usage of slavery as a metaphor for prostitution signified the sale of a woman's body, not the more specific meaning of forcible procurement of prostitutes through an international trade, which "white slavery" signified in the Progressive Era.

[67] "Tennessee," *New York Times*, June 2, 1865, 4; Surgeon General, United States Army, *The Medical and Surgical History of the War of the Rebellion*, pt. 3, vol. 1, *Medical History*, by Charles Smart (Washington, D.C., 1888), 891–96; quotes at p. 895; Ira Berlin et al., eds., *Freedom: A Documentary History of Emancipation 1861–1867*, ser. 1, vol. 3, *The Wartime Genesis of Free Labor: The Lower South* (New York, 1990), 317; see also pp. 232, 319, 380–81, 684–85, 814–15; Joseph Warren, ed., *Extracts from Reports of Superintendents of Freedmen*, 2nd series (Vicksburg, Miss., 1864), 20–23. See also James Boyd Jones, Jr., "A Tale of Two Cities: The Hidden Battle against Venereal Disease in Civil War Nashville and Memphis," *Civil War History*, 31 (1985), 270–76; Lawrence R. Murphy, "The Enemy among Us: Venereal Disease among Union Soldiers in the Far West, 1861–1865," *Civil War History*, 31 (1985), 257–69; Thomas P. Lowry, *The Story the Soldiers Wouldn't Tell: Sex in the Civil War* (Mechanicsburg, Pa., 1994), chs. 6, 7, 8, 10; Leslie J. Reagan, " 'About to Meet Her Maker':

A decade later the Civil War experiment stood as a model for plans to license and regulate prostitution in cities across the country. As one physician, Dr. W.M. Chambers, who had been an army surgeon in Nashville, stated to the American Medical Association in 1875, "If prostitution exists in a city, that disease can be, at least in a very great measure, stamped out by the police using the plan that was adopted in the army." Advocating involuntary medical inspection as well as arrest, he claimed that "official surveillance of prostitutes worked wonders." Doctors were among the leading proponents of licensed prostitution as a public health necessity, and though also citing European regulations adopted early in the century and the English Contagious Diseases Acts of the 1860s, they contended that the Tennessee measures showed that Old World rules could be applied in American cities. At an 1880 meeting of the American Public Health Association, physicians again held up the army plan as an example of the "wonderful amount of good" achieved by state regulation and contrasted European cities where licensing was in effect with "scandalous scenes" in "Philadelphia and Brooklyn and Boston, where the respectable woman is jostled in every street by unsuspected courtesans, and unfledged boys are lured to disease by young girls in the garb of decent poverty." There was no unanimity within these associations about the efficacy or the moral defensibility of licensing, but their discussions supported the diagnosis that streetwalkers' unregulated circulation was a major feature of the problem.[68]

The idea of an American license system had been raised before the war, but legislative initiatives only began in the late 1860s, with New York in the forefront. In response to an inquiry from the state assembly about laws to restrict prostitution, a joint 1867 report by the New York City boards of police and health proposed a system of government control and compulsory medical supervision. The report argued graphically that prostitution was ineradicable and a source of disease that afflicted both the pure and impure and every part of the body – "the skin, brain, eyes, throat, nose, lungs, and bones. The surface of the body becomes covered with sores and scars. . . . The blood itself is poisoned." Since strictly punitive measures had failed, "questions of conscience" must now give way to

Women, Doctors, Dying Declarations, and the State's Investigation of Abortion, Chicago, 1867–1940," *Journal of American History*, 77 (March 1991), 1240–64, quote at p. 1261.

[68] *Transactions of the American Medical Association*, 26 (1875), 238; American Public Health Association, *Public Health Papers and Reports*, 4 (Boston, 1881), 4: 410–11. See also Judith K. Walkowitz, *Prostitution and Victorian Society: Women, Class, and the State* (Cambridge, 1980).

public health. In 1867, 1868, and 1871 the state legislature debated licensing laws based on this report, but conscience remained paramount and none were enacted.[69]

Nevertheless, similar bills were introduced in the 1870s for almost all the nation's major cities, including Philadelphia, the District of Columbia, Chicago, and San Francisco. Though backed by police and medical officials, they were defeated by anti-licensing coalitions led by former abolitionists, feminists, and ministers who called themselves "new abolitionists" – by what an irate doctor saw as the "fanaticism" of the "clergy, old women, and others." Only in St. Louis was regulation briefly enforced, under a law enacted by the city council in 1870, which was repealed by the state legislature in 1874. Yet the licensing argument retained force. In New York, legislators continued to insist that state control would make the sale of women less offensive. This was the rationale offered by an 1875 state assembly report on the "Causes of the Increase of Crime in the City of New York." The report found that the criminal laws against streetwalking contained in the vagrancy codes were "absolutely nugatory" – "dead letters upon the statute book." Arguing that legislation should not be guided by higher law but "take the world as it is," these lawmakers maintained that only a license system could both limit disease and "prevent all street walking, all indecent exposure." For them, sound bodies and orderly streets were inseparable.[70]

Thus state efforts to legalize prostitution had the same object as the era's seemingly contradictory criminal enactments against begging – keeping roving, clamorous persons off the streets while also policing free market exchange. Not only were the city streets plebeian meetingplaces and places of commerce, they had also become a setting for elite practices such as promenading; the streets were traveled by men and women of all classes involved in all kinds of exchange relations. Accordingly, a central principle of licensing was to curb the street freedom of prostitutes, the "exposure permitted in public places to the most abandoned and unmistakable strum-

[69] New York City Police Department, *Communication from the Metropolitan Board of Police and Board of Health in Answer to a Resolution in Relation to Prostitution in the City of New York.* State of New York, Ass. Doc. No. 67 (Albany, 1867), 1, 2, 8. See also Aaron M. Powell, *State Regulation of Vice: Regulation Efforts in America, the Geneva Congress* (New York, 1878), 49–52; "Prostitution," *Revolution,* April 23, 1868; Ryan, *Women in Public,* 113–15; Pivar, *Purity Crusade,* 29, 51, 52; Gilfoyle, *City of Eros,* 139–41.

[70] *Transactions of the American Medical Association,* 26 (1875), 239, 238; N.Y. State Assembly, *Report of the Select Committee of 1875,* 31, 33. See also "Municipal Code Convention," *Ohio State Journal,* December 9, 1969, 4; John C. Burnham, "Medical Inspection of Prostitutes in America in the Nineteenth Century: The St. Louis Experiment and Its Sequel," *Bulletin of the History of Medicine,* 45 (May–June 1971), 203–18; Woolston, *Prostitution,* 26–30; Sanger, *History of Prostitution,* 638–43; Walkowitz, *Prostitution and Victorian Society.*

pets," and to forbid them "to approach or solicit men on the street." As one doctor complained after the repeal of the St. Louis law, "you cannot walk half a dozen blocks without being asked to come in." Most licensing advocates argued pragmatically that prostitution could never be fully suppressed because it arose from passions intrinsic to "Human nature," a theory not applied to begging, though these wrongs were otherwise considered equivalent. It therefore followed that the only way to abolish streetwalking was to regulate the sale of women in brothels sanctioned by the state.[71]

The perplexities of lawful prostitution were made plain by the Massachusetts Board of State Charities in its 1873 annual report. Offering more balanced judgments than most other government discussions, this report weighed the medical value of licensing against the affront to morality. Yet it also openly stated the antislavery concerns of the board's directors, the reformers Edward Pierce, Franklin Sanborn, and Samuel Gridley Howe. Though the board had promoted the new vagabond laws that governed both prostitutes and beggars, it admitted their failure to check prostitution. Yet it neither endorsed nor condemned the license system. It objected that the system of compulsory medical inspection allowed immorality and violated women's liberty but recognized the good of preventing "the infected from going at large to scatter fire-brands, arrows and death," even if that meant "occasional infringement upon personal freedom." It was troubled that the license laws were unequal, inviting men to sin with impunity, but asked if nothing should be done "because we cannot reach the whole?" On the one hand, the board wondered if licensing could be altered "to give its good without its evil fruits." But on the other, it could not be resigned to the "melancholy trade." Using the language of abolitionism, it underscored the difficulties of a system that authorized "a certain order of women – sisters of sin – to sell and traffic their bodies and souls in the public market."[72]

The charities board did not speak of slavery, but other commentators on the dilemmas of lawful prostitution drew explicitly on this

[71] American Public Health Association, *Public Health Papers and Reports*, 4: 413; Boston Chief of Police, *Annual Report* (1870), 57; George W. Walling, *Recollections of a New York City Chief of Police* (Montclair, 1972; orig. pub. 1887), 602; *Transactions of the American Medical Association*, 26 (1875), 239; N.Y. State Assembly, *Report of the Select Committee of 1875*, 31. See "Punishing Women Only," *Woman's Journal*, July 23, 1870; Warren, *Thirty Years' Battle*, 40; David Scobey, "Anatomy of the Promenade: The Politics of Bourgeois Sociability in Nineteenth-Century New York," *Social History*, 17 (May 1992), 203–27; Kasson, *Rudeness and Civility*, 112–46; Ryan, *Women in Public*, 62–94, 109–115.

[72] Massachusetts Board of State Charities, *Ninth Annual Report* (Boston, 1873), xxv–xxviii.

analogy. In a thoughtful 1871 article on the clergy's opposition, the Unitarian minister Octavius Frothingham argued that by regulating prostitution the state "legitimates it in the same sense as the Missouri Compromise legitimated slavery; by putting it under restriction, it of course recognizes its necessary existence where it happens to be." Frothingham was neither a critic nor a defender of the license system; what he disputed were categorical rejections based on moral opinions rather than objective inquiry. He wrote that to assume criminal law could suppress prostitution was to "talk nonsense" and that licensing was "well meant" in spite of its flaws: "just as nothing would have pleased the framers of the Missouri Compromise more than the total abolition of the system they could only succeed in confining within definite limits." In posing quandaries for law and morality, prostitution could be compared only to slavery.[73]

But the slavery analogy figured most powerfully in arguments that state sanctioning of the traffic in women had no virtue whatsoever. As Garrison wrote to leaders of the anti-licensing movement in 1879, "the world has never before seen such a morally sublime uprising against statutory licentiousness. . . . [I]t closely resembles the conflict that was so hotly waged in this country for the abolition of chattel slavery." This analogy did not animate all attacks on licensed prostitution. It did not appear, for instance, in a highly influential statement written by the St. Louis minister William Greenleaf Eliot, who argued that the system subverted public morality, individual liberty, and equal rights at law. Yet it was common for opponents of licensing to make the same arguments by relying, in one way or another, on the example of slavery. The moral reform journal *Alpha* even spoke hyperbolically of a "new 'irrepressible conflict' . . . against a system more unjust and oppressive than negro slavery."[74]

In the antebellum era the moral reformers who had crusaded against prostitution in the North rarely compared it to southern slavery. Perhaps, since they were often allied with abolitionism, they avoided analogies that could be exploited by slaveholders and that might undercut the argument that chattel slavery was an unparalleled wrong. Sometimes they referred to lust, the thrall of sexual passion, as a form of bondage, while often condemning the

---

[73] O.B. Frothingham, "The Pulpit and the Social Evil," *Golden Age*, April 8, 1871.

[74] "Protests against Licensed Vice," *Woman's Journal*, March 15, 1879; William G. Eliot, *A Practical Discussion of the Great Social Question of the Day* (New York, 1876; orig. pub. March 1873); *Alpha*, 1 (May 1, 1876), 7. See also British Continental and General Federation of the Abolition of State Regulation of Prostitution, *The New Abolitionists: A Narrative of a Year's Work, Being an Account of the Mission Undertaken to the Continent of Europe by Mrs. Josephine Butler, and of the Events Subsequent Thereupon* (London, 1876).

forcible procurement of prostitutes and the trade in women as
market commodities. For example, the 1832 tract *Magdalen Facts*
depicted a prostitute trapped by a "jailoress" who "sold chastity at
a price, and gloried over this new piece of the richest article in
the market." Yet in this era it was not the rule to term a prostitute
a "slave of vice" – she was almost never called a *white slave*, a
metaphor used by labor reformers to signify a hireling. Perhaps
precisely because prostitution was such a central symbol in the debate over chattel slavery, Yankee moral reformers hesitated to attack it as slavery outright.[75]

But after the war, reformers with an antislavery pedigree represented prostitution as slavery rather than the reverse. Not only was
this because emancipation had cleared the way ideologically for com-
paring other commodity relations that invaded the inner precincts
of the self – other trafficking in bodies and souls – to the peculiar
institution. It was because a system of licensing would have institutionalized prostitution, constituting a decisive break from past practice. And it was also because the laws regulating this trade would
have hedged the freedom of sellers but not buyers, defining women
as a separate and unequal class of persons and thereby tightening
the analogy between prostitutes and slaves. In the wake of abolition
the license system presented the prospect of women being designated commodities by the state. "It is the most infamous system of
slavery of womanhood and girlhood the world has ever seen," argued the antislavery reformer Aaron Macy Powell, who had become

[75] *Magdalen Facts*, 35, 57. Very infrequently, references to white slavery appeared in
reprints from British publications. See *Magdalen Facts*, 63; *McDowall's Journal*, February 1834, 15. But it was exceedingly rare for antebellum American moral reform
literature directly to equate prostitution with chattel slavery. See *McDowall's Journal*,
May 1834, 39. But on the common imagery of bondage to lust, see, for example,
McDowall's Journal, February 1834, 10; March 1834, 22; June 1834, 41; July 1834,
52; "Moral Reform. A Poem," *Fourth Annual Report of the New York Female Moral
Reform Society* (New York, 1838), 11–16. Reform publications containing no mention
at all of slavery or bondage include: Philadelphia Magdalen Society, *To the Members
of the Magdalen Society* (Philadelphia, 1818); Justin Edwards, *Sermon, Delivered in Park
Street Church Before the Penitent Female's Refuge Society* (Boston, 1826); *Guardian* (May
1838); *Fourteenth Annual Report of the New England Female Moral Reform Society, for the
Year Ending May, 1852* (Boston, 1852). On the changing usages of "white slavery,"
see entry for "white slave" in Peter Tamony Collection, Western Historical Manuscript Collection, University of Missouri-Columbia; Roediger, *Wages of Whiteness*, 65–
87. Regarding usage of the term "sexual slavery," Hobson appears to overstate the
case or perhaps neglects to distinguish carefully between allusions to the female
hireling and the prostitute. See Hobson, *Uneasy Virtue*, 61–66. My argument high-
lights the radicalism of antebellum antislavery feminists who did widely use the
concept of slavery of sex. On "white slave" symbolism in the early twentieth century,
see Rosen, *Lost Sisterhood*, 112–35; Connelly, *Prostitution in the Progressive Era*, 114–
35.

an anti-licensing leader. "It is slavery worse than the chattelism, in some of its details, which formerly prevailed."[76]

The outcry centered on the power of the state to regulate this dehumanizing commerce and the right of women to bodily integrity and freedom on the streets. Notably, antislavery newspapers had not reported on the wartime license system, raising no claim that it conflicted with emancipation. But the "new abolitionists" saw themselves as safeguarding freedom and equality in alliance with anti-licensing reform abroad. From old abolitionism they inherited not simply a vocabulary for indicting the treatment of human beings as objects of sale but also a world view preoccupied with the rule of law. Just as the *Liberator* had once declared that chattel slaves were "perfect merchandise" because "the vital principle of humanity is destroyed by law," so the new abolitionists protested, in the words of the minister William Greenleaf Eliot, that licensing would be unconstitutional "class-legislation." But others were more graphic in describing the details of the license system that made it like slavery. In the persons of policemen and doctors, argued Lucy Stone in 1876, the state would invade women's bodies in order to warrant them safe for buyers: "the plain language of the proposition is 'the law will shut you up for the use of men, who may come to you reeking with disease. . . . The hands of brutal men shall search your body to see whether it is safe.' " According to Stone's husband Henry Blackwell, "African slavery never had anything in it more horrible than this."[77]

The anti-licensing argument was premised on the principle of equal rights for the sexes. In this case even clergymen who opposed woman's enfranchisement attacked laws that discriminated by sex. The Chicago minister Robert Laird Collier explained that he would support "no law that did not apply to men as to women. We want no registry of sin, but . . . a law that will arrest a known libertine . . . just as it should a lewd woman." But again feminists most fully drew out the implications of this argument by reasoning in terms of both contract and slavery – just as they did with respect to marriage. "If the police must register the women, let them also register the men. Pros-

---

[76] Powell, *Personal Reminiscences*, 276, 277. See also Roediger, *Wages of Whiteness*, 167–84; Pivar, *Purity Crusade*, esp. pp. 67–73.

[77] "Difference between a Free Laborer and a Slave," *Liberator*, December 1, 1837; Eliot, *A Practical Discussion*, 20; "The Social Evil," *Woman's Journal*, June 17, 1876, 196; "Licensing Prostitution," *Woman's Journal*, February 26, 1876. See letter of W.G. Eliot to Caroline Dall, February 29, 1876, Caroline H. Dall Papers, Massachusetts Historical Society, Box 6, Folder 15. On the lack of wartime coverage of the license issue, see *Liberator*, June 1863–November 1864; *National Anti-Slavery Standard*, June 1863–December 1863, August 1864–November 1864; *Douglass's Monthly*, August 1863.

titution is committed on the basis of a business contract; and if one party thereto must give legal notice to the authorities, let the other do the same," declared the *Revolution* in 1870. "Woman's merchandise of her body – by which she makes a market of herself in the streets – is impossible without man's complicity in the hellish bargain." But the *Revolution* did not view prostitution as a free contract; rather it was always commerce in which a woman lost title to "body and soul" – a bargain based on "the ownership of woman by man, not merely the individual right of a man to his wife, but that of one sex to put to the basest uses a portion of the other." Even if the laws authorizing the sale assured formal equality, the claim was that prostitution would still define women as chattel property.[78]

Anti-licensing also defended woman's personal autonomy, particularly her freedom to walk through the streets. Under the proposed legislation anyone suspected of prostituting herself could be placed in confinement and have her body involuntarily examined, just as free blacks had been captured as fugitive slaves. The argument was not only that unlicensed streetwalkers would be "hunted down . . . as if they were vermin" but that all women would be liable to undergo the procedures required for prostitutes. Henry Blackwell warned, "Pass this law, and every poor working girl in New York will be at the mercy of every base policeman." Under the existing criminal laws police abuse of streetwalkers was already well documented; even police officials admitted the "wholesale blackmailing" of "poor degraded women who sell their bodies for gain," and reports were widespread that women mistakenly arrested as prostitutes were dragged through the streets and beaten until they were "black and helpless with pain." The license system's opponents granted that the street sale of women would be restricted, but at too great a cost. As Aaron Macy Powell calculated, "the freedom of all women is restricted." Thus new abolitionism fleshed out why slavery had become a symbol for prostitution.[79]

---

[78] Collier, *The Social Evil*, 7; "The Social Evil," *Revolution*, August 11, 1870; "The Shame of England," *Revolution*, January 12, 1871. Massachusetts was exceptional in enacting an 1876 statute providing for the punishment of male nightwalkers who invited illicit sexual intercourse, a law feminists heralded as an "equal rights" victory. See "Male Night-Walkers," *Woman's Journal*, May 20, 1876. On feminists anti-licensing arguments, see Paulina W. Davis, *A History of the National Woman's Rights Movement for Twenty Years* (New York, 1871), 22; *Revolution*, December 23, 1869, November 24, 1870, March 30, 1871, April 13, 1871; *Woman's Journal*, September 3, 1870, March 14, 1874, April 24, 1874, May 9, 1874, June 17, 1876, June 24, 1876, October 7, 1876, March 1, 1879; Letter of Isabella Beecher Hooker to Anna Dickinson, March 31, 1874, Anna Dickinson Papers, Library of Congress, Box 9; Isabella Beecher Hooker, *Womanhood: Its Sanctities and Fidelities* (Boston, 1874), 41–55.

[79] Eliot, *A Practical Discussion*, 11; "Licensing Prostitution"; Walling, *Recollections*, 602, 387; New York Senate, Counsel of the Committee of the New York Senate Ap-

It was a British anti-licensing tract, the *Purchase of Women,* that expounded with greatest clarity the logic of using chattel slavery as an analogy for prostitution. This 1886 tract contributed to the protest in England against the Contagious Diseases Acts, a cause that had emerged in the Old World just after the Civil War ended in the New and that had become a model for anti-licensing efforts internationally. Yet the tract was written by an American expatriate, Elizabeth Blackwell, a physician and feminist, and it reflected her Yankee abolitionist upbringing in a family of famous reformers. And it was read widely on both sides of the Atlantic. "What is involved in living by the sale of the human body?" Blackwell asked. This was living by the "slave principle," she answered. She mourned "the flood of women in the streets, begging to be bought" and argued that the state must treat this sale of self – "this terrible trade which converts the human body into a marketable commodity" – no differently than the market in slaves. She declared that the "human being . . . may not be made a thing of trade," that "freedom is violated by converting human bodies into chattels," that the "abolition of slavery forbade henceforward the purchase or sale of any individual." As "human merchandise" the prostitute was the living embodiment of the slave principle.[80]

The *Purchase of Women* thereby laid bare the profound ideological problems posed by prostitution in the aftermath of slave emancipation. Its attack on the continuing trade in human commodities ultimately called into question the legitimacy of contract freedom. In equating prostitution with chattel slavery, Blackwell expressed outrage at free market relations defended by abolitionists – at a political economy that "converts everything into money value," an ethos that "spares no relation of life" from the calculus of commodity exchange, a regime of "buying and selling" that was still "permitting one half the race to become the merchandise of the other half." She expressly attacked the ideal of contract that lay at the very core of the antislavery doctrine she otherwise honored. "Under a specious hypocrisy, falsely styled freedom of contract, a modern phase of slav-

pointed to Investigate the Police Department, "Examination of Trials by the Police Board from January 1, 1891 to May 1, 1894" (typescript, May 1, 1894), 108, 138; Smith, *Sunshine and Shadow in New York,* 300–306; Powell, *State Regulation of Vice,* 21. See also "Where Are the Police," *Revolution,* September 24, 1868; "Police as Protectors," *Revolution,* August 26, 1869; "Women and the Police," *Revolution,* February 1, 1879.

80 Elizabeth Blackwell, *Purchase of Women: The Great Economic Blunder* (London, 1916; orig. pub. 1886), 45, 41, 39, 37, 28, 46. See *Philanthropist,* March 1887, 4, April 1887, 5. Blackwell remained in the United States until 1867, participating in abolitionism and absorbing its language and theory. See Dumas Malone, ed., *Dictionary of American Biography* (20 vols., New York, 1936), 2: 320.

ery is still exercising its influence in our midst, for the slaveholding
principle that the human body may be an article of merchandise is
still applied to women." Blackwell condemned the idea that contract
distinguished prostitution from slavery, mocking as "sophistry" the
theory that the propertied and unpropertied could bargain as
equals, that starving persons could " 'consent' to be purchased, and
that therefore there is a radical difference between the purchase of
the bodies of men and women, which the anti-slavery movement has
pronounced illegal, and the purchase of women by men which we
are now considering." By the same token, she condemned the wages
of "cheap labor" that drove women to live by repeatedly selling their
bodies. The prostitute, therefore, was also the embodiment of contract freedom.[81]

The point was that the purchase of women falsified the absolute
difference between the commodity relations of slavery and freedom.
Blackwell paid homage to abolitionism for establishing the principle
that converting human beings into market commodities violated
freedom. Yet she debunked the abolitionist faith that contract freedom was the opposite of slavery by arguing that living by the sale of
self embodied both the essence of slavery and the illusion of free
contract.

If prostitution made ambiguous the difference between southern
slavery and Yankee freedom, what then of the difference between
prostitution and marriage as sexual contracts? That was the question
feminists forced into the debate about the sale of women in postbellum society, as they argued that prostitution was not as peculiar an
institution as chattel slavery but rather a relation based on the same
principles as a marriage contract between a free husband and wife.
Even as they protested that licensing prostitution would create a new
form of bondage, feminists claimed that marriage was lawful prostitution – that wives were market commodities no different from
streetwalkers or slaves. Their argument was that flesh trading extended to marriage and that the commerce in women was an institution as fundamental to free society as to slavery. Here prostitution
symbolized the unfreedom of marriage as a contract representing
both a paternal bond and a market relation.

This symbolism was not new to postbellum feminism, but it now
held a more central place in arguments for female emancipation
than in the past. It had been used in the eighteenth century by the
British thinkers Mary Astell and Mary Wollstonecraft, who had suggested that women prostituted themselves in marriage, and some

[81] Blackwell, *Purchase of Women*, 28, 32, 33, 35, 43.

American feminists in the early nineteenth century had stressed that economic need often led women into loveless marriages. But others were cautious at first about dealing with sexual exchange, as compared with other property relations between husband and wife. Unsure about how to discuss what she called "the *abstract question* of marriage" – that "a thousand aching and uncompanioned hearts and minds" were "wedded only in name" – Lucy Stone wrote to Stanton in 1855: "I am not one bit afraid of the censure which a discussion of this abstract question will bring. If I were only sure what was the *right*. . . . It does seem to me that *you* are the one to do it." In the following years Stanton did become a principal critic of the sale of women, openly attacking the "legalized prostitution of womanhood" and deploring all mercenary sex. "Oh! what a sham is the marriage we see about us, though sanctioned in our courts and baptized at our altars," she declared in 1869. By this era, however, many feminists argued similarly, perhaps emboldened by the rising concern with prostitution and a series of sensationalized trials involving adultery, as well as by the eroticized symbolism of the slavery debate.[82]

The feminist claim that sex was the primary currency of marriage was hardly a revelation. According to longstanding common law doctrine, sex was the gist of the relation between husband and wife; that doctrine defined sex outside marriage as illegitimate. Although marriage also entailed exchanging wifely service for husbandly support, only the "sexual connexion" went to the contract's foundation, comprising "the essentials of the relation." Nor was there anything exceptional in feminist claims that a marriage market existed. Advice books instructed both sexes about grooming for romantic competition, stories of male and female fortune hunters were common, and popular songs and jokes described buying a woman's love for merely "some bags of flour" and a "good supply of potted beef." What subverted prevailing assumptions was the feminist claim that mar-

[82] Letter of Lucy Stone to Stanton, October 22, 1855, Elizabeth Cady Stanton Papers, Library of Congress, Box 1; "The Naperville Tragedy," *Revolution*, February 4, 1869. See Mary Astell, *Some Reflections upon Marriage* (New York, 1970; orig. pub. 1730), 29, 40–41; Mary Wollstonecraft, *Vindication of the Rights of Woman* (New York, 1982; orig. pub. 1792), 165–66; Sarah Grimké, "Marriage," in *The Female Experience: An American Documentary*, ed. Gerda Lerner (Indianapolis, 1977), 97, 94; Elizabeth Cady Stanton, Susan B. Anthony, and Matilda Joslyn Gage, eds., *History of Woman Suffrage* (6 vols., Rochester, N.Y., 1887), 1: 166; "Retrogressive Progression," *Packard's Monthly*, January 1870, 41; "Marriage and Divorce," *Packard's Monthly*, February 1870, 85; Hendrik Hartog, "Lawyering, Husbands' Rights, and the 'Unwritten Law' in Nineteenth-Century America," *Journal of American History*, 84 (June 1997), 67–97; Richard W. Fox, "Intimacy on Trial: Cultural Meanings of the Beecher-Tilton Affair," in *The Power of Culture: Critical Essays in American History*, ed. Richard Wightman Fox and T.J. Jackson Lears (Chicago, 1993), 103–32.

riage and prostitution were essentially similar market relations that
converted women into human articles of merchandise – that marriage was a contract as unfree and sordid as prostitution. As Lydia
Maria Child proclaimed at a convention of the American Woman
Suffrage Association in 1870, "We all know that the institution of
marriage has been degraded and polluted by making woman a marketable commodity."[83]

Equating the wife and prostitute cast in doubt not only the sanctity of marriage but the moral legitimacy of free market society. In
using prostitution as a symbol for marriage, feminists discredited the
vaunted cultural and economic distance between the market and the
home. Contrary to the image of separate spheres, which worked to
validate free market relations by representing a boundary to their
sway, the symbolism of marriage as prostitution suggested that no
precinct of human existence was exempt from commodity relations –
that the cash nexus reached everywhere – even into the most private
exchange of husband and wife; that the market was unbounded, with
all for sale. This symbolism clashed with the abolitionist representation of the free household as a place that could not be violated by
the market, mirroring instead labor reform portraits of tenement
homes destroyed by wage labor and proslavery visions of Yankee domestic relations that were calculated in dollars and cents. The outcome of the economic dependence that made marriage involuntary
for woman, Stanton argued, was that the wife exchanged "her
charms of person" for the "bounty of man" in a bargain based on
necessity, not love – the very image of the wife as prostitute.[84]

This argument was meant to disclose that the slaveholding principle recognizing human beings as objects of sale persisted not simply in prostitution but in the free contract of marriage. Speaking to
an 1869 meeting of the American Equal Rights Association, which
was composed of abolitionists and feminists, Susan Anthony envisioned a time when women would "no longer be compelled to sell
themselves for bread, either in or out of marriage." For most feminists, there was no conflict between protesting licensed prostitution
and bringing to light the corruption of marriage: "the vast amount
of legalized prostitution, bearing the semblance of virtue, but . . .
rotten below the fair exterior." They used images of prostitution and
slavery interchangeably to assert woman's right to self ownership in

[83] Joel Bishop, *Commentaries on the Law of Marriage and Divorce and Evidence in Matrimo-
    nial Suits* (2 vols., Boston, 1873), 1: 151, 143; see also pp. 145, 279–81, 630; "The
    Practical Lover," in *The Book of Comic Songs and Recitations* (New York, 1875), n.p.;
    "Proceedings of the Convention of the American Woman Suffrage Association,"
    Woman's Journal, December 3, 1870.
[84] Elizabeth Cady Stanton, "The Women Question," *Radical,* 3 (1868), 20.

and out of marriage, decrying love as unfree when women sold themselves as commodities owned in perpetuity by husbands. Elizabeth Blackwell was unusual in rejecting the analogy between prostitution and marriage as a "spreading sophistry" and in looking to marriage law for a "measure of justice." Others played devil's advocate by arguing not simply that marriage was "sexual license" and prostitution a "natural name" for all loveless sex but that licensed prostitution was just as legitimate as marriage. "It is a distinction without a difference," claimed *Woodhull & Claflin's Weekly* in 1870, " 'young ladies' are set up, advertised and sold to the highest cash bidder"; while marriage was "a transfer – or sale – for life" and prostitution was "at the option of the contracting parties . . . both are for a consideration given by the man and received by the woman." The license system authorized "sin by statute" no more than laws upholding marriages representing "bargains and sales."[85]

In indicting northern commodity relations, apologists for slavery would have argued no differently. But slaveholders had held that dependence was the only basis for domestic affection, while feminists envisioned a marriage contract that would be modeled neither on market relations nor on paternalism – an ideal of love in which women would be neither articles of sale nor personal dependents of men. "Was love ever constrained, enforced, or purchased?" they asked. As a writer in the *Woman's Journal* stated in 1871, "*Freedom is of love.*"[86] Though few feminists went so far as to deny any difference

---

[85] Stanton et al., *History of Woman Suffrage* 2: 390; Davis, *History of the National Woman's Rights Movement*, 29; Elizabeth Blackwell, "Criticism of Gronlund's Co-Operative Commonwealth," 5, in Blackwell Family Papers, Library of Congress, reel 45, container 59; "What Is the Issue?" *Woodhull & Claflin's Weekly*, January 31, 1874; "Propositions in Sexual Science," *Woodhull & Claflin's Weekly*, February 8, 1873; "The Sixteenth Amendment," *Woodhull & Claflin's Weekly*, November 12, 1870; "The Social Evil," *Woodhull & Claflin's Weekly*, August 20, 1870; see also "The Scarecrows of Sexual Slavery," *Woodhull & Claflin's Weekly*, September 27, 1873; "The Social Evil," *Woodhull & Claflin's Weekly*, July 2, 1870; "Licensing Prostitution," *Woodhull & Claflin's Weekly*, August 27, 1870. See also Elizabeth B. Clark, "Matrimonial Bonds: Slavery and Divorce in Nineteenth-Century America," *Law and History Review*, 8 (Spring 1990), 25–54; Amy Dru Stanley, "Conjugal Bonds and Wage Labor: Rights of Contract in the Age of Emancipation," *Journal of American History*, 75 (September 1988), 471–500. Feminist arguments anticipated the theories of Charlotte Perkins Gilman and Emma Goldman about the political economy of marriage and the commercial nature of the marriage contract; see Charlotte Perkins Gilman, *Woman and Economics: A Study of the Economic Relation Between Men and Women as a Factor in Social Evolution* (Boston, 1899) and "Home Conditions?" *American Journal of Sociology*, 14 (March 1909), 592–605; Emma Goldman, *The Traffic in Women and Other Essays* (Albion, Calif., 1970; orig. pub. 1917). On the legacy of antebellum free love doctrine, see John C. Spurlock, *Free Love: Marriage and Middle-Class Radicalism in America, 1825–1860* (New York, 1988).

[86] Paulina W. Davis, "The Apollo Hall Resolutions," *Revolution*, June 15, 1871; Lydia Fuller, "Love versus Ownership," *Woman's Journal*, April 15, 1871.

between licensed prostitution and marriage, most saw no clear line between the illicit sale of women and the exchange sanctified by law. They argued that dependence on men meant that women would remain commodities, despite laws forbidding the open sale of their bodies on the streets. Like abolitionists, they used the prostitute as a figure for slavery, to symbolize by negation the ideal relation between the sexes. Yet like slaveholders, they also used the prostitute to symbolize the existing conditions of freedom.

The feminist argument inverted the law's interpretation of the prostitute's situation. The law also recognized an analogy between marriage and prostitution, but whereas feminists saw both as commodity relations, the law construed both as relations of personal dependence – one legal, the other a crime. For feminism, it was a woman's dependence that transformed her into a commodity. For the law, it was prostituting her body that defined a woman as an illegal dependent, as someone with nothing legitimate to sell in the labor market, someone no different from a beggar. Thus, under a Massachusetts law governing vagabonds, common nightwalkers, and other idle and wanton persons, Justice Oliver Wendell Holmes, Jr., speaking for the Massachusetts high court, upheld the conviction of a Boston woman accused of "soliciting men passing by" and "misspending her time." At the trial five policemen had testified that she did no "work of any kind." A jury might well infer, reasoned Holmes, that "she did not possess independent means of support, that she was physically able to work . . . but neglected to do so." In the eyes of the law the nightwalker was as dependent as a wife and as guilty as a beggar.[87]

Holmes's judgment equated two wholly different acts – the sale of a woman's body and the withholding of labor from sale. Under similar rulings issued from less lofty chambers by less eminent jurists, thousands of women each year were convicted as streetwalkers and punished for living by the sale of their bodies. Not only did this judgment define a market exchange – a contract relation – as a mark of unlawful dependency, it enforced the antislavery principle that in free society women could not be purchased as market commodities but only within marriage.

By the turn of the century, the prostitute as slave had become an icon of American culture. Audiences were transfixed by novels such as *The House of Bondage* and films such as the *Traffic in Souls*, which sensationalized the impressment of women into prostitution. The

---

[87] *Commonwealth v. Annie Doherty*, 137 Mass. 245 (1884), 246, 247. See also Mass. Pub. Stat. ch. 207, sect. 29, p. 1169 (1882); Freund, *Police Power*, 97–99, 226–30.

congressional enactment in 1910 of the White Slave Traffic Act barring interstate trade in prostitutes made this symbolism part of federal law. But the wage slave never became an icon in this way. With the 1914 enactment of the Clayton Act barring courts from enjoining collective labor activity as an illegal restraint on trade, Congress declared that "the labor of a human being is not a commodity." This act was heralded by labor reformers as securing freedom of contract, as representing "labor's Magna Carta." But it neither outlawed the traffic in human labor nor was known as a white slave law.[88]

This difference reflects how Americans understood the limits of commodity relations in free society. After abolition the prostitute became a negative exemplar of the legitimate trafficking in human bodies and souls, taking the ideological place of the chattel slave for a nation that enshrined contract freedom. Since the antebellum era some reformers had claimed that wage labor and marriage were contracts that fused market relations with relations of personal dependency and therefore resembled slavery. Following emancipation these claims grew more insistent but did not prevail outside the worlds of labor reform and feminism. Rather, with slavery's downfall prostitution came to appear as a singularly wrong sale of the self – a form of bondage as peculiar as the Old South's had been, one that validated wage labor and marriage as falling within the bounds of contract freedom despite the dispossession of self entailed in these relations. Not labor but sex represented the human essence whose sale as a market commodity transformed its owners from free persons into slaves.

[88] *The Statutes at Large of the United States of America, from March, 1909, to March, 1911,* vol. 36, pt. 1 (Washington, D.C., 1911), 825–27. See also Rosen, *Lost Sisterhood,* 112–18; D'Emilio and Freedman, *Intimate Matters,* 208–10; Connelly, *Prostitution in the Progressive Era,* 114–35; William E. Forbath, *Law and the Shaping of the American Labor Movement* (Cambridge, Mass., 1991), 128–58.

Afterword

In his 1890 study, the *Principles of Psychology,* William James questioned anew the meaning of selfhood – a philosophical issue embedded in his generation's endeavor to distinguish between slavery and freedom. The ideal of a society based on contract presupposed a self that could not be bought and sold, or owned by another, or enslaved. This free subject imagined by liberalism also interested James, though his inquiry was not into political economy but rather into the complexities of defining what was meant "by the name of me." In a chapter on "The Consciousness of Self" James began, "it is clear that between what a man calls *me* and what he simply calls *mine* the line is difficult to draw."[1]

In its own day the *Principles* was greeted as a masterpiece, and today it is recognized as foreshadowing James's later philosophy of pragmatism. Yet it reflected not only theory to come but debates that had gone before. James began writing it in 1878 and had been gathering materials for at least a decade earlier.[2] He was a thinker particularly aware of the historical contingency of ideas, and it seems likely that the questions he raised about self consciousness in the *Principles* were influenced by and responsive to postbellum arguments about the outcome of slave emancipation in a free market society. For the problem of drawing lines between *me* and *mine* – between what was unsaleable and what could be sold – had been the centerpiece of debate over the transition from bondage to contract freedom in James's Boston just as much as in the cotton fields of the Sea Islands.

The *Principles* did not explore the paradox of the Yankee culture that shaped James's thought – a culture that simultaneously con-

---

[1] William James, *The Principles of Psychology* (2 vols., New York, 1918; orig. pub. 1890), 1: 291.
[2] See Introduction by Ralph Barton Perry in *William James, Psychology* (Cleveland, 1948), vii; Introduction by John J. McDermott in *The Writings of William James: A Comprehensive Edition* (Chicago, 1977), xxxiii; James T. Kloppenberg, *Uncertain Victory: Social Democracy and Progressivism in European and American Thought, 1870–1920* (New York, 1986), 64–94; James Livingston, *Pragmatism and the Political Economy of Cultural Revolution, 1850–1940* (Chapel Hill, 1994), 158–59, 263–72, 289–94.

demned slavery as traffic in human beings and enshrined freedom
as social exchange in which persons were merchants and free labor
a market commodity. Rather, James offered an unequivocal affirmation of propertied individualism and envisioned wives as belonging
to husbands. Considering the "empirical self" as opposed to the
thinking self, he wrote:

*In its widest possible sense . . . a man's self is the sum, is the sum total of all that he
CAN call his,* not only his body and his psychic powers, but his clothes and
his house, his wife and children . . . his reputation and works, his lands and
horses, and yacht and bank-account.[3]

Clearly, James did not have a hireling in mind in providing this
inventory of affluence. Otherwise, he sounded much like an abolitionist listing the possessions of a newfound freedman. He dwelled
not only on a man's ownership of his body and soul but on his work,
reputation, and money. And he also stressed household entitlements, a man's claim to his wife as well as a home to "live in and
'improve.' " Even when James turned from matter to consciousness –
to the "sanctuary within the citadel" – he represented selfhood as
ownership. When we *"think of ourselves as thinkers,"* he remarked, the
elements of the empirical self seemed "external possessions"; but
the relationship between the thinker and the succession of *thoughts*
that James defined as "selves" was also proprietary. "There must be
a real proprietor in the case of the selves, or else their actual accre-
tion into a 'personal consciousness' would never have taken place,"
he argued.

We can imagine a long succession of herdsmen coming rapidly into possession of the same cattle by transmission of an original title by bequest. May
not the "title" of a collective self be passed from one Thought to another in
some analogous way?[4]

Just as abolitionists imagined self ownership as the taproot of contract freedom, so for James self ownership was the basis of human
consciousness.
   James's concern with title to body and soul drew on liberal conceptions of self and property that valorized labor. He held that the
property most "intimately ours" was "saturated with our labor" and
that its loss involved a "partial conversion of ourselves to nothingness" that made men "feel personally annihilated." To be dispossessed like this was to be "assimilated to the tramps and poor devils
whom we so despise." But as examples of property saturated with
labor because created by "hands or brains," James named an "en-

---

[3] James, *Principles of Psychology*, 1: 291.   [4] Ibid., 293, 297, 337, 339.

tomological collection" and a "work in manuscript" – examples far removed from the world of hireling labor, whether in northern tenement houses or on southern plantations. His purpose in the *Principles* was not to wonder if converting free labor into a commodity annihilated selfhood and home life. He asked neither if someone who sold time would be reduced to the "nothingness" of a tramp nor if wage labor and marriage sustained one another. Exploring self consciousness, he did not meditate on the transformations caused by industrial capitalism – on the philosophical consequences of a sprawling marketplace. Yet in later studies of pragmatism James often used commodity metaphors uncritically to explain the working of consciousness. His own thought was infused with market usages. Teaching that all values were contingent and not absolute, he spoke of "cash-value" in words and concepts. "We exchange ideas; we lend and borrow verifications" and "trade on each other's truth," he wrote. With regard to truth there was an "obligation to do what pays." His pragmatism extended the image of buying and selling to cognition, thereby affording new legitimacy to the market as a model of human relations.[5]

In the *Principles* the meaning of selfhood ultimately rested not on material determinants of *me* and *mine* but rather on processes of thought. Although James maintained that the "nucleus of the '*me*' " was "bodily existence," the endpoint of his inquiry was the stream of thought through which the self appropriated successive states of experience into consciousness. Skeptical about the existence of "an unchanging metaphysical entity like the Soul," he summed up his theory of consciousness of self with the idea that "*thought is itself the thinker*, and psychology need not look beyond."[6] For James, the thinking self remained more central than the empirical one.

But for most of James's generation, the problem of marking boundaries between *me* and *mine* was as much about commodities as about individual consciousness. What could be termed the metaphysics of market relations was never far from the minds of Americans preoccupied by the opposition between freedom and slavery. Reformers and lawmakers, moralists and social scientists, southern freedpeople and northern hirelings – these practical philosophers considered not only the self as body and soul but what could be bought and sold, owned and disowned. As they confronted the nexus of change generated by slave emancipation and burgeoning capitalism they argued over the limits of commodity exchange, measuring

---

[5] Ibid., 293. See also Livingston, *Pragmatism and Cultural Revolution*, 199–201, 206–210, 214–215, quotes at 208, 209.
[6] James, *Principles of Psychology*, 1: 400, 401.

the entitlements of wage labor and marriage against the promise of contract freedom. This momentous argument gave voice to efforts to distinguish absolutely between freedom and slavery. Yet it also revealed deep ambiguities concerning self ownership in a free market society as well as relations of dependence and dominion both at work and at home. These were the ambiguities for which prostitutes and beggars, housework and sweatshops became vivid symbols. The argument was premised on an understanding of slavery as traffic in human chattels; but the expansion of the postbellum market into personal spheres that had once been thought beyond a price obscured the stark line between freedom and bondage.

Why contract provided a worldview for making sense of these ambiguities owed to the joint legacy of abolitionism and liberalism. Though shaped by liberal contract theory that idealized propertied individualism and voluntary exchange, abolitionism altered that theory by making home life, together with labor, central to the conflict over slavery and freedom. Yet the essential philosophy of contract after slave emancipation remained much as Hegel had described it early in the nineteenth century, when he explained that contract "revealed and mediated" the complexities of property ownership and dispossession, ostensibly distinguishing between the commodity relations of freedom and slavery. Under a contract a person:

ceases to be an owner and yet is and remains one. It is the mediation of the will to give up a property, a single property, and the will to take up another, i.e. another belonging to someone else. . . .

And the "single property" at stake in this voluntary exchange could not legitimately be "my personality," or the "whole of my time, as crystallized in my work," or the "substance of my being."[7] It was thus contract that marked the fundamental line between *me* and *mine* – between what was unsaleable and what could be sold.

Not even the harshest critics of postbellum life imagined a world without market relations; nor did they disown the value of contract freedom. But from standpoints reflecting the particularities of their own circumstances, they assailed the unfreedoms of existing contracts, arguing against tributes to voluntary exchange that were blind to dependencies imposed by custom, law, and unequal property relations. They drew examples from worlds where freed slaves were forced to enter into contracts, where men with unsold time became beggars and were punished in workhouses, where husbands lost property in labor their wives sold as a commodity, where prostitutes walked the streets. Both former slaves and hirelings who had never

[7] T.M. Knox, trans., *Hegel's Philosophy of Right* (New York, 1979), 58, 54.

been chattel questioned whether it was possible to be self owning without owning other forms of property. Feminists claimed that entitlement to property was worthless without self ownership. Reformers of all kinds deplored the market's intrusion into the home. And virtually all who thought seriously about the meaning of slave emancipation believed that freedom must safeguard precincts where buying and selling was not the rule of human affairs. This was the ideological significance of the outcry over prostitution, an outcry that departed from the liberal inheritance of the Enlightenment in valorizing sex rather than labor as the essence of selfhood. In postbellum America the prostitute replaced the chattel slave as the ultimate symbol of illegitimate commodity exchange, defining by negation the ideal of contract freedom.

In some ways the dilemmas of bondage and contract were peculiarly a nineteenth-century problem, one evoked by slavery's downfall amid industrial capitalism's ascendence. By the turn of the century, the problem had become recasting liberalism so as to validate unprecedented state authority over both wage labor and home life, spheres once held to be self regulating. Here reformers and thinkers who laid the foundations for a modern leviathan looked not to classical ideas of contract but to the new philosophy of pragmatism. Yet in other ways arguments about contract freedom in the age of slave emancipation bequeathed enduring principles – that some things must never be for sale, that the legitimacy of the market rests on its moral boundaries. Arguments about those boundaries endure as well.[8] There still exists the paradox that slavery embodies the sale of human beings while freedom is imagined as commodity exchange.

[8] See Kloppenberg, *Uncertain Victory*; Margaret Jane Radin, *Contested Commodities* (Cambridge, Mass., 1996).

Index

abolitionism, 17–18, 52–54, 61, 104,
126, 131, 150, 160–61, 177, 201,
245–46, 248, 253, 255; and the
"new abolitionists," 251, 253–58.
See also antislavery thought
Adams, Henry Carter, 72, 74–75, 82,
167–69, 171
African Methodist Episcopal Church, 24,
49
agricultural labor, 35, 41, 47, 49, 69, 86,
123–24, 140–42, 173, 188–91, 204,
210, 264
Alexandria, VA, 45
alms. *See* charity
Alpha, 253
American Antislavery Society, 18, 30,
243
American Economics Association, 72, 74,
78, 82, 166
American Equal Rights Association, 50,
260
American Freedmen's Inquiry Commission, 35–36, 124–25, 129, 141, 156,
190
American Law Review, 200
American Medical Association, 250
American Public Health Association, 250
American Revolution, 7
American Social Science Association,
108
American Tract Society, 38
American Woman Suffrage Association,
184, 260
Anthony, Susan B., 177, 204, 205, 233,
260
antislavery thought, x, xii, xiii, 9, 17–35,
74–76, 88–89, 92, 131–32, 138–40,
142–43, 146–48, 153, 157–60, 163,
166, 168–70, 181, 186, 188, 217,
235, 237, 238–45, 248, 252, 257–
58, 260, 262, 265, 267; and bodily
imagery, 22–23, 25–31; and race
difference, 28, 30–31, 241; and sex,
25–27, 31–33, 240–45; and sex difference, 25–35, 142–43, 153;

thought of former slaves, 18, 20, 21–
26, 31–32, 34, 52–53, 139, 143,
201, 242; thought of free blacks, 21,
26–27, 30–33, 53–54, 241–43. *See
also* abolitionism; market, antislavery
critique of; slavery, ideological conflict over
Association for Improving the Condition
of the Poor, 100, 110, 137, 148
Astell, Mary, 258
Atkinson, Edward, 65, 79, 92, 122, 162

bakers, 155
Beaufort, SC, 40
Beecher, Henry Ward, 138–39
beggars, xi, xiii, 98–122, 128–37, 162,
194, 197, 225–27, 230, 251, 252,
267; and contract, 99–100, 105–7,
130, 135–37, 267; and deception,
103–4, 113; equated with streetwalkers, 218–21, 252, 262; profile of,
104; punishment of, 116–20, 128,
130–37, 252, 267. *See also* charity;
contract, and coercion; dependence, as a criminal status; forcible
labor; idleness; poverty; law, and
beggars; vagrancy laws; wage
contract, and legal coercion
Beman, Jehiel, 26
Benjamin, Walter, 222
Bishop, Joel, 180–81, 211
Black Codes, 55, 108, 125–27
Blackstone, William, 7, 10, 11, 14, 134,
176
Blackwell, Elizabeth, 257–58, 261
Blackwell, Henry, 255, 256
Bladen County, NC, 46
Boston, MA, 35, 61, 63, 76, 90–92, 99,
103, 104, 110, 111, 118, 129, 130,
147, 150–52, 155, 161, 181, 193,
207, 209, 220, 224–26, 230, 231,
236, 238, 250, 262, 264
Boston Daily Globe, 130
Boston Eight Hour League, 90
Boston Industrial Aid Society, 110, 129